Regoverning the Workplace

Regoverning the Workplace

From Self-Regulation to Co-Regulation

Cynthia Estlund

Yale University Press

New Haven & London

For Sam, Jessica, and Lucas

Set in Adobe Garamond type by The Composing Room of Michigan, Inc.
Printed in the United States of America.

Library of Congress Cataloging-in-Publication Data

Estlund, Cynthia.
    Regoverning the workplace : from self-regulation to co-regulation / Cynthia
Estlund.
        p. cm.
    Includes bibliographical references and index.
    ISBN 978-0-300-12450-7 (cloth : alk. paper)
    1. Industrial management—Employee participation—Law and legislation—
United States.   2. Employee rights—United States.   3. Labor laws and
legislation—United States.   I. Title.
    KF3369.E88 2010
    344.7301—dc22

                                                                2009023980

A catalogue record for this book is available from the British Library.
This paper meets the requirements of ANSI/NISO Z39.48-1992
(Permanence of Paper).

10 9 8 7 6 5 4 3 2 1

Contents

Preface

Like many teachers and scholars of the law of the workplace, I was first drawn to the field in part by the exhilarating and romantic history of the labor movement and by images of workers making common cause, standing together in solidarity, forming their own self-governing organizations, and democratizing workplaces and society. They were, as Lizabeth Cohen's book title had it, "making the New Deal," and they occupied center stage in the drama that remade American society, law, and politics.

By the time I came of age, labor's progressive image had become a bit battered and rusty in the wake of organized labor's retreat into "business unionism" in the 1950s; the persistence of pockets of corruption and thuggishness; and its mixed response to the civil rights movement, the anti-war movement, and the environmental movement in the 1960s and 1970s. But still in the early 1980s, for many of us, there remained something deeply inspiring about the possibility, and the history, of workers and their unions democratizing workplaces and reforming society through self-organization, peaceful self-help, and participation in governance rather than primarily through litigation. There was not yet much of anything called "employment law," either in the curriculum or in the profession. That was beginning to change, of course, with the growth of antidiscrimination law, the rise of public employees' constitutional rights, and the first few cracks in the wall of employment-at-will that surrounded non-union employment relations. But the law of the workplace was still basically the law of unionization and collective bargaining. And labor law became my calling, first as a practicing lawyer and then as a new law professor.

In the decades since, labor law has shrunk in its reach along with union membership, while "employment law" has grown ever more voluminous and sprawling. Much of the labor law professoriate began gradually, and often regretfully, to turn away from labor law and toward employment law—away from collective bargaining and toward the courts—much as workers and their advocates had been doing since the 1960s. In the meantime, the labor movement itself has become more diverse, more democratic, and more dedicated to organizing the unorganized—even as it has continued to shrink as a share of the workforce. As things stand, even a tripling of current levels of private-sector union density would leave nearly 80 percent of the private-sector workforce with no institutionalized form of collective voice at work. Labor law reform and union growth through new organizing, though more necessary than ever, have long ceased to seem sufficient to address the needs of workers.

Much has been lost for workers in the decline of collective bargaining and the rise of employment law. The unions themselves, in their effort to promote labor law reform, have understandably stressed the economic losses—the declining middle class, growing inequality, the erosion of wages and health benefits. Other losses are less tangible but no less profound. In particular, the democratic aspiration of labor law—the goal of empowering workers as citizens to shape a regime of self-governance and to participate in lawmaking and the adjudication of collectively bargained rights—has no parallel in the patchwork that is employment law. Solidarity gave way to solitary legal claims; collective self-help and self-governance gave way to individual recourse to lawyers and courts; voice and democracy at the workplace gave way to private rights of action. And yet the growing body of employment law beckoned, for the sheer disorder, dynamism, and diversity of institutions and actors within employment law seemed to offer possibilities for reform (and for scholarship) that were growing more scarce within the coherent but schlerotic body of labor law.

This book represents the culmination of my own effort to find new ways to advance the democratic aspirations of labor law using the many legal levers

—the tools, actors, institutions, and resources—that take part in the sprawling enterprise of employment law. The hope is not to supplant unions, collective bargaining, and industrial self-governance but to cultivate new channels for worker participation in which both unions and new worker institutions can thrive alongside each other.

Cultivation is best done in fertile ground, of course. And this book finds fertile ground for a renewal of workplace self-governance in existing trends toward self-regulation—toward using law to encourage firms to internalize public norms (of equality and workplace safety, for example) and to create internal structures for their realization. On the one hand, these internal self-regulatory schemes currently leave workers largely voiceless, for the trend toward self-regulation is taking hold at the same time that unions—the only institutions we have for representation of workers within firms—are shrinking in their reach. On the other hand, these developments portend a renewed commitment to internal lawmaking and law enforcement within a public law framework. If properly channeled, these trends might lead to new forms of governance in which workers have a real voice.

Some of the channeling might be done by workers and worker advocates themselves. For even as various arms of the state are encouraging firms to self-regulate, worker advocacy groups such as worker centers are creating a kind of "bottom-up" pressure to self-regulate. Those groups, sometimes in alliance with unions, are exerting pressure on firms to improve labor conditions and to adopt codes of conduct and monitoring regimes, both for the firms' own operations and for the contractors who supply them with labor. These experiments, still sparse and scattered, can be found in the restaurant and grocery sectors and in maintenance, agriculture, and other pockets of the economy.

This book aims to investigate these developments and to explore both their limitations and their promise as the potential makings of a new model of workplace governance. It will report on experiments in workplace self-regulation, large and small, and evaluate them against the demands of theory and experience, both in the United States and elsewhere. The book finds support in both theory and experience for the necessity of incorporating an effective institutional voice for employees—institutional structures that enable workers to overcome the collective action problems and the fear of reprisals that inhibit them from enforcing their own legal rights at work. If direct public regulation gives way to self-regulatory systems that lack an independent voice for workers, the result is likely to be a disguised form of deregulation and continued disempowerment of employees. But if public regulation operates to encourage forms of self-regulation that include these elements, the result may be a new model of workplace self-governance in which workers can reclaim their role as citizens at work.

These ideas first began percolating many years ago, while I was teaching at the University of Texas School of Law, upon first reading Ian Ayres and John Braithwaite's gem of a book, *Responsive Regulation: Transcending the Deregulation Debate*. It was not until several years and several projects later, after moving to the Columbia Law School, that I turned to this work in earnest. In part that was because Columbia colleagues such as Mark Barenberg, Michael Dorf, Charles Sabel, and Susan Sturm were exploring new "experimentalist" ways of thinking about law and regulation that intersected in intriguing ways with ideas that Braithwaite and others were continuing to pursue. In part it was because my semi-eulogistic article, "The Ossification of American Labor Law" (reprised briefly here in Chapter 2), crystallized in my own mind the contrast between labor law, with its built-in rigidities and barriers to change and experimentation, and the chaotic yet dynamic and protean body of employment law. The outlines of the project were set out in a subsequent *Columbia Law Review* article, "Rebuilding the Law of the Workplace in an Era of Self-Regulation," revised portions of which are incorporated throughout this book. The remaining research and writing were completed after I moved to my present, and eminently pleasant, perch at the New York University School of Law, where I have found extraordinary colleagues and resources, not to mention a lot of great food and espresso.

Now for a reckoning of my debts. I have had the rare good fortune of teaching at three great law schools—the University of Texas, Columbia, and NYU —where research is generously supported and where I had several colleagues who shared a primary focus on the law of the workplace. I have benefited from the generosity of all three law schools, their deans, and their donors. In particular, I would like to thank Dean Richard Revesz and the Filomen D'Agostino and Max E. Greenberg Research Fund at the New York University School of Law, as well as Catherine A. Rein, whose named chair I am proud to hold at NYU.

The list of colleagues to whom I am indebted for their contributions to this project is long and extends beyond the academy. It includes Jennifer Arlen, Miriam Baer, Mark Barenberg, Matthew Bodie, John Braithwaite, Jim Brudney, Lance Compa, Bob Clark, Sam Estreicher, Janice Fine, Matthew Finkin, Catherine Fisk, Willy Forbath, Lilia Garcia, Jack Getman, Jennifer Gordon, Janet Herold, John Howe, Alan Hyde, Sam Issacharoff, Saru Jayaraman, Bob

Kagan, Tom Kochan, Kim Krawiec, Orly Lobel, Deborah Malamud, Richard Moberly, Richard Nagareda, Christine Parker, David Rosenfeld, Brishen Rogers, Cathy Ruckelshaus, Chuck Sabel, Ben Sachs, Vicki Schultz, Judy Scott, Patricia Smith, Katherine Stone, Susan Sturm, and Jim Tierney. I benefited from comments and discussions at and after several workshops and lectures where I have presented parts of this book's thesis, including at the Chicago-Kent School of Law, Columbia Law School, Harvard Law School, Lewis and Clark School of Law, NYU School of Law, University of San Diego School of Law, and the Yale Law School. I also had the help of wonderful research assistants, including Theodore Geiger, Stephanie Herbert, Richard Kaplan, David Lawrence, Andrew Lichtman, Katherine Mastman, Maiko Nakarai, Max Preston, Anna Purinton, Shaun Sethna, Arun Subramanian, Keren Wheeler, and Yi Zhang. At Yale University Press I enjoyed the support and patience of my editor, Michael O'Malley, and the discerning comments of two anonymous reviewers.

Finally, I am deeply indebted to Sam Issacharoff and to our children Jessica and Lucas for all the really important stuff.

New York, New York, May 2009

Part One The Decline of Industrial Self-Governance and the Rise of Self-Regulation

Chapter 1 Introduction

The law that governs work in the United States is not working. Most notoriously, it is not enabling workers to participate collectively in workplace governance, as the centerpiece of the New Deal labor reforms, the National Labor Relations Act (NLRA), was meant to do. It is not providing a firm and decent floor on labor standards, as another pillar of the New Deal, the Fair Labor Standards Act (FLSA), and subsequent labor standards laws were meant to do. And it is not providing most workers with a practicable means of enforcing their legal rights to fair and equal treatment at work, as the 1964 Civil Rights Act and a steady stream of employee rights statutes and doctrines were meant to do.

The failings of "labor law" are evident in the growing gap between the small fraction of workers that has collective representation at work and the large majority that wants some kind of collective representation. The failings of "employment law"—the labor standards laws and individual rights regimes that have proliferated since the New Deal— are less pervasive; there are success stories as well as shortcomings, and we will return to them. But the cracks, crevices, and gaping holes in

3

the floor that the law establishes for labor standards are well chronicled in a spate of recent books whose titles tell the tale: *The Big Squeeze: Tough Times for the American Worker; Wage Theft in America: Why Millions of Working Americans Are Not Getting Paid and What We Can Do about It;* and *The Gloves-Off Economy: Workplace Standards at the Bottom of America's Labor Market.*[1] The blizzard of laws and doctrines that make up employment law have not only failed to fill the vacuum—the representation gap—left by the retreat of collective bargaining, but also much of that law has failed on its own terms to protect workers from substandard and unfair treatment.

In part, the law of the workplace has simply failed to keep up with powerful economic and technological forces—with the increasing speed and ease with which capital, goods, services, and information can be transported across boundaries and around the globe. Those forces have intensified competition in product markets, capital markets, and labor markets; strengthened the hand of capital vis-à-vis both labor and the state; and weakened every piece of the patchwork of rights, regulations, and collective bargaining that makes up the existing paradigm of workplace governance. That late twentieth-century American paradigm, like its cousins across the developed world, is losing its grip on the increasingly fragmented, fluid, and footloose organizations and networks through which goods and services are produced and distributed in the twenty-first century. What will take its place?

Many observers—some hopefully and others anxiously—point to the default regime of workplace governance in a capitalist economy: the market, based on individual contract and legally protected property rights. Of course that is the very regime whose harsh labor-market outcomes brought about the New Deal embrace of state regulatory power on behalf of both minimum labor standards and collectivized bargaining. At least for the majority of citizens who lack both capital and scarce skills, a twenty-first-century version of laissez-faire, unfettered by effective collective bargaining or enforceable labor standards, is not an appealing vision. But that may indeed be where we are headed unless we choose to construct some alternative regime.

What is that alternative regime? This book ventures an answer to that question that is one part prediction and one part prescription. It takes as its starting point the conviction that a new paradigm of workplace governance for the twenty-first century is not going to be constructed from whole cloth. While new thinking and new institutions are clearly needed, a twenty-first-century paradigm will have to be initially constructed with the tools and the materials that the twentieth century has bequeathed us, including what is left of our badly corroded New Deal institutions. The new paradigm will have to take root in the very ground out of which those older institutions grew and into which they are partly crumbling. So, too, a new paradigm of workplace governance cannot be built in sheer defiance of the forces that have corroded the twentieth-century paradigm and its signature institutions, for those forces continue to operate, not only in the U.S. but worldwide, and not only in the law of the workplace but across a wide spectrum of regulatory regimes. Reform efforts, to be successful, will have to channel and shape those forces rather than simply defy them.

So to see where we are headed, we have to look back at where we have been, and we have to look around us at how workers and their advocates and corporations and their managers, both in the U.S. and around the world, are responding to the changing labor landscape. For behind the rattling of a dysfunctional and crumbling New Deal regime we may hear the rumblings of reform.

RUMBLINGS OF REFORM IN SURPRISING PLACES

Wal-Mart, Inc., the world's largest private employer and reigning nemesis of organized labor and other worker advocates, has been touted by fans and foes alike for its masterful deployment of information technology and managed competition—among its thousands of suppliers worldwide, as well as among its thousands of stores—to generate relentless downward pressure on costs, especially labor costs. The world's richest company has generated its famous "Everyday Low Prices" in part through everyday low wages and labor law violations. In its retail stores alone, Wal-Mart has been hit with over fifty class-action lawsuits challenging off-the-clock work demands and overtime violations and a blizzard of lawsuits and legal complaints about the use of child labor and undocumented workers, illegal anti-union activity, and discrimination against women and older and disabled workers. A pending class-action lawsuit on behalf of an unprecedented 1.6 million employees and former employees charges Wal-Mart with sex discrimination in promotions.[2]

The barrage of bad publicity and litigation has provoked powerful labor and community opposition to Wal-Mart's expansion plans.[3] In 2007, Human Rights Watch issued a report lambasting Wal-Mart for its labor practices, especially its "sophisticated and determined" strategy to prevent or quash union organizing. Even in a pervasively anti-union climate in the U.S., "Wal-Mart stands out for the sheer magnitude and aggressiveness of its anti-union apparatus and actions."[4] Even some shareholders have rebelled. In June 2006 the Norwegian government barred its pension fund from holding Wal-Mart stock because, according to the pension fund's Council on Ethics, "[i]t appears to be a systematic and planned practice on the part of the company to operate on, or below, the threshold of what are accepted standards for the work environment."[5]

The onslaught of litigation and adverse publicity seems to have gotten Wal-Mart's serious attention around 2004. That year it announced the creation of a "corporate compliance team" and vowed to use its legendary organizational capabilities, along with new technology and compensation policies, to become "a corporate leader in employment practices."[6] According to the company, new software would ensure that workers were taking required breaks and not working "off the clock"; a new job classification and pay structure would ensure pay equity; and managers' compensation would reflect in part their achievement of "diversity goals." In early 2005, Wal-Mart issued a revised Statement of Ethics that addressed a number of areas in which Wal-Mart had been criticized or sued (though conspicuously absent was any mention of employees' right to join a union).[7] The document set out alternative avenues for employees to report ethics concerns, from "the Open Door" to an anonymous "Ethics Hotline," and offered repeated assurances against retaliation.[8]

What are we to make of Wal-Mart, Inc., vowing to remake itself into a model corporate citizen in its labor practices? Is this a superficial public relations gesture? A genuine and public-spirited embrace of corporate responsibility? Or perhaps simply a rational set of precautions against future accidents and attendant liability? Are these measures diversionary tactics to be exposed and discounted, or do they show the law working just as it should by inducing compliance? Or do they reflect something new and important in the evolution of the law of the workplace?

Wal-Mart's response to its legal and political troubles is not exactly novel; the corporate compliance bandwagon has been on the road for some time. What is comparatively new, at least within the labor and employment universe, lies in what companies may now hope to gain from such programs. Internal compliance structures are no longer merely prophylactic or liability-avoidance schemes instituted under the "shadow of the law;" rather, they seek to meet explicit demands of external law and to earn distinct legal benefits.[9] Wal-Mart and others hope to be judged not only on the basis of whether they have complied with substantive legal standards—for example, whether employees in fact worked off-the-clock and without pay—but also on the basis of whatever internal systems the firms have in place to try to ensure compliance with those legal standards. If internal reforms can indeed be relied upon to secure compliance with legal norms (or better), then it only makes sense for the government to focus its scarce enforcement efforts elsewhere and for courts to construct liability rules that encourage such reforms. But can we count on firms' compliance programs to do what they purport to do? It all depends, as we will see.

More rumblings of reform can be heard from seemingly distant quarters: Manhattan's fine restaurants. The Restaurant Opportunities Committee of New York (ROC-NY) was formed with union support to help downtown restaurant workers displaced in the wake of the September 11 attacks. But the group soon shifted its focus when it was inundated with complaints of mistreatment from the restaurant workers: unpaid wages and overtime, misappropriation of tips, discrimination, and harassment. On behalf of the mostly immigrant restaurant workers, ROC-NY has supported lawsuits and engaged in some rather theatrical protest tactics against targeted offenders, especially the large restaurant conglomerates—such as the Smith and Wollensky Restaurant Group (S&W)—which own a growing share of Manhattan's high-end restaurant market.

In January 2005, ROC-NY reached a settlement agreement with S&W, winning $164,000 for twenty-three workers who had sued, claiming unpaid overtime and racial discrimination at two restaurants. As part of the settlement, S&W agreed not only to reform its wage and hour practices but also to institute management training, paid vacations and sick days, progressive discipline, and a promotion policy, as well as to include these provisions in a handbook that would be distributed to all employees. ROC-NY serves as the informal monitor of the agreement and as the formal monitor of one of its provisions —a pledge not to fire any of the twenty-three plaintiffs without giving ROC-NY three days' notice and an opportunity to investigate the termination to ensure that it was not retaliatory in nature. In the few instances where workers have reported violations of the agreement, the issues have been promptly resolved. According to ROC-NY founder and former director Saru Jayaraman, "the fear of us returning" has kept violations to a minimum.[10]

Another major target, the Fireman Hospitality Group of five restaurants, fought off waiters' wage and hour and discrimination claims and denounced ROC-NY's publicity campaign for several years. But in 2008, the Fireman Group capitulated and agreed to a settlement that included not only $3.9 million in back pay (mostly for tips that waiters were illegally required to share with managers), but also prospective relief in the form of concrete policy changes and a grievance procedure for resolution of future worker complaints. Other targeted restaurant owners, after watching ROC-NY's successful campaigns against competitors, decided to make peace rather than fight. When ROC-NY kicked off one campaign against a prominent restaurateur, it received a phone call offering to meet the very next day. Restaurant owners knew what others in the industry had been through and wished to avoid it.[11]

In five years, ROC-NY mounted eight successful campaigns against targeted restaurateurs. Capitalizing on its success in these campaigns, it spearheaded the formation of the Restaurant Industry Roundtable, a nonprofit association of "high road" restaurateurs that is seeking to brand itself, with ROC-NY's support, as the industry's good citizens. The Roundtable is in its infancy still, but might become a vehicle for more ambitious reform efforts. In January 2008, the founders of ROC-NY launched a new nationwide organization, ROC-United, to build on the success of the New York project and to start up new branches across the country.[12]

From a twentieth-century viewpoint, an organization like ROC-NY appears to be either a precursor or an impediment to unionization—either as a kind of "pre-union," laying the groundwork for conventional union organizing in the future, or as a feeble substitute for unionization and collective bargaining, one that might make it harder for employees to get the real deal. But perhaps ROC-NY's strategy instead foreshadows a new model of collaborative self-governance with the potential to secure real gains—both improved labor standards and a collective voice in working conditions—for workers whose needs have not been met by the twentieth-century paradigm. Like Wal-Mart's compliance initiative, ROC-NY's settlement agreements embody a form of self-regulation—private initiatives that purport to internalize public law norms and values on behalf of workers and to go beyond mere compliance, aiming (from the employers' standpoint) to deflect external pressures, legal and non-legal, by doing so. Like Wal-Mart and the standard corporate compliance, program, ROC-NY's strategy seeks in part to tap the monitoring capabilities of employees themselves. Unlike Wal-Mart's initiative, the ROC strategy engages workers not only as individuals but also collectively, through an outside worker advocacy organization, in the process of monitoring compliance and governing facets of the workplace. Even with that crucial added component, the ROC-NY model may fail if the vectors of pressure that converged to induce employers to enter into the agreements falter. On the other hand, if the agreements work as envisioned, they may secure not only better compliance with legal norms than public enforcement promises to do, but also improvements beyond what public law requires.

Are these self-regulatory schemes just a minor twist on the twentieth-century paradigm? Or are they merely cushioning or even obscuring the collapse of that paradigm in favor of de facto deregulation? Or are they the wave of the future and the makings of a new paradigm of workplace governance? Again, it all depends.

FROM LABOR LAW TO EMPLOYMENT LAW

To understand and shape the divergent possibilities that are presented by the movement toward self-regulation in the workplace, it will be helpful to look back from whence it came. For the concept of self-regulation resonates with rather old ideas in workplace governance. The New Deal model of industrial relations, with its reliance on self-organization of workers and voluntary collective bargaining over most terms and conditions of employment, is itself a system of self-governance.[13] Industrial democracy through collective bargaining was to head off the need for extensive government regulation of wages and working conditions. It was designed to enable the "citizens" of the enterprise to use a reconstructed regime of contract to generate mutually agreeable, flexible, and workplace-specific solutions to labor-management problems and accessible mechanisms for the resolution of workplace disputes.

But in succeeding decades, American labor law's favored system of collective bargaining has faltered, and its reach has shrunk to a small fraction of the private-sector workforce. There are many complex and intertwined reasons for the decline of collective bargaining, including both employer resistance to unionization and the economic forces that motivate employers to resist unionization. Unions themselves bear a share of the blame, both for what they did well—negotiating rich wage and benefit packages that depended for their viability on employers' insulation from competition—and for what they did badly—failing for too long to organize the unorganized and tolerating pockets of corruption. But one reason for the decline of collective bargaining is that labor law itself has become an increasingly clumsy vehicle for workers' self-organization and increasingly impotent against intense employer resistance.

Labor law's ineffectuality, in turn, is due in part to its "ossification"—its extraordinary insulation for more than sixty years from both internal and external sources of renovation.[14] Labor law has been insulated from revision at the national level by Congress; from "market"-driven competition by employers; from the entrepreneurial energies of individual plaintiffs and the plaintiff's bar and the creativity they can sometimes coax from the courts; from variation at the state or local level by representative or judicial bodies; from the winds of changing constitutional doctrine; and from emerging transnational legal norms. Even without knowing where any of these potential paths of change might have led, one can surmise that change or experimentation through one or more of these channels might have produced, over the past half-century, a body of labor law that was more responsive to the very different economic and social conditions that workers and employers face today. Instead we are left with the legacy of the New Deal and the immediate postwar backlash.

The tale of labor law's ossification bears emphasis here, as it is bristling with warning signs and lessons for those who would construct new mechanisms for governing the workplace and work in the U.S. One of the lessons is that the raw materials for reform are less likely to be found within the fairly coherent but fossilized body of labor law than within the unruly but dynamic patchwork of employment law that has grown up in its wake. For even as the New Deal model of industrial self-governance has faltered, the problems to which collective bargaining was to be the answer have not disappeared. Nor has the law ceased to grapple with them. On the contrary, the role of external law—litigation, legislation, and regulation—has burgeoned as the New Deal system of internalized lawmaking and dispute resolution has shrunk.

Since the 1960s, the New Deal collective bargaining system has been supplemented, and largely supplanted, by other forms of workplace governance: a regulatory model of minimum standards, enforceable mainly by administrative agencies, and a rights model of judicially enforceable individual rights. The former is exemplified by the wage and hour laws and the Occupational Safety and Health Act (OSHA); the latter, by civil rights laws and the employee rights underlying the law of wrongful discharge. These two branches of "employment law" each mobilized institutions and resources that were not central to the collective bargaining model constituted by labor law. The regulatory model harnessed the coercive power and resources of the government, while the rights model made courts central to the articulation and enforcement of employee rights and tapped into the self-interest and indignation of aggrieved individuals and the professional and entrepreneurial energies of their attorneys. Both regulations and individual rights have emanated from state and even local governments—those famed laboratories of reform that have been banished from the field of labor law—as well as from Congress.

As a result of these enactments, the law of the workplace, once dominated by New Deal labor law and the collective bargaining model it established, is now dominated by regulatory statutes administered by government agencies and by individual rights enforceable through private litigation. In principle, the legal rights of employees and the corresponding limitations on employer power that have developed since 1964 provide rudimentary analogs to the constitutional rights of citizens as against the government—"equal protection" rights, free speech rights, even some scattered due process rights. One may be tempted to see in these doctrines a revival of the New Deal conception of employees as "citizens" of the workplace. But it is at best a highly truncated conception of citizenship. The regulatory model renders employees the passive beneficiaries of the government's protection. The rights-litigation model of wrongful discharge law casts employees as rights bearers but also—and perhaps more visibly—as victims seeking redress for past wrongs. Neither conceives of employees, as the NLRA does, as citizens of the workplace actively participating in its governance. Especially in the wake of union decline, the modern workplace suffers from a serious "democratic deficit," for labor law has failed to deliver a mechanism that allows employees to participate in workplace governance, and employment law does not even try to do so.

. . . AND FROM COMPLIANCE TO
REGULATED SELF-REGULATION

So employment law has not grown into a worthy successor to the New Deal model of workplace self-governance. But it has become an unruly hydra head of duties and liabilities for employers, and those liabilities had to be managed. Title VII of the Civil Rights Act of 1964 and the wave of discrimination litigation that followed generated the growth of internal grievance procedures and equal employment offices within firms, with the aim of preventing or redressing potential discrimination complaints and avoiding lawsuits. The enactment of OSHA spurred the growth of internal health and safety departments. Corporate compliance structures were put in place to manage potential employment law liabilities, as well as liabilities under environmental, securities, consumer safety, and other regulatory regimes. At their best, corporate compliance efforts aspire not only to avoid liabilities but also to embrace corporate responsibility and internalize the public values and goals behind these various legal regimes. At their worst, these programs may be mere window dressing— a glossy façade behind which business goes on as usual.

Whether mere window dressing or otherwise, these programs are increasingly prominent features of the public face that big corporations seek to present. Firms vow not just to comply with legal standards but to exceed them—to be not just a law-abiding corporate citizen but a model citizen. These public commitments are prominently displayed on corporate Web sites, typically on the opening page or at most one click away. Here is what we find, by way of illustration, starting at the top of the 2008 list of Fortune 500 companies:

- Wal-Mart portrays as its top concerns community development, economic opportunity and "health and wellness" of customers and employees, and environmental sustainability.[15]
- Exxon-Mobile's "Corporate Citizenship Report" details contributions to education, the environment, world health, employee safety, community development, and "worldwide giving."[16]
- Chevron, Inc.'s "Corporate Responsibility Report" describes programs on human rights, economic and community development, and environmental protection.[17]
- General Motors' corporate responsibility report highlights environmental commitment, safety, diversity, and community.[18]

The proclaimed commitment to corporate citizenship, and to going above and beyond compliance, extends invariably to employee well-being, especially health, safety, and diversity. Continuing down the Fortune 500 list:

- ConocoPhillips states: "We will not be satisfied until we succeed in eliminating all injuries, occupational illnesses, unsafe practices and incidents of environmental harm from our activities."[19]
- General Electric reports on systems for continuous improvement of workplace health and safety, work-life balance, and diversity and inclusiveness, among other areas of social responsibility.[20]
- Ford Motor Company says of its occupational health policy: "We're committed to meeting and exceeding . . . regulatory requirements. When necessary and appropriate, we establish and comply with standards of our own, which may go beyond legal mandates. . . .[O]ur priority is achieving the greatest anticipated practical benefit while striving for continuous improvement."[21]
- Citigroup articulates its belief "that every employee should be treated with respect and dignity and work in an environment that is free from discrimination," embraces principles of international law, and advertises its programs for

diversity and inclusiveness, safety, and even meeting employees' childcare needs.[22]

Hundreds more such pronouncements could be readily gleaned from the public relations materials of leading corporations. Of course, all one can confidently conclude from this superficial survey is that corporations—at least large, brand-conscious corporations—wish, or even feel compelled, to cultivate a reputation for good citizenship and to create at least the semblance of an institutional commitment to public values.

Yet even as employers publicly embraced corporate compliance and social responsibility, they continued to push back politically and legally against the burdens of regulatory compliance and litigation (much as they resisted the constraints of collective bargaining). Consider, for example, the U.S. Chamber of Commerce's "Policy Priorities for 2009" in the labor arena, which have a distinctly deregulatory cast:

- Oppose unreasonable expansion of workplace mandates and craft alternatives when necessary.
- Aggressively oppose initiatives to make union organizing easier, including union-backed proposals to abolish secret ballot elections in favor of card-check majorities for union recognition.
- Oppose efforts to expand the Family and Medical Leave Act by covering smaller businesses and oppose making leave paid.
- Oppose efforts to mandate paid sick leave.
- Oppose efforts to expand civil rights laws by increasing the amount of punitive and compensatory damages available, the potential for frivolous litigation, and unjustified administrative burdens.
- Block attempts to unreasonably increase penalties for criminal violations of OSHA.
- Protect the use of binding arbitration in employment. . . .
- Oppose any attempt to revive an OSHA ergonomics regulation.[23]

To be sure, there is no great difficulty in logically reconciling a plea for deregulation with a corporate commitment to social responsibility and employee welfare. Translation: "Leave us alone, as we're already committed to doing the right thing by our workers and the public." But other less sanguine interpretations come readily to mind: "Leave us alone so that we can decide just how much or how little to live up to our public commitments."

Employers' pleas for deregulation over the decades have yielded rather little actual deregulatory legislation, but they have taken their toll on regulatory efficacy through underfunding and understaffing, procedural delays, and (especially during antiregulatory administrations) heightened demands for justification.[24] Similarly, employer tirades against the "litigation crisis" have yielded few legislative cutbacks on employee rights, though they have yielded doctrinal and procedural hurdles that stymie most plaintiffs.[25] Moreover, employers have secured judicial approval for a strategy of muffling the threat of litigation through mandatory arbitration.[26] Informal deregulation has proceeded in other ways as well. Employers in the lower reaches of the labor market have opted for evasion, hiding below the regulatory radar and beyond the effective reach of litigation, in part by employing workers who do not know their rights or fear to assert them. At the same time, American employers have put quite a lot of jobs —especially in manufacturing—beyond the reach of American law through the relocation and outsourcing of production to lower-wage (and less regulated) jurisdictions.

Challenges to the efficacy of regulation and litigation of workplace rights and labor standards have come not only from employers, however, but from scholars and employee advocates as well. Observers from a range of perspectives have argued that the postwar regime of "command-and-control" regulation is losing its grip in the face of rapidly changing markets, technology, and firm structures;[27] that uniform national (or even state or local) labor standards do not and never will address the range of concerns and the variety of contexts that workers face;[28] and that "adversarial legalism" and "regulatory unreasonableness" are undermining the pursuit of public regulatory goals.[29] The poster child for many of these critiques is OSHA, with its thousands of pages of detailed regulations anchored to the technologies that existed decades ago at the time of their adoption. Even the comparatively flexible and dynamic regime of individual employee rights and private rights of action has come in for its share of criticism from scholars and employee advocates. Civil litigation has been a potent spur to internal corporate reform and compliance activity, but it has proven to be a costly, slow, and often inaccessible mechanism for securing workers' rights and adjudicating disputes.[30]

Some of these critiques echo the very arguments that led New Dealers to turn away from extensive public regulation of the workplace and toward unionization and collective bargaining—toward shared self-governance—as the primary vehicles for addressing workplace disputes and the inequities of the labor market. This time around, however, with labor unions in seemingly steady decline, many critics, courts, and regulators have converged instead on the con-

cept of "self-regulation." They point to the growth and increasing sophistica-
tion of corporate compliance structures as evidence that corporate self-regulation is a real phenomenon and can be made an effective instrument of social
control. The call for self-regulation takes many forms, some of which are hard
to distinguish from employers' own arguments for deregulation. But the more
sophisticated proponents of corporate self-regulation—particularly those who
have gathered under the broad umbrella of "New Governance"—argue not for
the abandonment of public regulation of corporate conduct but for its rede-
ployment: external law should be designed to encourage employers to internalize public values and regulate their own practices rather than serving primarily as a direct instrument of control. In other words, the law should not
merely step aside in favor of voluntary self-regulation; it should regulate self-
regulation.

The concept of regulated self-regulation has begun to make its mark on the
law of the workplace (though not only on the law of the workplace). Agencies
responsible for enforcing labor standards—OSHA, for example—have experimented with cooperative programs designed to induce self-regulation and voluntary compliance and to make more efficient use of regulatory resources.
Courts responsible for enforcing employee rights have begun to formalize the
role of internal compliance procedures, granting employers a partial shield
against litigation and liability based on those schemes. So firms that maintain
an acceptable internal antidiscrimination policy and grievance process may
have a legal defense, partial or total, against some Title VII claims by employees, and firms that maintain an acceptable private arbitration regime may secure near-immunity from civil litigation. These developments bring the main
locus of enforcement of both rights and regulations inside the firm or under the
firm's control. The internal compliance regimes of Wal-Mart and many other
employers must be seen in that light: as efforts not simply to comply with the
law but also to secure the legal advantages of self-regulation and a partial shield
against regulatory and judicial intervention.

Superficially, one might see these developments in employment law as a reen-
actment of the New Deal embrace of self-governance over public regulation as
the primary mode of protecting workers and improving wages and working
conditions. We are again moving toward internal lawmaking and law enforcement within a public law framework and away from direct public regulation
or judicial resolution of workplace disputes. But one striking difference between New Deal–style self-governance and twenty-first-century-style self-regulation is that, this time around, workers have been largely cut out of the in-

ternal governance schemes. The trend toward self-regulation, and toward public regulation of and reliance on self-regulation, has been gaining ground at the same time as the system of self-governance through union representation and collective bargaining has been shrinking in scope. The corporate "self" that is increasingly gaining the prerogative to regulate itself is less likely than ever to encompass employees other than as individuals, who face familiar and daunting impediments to effective bargaining or intervention on their own behalf.

At the same time, however, there has been a surge of innovation and experimentation among and on behalf of employees themselves, especially low-wage employees who have benefited least from the rise of corporate compliance schemes and suffered most from the decline of unions and the shortfall of public enforcement. Labor unions themselves have experimented with new organizing strategies, and have won some impressive gains among and for low-wage workers, by abjuring the NLRA's notoriously cumbersome and conflict-ridden representation process in favor of a privately negotiated path to collective bargaining. Alongside conventional labor unions, and sometimes in alliance with them, worker centers such as ROC-NY, with their energetic membership, creative leadership, and impressive capacity for learning and coalition building, have brought a jolt of energy to the labor movement and a spate of experiments to improve working conditions. Partly inspired by the global anti-sweatshop movement, some worker centers have turned to the eminently flexible framework of contract to create their own mechanisms for improving labor standards. They have induced employers to enter into codes of conduct, with promises of not only compliance but often better-than-compliance with labor standards and with provisions for formal or informal monitoring of compliance.

These bottom-up experiments may seem far removed from the corporate boardrooms where social responsibility commitments are proclaimed and corporate compliance systems are hatched and overseen. But both the corporate social responsibility and compliance schemes and the bottom-up worker-centered efforts are hybrid forms of public-private regulation by which employers, responding to a combination of legal and nonlegal pressures, make voluntary commitments that go beyond what external law demands and put private organizational resources in the service of public regulatory goals. Many of those efforts have at their center a contractual or quasi-contractual commitment along the lines of a code of conduct. And law in its conventional guises—litigation and legal complaints, legislation and regulation—plays a variety of roles, both behind the scenes and on stage, in inducing firms to enter into both kinds of above-and-beyond commitments. The two developments must take their places alongside each other in the emerging constellation of "New Governance" strategies for workplace governance.

The trend toward more and less regulated versions of self-regulation is not unique to the law of the workplace. It follows a trajectory that has become increasingly familiar, and widely analyzed, in corporate criminal law, securities law, and environmental law, among other areas. In all of these areas, across much of the world as well as in the U.S., there has been a shift away from direct mechanisms of legal control and toward what some scholars call "reflexive" mechanisms of legal control that encourage effective self-regulation, and the internalization of public values, by organizations.[31] Many of these mechanisms, including most of those extant in the law of the workplace, take a conditional or quasi-contractual form: self-regulation is not mandated but is encouraged and rewarded, most tangibly by the promise of relief from some aspect of the background enforcement regime. Those self-regulatory privileges are conditioned on what the law recognizes as adequate self-regulatory activity.

Detractors see the move away from direct state enforcement and toward self-regulation as a more or less disguised form of deregulation, one that allows firms to deflect public scrutiny by engaging in "cosmetic compliance" and window dressing.[32] Proponents see the evolution of more efficient and effective systems for enforcing legal norms.[33] Much in the debate turns on whether courts and regulators can be counted on to distinguish effective from ineffective systems of self-regulation. Effective self-regulatory processes can introduce flexibility and responsiveness into the regulatory regime and reduce the costs and contentiousness associated with litigation while promoting the internalization of public law norms into the regulated organization itself. But if we cannot be confident that courts and regulators can or will distinguish real from cosmetic compliance, then regulated self-regulation may become a thinly disguised form of deregulation.

Whatever may be the evolving wisdom on self-regulation and corporate compliance schemes generally, their diffusion within the law of the workplace deserves special attention. The shift toward self-regulation is based in large part on the recognition that those who are best situated to detect, report, and avoid organizational misconduct are the insiders employed by the organization. Systems that activate the monitoring potential of insiders can improve corporate compliance far beyond what ordinary law enforcement can do. In the case of labor standards and employee rights, the firm's employees are not only the best potential monitors of misconduct but are also the primary beneficiaries of the law. That fact, unique to the law of the workplace, creates both distinct opportunities and distinct risks in the self-regulation of employee rights and labor standards.

The distinct opportunities are quite obvious: employees within self-regulating firms have both interest and information—motive and means—to monitor labor standards and respect for employee rights. Employee reporting mechanisms are central to programs of effective compliance with environmental law or of financial requirements; how much more important and valuable must such mechanisms be in a system of self-regulation of worker health and safety, for example? Whatever altruistic or organizational motive employees have to report dangerous consumer products or financial shenanigans, for example, they have an additional intrinsic and self-interested motive to report dangerous working conditions or denial of overtime pay. At least in the non-union workplace, employees still face collective action problems, for most of what the law of the workplace requires are "public goods" within the workforce or some subset of it. They affect employees as a group, and the benefits of compliance to employees as a group, as well as the costs to the employer, are much larger than are the benefits to any one employee. So individual employees do not have enough incentive to speak up, even apart from their fear of reprisals. But if that problem can be overcome, the activation of employees within internal compliance systems has a huge potential payoff.

Yet distinct risks arise from employees' economic dependence on the employer whose compliance is sought, for at least non-union workers may fear that they will be fired or otherwise penalized if they report or complain about employer misconduct. Of course that is a challenge to any effort to activate employees as monitors and "whistleblowers," whether on behalf of environmental or consumer safety or securities laws. But those laws do not put all their private enforcement "eggs" in one basket. The laws' beneficiaries, who are outside the organization, generally have some independent mechanism for challenging the organization's misconduct—for example, a securities fraud suit by shareholders, a private right of action under environmental laws, or a tort action by consumers for injury from unsafe products or practices. Recourse to private enforcement mechanisms by shareholders, citizens, or consumers may be difficult or costly and it may be hindered by the lack of inside information, but it is not encumbered by the economic dependence of an employment relationship. In the case of employment laws, however, employees may be inhibited in both their internal whistleblowing and their private enforcement efforts by the fear of reprisals (unless they have already quit or been fired). That is where the state, and public enforcement, traditionally come in. But to the extent that self-regulation goes hand in hand with a reduction in direct state oversight, employees' fear of reprisals may be the Achilles' heel of the system. It may allow employers to fend off liability or regulatory scrutiny on the basis of compliance systems that do not do the job.

The legal literature on corporate compliance and self-regulation has generally overlooked these peculiar complexities posed by the law of the workplace. Neither the economically oriented analysts of corporate compliance nor most exponents of New Governance have come to grips with the vulnerability of employee beneficiaries within the workplace: non-union employees lack any external enforcement agent other than the state, whose retreat from the front lines of enforcement is the assumption behind, if not the very purpose of, these self-regulatory systems. The extension of regulated self-regulation to the law of the workplace thus has the potential to divert crucial public resources from the task of securing compliance with public norms and to enfeeble the few fearsome legal weapons that worker advocates have in their efforts to enforce basic employee rights and labor standards.

The momentum in favor of self-regulatory solutions and against sole reliance on direct state regulation is growing. Both corporations and their stakeholders are pouring prodigious resources into improving the state of the art in designing and assessing self-regulatory compliance systems. There is still a lively and important debate over the virtues of self-regulatory approaches to workplace regulation. But in the meantime, this train has left the station. Workers and their advocates have more to gain, I believe, from getting on the self-regulation train and trying to steer it than from trying to flag down the train or blow up the tracks.

LOOKING AHEAD: FROM SELF-REGULATION TO
SELF-GOVERNANCE BY WAY OF CO-REGULATION

If all workers had to gain from effective forms of self-regulation were the better enforcement of the law's minimum standards, then that would be worth something, and perhaps a great deal for workers at the bottom of the labor market. But it would hardly promise an alternative vehicle for self-governance akin to the system of collective bargaining that it promises (or threatens) to overtake. Fortunately, self-regulation programs aspire and often do push substantive standards above the legal floor. The internal corporate codes of conduct that have proliferated in recent years almost invariably pledge to reach beyond legal standards toward higher standards of social responsibility. And in nearly every code of conduct that is negotiated by worker advocates, employers commit to doing more or better than the law requires.

So the rise of regulated self-regulation is a potential vehicle not only for improving enforcement of underenforced minimum legal standards but also for improving standards beyond the legal minimum. I say "potential" because many questions remain about the viability and efficacy of existing self-regulatory undertakings, both unilateral and contractual. But realizing that potential for exceeding legal standards is crucial, in part because that feature of regulated self-regulation responds to some of the shortcomings of the system of command-and-control regulation that it is supposed to supplant.

Two of the inherent weaknesses of uniform minimum standards are their rigidity in the face of changing conditions and their uniformity in the face of firms' widely varying capabilities and workers' varying needs and interests. Uniform minimum standards invariably demand too little of some firms that can do better and provide too little for workers who want more. Of course, that is in the nature of minimum standards. Their introduction in the New Deal was meant to provide a floor from which workers, as individuals and through unions, could bargain up. With the drastic decline of collective bargaining, it is crucial to find additional mechanisms by which workers—and not only those with scarce skills and individual bargaining power—can secure improvements in their wages and working conditions above the legal floor. We will have the makings of a new form of workplace self-governance only if we can realize the potential of regulated self-regulation to improve upon substantive minimum standards in ways that respond to workers' varied and changing needs and desires. But before building up from the legal floor, we must figure out how to ensure that the floor is sound—that mechanisms of self-regulation, at a minimum, can be made effective in securing compliance with existing legal mandates.

What will it take to create an effective system of self-regulation in the workplace? In its particulars, the answer will vary from one legal regime to another and from one industry or firm to another. It will be different for employment discrimination laws than for workplace safety laws, and it will be different for a large corporation like Wal-Mart than for a small janitorial contractor. One of the lessons of labor law's ossification is that any single system of workplace governance is likely to be, or to become, dysfunctional over time and across the range of workplaces and industries that are in need of better governance. Still, particular solutions should be informed by more general principles. In seeking those general principles, I turn first to the model of Responsive Regulation, championed especially by John Braithwaite.[34] Braithwaite and others, drawing on a wealth of experience across an array of regulatory arenas, maintain that effective self-regulation must be tripartite in structure. It requires the participation of the regulated firm, the government, *and* the primary beneficiaries of the relevant legal norms, or "stakeholders."[35] And whether the beneficiaries of the relevant legal norms are consumers, patients, shareholders, air breathers, or workers, they must be represented in some organized form that allows them to influence and monitor self-regulatory processes.

Effective employee participation in self-regulation requires not only avenues for individual reporting by employees—which are part of any functioning self-regulatory process whatever laws are concerned—but also some form of collective representation. That is true, first, because individual employees—especially those without strong job security—are bound to be inhibited from monitoring by fear of reprisals. Organizations with an existence outside as well as inside the workplace have independence and insulation against reprisals that individual employees lack. Second, compliance with many employment laws is a "public good" within the workforce—a benefit that is shared across the group such that individual workers have an inadequate incentive to invest in it. Organizations of workers may help overcome this collective action problem. Third, effective participation in self-regulation requires power to affect decision making and to counter the opportunistic impulses that may lead firms to cheat and defect from their self-regulatory commitments; individual employees rarely have that power. So some form of collective employee representation that has one foot outside the employer's domain, such as a union, appears to be essential to effective self-regulation of labor standards and employee rights.

The problem, as noted, is that the move toward self-regulation has coincided with a drastic decline in unionization, and unionization is the only legally sanctioned vehicle in the U.S. for organized employee representation within the firm. Even apart from the trend toward self-regulation, both employee rights and workplace regulations are often underenforced in the absence of union representation, especially where employers are committed to competing through the minimization of labor costs.[36] The movement toward self-regulation and the attendant retreat of public agencies and courts from the front lines of enforcement exacerbate this vulnerability. Indeed, some critics fear that the rise of self-regulation will contribute to the further erosion of institutions of employee voice: "By diverting attention to management monitoring systems, and away from classic voice mechanisms . . . , self-regulatory initiatives run the risk of supplanting rather than buttressing democratic participation in the work-place."[37] Yet the prospects for reviving and dramatically extending the New Deal collective bargaining model in the U.S. seem bleak.

One might well tell a fatalistic version of this story (as perhaps befits a labor law story these days): unions and collective bargaining have been battered and eroded by relentless forces of competition and capitalist opportunism (in what-ever mix one favors). Those same forces have also led employers to push with some success for the state's retreat from the front lines of adversarial enforce-ment in favor of the internalization and domestication of both rights and reg-ulatory standards. Those processes in turn have exacerbated the vulnerability of employees who lack a collective voice within firms and threaten in that un-organized setting to collapse into deregulation.

I aim to retell the story as one of possibility, for the partial migration of em-ployment law and its enforcement inside firms creates not only the need but also the opportunity to revive employees' voice inside firms. That is because the law can and does impose conditions on firms' ability to secure the legal ad-vantages of self-regulation. To the extent that firms construct compliance sys-tems with an eye not only to improving compliance but also to securing favored legal and regulatory treatment, they must meet conditions set by law, and those conditions are meant to ensure the efficacy of self-regulation. One of those conditions should be the effective and collective participation of the employ-ees whose rights and working conditions are at stake. So when public agencies set the conditions for admission to a less adversarial enforcement track based on self-regulatory programs, or when courts set the conditions for a partial de-fense against liability, they should ensure that the affected employees have an effective organizational voice in the self-regulatory process. So, too, when pri-vate actors deploy legal and nonlegal pressures to induce firms to enter into contractual commitments to self-regulation, they should include provisions for effective collective involvement by employees in the self-regulatory scheme.

I will use the term "co-regulation" here as shorthand for a regime of effec-tive employer self-regulation in which employee beneficiaries have a genuine collective voice. Any self-regulatory privileges that the law and legal actors deal out in the employment arena—partial defenses to liability, more congenial and cooperative enforcement tracks—should be reserved for firms that maintain a system of co-regulation. Unlike much of what now passes for corporate self-reg-ulation, a system of co-regulation provides safeguards against cosmetic com-pliance and self-deregulation that critics legitimately fear.

This is not the first proposal to improve compliance with employment mandates by fostering new vehicles for employee representation. The concept of co-regulation proposed here resonates strongly, for example, with David Levine's proposal in the late 1990s for "conditional deregulation."[38] That proposal would offer firms the opportunity to opt out of certain aspects of the default regime for enforcement of labor standards and employee rights—including many of the law's detailed rules, regulations, and enforcement mechanisms —if they maintain employee representation committees, chosen by employees and insulated in certain respects from managerial control, to oversee the firms' pursuit of regulatory goals. Like the proposal advanced here, Levine's proposal pursued the dual aims of greater flexibility and efficacy on the regulatory side and greater employee voice in the non-union workplace, and it did so by trading off elements of external regulatory enforcement for better internal governance mechanisms. But during the ten years that have passed since Levine's proposal, the ranks of organized labor have both continued to decline and reinvigorated themselves; new institutions for worker representation and experiments in workplace reform have multiplied across the country; compliance activity and the imperative of social responsibility have taken firmer hold and gained salience within the corporate firmanent; command-and-control has continued to lose its grip and public enforcement of labor standards has deteriorated; and both theories and empirical studies of alternative, governance-based approaches to regulation have gained traction among regulators and scholars. This book aims to chart a path toward co-regulation that takes account of these developments—to understand how co-regulation fits with trends that are already well under way and to capitalize on their momentum, while highlighting the critical dangers and challenges that lie within some of those trends.

A gap still remains between co-regulation and shared governance. But the former may be a stepping stone to the latter. If workers have an effective collective voice in a system of self-regulation—that is, enough power to monitor compliance and to counter firms' opportunistic impulses—then they will often have the power to seek more than compliance. The information, skills, channels of communication, and points of leverage that are needed to ensure compliance with, or trigger enforcement of, minimum standards can also be deployed to seek additional improvements. There are no guarantees. But then there were no guarantees that unions would be able to bargain collectively for wages, benefits, and working conditions beyond what the law required. Labor-market and product-market conditions matter—and are probably less favorable for most workers now than they were in the 1940s and 1950s. But if workers can achieve an effective voice within the workplace for purposes of enforcing their legal rights, that voice may carry over to other objectives too. That is how co-regulation could grow into a form of workplace self-governance and could begin to address the "democratic deficit" opened up by the retreat of collective bargaining.

A ROADMAP OF THE BOOK

The book is organized as follows: Part 1 surveys the terrain in which any new paradigm of workplace governance in the U.S. will have to take root: the complex past and present of workplace self-governance and self-regulation. Chapter 2 recounts the ossification and decline of the New Deal system of industrial self-governance through collective bargaining. That tale introduces some important architectural components of the existing law of the workplace and suggests some constraints on, and lessons for, future reforms. Chapter 3 briefly charts the proliferation of labor standards laws (epitomized by those regulating wages and hours and occupational health and safety) and individual employee rights, especially the equality rights of the Civil Rights Act and its progeny. Both of those chapters cover ground that will be familiar to those who teach or practice labor and employment law.

Chapter 4 turns to some less familiar developments: the rise of forms of "regulated self-regulation"—that is, public laws and doctrines that seek to encourage self-regulation and, within the regulated firms, self-regulatory mechanisms that aim not only to improve compliance but also to satisfy explicit legal standards and secure explicit legal concessions. While Chapter 4 focuses on the forms of self-regulation that have developed within larger and more complex firms out of the interaction between regulators (including courts) and regulated firms, Chapter 5 turns to self-regulation at the lower layers of the labor market. That includes creative public enforcement programs as well as a number of bottom-up experiments in self-regulation initiated by workers and their organizations, traditional and nontraditional. In response to the failings of both firms and regulators in some low-wage sectors of the economy, workers in a variety of settings have turned again to the basic architecture of contract: codes of conduct and monitoring agreements in which worker organizations are direct participants. In these experiments one can see both something old and something new—echoes of the American labor movement's voluntarist roots and its reliance on contract, as well as efforts to integrate enforcement of labor standards and enhancement of worker voice outside of the traditional domain of labor law and collective bargaining.

Part 2 turns to the future and to the question of how to steer the self-regulatory juggernaut away from the spectre of *de facto* deregulation and toward new forms of workplace governance that serve the interests of workers, respect their rights, and enhance their voice at work. I begin in Chapter 6 with the theoretical model for effective self-regulation set out in "Responsive Regulation." In seeking to retool its tripartite system of regulated self-regulation for the setting of chronic underenforcement and low union density that we face in the U.S., I draw additional insights from two main sources: the theory of "ratcheting labor standards," which envisions a system for effective regulation of global supply chains in the virtual absence of public regulation and union representation, and the American system of "audited self-regulation" under the corporate securities law, as refined in the wake of corporate financial scandals. The three different models of regulation are instructive especially for what they agree on—for example, the crucial regulatory role of independent nongovernmental bodies—but also for where they differ—for example, on the centrality of state power and organized stakeholder representation. Chapter 6 concludes with a sketch of the model of co-regulation, which the remaining chapters fill in.

Central to co-regulation is employee representation. Employee representation is not the only condition for effective self-regulation of workplace rights and standards, but it is the one that is most challenging to implement in the overwhelmingly non-union environment that exists, and is likely to persist, in the United States. That is especially so under the existing labor law regime, which not only fails to enable employees to form their own traditional labor organizations, but also creates impediments to some nontraditional forms of employee representation. So Chapter 7 begins to carry the lessons of theory a few steps closer to realization in the American workplace setting by surveying the landscape of possible institutions of collective employee representation—not only unions but also internal employee committees and worker centers.

Chapter 8 turns to other major components of co-regulation, beginning with the contractual or quasi-contractual architecture that underlies both the main theories and much of the experience with regulated self-regulation. It then turns to key actors within a system of co-regulation: employers, including what I call "super-employers" at the top of the supply chains within which many low-wage workers labor; employees, acting both as individual whistleblowers and through old and new institutions of collective representation; and independent monitors. Chapter 9 moves from basic architecture and actors to strategies for implementation, first in an imagined first-best world in which there are no political or bureaucratic hurdles to enacting a comprehensive federal regime of co-regulation for the law of the workplace, and then in the more likely world in which progress is piecemeal and pressed forward on various narrower fronts and in part through private litigation. Chapter 10 concludes.

My aim here is to chart a strategy for reforming the law of the workplace that straddles the conventional divide between labor law and employment law— one that finds footholds within employment law for the pursuit of the core normative commitment of New Deal labor law to workplace democracy. It is grounded in the observation that workers' freedom of association and self-determination are not only of intrinsic value in a democratic society but also of instrumental value in realizing the rights and regulatory norms governing the workplace. That is especially true in an era of self-regulation in which the locus of enforcement is moving inside the workplace and away from direct public oversight. Giving employees an institutionalized role in self-regulatory processes will help both to make rights more real and regulatory standards more effective, as well as to rebuild mechanisms for effective worker participation in self-governance. In other words, the paradigm of workplace governance that has emerged in the wake of the decline of the collective bargaining model can be both improved by and turned to the cause of promoting democratization within the workplace.

Chapter 2 The Ossification

of Labor Law and the Decline

# of Industrial Self-Governance

This book seeks to chart a path toward self-governance in the workplace for twenty-first-century America. But that path cannot be constructed from scratch. The legacy of the New Deal and the NLRA, with its embrace of a particular form of industrial democracy, offers resources and tools that should not be left behind, and it erects hurdles and teaches cautionary tales that it would be perilous to ignore. This chapter covers a landscape that will be familiar to scholars, teachers, and practitioners of labor law, but it aims to throw a new light on that landscape and to highlight some of its features that are of particular importance as we look to the future.[1]

WHAT WENT WRONG WITH
AMERICAN LABOR LAW?

The original NLRA, or Wagner Act, of 1935—enacted in the throes of the Depression, in the face of rising labor militancy and in the wake of an overwhelming electoral mandate in favor of the New Deal— declared an affirmative national policy in favor of collective bargaining. Section 7 recognized the right of employees "to self-organization, to form, join, or assist labor organizations, to bargain collectively through representatives of their own choosing, and to engage in concerted activities, for the purpose of collective bargaining or other mutual aid or protection." Section 8, now 8(a), banned five employer "unfair labor practice[s]": interference, coercion, or restraint of employees in the exercise of Section 7 rights; domination or assistance of labor organizations; discrimination based on union membership; discrimination based on participation in proceedings under the Act; and refusal to bargain in good faith with a union representing employees. The Act established a mechanism for the election and certification of representative labor organizations based on the principle of majority rule, and it created the National Labor Relations Board (NLRB or the Board) to administer representation proceedings and enforce the Act, subject to judicial review in the federal courts of appeals. The Supreme Court's surprising constitutional vindication of the Act in 1937 as a proper exercise of Congress's Commerce Clause powers inaugurated the modern era of American labor law.[2]

The NLRA effectively established a "constitution" of the private-sector workplace—a framework for self-governance supported by a set of individual and group rights and an administrative enforcement scheme.[3] That framework sought to permit workers, acting through unions, and management to engage in "politics" in the form of bargaining and lawful self-help, to enact "legislation" in the form of a collective bargaining agreement, and to set up a system of adjudication and interpretation through grievance arbitration. The New Deal labor scheme was supposed to take most labor disputes and struggles for improved working conditions out of the courts and legislatures and into a reconstructed domain of contractually based self-governance, in which workers were citizens, with rights of association and freedom of expression, and the workplace was a site of self-determination.[4]

By comparison with the federal Constitution, the original New Deal constitution of the workplace was missing some important provisions. It did not "guaranty . . . a republican form of government," or its industrial equivalent, instead leaving to majority rule and the precarious organizing process the question of whether workers would be represented at all. It lacked an "equal protection clause" banning discrimination because of race or other ascriptive traits. Missing, too, was a requirement of due process: Unions typically bargained for "just cause" protection and "industrial due process" through grievance arbitration, but non-union employees remained terminable at employer will without notice of the reasons or an opportunity to contest them. The very partiality of the New Deal constitution of the workplace—especially the opportunity it afforded for employer resistance to unionization—paved the way for the subsequent decline of unions and collective bargaining. Still, the New Deal constitution designated the workplace as a proper domain of democracy and civil rights and liberties. It established the legitimacy of legislative intervention into the internal workings of private firms, and against the employers' sovereignty over the workplace, in order to further employees' freedom and self-determination.

But this was not the unfinished agenda that Congress took up when it revisited the Wagner Act in 1947. By that time the labor movement had quintupled in size since 1935 and had, in the eyes of some, "abused" its newfound power.[5] With the Taft-Hartley Act, Congress turned away from the forthright endorsement of collective bargaining and recast the basic policy of the Wagner Act as favoring employee "free choice" with respect to unionization. It amended Section 7 to affirm employees' right to *refrain* from as well as to engage in concerted activity and added section 8(b), which prohibited unions from engaging in secondary picketing and boycotts and other "unfair" practices.[6] Still, the 1947 amendments worked largely by addition, not subtraction; they left the core provisions of the original New Deal text—and in particular the employer unfair labor practices—essentially intact.

Changes since 1947 have been comparatively minor. The Landrum-Griffin Act of 1959 imposed a regime for the regulation of internal union affairs, including crucial rights for union members and provisions for union democracy.[7] But it only tinkered with the labor-management provisions of the NLRA, mainly by expanding the prohibition of secondary boycotts and regulating recognitional picketing.[8] With those few exceptions, the text of the NLRA that today governs workers' efforts to advance their shared interests through self-organization and collective bargaining is essentially as Congress left it in 1947.

Since then, organized labor's share of the private-sector workforce has shrunk to about 8 percent.[9] The collective bargaining system that the labor laws intended to serve as the primary mechanism for determining terms and conditions of employment and settling workplace disputes has become nearly irrelevant to the vast majority of private-sector American workers. That is not because of any fundamental mismatch between the nature of contemporary work life and the basic concept of collective bargaining between employers and their workers' representatives. American workers still express a desire for collective representation in workplace governance.[10] Moreover, collective bargaining in its essence responds to current demands for accommodation to the market, to local conditions, and to change; it is at least potentially decentralized, flexible, and democratic.[11] While the reality has often fallen short of the ideal, collective bargaining potentially holds out a promising "third way" between the harsh regimen of individual contract and the much-maligned paradigm of centralized "command-and-control" regulation, much as it did in the New Deal itself.[12]

So why is the system of union representation and collective bargaining so moribund?[13] Scholars have advanced several answers, not mutually exclusive but competing for emphasis: structural economic change, including deindustrialization and increasingly global and competitive product markets;[14] a mismatch between the interests of both employees and employers and traditional adversarial unionism;[15] the unions' own complacency and lack of commitment to organizing for several crucial decades;[16] pockets of thuggery and corruption that have tarnished unions' public image and appeal;[17] and increasingly brazen employer resistance to unions.[18] We will return in Chapter 7 to the causes of union decline. But any explanation that points to changes in the last half century—changing economic conditions or changing needs of employers or workers—beg another question: Why hasn't the law that governs labor relations itself changed to keep pace with those changes in the world?

The core components of American labor law have been essentially sealed off both from democratic revision and renewal and from local experimentation and innovation. The basic statutory language, and many of the intermediate-level principles and procedures through which the essentials of self-organization and collective bargaining are put into practice, have been nearly frozen, or ossified, for over fifty years. By a variety of political and legal mechanisms, labor law has been remarkably insulated from significant change for a remarkably long time. American labor law has been crippled in part by its ossification.

The significance of this many-faceted phenomenon of ossification for this mostly forward-looking project is that, for the foreseeable future, proposals to improve the governance of the workplace are unlikely to find a toehold within the traditional domain of "labor law," and even proposals for reform from without will need to steer clear of the rather large and durable roadblock that labor law creates. Moreover, the story of labor law's ossification may serve as a cautionary tale for reformers. It is often tempting, and sometimes even wise, for reformers to seek to entrench their victories against easy dislodgement by shift-

ing political currents. But one can succeed too well in this aim. Even the greatest of reforms must be reformable, revisable, and adaptable, especially in a
world in which the pace of change seems only to accelerate.

THE CONGRESSIONAL IMPASSE OVER
LABOR LAW REFORM

One of the most striking features of American labor law is the age of its basic
governing text. The current National Labor Relations Act (NLRA or Act) consists almost entirely of the original Wagner Act of 1935, together with the major
Taft-Hartley amendments of 1947 and the relatively minor changes of the Landrum-Griffin Act of 1959. The text has remained virtually untouched since
1959. That is not because it has served its purposes so well but because efforts
to amend it have been repeatedly stymied.

Needless to say, much has happened since the 1950s. The labor force has
changed as women have flooded into the workforce and racial and ethnic diversity has burgeoned. The economy has changed as manufacturing has shrunk
relative to the service sector and the new "information" sector and as the technology of transportation and communication has increasingly eroded geographic constraints on product markets and the location of production. The organization of work has changed as mass production and stable workplace
hierarchies have given way to more flexible, customer-centered production
methods and semiautonomous, team-based organizations. And the surrounding legal landscape has changed as laws regulating substantive terms of employment and granting individual employee rights have proliferated. In the
meantime, the collectivist premises of the NLRA have acquired the patina of
a historic relic. So how is it that no significant reforms have made their way into
the statute books since 1959?

Part of the Act's durability may come from the enduring power and open-tex-
tured quality of its basic provisions. The Act is studded with terms like "discriminate," "interfere," and "coerce," which could be given different meaning
over time. Many crucial interpretive decisions were rendered by the Supreme
Court in the early years of the Act's existence and have been in place—amendable only by Congress—since at least the 1950s. Those early Supreme Court decisions have been criticized for "deradicalizing" the original Wagner Act and for
reintroducing into the labor law many of the common law doctrines that the Act
was meant to repudiate.[19] But everything the Court did by way of interpreting

the Act could have been undone by Congress. The congressional impasse has thus entrenched those early decisions as well as the text itself. So while the basic principles of the Act continue to command a broad political consensus, many intermediate-level doctrines and procedures—some of them embedded in the text and some in long-standing judicial precedents—have attracted much criticism and might have warranted another look in the last half century.

Unions and their allies have been especially critical of the rules governing union organizing activity and employers' typically tenacious opposition to that activity.[20] The law not only protects employers' right to express their opposition to unionization, but it also recognizes their right to compel employees to listen to them in "captive audience" meetings while excluding union representatives from the workplace altogether.[21] Moreover, by granting employers the right to an NLRB election, as opposed to more informal methods of verifying majority support, the law affords employers time to campaign against union representation and opens the door to the use of coercive and dilatory tactics.[22] So, too, the law fails to effectively prevent or punish coercive and illegal forms of employer opposition, the incidence of which appears to have risen significantly since the 1970s.[23] In particular, the Act has been faulted for its paltry and easily delayed remedies for anti-union discharges. Those remedies—basically reinstatement and back pay, minus wages that were (or should have been) earned in the interim—are a minor cost of doing business for an employer committed to avoiding unionization. Yet legislative efforts to fortify the Act's remedies and speed up the representation process have failed.

A frequent target of criticism has been the law's failure to afford unions physical access to the workplace during an organizing campaign.[24] Since the 1950s, unions' supposedly equivalent opportunity to reach employees in their homes or at union halls has become increasingly impracticable in an age of suburban sprawl and overextended working parents, and employers' right to exclude others from property that has been opened to workers, customers, or the public has been eroded by the antidiscrimination laws and regulatory regimes put in place since the 1950s.[25] Yet the Supreme Court has rejected Board decisions affording even limited union access to nonwork areas of the workplace under the existing statute, and efforts to legislate access have failed.

Another much-criticized aspect of the NLRA is the "*Mackay Radio* doctrine," under which employees engaged in an economic strike that is "protected" by Section 7 are nonetheless subject to permanent replacement by their employer.[26] The employer's right of permanent replacement—established in 1938 by Supreme Court dicta but little used until the 1980s—has become the

key to aggressive de-unionization campaigns. It has rendered the strike virtually suicidal for many employees and has become employers' Exhibit Number
One in union organizing campaigns.[27] The doctrine has been excoriated by
scholars and public officials; it has not been overruled by Congress.

All of these changes have been sought by labor and its allies. Since Taft-Hartley, employers have had far less to complain about. But they have sought legislative relief from the law's nearly seventy-year-old ban on employer-initiated
"employee representation" plans. Employers have been urged and have sought
in recent decades to tap the collective creativity and knowledge, and to respond
to the shared interests, of their workers. Yet Section 8(a)(2) of the NLRA prohibits them from sponsoring any organization of employees that "deals with"
the employer regarding terms and conditions of employment. This ban has
provoked volumes of scholarly criticism and reform proposals, yet nothing has
emerged from Congress.[28]

Another sort of labor law reform one might have expected from Congress is
the recognition of a role for unions, or for some institution of employee representation, within the numerous federal employment statutes enacted since
1964.[29] Those statutes recognize that employees play an important role in the
enforcement of workplace rights and regulations: they protect employees
against retaliation for their participation in enforcement and often give them
the right to sue for enforcement and for individual remedies.[30] But unions appear primarily as potential wrongdoers under the new statutes, especially the
antidiscrimination statutes.[31] With a few minor exceptions, Congress has assigned no formal role to employees' collective representatives in identifying violations, monitoring compliance, or tailoring regulatory requirements to particular workplaces. That is an oversight to which we will obviously return.

What explains congressional inaction in the face of decades of social, economic, and legal change and persistent criticism? In short, both organized labor
and especially employers have long had enough support in Congress to block
any significant amendment that either group strongly opposes. "Enough support" does not mean a majority; it means a minority that is big enough, well
organized enough, and committed enough to tie up a bill through the arcane
supermajority requirements of the Senate (for example, through filibuster) or
to sustain a presidential veto.

For example, the Labor Law Reform Act of 1977 sought to mitigate some of
the overwhelming advantages that employers enjoy in union campaigns and
to beef up remedies against employer misconduct.[32] In spite of gaining majority support, the bill died in the Senate after a five-week Republican filibuster

and six unsuccessful efforts to end debate.[33] Similarly, bills to prohibit the permanent replacement of strikers gained majority support in both houses of Congress in 1992, and again in 1994, but succumbed to a filibuster.[34] Organized labor, too, was able to stymie a congressional majority on the single occasion in recent decades when employers pressed for a significant amendment of the NLRA. The Teamwork for Employees and Managers Act (TEAM Act) would have loosened the NLRA's ban on employer-sponsored employee representation plans.[35] Employers claimed that these plans would help enable them to compete in the global marketplace, but organized labor held fast to its view of these schemes as additional weapons in the employers' already bulging arsenal of anti-union tactics.[36] The TEAM Act narrowly passed both houses of Congress in 1997, but supporters were unable to override President Bill Clinton's veto.[37]

The latest union-sponsored effort at labor law reform, the Employee Free Choice Act (EFCA), had gained majority support, but not the necessary veto-proof supermajority, in both houses of Congress as of 2007. Even with a pro-labor Democrat in the White House, it will still take sixty votes in the Senate to overcome the inevitable Republican filibuster. And that may take crossover support from Republicans, which has become increasingly rare for pro-union labor law reform proposals.

Labor law reform has thus far failed because existing institutional arrangements make it possible for committed and well-organized congressional minorities to block or hijack statutory reforms they oppose. But why does labor law reform in particular provoke such committed and cohesive opposition? Some of the answers—particularly those from the field of "public choice"—suggest a certain symmetry. Both sides are well organized and both perceive high stakes: employers are fighting for flexibility and managerial prerogatives that they claim are crucial to their economic survival, while unions are fighting for their very existence in the face of aggressive managerial resistance and long-term attrition.[38] Only a serious crisis in industrial relations or a political realignment of epic proportions seems capable of breaking through the resulting impasse.[39]

But the seeming symmetry is misleading. Much like the pitched battle that is enacted in the typical private-sector organizing campaign, the battle for labor law reform takes place on an uneven playing field. The political power of employers to resist labor law reform in Congress is grounded in capital's indispensability to our economic well-being and its mobility within and across national borders, and it is fortified by the unusual unanimity with which business opposes reforms that might facilitate unionization.[40] Business is far more united in its opposition to pro-union labor law reform than in its opposition to other forms of regulation—even workplace regulation—which often divide large and small employers or employers in different sectors.[41] A deeper asymmetry is reflected in both the legislative process and the typical labor dispute: unions cannot live if they kill their "hosts"; they cannot thrive if employers do not. But employers can thrive without unions; indeed, many would prefer to see unions disappear altogether, and they are willing to do their part to bring that about. It is hard to find common ground in that sort of contest.

Organized labor is faltering badly under the existing antiquated regime. It has a far greater need for labor law reform, and less political capacity to secure it, than employers have. So while organized labor has mounted several major efforts at labor law reform in the past thirty-five years, employers—equipped though they are with the political advantages of organization, internal unity, access, and wealth—have made almost no such efforts since 1959. For the most part, employers that oppose unions and collective bargaining are willing to bide their time in the political process, batting down periodic reform proposals that might tip the scales in unions' favor and watching union strength ebb away.

PATHWAYS NOT TAKEN: INNOVATION FROM EMPLOYERS, FROM COURTS AND LITIGATION, AND FROM STATE AND LOCAL EXPERIMENTATION

National legislation is not the only possible channel of legal change, of course. But the New Deal Congress that enacted the Wagner Act did not mean for its hard-won victory to be easily undone; it built in some barriers to change. In particular, Congress sought to insulate the new labor relations regime from some highly suspect sources of change and variation—employers and the courts —and to entrust the administration of the Act to a new federal agency, the NLRB. Over the past seventy years, those built-in obstacles to change have grown anomalous and out of sync with surrounding legal and economic developments, yet they remain entrenched.

Insulation from Employer-Sponsored Alternative Forms of Employee Representation

One potential avenue of extralegal renewal and experimentation was deliberately shut down by Congress in 1935 and never reopened. Employers seeking to meet (or deflect) workers' demands for a voice in their working conditions while advancing their own interests in productivity and profits might have devised—and did devise, before 1935—a variety of alternative mechanisms for employee representation. Those mechanisms might have competed with independent unions for employee loyalty and perhaps spurred innovation within the labor movement. We might think of this as a "market" mechanism of reform. But the single most controversial provision of the Wagner Act closed down that potential avenue of change.

Company unions—employee organizations that were established and controlled by management—loomed in 1935 as among the chief barriers to independent union representation.[42] Section 8(2)—now Section 8(a)(2)—of the Act thus made it unlawful for an employer "to dominate or interfere with the formation or administration of any labor organization." Section 2(5), in turn, defined "labor organizations" broadly to include "any organization of any kind, or any agency or employee representation committee or plan, in which employees participate and which exists for the purpose, in whole or in part, of dealing with employers concerning grievances, labor disputes, wages, rates of pay, hours of employment, or conditions of work." The ban thus reached not only organizations that purported to bargain collectively, or that masqueraded as unions, or that operated to coerce employees or discriminate against union activists or to evade the duty to bargain with the labor organization chosen by the majority; it also reached some employee representation plans that were favored by employees and that worked well, by all accounts, within the particular organization.[43] The broadly worded ban was based on ample evidence before Congress that many—probably most—employee representation plans were a sham, a pretext for resistance to employee demands for independent representation through unions, and a vehicle for discrimination and coercion against employees who favored such representation.[44]

The result was a choice—though far from a free choice, given employer resistance—between full-fledged independent representation and no collective representation at all on terms and conditions of employment. Given the congressional impasse that has solidified since then, employees are still faced with this all-or-nothing choice. Both employees and employers have reason to question the continuing justification for the broad prohibition of Section 8(a)(2). Even the diluted and domesticated forms of employee voice that are likely to be initiated by employers may be better than no collective employee voice at all for the 90-plus percent that is unorganized. And many employers have become convinced of the productivity benefits, even the necessity, of employee involvement in workplace decision making.[45]

To be sure, the law does not prohibit all forms of employee involvement. It permits programs aimed at improving "quality" and "productivity," as long as they do not deal regularly with terms and conditions of employment—that is, employee compensation, schedules, job descriptions, promotion policies, and any number of issues that are inextricably implicated in the more efficient organization of production.[46] The law also permits one-way communication and suggestion schemes, as long as they do not involve give-and-take between employees and management.[47] And it permits schemes that go so far as to delegate to groups of employees full managerial authority over hiring, scheduling, promotions, discipline, or other employment issues.[48] In short, it makes room for schemes that allow employees to do either more than or less than "deal with" employers; but it does not permit employer sponsorship of institutionalized forms of give-and-take, consultation, or negotiation over the things that matter most to employees at work. It rules out a wide swath of potentially valuable forms of employee involvement in workplace decision making.

One might question the impact of Section 8(a)(2) in discouraging such innovations, for that section is about as toothless as the rest of the Act. At least where there is no union on the scene, unfair labor practice charges against employee involvement schemes are rare; remedies are weak; and here as elsewhere, the Board lacks the power to punish violations of the Act.[49] So, for example, the Employees' Committee (EC) at Polaroid Corp. operated from the late 1940s until 1992, apparently with widespread support from employees; despite its "indisputable illegality," no Section 8(a)(2) charge was ever filed.[50] Given the low risk and limited cost of a legal challenge, some employers appear to be experimenting with alternative forms of employee representation that may violate the ban or at least push the limits of legality.[51]

Even so, a significant narrowing of Section 8(a)(2) would produce more experimentation with new forms of employee voice.[52] The plans would be employer-initiated and would presumably be designed to give employees some voice while retaining managerial control. They would be "cooperative," and arguably co-opted, by design. But that is roughly what most employees say they want, according to the findings of Richard Freeman and Joel Rogers. Over 70 percent of all workers surveyed believed that an employee organization could be effective only with management cooperation, and over 80 percent of nonmanagerial employees preferred an employee organization that was "run jointly" by employees and management.[53] Indeed, nearly 60 percent preferred "joint employee-management committees that discuss and resolve workplace problems," a form of organization that is clearly illegal in the non-union workplace under Section 8(a)(2).[54] Of course, those employee preferences are at least partly a

product of managerial resistance to independent employee representation and
the price employees anticipate paying for that resistance.[55] Employee ambiva-
lence about unionization reflects not only fear of reprisals but also anxiety about
confrontation and conflict, which employers commonly predict—and can ensure—will follow from unionization.[56] But the widespread sentiment among
employees for "cooperative" and "jointly run" mechanisms of collective employee influence should give pause to the defenders of existing law.

Maybe the unions are right. Eliminating or significantly narrowing the ban
on employer-dominated labor organizations might simply deal management
additional trump cards in the fight to remain non-union and accelerate the decline of genuine independent employee representation. At best, employer-initiated plans might well promise more than they deliver; they might give the appearance of influence without any real power to effect change. But that is
something employees are likely to discover for themselves. As long as they remain free to explore the union alternative, it is hard to see why employees need
to be protected from representation plans that may turn out to be ineffectual.
Indeed, unions might find rich organizing opportunities in the wake of failed
or disappointing employer-initiated representation plans. This may be the real
reason experimentation with employee representation is limited: employers
may fear giving employees a "taste" of influence, along with a sense of entitlement, that outruns management's willingness to satisfy it. It is worth recalling
the history of pre-NLRA employee representation plans, some of which es-
caped employer control and evolved into independent unions.[57] In any event,
some collective voice seems preferable to none, which is what over 90 percent
of the private-sector workforce has under the current all-or-nothing regime.

The issue of Section 8(a)(2) reform is complex, plagued by limited and conflicting empirical evidence and loaded with symbolic import. One thing is clear:
the choice made by Congress in 1935 has clogged if not blocked the proliferation
of employer-initiated forms of employee participation. It has impeded what we
might call a market response to both employee and employer demands for viable forms of employee representation in workplace decision making. Of course
that is what the original Wagner Act set out to do. And that choice, whether or
not it serves us well over seventy years later, remains in effect.

Insulation from Private Litigation and Lawyering

For the modern observer of the law of the workplace, an obvious channel of law
reform is private litigation. Costly and burdensome though it may be, litiga-

tion is a powerful cauldron of legal change, in which aggrieved individuals combine forces with zealous and creative attorneys to test out new legal theories on sometimes-receptive courts. The aggregate impact of private litigation under broadly worded federal and state statutes and hospitable common law doctrines has utterly transformed the landscape of "employment law" and has drawn the anxious attention of employers seeking to avoid its snares. But while employment law has electrified employers, labor law has proven to be a rather low-voltage instrument. Why?

The NLRA's ban on anti-union discrimination was the nation's first major "wrongful discharge" law. Enacted in an era of swelling confidence in the administrative state, it contains no private right of action. Rather, an aggrieved person may file a charge with the NLRB's prosecutorial arm, which makes an unreviewable decision whether to file an unfair labor practice complaint with the Board.[58] The New Deal choice of administrative rather than judicial adjudication largely dictated the range of remedies: reinstatement, back pay, and other equitable remedies, but no compensatory or punitive damages of the sort that only juries could award.[59] As a historical matter, the original choice of administrative enforcement is understandable. In 1935, the courts were the last places to which New Dealers and union activists would have turned for the enforcement of labor rights.[60] On the contrary, much of the Act was shaped by its framers' aim of keeping the role of courts—and especially the lower courts, which were so tarnished by the history of the labor injunction—to a constitutional minimum.[61] Even apart from this history, a private right of action to enforce employee rights would have been thought quite worthless and certainly less potent than the chosen remedy of enforcement by a federal agency.

Since the New Deal, however, wrongful discharge law has come into its own.[62] The Civil Rights Act of 1964,[63] which included both private and administrative remedies, ushered in an era of expanding employment legislation and litigation, especially under the aegis of the antidiscrimination principle.[64] The availability of attorneys' fees and substantial damages under a growing array of federal and state statutes spawned the growth of a small but energetic plaintiffs' bar in the private and nonprofit sectors. In the wake of the civil rights revolution, state courts began to develop common law tort doctrines of wrongful discharge in violation of public policy. Both discrimination actions and state wrongful discharge actions occasionally generate the kind of six- or seven-figure verdicts that get employers' attention.

Yet the explicit and long-standing federal policy favoring workers' freedom of association and self-organization, and banning employer retaliation for the exercise of that freedom, is still backed only by an administrative complaint procedure and a comparatively paltry financial threat. On the other side, the perceived value of remaining non-union gives management a huge incentive to try to squelch an incipient union drive by firing a union advocate or two before the drive gains momentum. The weakness of the Act's remedies in the face of employer resistance has proven to be the Achilles' heel of employee rights. Notwithstanding their expansive expression and rather far-reaching substantive interpretation, employees' Section 7 rights are notoriously underenforced.[65] The right to be free from coercion and retaliation based on union organizing or other collective dissent is widely flouted by employers, who perceive too great an economic threat in the rumblings of union talk and too easy and cheap a response in the discharge of union adherents. Federal law not only provides inadequate remedies and inadequate deterrence; as we will see below, it also shields employers from *state* damages remedies for anti-union discharge. As things stand, most employers can treat the small and confined risk of an unfair labor practice charge as a minor cost of doing business.

What if labor law had kept up with the times and added a private right of action for anti-union discrimination that the law already condemns? We might have had a "common law" of anti-union discrimination, with cross-fertilization from other wrongful discharge doctrines. Imagine, for example, if the ban on employer discrimination against union members had given rise to a ban on "anti-union harassment" or creation of a hostile anti-union environment, much as Title VII's ban on employer discrimination on the basis of sex gave rise to sexual harassment law. And if the resulting doctrines and remedies packed enough of a punch, they might have induced employers to choose carrots over sticks in fighting unionization or even to let employees decide the matter for themselves. It might, in other words, have helped to do what the law already purports to do. That would have shaken up labor relations considerably.

Insulation from State and Local Reforms

So the basic federal scheme of labor relations contains some built-in obstacles to innovation that have become entrenched at least since the 1950s by a political logjam in Congress. But our system of government distributes and diffuses power and the potential to bring about legal change both to other subordinate sovereigns through principles of federalism and to other branches of government through constitutionalism and the separation of powers. Moreover, domestic law is potentially subject to the commands of international law. Yet there has been little or no innovation from these quarters either. The NLRA's scheme of labor relations has been rendered largely impervious to change at the margins by state and local lawmaking and to challenges from "above"—from constitutional and international law. We will focus here on the first of these closed doors.

For decades, labor law reform was blocked in Congress. But what about adaptations at the state and local level? In a federal system, state-by-state variations might ordinarily be expected and might permit a kind of experimentation around the edges of the national scheme. As Justice Louis Brandeis famously observed, "[i]t is one of the happy incidents of the federal system that a single courageous State may, if its citizens choose, serve as a laboratory; and try novel social and economic experiments without risk to the rest of the country."[66] Successful local experiments might spread to other localities and might even provide credible models for national reform. State and local lawmaking might also give voice to popular discontent with the existing labor law regime that has no effective outlet at the federal level; it might make room at the local level for democratic reform efforts that are stymied in Congress.

As a clue to the possible shape of state-level reforms, we might look to the public-sector labor laws that have produced a much higher level of unionization among public employees—especially in the labor-friendly states of the Northeast, upper Midwest, and West Coast—than exists among private-sector employees under the NLRA. Some public-sector statutes have provisions like those on labor's wish list for the private sector, such as employer neutrality toward representation campaigns and arbitration of first contracts. These laws suggest some of what might happen at the state level in private-sector labor law, if only. . . .

. . . .If only state and local reform efforts did not run headlong into the wall of federal labor law preemption.[67] The NLRA contains no express preemption provision.[68] But the constitutional supremacy of federal law dictates the preemption of state law that is in "conflict" with federal law. The question is how broadly federal law is deemed to extend so as to conflict with state law. At a minimum, for example, state law may not prohibit that which is protected by the Act or require that which is prohibited. So the states may not ban union membership or federally protected labor picketing; nor may the states require employers to create employee representation committees that would violate Section 8(a)(2) of the Act. Such state laws would be "repugnant" to the express provisions of federal law.[69] That was roughly the shape of federal preemption of state labor law until the 1950s.

Once the Taft-Hartley Act extended the reach of federal regulation to union as well as employer conduct, however, Congress came to be seen as having "occupied the field," implicitly preempting a much broader range of state laws. Modern labor law preemption essentially ousts states and municipalities from tinkering with the machinery of union organizing, collective bargaining, and labor-management conflict.[70] Under what is known as "*Garmon* preemption,"[71] by and large, a state may not regulate activity that is arguably protected or arguably prohibited by the Act.[72] And under what is known as "*Machinists* preemption," states and municipalities may not weigh in on one side or the other of labor disputes by regulating activity that is clearly *unregulated* by the Act—that is, clearly neither protected nor prohibited.[73] *Machinists* preemption creates, in effect, an employer "right" to use its unregulated economic weapons—the "right" to permanently replace strikers, for example—as against state regulation of those weapons. *Garmon* and *Machinists* together virtually banish states and localities from the field of labor relations.

Under that broad preemption doctrine, for example, states may not award additional remedies for conduct the act prohibits; nor may they impose additional punishment on labor law violators, or even disfavor them in the award of state contracts.[74] States may not, therefore, extend a private right of action, with make-whole remedies, to an employee fired for seeking union representation.[75] That tort remedy would fit comfortably within the contours of the tort of wrongful discharge in violation of public policy in many states.[76] Yet labor law preemption doctrine prevents the states from enforcing their own public policy against anti-union discrimination, even in a manner consistent with federal law.

There are exceptions to labor law preemption. States are largely free to enforce general laws against violence, intimidation, and trespass in the context of labor disputes, though they may not otherwise regulate collective bargaining, industrial conflict, or labor organizing.[77] The net effect of these exceptions is to skew an apparently "neutral" preemption doctrine in favor of employers. For outside the limited context of public projects, states' role in the labor relations sphere is largely confined to protecting property and public order. Employers have the property that is thus protected, while organized labor traditionally relies on the power of numbers and of more or less disruptive concerted activities such as picketing. So when states and localities do permissibly intervene in private-sector labor disputes, they usually do so against union activity.

More promising from labor's perspective is the latitude that states have, when acting in their "proprietary" capacity, to make contracts favorable to organized labor, and to avoid the costs associated with labor unrest, on public projects.[78]

But even the states' power of the purse is sharply limited. States may not use their spending power to effectively "regulate" labor relations, for example, by linking general state procurement policies to the labor relations practices of contracting firms.[79] The Supreme Court's latest brick in the wall of preemption limits state efforts to ban even the *use* of state funds by contractors for certain labor-related purposes. California had enacted a statute prohibiting the use of state funds to oppose (or support) unionization. But in *Chamber of Commerce v. Brown* in 2008, the Supreme Court struck down the statute on preemption grounds.[80] The Court held that the procedures for demonstrating compliance with the ban on impermissible use of state funds were so burdensome as to deter firms from engaging in the conduct altogether; the law amounted to an impermissible effort to regulate labor relations. *Brown* may leave room for similar legislation that is less burdensome to comply with, but it underscores just how little room there is for state regulation of labor relations. Preemption doctrine has become nearly as entrenched as the text of the NLRA itself, even as the Supreme Court has revived federalism limitations on Congress's *express* exercise of federal power.[81]

It is hard to say for sure whether labor or management would have gained more from a narrower preemption doctrine because it is hard to say how state and local governments would have exercised their broader authority over labor relations.[82] One can safely guess that organized labor would have gained legal ground in those states and localities in which it is strongest politically—especially the Midwest, Northeast, and West Coast—and lost it in those states in which organized labor is weak—especially the South.[83] That may look like a draw (or worse, given labor's waning strength). But it is not. That is because labor's basic rights are explicitly protected in the NLRA itself and would be protected from infringement by even a narrow preemption doctrine that hewed more closely to the minimum demands of the Supremacy Clause. Management's most important rights, by contrast, are not found in the Act but originally in the state law of property—the right to exclude others from property, for example. A narrower preemption doctrine would thus predictably afford more room for the states' regulation of employer conduct than for the regulation of employee and union conduct.[84]

Consider, for example, a labor law preemption doctrine that distinguished between the Act's basic rights of self-organization and its rules of engagement for the organized workplace. As to the latter, it can perhaps be said that Congress has struck a balance, choosing to permit some tactics and to prohibit others by both parties in the economic contests between them. But as to the former—in particular the rights of unorganized employees to discuss workplace issues and the merits of unionization, free from retaliation—the metaphor of a "fair contest" or a battle, with carefully calibrated rules of engagement, is utterly out of place. The basic rights of unorganized workers and the remedies established by the Act could be conceived of as minimum standards, which states may supplement so long as they do not come into direct conflict with the federal scheme or with the Constitution. States could, for example, create broader rights of access to the workplace for organizers and stronger remedies and penalties for the discharge of union activists. That approach would place the basic federal associational rights of workers on much the same footing, vis-à-vis state lawmaking, as the federal antidiscrimination rights of workers. States would be free to add to the protections of federal law, even though doing so would necessarily strike a different "balance" and increase the burdens on employers. In other words, federal law would place a floor but not a ceiling on the basic "civil rights" of employees to associate and organize themselves.

Under the broader preemption doctrine that we have instead—and that is firmly entrenched in the absence of congressional action—there is no room for these variations. That means that states have lost some of the flexibility they might have had, consistent with federal law, to implement their own policies. It means that the popular impulses that are stymied at the federal level have no outlet at the state and local level either. And it means that whatever lessons might have been learned from state-by-state experimentation with the intermediate-level principles of labor relations have gone unlearned.

INSULATION FROM CONSTITUTIONAL AND INTERNATIONAL LEGAL SCRUTINY

Two potential avenues of labor law reform come not from within the statutory scheme but from "above": the federal Constitution and international law both embody evolving fundamental norms of civil and human rights that might have cast a critical light on, or even supported a legal challenge to, aspects of American labor law. That has not happened.

Before 1937, labor law in the U.S. had everything to do with the Constitution. The laissez-faire construct of "liberty of contract" posited a constitutional right to sell one's labor, and to buy the labor of others, on such terms as the market permitted, free from interference by the state (or, for that matter, by organized labor).[85] This was the unique American version of constitutional labor rights: the right to be free from the shackles of protective labor legislation. But since the NLRA's constitutional vindication helped to close the door on the era of substantive due process, the courts have had little resort to the Constitution as a source of critical scrutiny of the federal labor law regime.[86] In particular, the Constitution has played virtually no role in expanding the protection, or challenging the suppression, of collective action and expression by employees.

The story might have turned out differently. The Thirteenth Amendment's ban on involuntary servitude, the Fourteenth Amendment's equal protection and privileges and immunities clauses, and the First Amendment all might have supported the development of workplace rights.[87] But the basic rights of American workers were won in a battle for legislative supremacy and against the courts' constitutional power of judicial review. For a few years, it seemed that labor rights might take their place within the Supreme Court's post–New Deal constitutional project of safeguarding individual liberties and the channels of political discourse and change.[88] For example, when the Court struck down a state ban on peaceful labor picketing under the First Amendment, proclaiming the facts of a labor dispute to be undeniably "matters of public concern," it seemed to treat organized labor as a movement for economic justice and equality deserving of energetic constitutional protection.[89] But labor's brief moment in the constitutional sun came to a close once Congress extended its regulatory reach to unions in 1947—and perhaps in step with organized labor's own transformation during the 1950s. As unions looked increasingly like market actors jostling for a bigger share of the economic pie, labor protest was largely relegated to the domain of economic activity, where deference to the legislature ruled the day.[90]

Deference in the labor sphere prevailed even after picketing and boycotts came to be recognized in the 1960s as constitutionally protected forms of protest in the hands of civil rights activists.[91] Organized labor's role as the voice of the downtrodden during the 1940s had helped to spur the initial recognition of constitutional protest rights, which were then expanded in the civil rights era.[92] But labor enjoyed little return on those expanded rights, at least for picketing, its signature form of expression.[93] Congress had struck a "delicate balance," and the Court was loath to disturb it.[94] The contrast between the Court's vigorous protection of peaceful civil rights picketing and boycott activity and the deference to Congress's ban on virtually identical activity by unions suggests a little of what has been lost in the deconstitutionalization of labor law.

Lest we romanticize the potential of constitutional law to shake up labor law, however, we must recall its double-edged quality. Among the few constitutional challenges to the NLRA that have garnered serious attention, most have come at the behest of individual employees against unions. In particular, the Supreme Court has elaborated a robust First Amendment "right to refrain" from compelled association and political activity.[95] On those grounds, the Court has construed the statute to prohibit the compelled exaction of dues to support unions' lobbying and most organizing activity.[96] The quasi-constitutional "right to refrain" and its expansion over the years has worked a change in labor law—a change in the direction of greater individual rights and weaker collective institutions. It shows one way in which the process of "ossification" is qualified, complicated, and uneven. And it shows that the Constitution is still a double-edged sword in the domain of labor law. It is thus difficult to predict how the more frequent deployment of that sword might have reshaped labor law. But it would have at least opened pathways of legal challenge and change that have instead remained closed.

Another potential source of "higher law"—international human rights law— has made no discernible mark (as yet) upon American labor law. To be sure, the U.S. has long recognized the international status of workers' rights to associate freely, form unions, and bargain collectively.[97] But international human rights laws require more of states than abstaining from direct repression of associational activity and more than the formal protection of such activity; they require that states affirmatively and effectively protect the freedom of workers to associate and to form unions.[98] The U.S. government has not embraced the affirmative dimension of international labor rights (though it is bound by the instruments that establish it), and it is primarily on that score that American law falls short.[99] The critical bite of international law depends, in other words, on whether one examines American labor law on the books or the law in action.

International human rights advocates have thus criticized the notoriously patchy enforcement of basic rights, even for those workers covered by the NLRA. The criticisms are familiar. Given paltry remedies and long delays, "[m]any employers have come to view [legal sanctions] as a routine cost of doing business, well worth it to get rid of organizing leaders and derail workers' organizing efforts. As a result, a culture of near-impunity has taken shape in much of U.S. labor law and practice."[100] According to human rights observers, "[i]n a system replete with all the appearance of legality and due process, workers' exercise of rights to organize, to bargain, and to strike . . . has been frustrated by many employers who realize they have little to fear from . . . a ponderous, delay-ridden legal system with meager remedial powers."[101]

American legal institutions and decision makers have thus far been deaf to the claim that international labor law provides a potential model for American labor law, or even a critical vantage point from which to view American labor law. Of course, the insulation of American labor law from transnational and international legal scrutiny is not peculiar to labor law. The same official resistance to the application of international human rights standards within American borders meets international criticism of the death penalty or police brutality.[102] As things stand, the labor arena is simply one of many in which the critical and transformative potential of transnational law remains untapped by domestic American legal institutions.

The potential of international human rights law as a vehicle of pro-worker reform in the U.S. is growing as the international community has fought for a legal conception of human rights that has traction against private actors and as nongovernmental organizations and contractual instruments have become increasingly important institutional agents of human rights principles. These developments, to which I will return below, contain rich potential for the reshaping of workplace rights in the U.S. and elsewhere. But these developments have not yet made any impact on the content or enforcement of American labor law.

OSSIFICATION OR RETRENCHMENT?
A NOTE ON THE BUSH NLRB

It may seem jarring to decry the ossification of labor law after eight years of the Bush NLRB, which has been widely criticized by labor's allies for its voluminous output of anti-labor decisions, many of which overturned prior precedent. To quote a letter to Congress that fifty-seven labor law professors signed (and that I helped draft), "In periodic waves of closely divided, highly partisan decisions, the current Board majority has effectively removed whole categories of workers from the Act's coverage; stripped away protections promised by the Act; and further diluted the strength of already inadequate remedies."[103] A little more ossification might have been welcomed by organized labor during the Bush years.

On the other hand, decisions rejecting innovative remedies and erecting hurdles to even basic back pay remedies,[104] or excluding groups of workers from the protections of the Act altogether,[105] hardly count as renovation or reform. On the contrary, several of these decisions increased, or at least underscored, the Act's rigidity in the face of changing ways of organizing work. Such was the case with the *Oakwood* trilogy's treatment of nurses and other professionals as supervisors based on their participation in less hierarchical work arrangements. So, too, excluding graduate teaching assistants from the Act in *Brown University* was traced by dissenters to an outdated vision of the modern university and squelched organizing activity that was emerging in unfamiliar places. The *Register-Guard* decision declining to find a Section 7 right of employees to communicate with each other through employers' e-mail systems is of a piece with these decisions.[106] Similarly, the Board's decision in *Dana Corp.,* imposing new restrictions on voluntary recognition based on card check, while it reversed long-standing precedent, did so to put the brakes on an innovative and widespread union strategy to organize outside of the NLRB election scheme (to which we will return).[107]

If this is innovation, it is innovation in the service of ossification. So while the Bush Board issued an unusual number of decisions overturning settled doctrine, it did nothing to respond to changing conditions in the workplace or to address the long-standing criticisms of the Act's scheme for union organizing and bargaining. The most that can be said is that some of those decisions might in turn be reversed by a future Board that is more intent upon squeezing out of the Act whatever adaptability can be found there.

THE CONSEQUENCES AND LESSONS OF LABOR LAW'S OSSIFICATION FOR THE FUTURE

American labor law has been largely insulated from both internal and external sources of renovation. It has been cut off from revision at the national level by Congress; from "market"-driven competition by employers; from the entrepreneurial energies of individual plaintiffs and the plaintiff's bar and the creativity they can sometimes coax from the courts; from variation at the state or local level by elected or judicial bodies; from the winds of changing constitutional doctrine and emerging transnational legal norms. Even without knowing where any of these potential paths of change might have led, one can surmise that change or experimentation through one or more of these channels might have produced, over the past half-century, a body of labor law that was more responsive to the very different economic and social conditions that workers and employers face today.

Perhaps a tectonic political shift toward labor's allies will dislodge the formidable barriers to legislative reform of the labor laws and produce something like the Employee Free Choice Act. Unions might then set their sights on organizing a larger portion of the private-sector workforce. Whether or not that happens, however, a half century of ossification has left its mark and carries important lessons for those who seek to improve workplace governance and enhance workers' role in governance. I will simply flag the major lessons here and postpone until future chapters their elaboration.

First, an ossified labor law regime has promoted and may continue to promote efforts, especially by unions and other worker advocacy organizations, to work around and outside of (if not against) the law through forms of private and quasi-private ordering. The rise of worker centers and private "codes of conduct," which are a major focus of this book, is among those efforts. But private ordering is crucial to the strategy of traditional unions as well. Most important, unions are seeking to persuade and pressure employers to enter into "neutrality agreements" or "codes of conduct" that establish ground rules for the representation campaign that are designed to allow employees to make their choices in a less heated and less adversarial setting.[108]

A voluntary recognition agreement typically aims to achieve by contract many of the reforms that unions have failed to secure by statute, such as organizer access to the workplace and restrictions on anti-union campaigns and "captive audience" meetings. Many agreements provide for card-check recognition in lieu of elections (though some do culminate in a consent election), and most provide for arbitration of disputes under the agreement. Some agreements commit the employers to extend the same rules of engagement to employers with whom they do business. Probably more than half of the workers who have been organized in the private sector in the past six to eight years have been organized under neutrality agreements rather than through the traditional NLRB election process.[109] Neutrality and card-check agreements have been hailed as the harbingers of a "new paradigm" for the conduct of organizing and representation campaigns—one that both smoothes the path to union representation and lays the groundwork for a more cooperative labor relations climate.[110]

The success of neutrality agreements has provoked a number of legal objections that brought them before an NLRB majority that has been assailed for its barrage of anti-union decisions.[111] That brings us to the second lesson of ossification: ossified though it may be, the federal labor law regime still has the potential to squelch private experimentation in labor relations.[112] The risk that innovative private initiatives will be caught in the force field of labor law extends beyond the sphere of conventional unions and collective bargaining. As we will see in Chapter 7, some worker centers may be at risk of being labeled "labor organizations" and drawn into the ossified regime of federal labor law. But for now, consider how the NLRA may imperil labor's voluntary recognition strategy (much as the application of Section 8(a)(2) threw a wet blanket over some emerging forms of labor-management cooperation and employee involvement).

Some objections to neutrality agreements question their voluntariness and target the allegedly coercive tactics by which unions secure these agreements.[113] The most troubling challenges to neutrality agreements, however, question whether it is lawful for employers to agree to them, however voluntarily. Do employers who give up the right to oppose unionization unlawfully deprive workers of their "right" to a vigorously contested representation campaign?[114] Does an employer unlawfully favor or assist the signatory union in violation of Section 8(a)(2) by accepting a neutrality agreement that includes some proposed terms of an eventual collective bargaining agreement—thus allowing both employees and employers to make a more informed choice about their posture toward the union?[115] Does an employer's agreement to do business only with other employers that sign a neutrality agreement constitute a "hot cargo" agreement in violation of Section 8(e) of the Act?[116]

Thus far the NLRB has addressed one major question: Is the voluntary recognition of a union pursuant to a neutrality agreement entitled to the standard one-year moratorium on decertification or competing election petitions?[117] Under long-standing precedent, the answer was yes. But the Board's new answer in *Dana I* was "not so fast." Employers who voluntarily recognize a union based on a card check must report the recognition to the NLRB and post a notice informing employees of their right, within forty-five days, to seek an election to dislodge the union. Under *Dana I,* after a majority of employees has already proclaimed its choice to be represented by the union, a minority—as little as 30 percent of the bargaining unit—has a second chance to reverse that decision by demanding an NLRB representation election. The Board's aggressive assertion of regulatory authority over voluntary recognition could have been a first step toward deploying the Act—much criticized for its rigidity in the face of changing labor relations and labor markets—to disable the single greatest source of dynamism in the contemporary labor relations scene. That scenario seems less likely after the 2008 election.

The third lesson of labor law's ossification is that law reform efforts are more likely to bear fruit if they are pursued through other channels, particularly through what is known as "employment law." We have already glimpsed the sprawling collection of employment laws that has grown up since 1964 and have begun to see that those laws, imperfect though they are, are far more open to evolution and variation than is the law of collective labor relations. In particular, the federal employment laws seem to be periodically amendable by Congress; they generally allow for state variation above a federal floor; and many of them include private rights of action that bring a highly decentralized and diverse array of courts, lawyers, and litigants into the process of lawmaking. Chapters 3 and 4 will take up in greater detail the law that has resulted and the possibilities for further reform.

But even some reform efforts that are grounded in "employment law" outside of the labor relations universe will be constrained by the ossified labor law regime unless and until Congress acts to dislodge those constraints. Hence a fourth lesson of ossification. In particular, the labor law, and some of its oldest and most criticized provisions, may frustrate efforts to improve labor standards (such as wages or job safety) or promote employee rights (against discrimination, for example) by enhancing workers' collective involvement in those matters. So, for example, efforts at the state level to improve workplace health and safety by requiring collective employee involvement face a potential hurdle in the form of Section 8(a)(2)'s ban on employer-dominated "labor organizations," together with the preemption of state regulation.

So the ossification of labor law is both a spur and a potential impediment to innovation in workplace policy and practice outside the traditional boundaries of labor law. With due regard for those impediments, it is mainly outside those boundaries where we will be looking for openings for reform.

Chapter 3 The Rise of Employment Law: Labor Standards and Employee Rights

In part as a consequence of labor law's ossification, the domain of collective bargaining and industrial self-governance established by New Deal labor law has shrunk in its reach and in its stature as the constitutive law of the workplace. In its wake has arisen a growing array of statutes and common law doctrines regulating various terms and conditions of employment and establishing employee rights. These regulations and rights aim to supply for workers some of what the NLRA had sought to enable workers to secure for themselves—dignity, fair treatment, decent working conditions—as well as some of what was missing from the New Deal scheme—especially equal protection rights. These employment law rights and standards do not, however, aim to advance the core objective of the NLRA of enabling workers to participate collectively in workplace decision making and governance.

This chapter will chronicle these developments in two parts: first, the proliferation of legislated minimum labor standards, especially laws regulating wages and hours and those regulating occupational health and safety, and second, the growth of individual employee rights, especially those under employment discrimination laws. Roughly speaking, minimum labor standards were meant to be enforced primarily by regulatory agencies, while rights vest in individual employees and are mainly enforced through private litigation. The line between rights and labor standards is indistinct or even arbitrary at times. Employees can of course be said to have a right to be paid a minimum wage or to have a safe workplace, though I include both among "labor standards." Some employee rights against discrimination or retaliation are enforceable by administrative agencies; and some labor standards, especially minimum wages and overtime requirements, are enforceable not only by government agencies but also, and increasingly, by employees themselves through private litigation. But the division between labor standards and rights will nonetheless be helpful in organizing the story that is told here. Much as with Chapter 2, this chapter covers a legal landscape that will be familiar to the teacher, scholar, or practitioner of employment law. But it lays a necessary foundation for what is to come.

MINIMUM LABOR STANDARDS ON
THE BOOKS AND IN ACTION

Public doubts about the fairness and efficiency of labor markets and the deals struck within them have produced wave after wave of reform, many of which have taken the form of mandated minimum standards, and many of which have been controversial. Since the nineteenth century, many employer advocates and economists have contended for the superiority of unregulated markets and individual contract for setting terms and conditions of employment. Regulation of wages above what the market would bear—above, that is, the level at which some worker would be willing to work given his or her alternatives—would simply push some employers out of business and some workers off the bottom of the economic ladder altogether. In the early twentieth century that belief was one justification for the "liberty of contract" that formed a constitutional barricade against most regulation of wages and hours.[1]

Although the constitutional barricade against labor standards laws succumbed to the Depression and the New Deal "switch in time," the same basic arguments, illustrated with supply and demand curves, underpin neoclassical economic critiques of the social utility of the minimum wage and other employment mandates.[2] Then and now, some free market enthusiasts have contended that attaching costly mandates to employment—while necessarily leaving employers free to decide whether to employ and at what wage (above any minimum)—inevitably distorts the efficient allocation of resources. Indeed, they maintain that employees themselves, rather than benefiting from employer mandates, will suffer as employers either employ fewer workers or pay them less. A minimum wage, for example, is bound to depress employment levels, especially among the least skilled (and often the poorest, youngest and oldest, and disproportionately minority and female) workers, whose marginal productivity and market wage would be below the legal minimum. Better to leave employees themselves to bargain or shop around for the terms and conditions they want and may be able to get in competitive labor markets.[3] For these critics of regulation, even the matter of job safety could be left to the market, for workers themselves would demand a wage premium for dangerous work that exposed them to injury or illness that was not fully compensated after the fact.[4] They argue that such wage premiums alone would be enough to induce "efficient" levels of safety precautions. There are some "ifs," of course: if labor markets are frictionless and efficient, if workers are fully informed and fully rational about occupational risks, and if they internalize all the costs of injuries and disease and destitution. Scholars have questioned all of those "ifs" and argued on efficiency grounds for the kinds of regulations that the public has in any event demanded.[5]

Economists continue to study and debate the efficiency and consequences of employer mandates and minimum labor standards. They debate whether either human beings or labor markets behave as the neoclassical model predicts and whether deviations from its standard assumptions are substantial and systematic enough to call for new models. These debates are complex and undoubtedly relevant to decisions about whether to adopt or alter minimum wages or other labor standards. For the most part, however, this book will bracket those debates and take as given the substance of the employment mandates that the public has demanded and that are on the books. The focus here will be on issues of governance, enforcement, and compliance. For once labor standards laws are on the books, the society has an interest in ensuring compliance with them so that lawbreakers do not gain a competitive advantage over law abiders. Let us begin by briefly surveying existing labor standards laws, both on the books and in action.

The Proliferation of Labor Standards Laws

After the Depression dealt its crushing blow to public confidence in "free markets," the New Deal was founded on the conviction that market mechanisms for the organization of the economy, though perhaps superior to the alterna-

tives, were intrinsically flawed and prone to failure.[6] Competition could be de-
structive as well as productive and needed to be channeled and disciplined lest
it generate a "race to the bottom" in which responsible firms were undercut
and the public interest injured by opportunistic cost cutters. Competition
needed to be "fair" rather than "free."[7] After a short-lived experiment with cor-
poratist-style management of the economy, the New Dealers turned instead to
regulation—the enactment and centralized enforcement of uniform rules and
standards, later denominated "command and control"—as the primary mechanism for protecting the public interest against market malfunctions and de-
structive competition.[8]

In the labor arena, the idea of collective action and self-governance as an alternative to direct state regulation survived in the form of collective bargaining. Collective bargaining was meant to serve as the main mechanism for ensuring "fair competition" and improving labor standards in much of the
economy.[9] But it was not meant to be the only such mechanism. Alongside
the NLRA's reconstitution of the framework for private bargaining and contract, substantive labor mandates gained a foothold in the New Deal workplace with the Fair Labor Standards Act of 1938 (FLSA).[10] The FLSA provided
for a nationwide minimum wage and an overtime premium for leading sectors of the private labor market.[11] Enforcement was chiefly by the Department
of Labor, though employees could also sue on their own behalf, collecting attorneys' fees and, in cases of willful violations, liquidated damages in the form
of double back pay.[12] Unlike the federal law of labor relations, the federal wage
and hour laws were deliberately and explicitly framed as minimum standards;
states were left free to set higher standards and to establish their own enforcement regimes.

So substantive regulation of labor standards was no more foreign to the New
Deal scheme than was the recognition of employee rights. Still, the FLSA was
seen as secondary to and largely supportive of collective bargaining, which was
to be the primary vehicle for improving wages and working conditions in the
leading economic sectors.[13] The minimum wage was meant to supplement
that regime but was expected to have little direct effect in the rapidly unioniz-
ing core industries.[14] Along with the new Social Security system, the New Deal
wage and hour legislation established a nationwide floor on some basic economic terms of employment; above that floor the parties to the employment
relationship were free to bargain, either through the newly established regime
of collective bargaining or, outside the union sector, by individual contract.
Moreover, states and, depending on state law, some municipalities took ad-

vantage of their power to set higher wage and hour standards and enforce those standards themselves. Some states, especially in the industrial North, have historically maintained higher minimum wages. In recent decades, "living wage" campaigns have established minimum wage levels more than twice the federal minimum for some employers in some cities.[15] Most important for present purposes, the varied and often stronger enforcement provisions of those state and local laws have created opportunities for reform and experimentation to which we will return in Chapter 4.

The distinct problem of workplace hazards and accidents was a recurring source of legal and political turmoil from the Civil War to the New Deal.[16] The problem had two sides: how to compensate for or remedy occupational injuries after the fact and how to prevent or reduce accidents and injuries. Both sides of the problem were left essentially untouched by federal New Deal legislation. Compensation for workplace injuries had only recently been the focus of a monumental state-by-state reform effort to channel claims for compensation for industrial injuries out of the then inhospitable common law tort system into state workers' compensation systems. Under the workers' compensation "bargain," employers gave up formidable common law defenses to liability, and workers gave up the prospect of fully compensatory tort remedies, in favor of more limited but more reliable and accessible administrative remedies. Once the constitutionality of the workers' compensation bargain was finally settled in 1917, the reforms swept through the state legislatures.[17]

To the extent that workers' compensation schemes were supposed not only to compensate injured employees but also to prevent injury and disease by encouraging employers to improve health and safety, they did not do enough. By design, compensation was partial; that is what employers got in return for giving up their common law defenses.[18] (Over time, the benefit of the workers' compensation bargain tilted more strongly toward employers as tort doctrine, from which workers had been largely cut off, continued to evolve in a plaintiff-friendly direction.) The workers' compensation schemes proved particularly inhospitable, as did tort law initially, to claims of occupational disease that resulted from the cumulative exposure to toxic substances rather than to a single observable accident.[19] So workers' compensation was far from fully compensatory, and workers' compensation insurance rates therefore did not induce adequate precautions on employers' part. Nor were most employers reliably rewarded through the compensation system for any precautions they did take, as those insurance rates were not "experience rated" for most employers; a safety-conscious employer might pay the same insurance premiums as a careless competitor.[20] For a variety of reasons, the problem of how to prevent occupational injury and disease took on a political and policy life of its own.

Through the 1960s, the prevention of occupational hazards, like compensation, was left to the states. Some states rose to the challenge by regulating hazards, inspecting workplaces, and penalizing employers for dangerous practices; other states did little or nothing by way of prevention. In some firms and some industries, unions bargained for health and safety measures; in others, unions were either absent or unable or unwilling to bargain effectively over health and safety issues.[21] By the late 1960s, the problem of workplace disease and injury again loomed large on the national agenda.

With organized labor as its leading proponent, the Occupational Safety and Health Act of 1970 (OSHA) sought to take workplace safety out of competition by establishing minimum standards and a public enforcement apparatus.[22] The central provision of OSHA was its "general duty clause," which required every covered employer to keep the workplace "free from recognized hazards that are causing or are likely to cause death or serious physical harm to his [sic] employees."[23] But OSHA also attempted to regulate specific hazards through detailed uniform rules or standards, and that is what made it the poster child of "command-and-control"-type regulation. Many of the existing standards of the Occupational Safety and Health Administration (also OSHA) date from its start-up period, when the agency adopted hundreds of standards previously developed by the American National Standards Institute, the National Fire Protection Association, and the old federal Walsh-Healey program.[24] Both old and especially new OSHA standards became the focus of bitter contestation. Rule-making proceedings to regulate toxic substances that were endemic to certain industries—asbestos, cotton dust, lead, benzene, and other poisons—launched some of the biggest legal battles over the reach of the new regulatory state and the meaning of administrative due process, while the minutiae of OSHA's safety rules and record-keeping requirements generated a steady current of grumbling about its bureaucratic rigidity and intrusiveness.[25]

Unlike the FLSA, OSHA did largely preempt state regulation of occupational safety and health—except where OSHA explicitly authorized state regulation. For the Act allowed the federal agency to delegate regulatory authority to state occupational health and safety agencies that it found were meeting or exceeding federal standards in both substance and rigor.[26] Twenty-four states

sought and gained regulatory authority over workplace safety through this provision, but none has either left or entered that group since 1970.[27] Notwithstanding Congress's evident purpose of setting a federal minimum in this area,
workplace health and safety has become an arena with some striking state-by-
state disparities both above and below the federal regime. With OSHA's ac-
quiescence, some states have taken a rather lax approach to workplace safety,
not through lower substantive standards (which OSHA would preclude) but
through inadequate enforcement. But other states—notably California—have
been able to pursue much more aggressive and innovative regulatory policies.[28]
We will return below to the good, the bad, and the ugly in the domain of occupational safety.

More labor standards laws were in the offing. In 1974, after a spate of highly
publicized pension plan collapses, Congress confronted chronic failings of the
private pension system with the Employee Retirement Income Security Act
(ERISA), which put in place detailed regulations for the administration and
funding of employee pension and benefit plans, along with an insurance-based
scheme for the partial rescue of failed pension plans.[29] Unlike the FLSA and
OSHA, ERISA did not mandate anything; employers were not required to
provide pensions or other employee benefits to their employees. But if they did
choose to offer such benefits, ERISA aimed to ensure that they were properly
funded and administered.[30] Later came the Worker Adjustment and Retrain-
ing Notification Act of 1988, which required employers to give employees advance notice of plant closings and mass layoffs,[31] and the Family and Medical
Leave Act (FMLA) of 1993, which regulated and expanded parental and medical leave policies.[32]

The American electorate's appetite for employer mandates does not yet appear sated, notwithstanding persistent complaints from employers about the
burdens they impose. Among current proposals for new federal labor standards,
the Healthy Families Act would guarantee employees up to seven days of paid
sick leave to care for themselves or a family member,[33] and amendments to
the FMLA would expand the availability of leave to include elder care and children's school-related events. More labor standards (or employer mandates) can
be found at the state level.

Each of the existing federal enactments, from the FLSA through the FMLA,
was a major victory for organized labor, which has long been the leading legislative advocate for employees, union and nonunion alike. At the same time,
however, these regulatory statutes foreshadowed or perhaps even hastened the

eclipse of the collective bargaining model and the centrality of collective self-governance.[34] The statutes give unions barely a nod of recognition and at most a token role in enforcement. And for employees without a union, the statutes afford no avenue for collective participation in enforcement except for the individual right to file a complaint or contact regulators.[35] The politics behind those omissions recalls the congressional impasse at the heart of labor law's ossification: employer allies resisted giving unions any added powers or rights via these statutes, while both employers and organized labor resisted (for opposite reasons) any form of non-union employee representation. Behind the political scenes is a legal obstruction—the NLRA's broad ban on "company unions"—which Congress could have modified but not without triggering the chronic gridlock over labor law reform.

These dynamics were on display in Clinton-era efforts to reform OSHA (to which we will return). One element of the reform would have mandated the creation of workplace health and safety committees at most workplaces.[36] Such committees were proposed as a way of extending the reach of an overextended enforcement apparatus—of carrying information about unsafe workplace conditions upward to enforcement agencies and bringing regulatory requirements down to the shop floor. But employers feared that independent committees would become a point of entry for union organizing, while some unions feared that the committees would be dominated by management and would become tools for manipulating employees and fending off union sentiment.[37] The reform bill failed.

The whole body of federal labor standards legislation thus virtually ignores the institutions that do or could represent employees themselves, while federal labor law preemption severely constrains what states can do to encourage or mandate employee representation in improving labor standards (though some states have pushed the envelope in this regard, as we will see below). The cumulative message of this rash of labor standards statutes was that it was through legislation, not collective bargaining or other collective self-help, that the most politically salient workplace issues were being addressed for most workers. The collective bargaining model appeared increasingly inadequate to deal with some of the most pressing problems of workers, not only outside of the shrinking ambit of collective bargaining, but even within the organized workplace. Indeed, on some accounts, the growing array of legislative mandates and employee rights (on which more below) has functioned as a "union substitute" and has hastened the decline of collective bargaining by dampening employee desires for unionization.[38] Whether or not employment law has *contributed* to the decline of collective bargaining, it has effectively *taken the place of* collective bargaining as the primary source of protection against the vicissitudes of the market for most employees.

Cracks, Crevices, and Holes in the Floor: The Problem of Underenforcement

The regulatory regimes that have effectively displaced collective bargaining as a mode of governing labor standards have themselves proven inadequate to the task of regulating labor standards in millions of workplaces across the country. In part that is because of the impossibility of setting uniform standards that meet the needs of workers and the capabilities of employers across the breadth of the labor market.[39] But in part it is because of the decline of union representation, without which employees lack any collective voice or power to demand more than the underregulated market will bear. I will focus here, and throughout this book's discussion of labor standards, on the regulation of wages and hours and occupational health and safety.

"WAGE THEFT": UNDERENFORCEMENT AND NONCOMPLIANCE UNDER THE WAGE AND HOUR LAWS

The basic problem is simple: Whenever there are workers willing to work for less than the law requires—and the growing corps of poor and undocumented immigrants has swelled the supply of low-wage labor—employers have a dauntingly predictable incentive to pay them less. Traditional enforcement mechanisms have failed to raise the cost of noncompliance high enough to outweigh the immediate savings from noncompliance. Compliance is undermined by "widespread fear among low-wage workers and ignorance of the law among both employers and workers."[40] Most enforcement actions, when they occur at all, secure only the back wages owed to employees (or, in the vast majority of cases that are settled, just a fraction of these). Opportunistic employers risk very little by underpaying employees and hoping—quite realistically—to avoid enforcement, by either inspection or complaint.[41] One study found that the basic cost of noncompliance in the apparel industry—the average civil penalty discounted by the probability of inspection—was less than 12 percent of the cost of compliance—that is, the cost of paying employees the lawful wage.[42] As a result, compliance is "largely voluntary" and below 50 percent in some low-wage industries.[43]

Given these hard realities, simply ignoring the law is a tempting strategy, especially for marginal producers at the bottom of the production chain who have little fixed capital or stake in their reputation, who tend to operate under the regulatory radar, and who often rely heavily on undocumented immigrant workers who are too fearful or desperate to complain.[44] This layer of the labor market has been expanded by the powerful trend among larger companies to outsource work that is peripheral to their "core competencies."[45] Outsourcing allows those larger companies to reduce costs for services such as maintenance, security, and laundry by putting contractors in competition with each other for the work and, not just incidentally, by insulating the larger company from responsibility for the employment law violations that often follow from this "race to the bottom" among contractors.[46]

When it comes to evasion of wage and hour laws, where there is a will, there is a way. Actually, there are many ways, as explored in a rash of recent publications.[47] Some employers simply refuse to pay workers the promised wage after the work is done; that sort of "wage theft" is surprisingly common in marginal and casual employment.[48] Others ignore minimum wage and overtime laws (as well as employment tax laws), paying instead whatever the market, and its most desperate denizens, will bear.[49] Steven Greenhouse tells the story of Julia Ortiz, who spent years working for a discount store called Save Smart, which demanded over ten hours a day, six days per week, and paid just $35 a day—less than $3.35 an hour. Save Smart coupled low pay with abusive treatment and kept its undocumented workers from seeking better jobs by threatening to get them fired or to reveal their status to immigration authorities.[50]

Ignoring employment laws is also common in janitorial services, a labor-intensive sector that employs many poor and undocumented immigrants. The Service Employees International Union (SEIU), which has organized thousands of janitors in several major U.S. cities, has calculated that employers who ignore minimum wage and overtime laws and payroll taxes have labor costs as much as 40 percent below the minimum required by law. Those contractors can underbid lawful contractors (including union contractors) and still put extra money in their pockets. Well-known grocery and retail chains such as Albertsons, Ralphs, Target, and Wal-Mart are among the companies that have used such contractors for their cleaning services in recent years.[51]

Among the more devious pay practices that have come to light is "time-shaving": managers simply alter employees' time cards, often by small amounts in each case but enough in the aggregate to matter.[52] Greenhouse tells of a supervisor, Drew Pooters, who confronted the practice of time-shaving in three consecutive jobs at Toys "R" Us, Family Dollar, and Rentway. At Toys "R" Us,

Drew walked in on a manager who was editing down the hours clocked by the store's employees. When Pooters noted such time-shaving was "not exactly legal," the manager told him "it's none of your business" and began a campaign of threats, demotion, and harassment that eventually led Pooters to quit.[53] At his next job, managing a Family Dollar, he faced such intense pressure to cut payroll costs that it became impossible to effectively staff the store. His district manager told him to solve the problem by simply deleting hours that employees worked; when Pooters refused, she did it herself: "She started rejiggering the hours right in front of me. . . . I said, 'But that worker didn't take a lunch that day,' and she said, 'Now she did.'" Pooters encountered the same scheme once again at Rentway, this time affecting his own pay. Although he worked through lunch every day of his first week, his time sheet indicated he had taken daily lunch breaks. Pooters told his supervisor he wouldn't sign off on a doctored time sheet and was told, "If you don't sign, you don't get paid. If you don't sign, you'll be looking for work somewhere else."[54]

Employers also try to reduce wage costs and avoid paying overtime by exacting "off-the-clock" work from employees.[55] Wal-Mart has been sued repeatedly for its managers' practice of requiring employees to "clock out" before completing cleanup or inventory work; the practice was contrary to the company's written policies but allegedly tolerated and even necessitated by Wal-Mart's demands for minimizing labor costs.[56] To meet their draconian payroll, Wal-Mart managers report that they must often choose between working fifteen or more off-the-clock hours each week themselves and pressuring their employees to do so.[57] Wal-Mart and its offshoot, Sam's Club, often coupled off-the-clock demands with the practice of locking night-shift workers into stores overnight.[58] Workers on Farris Cobb's night shift at Sam's Club, for example, were required to clock out at two a.m. on Fridays but were locked into the building until four; when managers found them waiting by the door, they chastised them: "You should be working. Period."[59] Farris himself regularly arrived early and stayed late to finish work, but his time cards reflected only a portion of what were often sixteen-hour days. Farris kept quiet about the unpaid wages for years, fearing that complaining would impede promotions or get him fired.[60]

Another kind of off-the-clock practice reached the Supreme Court recently in what may prove to be the final act in almost two decades of litigation over meat processor IBP's refusal to pay workers for minutes spent "donning and doffing" safety and hygienic clothing and gear, sharpening knives, and doing other preparatory work. The dispute would not have been worth litigating for any one worker, but when the workers' position was largely vindicated in a class-action lawsuit, the total back pay liability for IBP amounted to over $7 million.[61] Pre-shift work in call centers has also come under scrutiny. A lawsuit is pending against one such call center operation, TeleTech, which handles customer service for Verizon and which required employees to arrive fifteen minutes early to boot up their computers and read up on product changes before their shift (and their wages) began.[62] Cingular and T-Mobile settled similar pre-shift work complaints for $5 million apiece after the Labor Department questioned their practices.[63]

Another common practice is to misclassify employees as "independent contractors," a category that is exempt from the FLSA's minimum wage and overtime requirements.[64] The category, intended for independent entrepreneurs operating their own businesses, has been misapplied to low-wage workers such as janitors, grocery delivery workers, sewing machine operators in the garment business, and pickle pickers.[65] Some employers use the "independent contractor" label after the fact, as a last-ditch effort to defend employment that was off-the-books, paid in cash, and essentially unregulated. Sometimes the "independent contractor" label is affixed deliberately and with all the corresponding documentation—though still to the end of evading compliance with employment and payroll tax laws (and denying workers the right to form a union).

FedEx Ground, for example, classifies its delivery truck drivers as independent contractors, claiming they are business people who set their own hours and buy their own routes (and have no right to unionize).[66] The arrangement saves FedEx Ground an estimated $400 million per year and gives FedEx a competitive edge over rival UPS, which treats its drivers as employees. For driver Jean Capobianco, her classification as an independent contractor meant she had to buy her own truck—for over $37,000—and pay for her own gas, insurance and maintenance, uniform, and other mandatory equipment. She worked sixty hours per week to net $32,000 per year. When she got sick, she had to find and pay a replacement driver to cover her route, for a net loss of $200 per sick day.[67] When she was diagnosed with cancer and was unable to work or find a replacement, FedEx fired her, claiming that because Jean was not an employee, it had no duty to accommodate her illness under the ADA.[68] In several class-action lawsuits, FedEx drivers have argued they are employees since FedEx strictly controls their work, requiring them to buy FedEx trucks, wear FedEx uniforms, and deliver FedEx packages when and where FedEx tells them to go. In August 2007, a California appeals court ruled for the drivers, noting that FedEx controlled "every exquisite detail of the drivers' performance, including the color of their socks and the style of their hair." Later that year, the IRS assessed FedEx $319 million in penalties and back taxes for 2002 alone, based on the company's misclassification of employees as independent contractors.[69]

The IBP and FedEx cases highlight the importance of aggregate litigation in enforcing employment laws, an issue to which we will return below. Indeed, many of the foregoing examples are drawn from cases in which either public or private enforcement actions were brought. But many more examples of such practices remain undiscovered or unprosecuted, either by enforcement agencies (with their inevitably inadequate inspection resources) or by employees themselves. Unfortunately, many employees do not know they are being misclassified or otherwise cheated, and many do not know their legal rights. Others may fear—and their employers may threaten—that a complaint may get them fired (an action that would be illegal but not easily remedied) or even deported in the case of undocumented immigrants.[70] As one employee said, "There's no one backing you, no government agency you can go to, so you're at the mercy of [the employer]."[71] Further, some of these pay practices cheat each individual employee by a rather small amount—too little to be worth the cost and risk of complaining—even though they add up to substantial savings to the employer. Unless someone has the incentive and ability to aggregate claims (and to pursue them without fear of retaliation), those violations will continue, depriving workers of their lawful pay and undercutting law-abiding competitors.

RISKING LIFE AND LIMB: UNDERENFORCEMENT AND
NONCOMPLIANCE IN HEALTH AND SAFETY

Occupational health and safety laws confront a more complex economic calculus than do the wage and hour laws. There is no simple baseline of "what the market will bear" in terms of health and safety. Nor is it as simple for a firm to ensure compliance with the law, given the complexity and multiplicity of both hazards and regulatory standards (though most hazards fall under the "general duty" provision of OSHA and not any specific rule or standard). Some health and safety precautions transparently raise production costs (for examples, those that require slowing down production); others may cost the employer less than they save by promoting productivity or avoiding lost-time accidents. Even if we ignore for now the fact that at least some managers and some firms actually care about their workers' physical well-being, the law is not all that drives firms to invest in safety.[72] We will return to those internal safety programs in Chapter 4.

But to the extent that the law does supply an important incentive to maintain safe and healthy working conditions, it is not up to the job. We have already observed that the system of workers' compensation sets up predictably inadequate incentives to reduce risk. In most states, compensation levels are too low; "experience rating" of workers' compensation insurance is often crude at best; and some employers effectively opt out of the system in whole or in part by failing to secure coverage or by discouraging workers from filing claims.[73] While the deterrence function of tort law has been largely disabled and replaced by a weaker administrative substitute, OSHA's preventive regime has not picked up the slack. Occupational health and safety standards are chronically underenforced in many industries and regions. OSHA enforcement is plagued by low penalties, rare inspections, and long delays, which combine to produce inadequate incentives to take precautions.

First, OSHA penalties are capped at levels that are way out of step with both the human costs of workplace hazards and the savings that employers might anticipate from cutting corners. Criminal prosecution is rare, and fines, civil and criminal, are usually modest; the maximum fine for a "willful" violation is $70,000, and for a "serious" violation, $7,000.[74] These compare to, for example, fines of up to $250,000 per day for violations of the Clean Water Act that knowingly endanger the public.[75] And unlike the Clean Water Act, OSHA does not provide for private civil enforcement.[76]

Second, OSHA is notoriously hobbled by a lack of inspectors and resources. One recent study calculated that to inspect each workplace within its jurisdiction would take OSHA and its existing staff 119 years.[77] The actual frequency of inspection varies by industry and by state; both OSHA and state agencies make some effort to target the most dangerous industries and firms. Even so, regulators are stretched way too thin. As one union safety expert noted, "OSHA only shows up when the building falls down."[78] The combination of rare inspections and modest penalties means that OSHA does little to offset whatever economic incentive employers may have to disregard health and safety requirements that impose costs.[79]

Third, that crude cost calculus must be further discounted because of chronic delays. The large number of appeals and the length of time required for the Occupational Safety and Health Review Commission (OSHRC) to decide a case have created a growing backlog of cases. For example, in 2007, OSHRC decided twenty-eight cases, some of them dating from 1991, while approximately two thousand new cases were filed with the commission that same year.[80] This long decision time is due in part to understaffing and the complexity of cases, but it also reflects a perverse feature of the law that encourages employers to string out the enforcement process: filing a notice of contest suspends an employer's duty to abate the hazard pending final resolution.[81]

The combination of underenforcement, low penalties, and delay means that firms seeking to minimize labor costs may be sorely tempted to do so in part by failing to protect workers from dangerous conditions or by driving workers at a pace that forces them to ignore safe practices. Some of the most dangerous jobs are in mining and construction, where shortcuts and poor training, especially in the growing non-union sectors, produce hundreds of deaths and thousands of serious injuries each year.[82] But workers in a variety of low-wage occupations are subject to chronic hazards. Steven Greenhouse reported, for example, on workers at Landis Plastics who operate the injection-molding machines that produce yogurt and cottage cheese containers and the printing presses that ink their labels. Inadequate training, long hours, repetitive motions, heavy lifting, and a frenetic pace of production resulted in a very high accident and injury rate at the plant. In one thirteen-month period, four workers lost fingers.[83] When OSHA inspectors finally came in response to worker complaints, they found seventy-four safety violations. The inspectors also discovered that Landis had unlawfully failed to record sixty-three worker injuries in the plant's safety log. In an unusually prompt and successful enforcement action, OSHA fined Landis $720,700, one of the biggest safety fines ever imposed in New York State, just six months after workers filed their complaint.[84]

Occupational hazards also abound in the meat- and poultry-processing factories that are scattered across the country but concentrated in the South. In these industrial feeding and processing facilities, workers are exposed to "manure gases, odours and degradation products; bacteria; endotoxins; and dust," leading to chronic respiratory diseases. Processing workers are also prone to flesh wounds and repetitive motion injuries.[85] Other hazards are less endemic to the poultry business as such than they are evidence of a lax attitude to workplace safety. A fire in a Hamlet, North Carolina, chicken-processing plant in 1991 killed twenty-five workers and injured fifty-six, in the worst industrial accident in American history since the Triangle Shirtwaist factory tragedy in 1911.[86] Two facts about the 1991 fire gained some notoriety: the fire escapes were locked, apparently to prevent workers from stealing chickens, and the Hamlet plant had *never* been inspected by the state safety and health agency to which OSHA had delegated regulatory authority.[87]

A leading hazard in meat and poultry processing, aside from the unavoidable presence of sharp instruments, is the speed of the processing line, which leads to rampant repetitive motion injuries as well as lacerations and lost digits. Yet slowing down the line translates directly into higher cost per unit of output. There is just not enough on the other side of companies' ledgers to make that worthwhile. Injured workers can be cheaply replaced and trained, and the cost of compensating workers for injuries is low, especially in the South. In most plants there is no union to put collective muscle behind workers' own demands for a safer workplace and work pace.[88] And there is little threat of public intervention, as inspections are rare and ergonomic hazards are in any case virtually unregulated.

THE GROWTH OF "UNREGULATED WORK"

The problem of noncompliance with labor standards laws and regulations—especially wage and hours laws and health and safety standards—is obviously most serious in the low-wage layer of the economy, where capital investments and barriers to entry are often low, firms are often small and marginal, and the skill and experience that is required of workers is limited (at least given the way work is organized). A large pool of poor and often undocumented immigrants, who very rarely call upon public agencies for help, along with growing competition from low-wage countries, especially in manufacturing, has contributed to a resurgence since the 1960s of sweatshop conditions that the regulatory agencies have failed to combat effectively. "People have to make choices between a job and their health, and most of the time they choose their job. . . . [E]ven when there is a serious risk, . . . they do it anyway because they're already there . . . and they need the money."[89]

In this gray economy, work is regulated neither internally by unions nor externally by public regulators. The only "regulatory regime" with real bite is the market. So contractors compete with each other based on labor costs. Once any contractors drop below the legal floor, competitors feel pressure to follow suit, and whenever employers operate below the legal floor, they are desperate to fend off unionization, which would force them out of the gray economy. As one recent report explains, "[u]nregulated work creates more unregulated work."[90] And the prevalence of unregulated work creates a demand for unregulated workers, especially undocumented immigrants. As a longtime New York City reporter stated, "The minimum wage is an abstract idea for immigrants."[91] The Immigration Reform and Control Act of 1986 made it unlawful for employers to hire undocumented immigrants; but at the same time it criminalized working as an undocumented immigrant, and that gave employers more power over such workers by magnifying the threat of discharge or deportation. Recall the story of Julia Ortiz, whose employer got away with paying her less than $3.35 per hour by threatening to call the immigration authorities if she complained.

Given that unregulated low-wage workers are disproportionately people of color, women, and immigrants, it should not be surprising that discrimination often accompanies other workplace violations. Employers frequently sort workers into jobs on the basis of race, gender, and ethnicity. For example, black and Hispanic job applicants at restaurants often find themselves directed toward positions as dishwashers rather than servers, regardless of skill.[92] Widespread discrimination helps to keep minorities and immigrants locked into low-wage work—fearful of discharge and confined to a narrow segment of the labor market—and thereby strengthens employers' power over unregulated employees. That brings us to the other half of the sprawling employment law regime, the proliferation of employee rights, while reminding us that the problem of underenforcement recurs there, especially—again—at the bottom of the labor market.

THE CIVIL RIGHTS ACT OF 1964 AND THE
EMPLOYEE RIGHTS REVOLUTION

Integral to the New Deal constitution of the workplace and its centerpiece, the Wagner Act, was a set of employee rights that were enforceable by the state against employers through the NLRB. Section 7 of the NLRA protected employees' right to support a union; to discuss matters of mutual concern with co-workers and others; and to engage in peaceful concerted activity in support of workplace objectives, including strikes, picketing, and other forms of economic pressure. So rights were central to the regime of collective bargaining from the beginning. But these rights were limited to those that supported the regime of collective bargaining and were not enforceable by employees in court, but only by the NLRB through its administrative processes.

The idea of the workplace as a domain of civil rights and liberties was extended dramatically in 1964, when Congress enacted an "equal protection clause" for the workplace. The idea of prohibiting employment discrimination had been put forward in the New Deal by early civil rights activists but was pushed off the agenda in the 1930s and 1940s as part of the price paid by the progressives to hold together their legislative coalition with the Southern Dixie-crats.[93] Growing pressure for reform soon came from many directions—from civil rights activism, Cold War diplomacy, and the conscience of liberal legis-lators.[94] Eventually, after escalating unrest and the longest filibuster in Senate history, Congress passed the Civil Rights Act of 1964, Title VII of which pro-scribed discrimination in terms and conditions of employment based on race, sex, religion, color, and national origin.[95]

The banner of equal opportunity has proven to be both politically formi-dable and protean. In contrast to the political gridlock that labor law faces, Congress has extended the equality mandate in stages to reach discrimination based on age, pregnancy, disability, and most recently genetic makeup; to add new remedies; and to overrule Supreme Court decisions that restricted liabil-ity.[96] All of these federal laws, like the FLSA and again unlike the labor rela-tions laws, disclaimed any preemptive effect. That has left the states free to ex-pand upon their protections—to add new protected classes, such as those based on sexual orientation, and to provide their own enforcement apparatus. Nearly all of these statutory equality rights, state and federal, were made enforceable in court both by public agencies and by private individuals. Critically, indi-viduals can sue on their own behalf and recover attorneys' fees if successful. They can seek a jury trial and can recover compensatory and exemplary dam-ages, not just back pay.[97]

So while the vindication of employee rights in the New Deal, and especially under the NLRA, was channeled away from courts and lawyers, the Civil Rights Act appointed courts and lawyers as leading agents of civil rights en-forcement. Inevitably that brought those actors into the process of defining employee rights. Creative lawyers translated the experiences of aggrieved indi-viduals into new legal theories of discrimination, and courts sometimes re-sponded, striking down employer policies with a statistically disparate impact on protected groups, the imposition of sexual demands on employees, and the creation of a discriminatory hostile environment.[98]

Employment discrimination law gave birth to a plaintiffs' employment bar and gave momentum to the idea of the workplace as a domain of legally cog-nizable rights and liberties. That idea in turn inspired a wave of legal demands for protection of privacy, dignity, and freedoms of belief, association, and ex-pression at work. Of course, those claims were up against the venerable doctrine of employment at will and employers' presumptive power to terminate employment at any time for good reason, bad reason, or no reason at all.[99] But the civil rights laws had dealt a mortal blow to the legitimacy of employers' claimed right to fire employees for "bad reasons" and opened the door to legislative and judicial recognition of other unacceptably bad reasons for discharge and other employee rights on the job.

By the 1970s it had become almost routine for legislatures, when enacting any kind of law regulating private firms' conduct, to include a prohibition of retaliation against employees who reported violations of the law. OSHA itself contains such a provision, as does Title VII; but so do environmental, consumer protection, and tax statutes. These statutory "whistleblower" protections are often narrowly framed and often lack both private enforcement provisions and fully compensatory remedies. (OSHA's antiretaliation provision displays both weaknesses, while Title VII's antiretaliation protections are both broader and privately enforceable.) But they represent a growing recognition that firms' compliance with their legal obligations—obligations that run to workers, consumers, the environment, shareholders, and the public at large—is dependent upon the willingness of the individuals within those firms to abide by the law and report violations. And that recognition in turn required the protection of employees who did their part and then suffered reprisals. We will return to the "whistleblower" laws below.

Following similar logic, common law courts began to elaborate the tort of wrongful discharge in violation of public policy.[100] Many wrongful discharge claims reinforce other laws governing the workplace (as well as laws regulating pollution, product safety, financial fraud, or other harmful business practices). For example, courts have made it a tort to fire an employee for refusing to violate the law (for example, refusing to underpay fellow employees) or for claiming a legal right (for example, filing a workers' compensation claim) or for reporting employer violations of the law (for example, complaining to OSHA about unsafe conditions). Through the backdoor of wrongful discharge law, employees essentially gained rights to act consistent with public law, free from the most onerous of employer reprisals, and the public gained potential allies in the enforcement of legal constraints on corporate conduct in the workplace and beyond. Employment at will became riddled with statutory and common law exceptions beginning in the 1960s.

As employers' right to fire employees for "bad reasons" came under assault, so did the right to fire employees for "no reason." The idea that employees enjoyed a kind of property right in employment began to take hold in the public sector, where the due process clause provided a doctrinal hook.[101] In the private sector, claims for job security were framed within the law of contract. First came broader enforcement of oral and implied promises.[102] Then came decisions enforcing policy statements about job security, fairness, and due process in employee handbooks—the sort of representations that employers were increasingly advised and inclined to make as a matter of both union avoidance and liability avoidance.[103] By 1980, one might have seen a trend toward recognizing an employee entitlement to job security. But the trend soon stalled, for just as the law became more receptive to contract claims based on employers' explicit or implicit assurances of job security, employers became less inclined to give such assurances.[104] The doctrine eventually provided employers with a road map for how to avoid liability while assuring employees of their good and fair intentions, as we will see in Chapter 4. The net result has been to give greater legal effect to employers' voluntary representations about job security; that is not nothing, but it is not much for most employees.

On the whole, it is important not to overstate the transformation of employee rights. Most of the law of wrongful discharge and of individual employee rights outside of antidiscrimination law is state law, and much of it is judge-made common law; employee rights thus vary dramatically from state to state and often unpredictably from case to case.[105] Moreover, employee rights —including those under antidiscrimination law—are circumscribed by deference to managerial prerogatives. Given the cost of litigation and the difficulty of proving an unlawful motive, many employees are still unable or unwilling to mount a legal challenge to a discharge they believe to be illegal.[106] And some groups of employees, especially low-wage immigrants, are so predictably unable to sue to enforce their rights that employers can safely ignore those rights.

Still, employees face a vastly more congenial legal regime than they did before 1964. Contract law has shed its exaggerated attachment to the presumption of employment at will. Tort law, fueled by the interests of aggrieved individuals and their entrepreneurial attorneys, has produced a dynamic body of wrongful discharge doctrine and a rudimentary set of employee rights against employers. And the protean antidiscrimination principle has generated a menu of potential legal claims. At least in the regulated parts of the labor market, it is clear that wrongful discharge liability, whether grounded in tort law or in the tort-like vehicle of antidiscrimination law, has had some of the deterrent impact that tort liability is supposed to have: it has induced employers to take precautions against liability. Some employer precautions aim to minimize "accidents"—that is, decisions that might be found wrongful—by creating internal procedures for the review and appeal of disciplinary and discharge decisions. There is little doubt that the threat of employment litigation and liability has helped to transform personnel practices and workplace demographics. I will return to this development in Chapter 4.

But first there is a bit more to say about the relationship between the rise of employee rights and wrongful discharge law and the decline or failings of collective bargaining. That relationship is not a simple one. The Civil Rights Act of 1964 responded in part to one failing of collective bargaining: the failure of many unions, majoritarian by design, to stand up for the "equal protection" of minority groups within the workforce. Many craft unions pursued an exclusionary economic strategy of controlling access to the trade, a strategy that had historically gone hand in hand with nepotism, nativism, and racism in their membership policies.[107] The industrial unions were much more inclusive in their own policies, at least at the national level. Still, many local unions, especially in the South, proved unwilling to combat widespread employer discrimination and segregation and sometimes contributed to it with discriminatory bargaining demands and grievance practices.[108] Majoritarianism without minority rights proved to be a deeply flawed form of democracy in labor unions as well as in the polity.

The wrongful discharge doctrines that developed in the wake of the Civil Rights Act arose less out of the shortcomings of unions and the collective bargaining system than out of their limited reach. Almost all of the claims of arbitrary and retaliatory treatment that generated common law tort exceptions to employment at will arose out of non-union workplaces. A functioning collective bargaining agreement would generally have subjected such discharges to the demanding standard of "just cause" within a jointly administered grievance arbitration process. Those grievance systems were hardly perfect, and unions were not uniformly willing to press such claims. But the union setting provided a modicum of procedural and substantive protection against arbitrary treatment along with a fair degree of job security. It was largely the plight of non-union employees, who were terminable at will, that moved courts to carve out exceptions to the employment-at-will doctrine.

Even more obviously, the softening of the employment-at-will presumption as against contractual claims of job security came in response to the claims of non-union employees. Often these were long-term employees who had developed reasonable but heretofore unenforceable expectations of continued employment—employees who, in the union context, would have been protected by a just cause provision as well as by seniority rights.[109] Some of these cases were brought by managers, who were outside the expected reach of the collective bargaining model. But many were brought by mid-level white-collar employees who, in the heyday of the New Deal, had been expected to turn to unions for protection as they realized their vulnerability and limited bargaining power as individuals within the modern organization.[110] The fact that these individuals remained almost entirely outside the realm of collective bargaining was part of the subtext, and sometimes the text, of judicial opinions and commentary in support of these contract claims.[111] The notion that non-union employers should be held to their promises in court gained appeal as the practical ability of employees to secure enforceable promises of job security through unionization became increasingly remote.

On the other hand, some of these cases reflected not just the absence of unions but also their presence elsewhere in the labor market. For the adoption of internal systems of "due process" was a standard component of both a "union substitution" strategy of averting employee discontent and a "union competition" strategy of attracting the best applicants away from unionized firms. Some courts recognized that employee handbooks, with their explicit assurances of fair treatment, were often designed to assure employees that they did not need a union. And some observers have argued that the rise of these internal due process systems accounts for part of the decline of unions.[112]

The rise of wrongful discharge law is also linked to the decline of collective bargaining by way of an ideological shift away from collective self-help and toward individualism.[113] By the lights of the New Dealers and in the midst of the Depression, individuals lacked genuine freedom and bargaining power vis-à-vis their employers. The remedy lay not in the courts, which had only recently put aside the radical individualism of *Lochner*'s liberty of contract, but in collective institutions for self-governance and group action. But the broad political appeal of collectivist institutions and ideals waned; within a decade or so, unions were the major surviving institutional reminders of the nation's short-lived romance with collectivization as a fundamental tenet of social policy.[114] The remedy for individual vulnerability was sought increasingly in the recognition of individual rights.

There are, in short, many interrelated connections between the decline of collective bargaining and the rise of individual employee rights and wrongful discharge law. Only one of them is the regulatory vacuum left by the limited and shrinking reach of collective bargaining and the system of workplace self-governance that it was meant to create. But even if the rise of employment mandates, both rights and labor standards, filled part of the vacuum left by the decline of unions, it left unaddressed the "democratic deficit"—the lack of any mechanism in most workplaces for collective employee participation in workplace governance. It is tempting to describe this as a "governance gap," but that would not be quite accurate. For organizations do govern themselves, and they do so under the shadow of the law. While the forms of workplace governance prescribed by labor law declined, the rise of employment law brought about another sort of workplace governance. Let us turn now to those developments.

Chapter 4 The Rise of Regulated Self-Regulation in the Workplace (and Beyond)

As workers' ability to bargain collectively for rights and improved labor standards has declined, the courts and legislatures have stepped in and generated a growing body of employee rights and minimum standards. The resulting body of "employment law," though it has surpassed the field of "labor law" in its practical impact, does nothing to restore or refurbish the New Deal commitment to workplace democracy and nothing to fill the democratic deficit left by the decline of unionization and collective bargaining. Still, the vast, hydra-headed body of employment law may be a more promising place to look for the building blocks of reform than is the aging and ossified body of federal labor law. First, the sheer diversity of governmental and private actors and institutions that operate within "employment law" creates many more levers and footholds for reform and experimentation. Second, much of the reform and experimentation that has taken place follows a potentially encouraging trajectory: rights and regulations create liabilities; liabilities beget precautions in the form of self-regulation; as self-regulation has drawn the attention of regulators, they have sought to shape self-regulatory structures into more effective regulatory mechanisms. In these emerging forms of "regulated self-regulation," we can see the glimmer of new mechanisms of workplace governance.

CORPORATE COMPLIANCE:
THE VIEW FROM THE TOP

The viability of command-and-control regulatory schemes has, since the 1970s, come under challenge from many directions. Many employee advocates focus on the problem of underenforcement, of which there is plenty: not enough inspectors, not enough penalties, not enough deterrence or compliance.[1] The opposite critique—too many rules, too much regulation—has been at least as voluble.[2] Business interests in particular have pleaded for deregulation in the interest of competitiveness and flexibility.[3] They did not get much formal deregulation, even during the Reagan administration.[4] But the deregulatory drumbeat from business has continued. On the other hand, for many thoughtful proponents of public regulation, the problem is neither too little regulation nor too much. The problem is that centrally administered uniform standards and the lengthy process for developing those standards are too rigid and unresponsive to industry and organizational conditions and out of step with increasingly agile forms of production, porous product markets, and transnational corporate structures.[5] These developments have converged to yield a growing conviction that traditional command-and-control regulatory approaches are anachronistic—ineffectual at best, counterproductive at worst.[6]

As the prestige, or at least the seeming inevitability, of markets and private ordering surged in the 1990s, the climate for these complaints began to change. At the same time, some in the mainstream business community changed their tune from the tendentious demand for deregulation to a kinder and gentler call for self-regulation and voluntary compliance backed by a growing investment in internal compliance machinery.[7] The growth of sophisticated internal compliance structures has enhanced the credibility of firms' demands for more cooperative regulatory approaches and for more latitude to self-regulate their labor practices.[8] If these compliance systems were simply the predictable efforts that firms made to avoid regulatory violations and associated liabilities, then we might not expect to see much by way of internal compliance investments in the case of labor standards, for the threat and cost of public enforcement are often too low to induce compliance as a simple economic matter. But the rise of corporate compliance programs has more and deeper roots than a simple computation of probability and cost of enforcement.

The Rise of Corporate Compliance
and Regulated Self-Regulation

Corporate self-regulatory programs, and legal initiatives to channel those programs, have been around almost since the rise of the modern regulatory state. There is of course the granddaddy of American corporate self-regulatory programs, the system of mandatory disclosure and audited self-regulation prescribed by the securities laws in the wake of the Great Depression, to which we will return in Chapter 6. But across a range of areas, especially for the past fifty years, history reveals a recurring cycle of corporate scandals—from price-fixing in the 1950s and '60s to bribery of foreign officials in the '70s to insider trading and defense procurement fraud in the '80s—followed by either legislation mandating expanded self-regulation or preemptive self-regulatory initiatives from industry to fend off indictments or legislation.[9] This pattern set the stage for the Federal Sentencing Guidelines for Organizations in 1991 and the burgeoning of corporate compliance programs. Under the Sentencing Guidelines, the existence of an "effective compliance program" may significantly mitigate, though not eliminate, criminal penalties imposed for corporate legal violations.[10]

The Sentencing Guidelines set out seven basic requirements for an "effective compliance program." The organization must have (1) codes of conduct that prescribe at least compliance with the relevant law; that are (2) communicated to employees, often via training; and that are (3) overseen at a high level (4) by individuals without a history of legal or ethical violations. The organization must also have in place (5) systems to monitor the effectiveness of the program, including confidential reporting systems that reduce risk of retaliation and (6) appropriate incentives and disciplinary procedures to enforce the compliance program, and it must (7) respond to any violations that are discovered.[11]

It is worth emphasizing at the outset that employees play nearly all the crucial roles in "effective compliance programs" under the Sentencing Guidelines, regardless of what laws are at issue. High-level employees oversee the system; employees are the would-be transgressors who must be trained in compliance and disciplined in case of noncompliance; and employees are the primary monitors of compliance through confidential reporting.

The Guidelines' self-regulation model quickly spread beyond criminal sentencing to prosecutorial decision making—effective compliance programs may allow a firm to avoid prosecution altogether[12]—and beyond the criminal law.

The Guidelines approach was replicated in several areas of civil liability, including environmental law, health care law, and occupational safety and health law.[13] The basic model of mitigating corporate civil liability on the basis of "effective compliance programs" got a boost from the Delaware Chancery Court's *Caremark* decision, which encouraged corporate directors to institute corporate compliance structures as part of their fiduciary duty to shareholders.[14] It soon became conventional wisdom that meeting the standards of the Sentencing Guidelines for "effective compliance programs" would leave a company "best equipped to contend credibly—in any forum—that the misconduct was the work of an errant employee, despite the company's best efforts."[15] These "voluntary" programs have become so indispensable to corporations' defense against a wide range of liabilities as to become virtually mandatory.[16]

Much of the legal reform activity and literature on corporate compliance relates to corporations' duties toward shareholders and investors, not toward workers, consumers, or the general public. That is the case with both the *Caremark* decision and the Sarbanes-Oxley reforms (to which we will return in Chapter 6). But to the extent that corporate wrongdoing against workers, consumers, or the general public can trigger costly liabilities that harm the corporation and its shareholders, those developments in corporate governance reinforce the legal inducements toward self-regulation of employment, environmental, and other practices.[17]

Growing corporate capabilities and commitments have converged with growing doubts about the efficacy and adequacy of traditional regulatory approaches to produce strong arguments for lifting some public regulatory burdens in exchange for firms themselves undertaking much of the regulatory work. The move toward self-regulation has not been accompanied thus far by significant amendments to the basic federal labor standards statutes. Still, both state and federal regulatory agencies have begun to experiment with forms of self-regulation within the confines of these command-and-control statutes.[18] A few examples in the health and safety arena will help ground the discussion going forward.

CORPORATE COMPLIANCE AND REGULATED SELF-REGULATION OF LABOR STANDARDS: THE CASE OF HEALTH AND SAFETY

Given the weakness of the enforcement regime for occupational health and safety, what may seem most surprising is that many employers do try to comply with safety standards most of the time.[19] Especially larger companies with valued reputations and ample resources of their own have invested in compliance and improvement of workplace safety, with internal health and safety departments and preventive programs.[20] We have all seen the signs outside factories: "187 days without a lost-time accident." Some of this may literally be window dressing, but some of it attests to the efforts some companies make to keep workplaces safe.

Internal health and safety programs, if they are supported by a managerial commitment to employee safety—by what insiders call a "culture of safety"—appear to make a real difference to employee well-being, and regulatory programs that support a "culture of safety" do more to promote occupational safety and health than more aggressive top-down enforcement alone.[21] In recognition of these efforts, OSHA, a political lightning rod since its birth in 1970, has undertaken cautious yet controversial experimentation with cooperative and self-regulatory approaches to improving workplace health and safety.[22] Professor Orly Lobel has ably canvassed those developments and placed them within the New Governance firmament.

OSHA's first major self-regulatory program is the Voluntary Protection Program (VPP), first established at the height of deregulatory fervor in 1982.[23] Under the VPP, employers who demonstrate the commitment and internal organizational capacity to comply with health and safety standards and to improve their safety records can be taken off the ordinary inspection schedule and put onto a more conciliatory enforcement track.[24] Participating employers must establish an approved written safety program, a framework for employee reporting of safety hazards, and an organized response to those hazards.[25] And they must involve employees in the program. In a unionized workplace, employee involvement means union involvement; in a non-union workplace, the nature of employee involvement is largely at the individual level.

The VPP is a modest program squeezed into the interstices of a command-and-control statute. Yet the program proved to be both effective and politically popular, drawing support from both proponents and skeptics of workplace health and safety regulation.[26] Even more encouraging was an OSHA pilot program called Maine 200, which targeted the most injury-prone employers in Maine and offered them a choice between traditional enforcement, including immediate detailed inspections, and a more cooperative approach centered around the employers' creation of workplace health and safety programs based on guidelines set by OSHA. The program produced dramatic improvements in both the identification of hazards and the reduction of injuries.[27]

The VPP and Maine 200 became building blocks of a more comprehensive reform effort in the Clinton administration as part of its "Reinventing Government" initiative. Recognizing that the existing statute was a clumsy vehicle for cooperative compliance programs, the Clinton administration first proposed OSHA reform legislation in the 1990s. Among other things, the law would have mandated the creation of comprehensive workplace health and safety programs, including employee health and safety committees, at most sizable workplaces.[28] Such committees might have played a crucial role in extending the reach of an overextended enforcement apparatus by activating regulatory resources and impulses within firms.[29] That aspect of the legislation became entangled in the chronic gridlock of labor law reform: the idea of mandatory employee safety committees triggered both employer fears of union organizing and union fears of employer domination and manipulation.[30] Employer opposition to the bill as a whole led to its abandonment.

Reformers did not give up, however, on the idea of improving workplace safety by stimulating regulatory activity inside the firm. Soon after the failure of OSHA reform legislation, the focus of reform efforts moved inside the agency itself. The Clinton administration announced in 1995 that "OSHA will change its fundamental operating paradigm from one of command and control to one that provides employers a real choice between a partnership and a traditional enforcement relationship."[31] With its new Cooperative Compliance Program (CCP), OSHA offered partnership, cooperation, and compliance assistance to employers who maintained a good safety record and an effective safety program, while it strengthened enforcement against employers who put workers at risk. Through the CCP, OSHA committed itself to shifting its focus away from merely "rack[ing] up their numbers of inspections, citations, and fines" toward actually reducing injuries.[32] Participating employers were required to develop and implement a comprehensive safety and health program that included regular internal inspections, channels for employee complaints and participation, and comprehensive surveys assessing risks. Employers who voluntarily participated in CCPs were placed on a secondary inspection list and exempted from routine inspections, with OSHA providing support and information.[33]

Perceiving the reforms as part of a strategy to strengthen overall enforcement, a coalition of business interests led by the Chamber of Commerce challenged the CCP rule in the federal Court of Appeals for the District of Columbia, which struck down the rule on procedural grounds in 1999.[34] After that setback, instead of revving up the comparatively ponderous formal rule-making procedures demanded by the court's ruling, OSHA retreated from comprehensive regulatory reform efforts. But lower-profile, more limited moves toward the encouragement of internal workplace health and safety activity— including expansion of the VPP—have continued.

So wholesale reform efforts that embrace the idea of regulated self-regulation in occupational health and safety have hit a number of legal and political road-blocks. Lobel has argued convincingly that the major legal roadblocks take their shape from established yet dysfunctional conceptions of the appropriate relations between corporations and the state and between corporations and their workers—from administrative law principles that fit a command-and-control regulatory strategy and labor law principles that called for a sharp di-vision between employers and any mechanism for collective participation by workers.[35] Yet even the limited and halting experimentation with more coop-erative and self-regulatory strategies in health and safety has been a qualified success and is certain to be part of future reform efforts.

States have also innovated. While OSHA preempts some state regulation of workplace health and safety, it expressly authorizes states to operate their own safety and health plans pursuant to OSHA approval and leaves states with con-siderable authority and room for innovation in this area.[36] States' responsibil-ity for workers' compensation systems provides another arena and incentive for reform. Some states have used their leverage and authority to promote or even mandate self-regulatory activity by employers. Nearly a dozen states have passed laws requiring employers to maintain workplace health and safety com-mittees.[37] Given that health and safety committees are already standard for most larger companies, the effect of these laws may be to push that innovation down toward some smaller and medium-sized firms. Where the committees exist, they seem to ratchet up agency enforcement activity.[38] Though the data do not go so far, such committees might also promote better internal compli-ance and safer workplaces by abating hazards without agency involvement. But these state mandates are themselves underenforced: the mandatory commit-tees are more likely to be created (and they appear to do more to improve en-forcement) in workplaces where a union is present.[39]

The most ambitious and innovative of state workplace health and safety pro-grams is in California.[40] Since 1991, Cal-OSHA has required all covered em-ployers to put in place a Workplace Injury and Illness Prevention Program that includes regular self-inspections, identification and abatement of hazards, train-ing of and regular communication with employees, and establishment of a sys-tem for confidential employee reporting of hazards. An employer whose program meets statutory requirements will avoid civil penalties for a first violation.[41] Similarly, New York mandates a program of self-regulation for employers with worse than average injury rates.[42] The regulatory hook in New York is not a state OSHA program but the workers' compensation system. Workplace health and safety programs like those mandated in California and New York, and like OSHA's Maine 200 program, recognize and reward the regulatory potential within firms—the particularized expertise and awareness of hazards and the potential for customized forms of hazard abatement.

So the move to push health and safety regulation into the regulated firm itself, while it has confronted serious obstacles, has been pursued in different forms by regulators, scholars, employers and their advocates, and worker advocates. Among worker advocates, the idea of self-regulation was dealt a serious setback, and will need to be rehabilitated, in the wake of the Bush administration's widely advertised shift within OSHA from enforcement to guidance and compliance assistance.[43] That reaction speaks to a deeper concern that legitimately dogs the proponents of self-regulation: one should be skeptical of calls for self-regulation by those who once touted the virtues of deregulation. But it would also be a monumental mistake to simply return to old-style command-and-control centralized enforcement of detailed, mandatory, uniform health and safety standards formulated in Washington, D.C. As will be developed further in Chapter 6, the idea of shifting regulatory activity into the firm itself has strong progressive bona fides, and when it is done well, it has proven effective. That is not to say that mandates, fines, and public inspections have no role to play in a progressive future labor standards regime; on the contrary, more inspectors and larger penalties are clearly needed. But they are not enough. Traditional coercive enforcement mechanisms, to be effective, have to be recalibrated and redeployed as leverage to induce firms to engage in serious and effective self-regulation, to reward and support firms that do so, and to reach firms that are unwilling or unable to regulate themselves.

FROM COMPLIANCE TO REGULATED SELF-REGULATION IN RIGHTS ENFORCEMENT

Much as employers have protested growing regulatory requirements, they have decried the proliferation of employee rights, with the attendant costs of liability and litigation and constraints on employer discretion and second guessing by judges and juries. But employers have also responded in constructive ways, internalizing some norms of public law even while seeking to minimize their legal exposure. These internal accommodations to the rise of employee rights began as what we might call "managing under the shadow of the law," but they have evolved toward forms of regulated self-regulation in which the law explicitly encourages and rewards employers' self-regulatory efforts. These developments have been most pronounced in the equal employment arena.

From Litigation Avoidance to Liability Shield: The Legalization of Corporate Antidiscrimination Policy and Procedures

The threat of large damage awards and bad publicity in employment litigation has undoubtedly captured the attention of employers. They have responded to the growth of employment litigation with complaints about escalating costs, burdens, and threats to American competitiveness, as well as with appeals for legislative relief.[44] But the substance of employee rights, especially rights against discrimination, has been surprisingly resistant to those appeals. Indeed, the formal reach of antidiscrimination law in employment has only expanded in the last forty years to reach new groups, new forms of discrimination, and new remedies. The near-unanimous enactment in 2008 of the Genetic Information Non-Discrimination Act is a case in point.[45] In the congressional arena, the antidiscrimination principle has proven to be a one-way ratchet: expansion has not been easy or automatic—consider the long-running effort to ban discrimination based on sexual orientation—but it has happened many times, while there is no history of explicitly cutting back on federal antidiscrimination rights.

As a consequence, employers' efforts to tame the threat of litigation have taken different forms. In particular they have invested in litigation avoidance and management. It may be useful to divide employer strategies into two categories: systemic strategies, which seek to avoid actionable claims of discrimination by internalizing compliance and complaints, and contractual strategies, which seek to minimize litigation by securing from individual employees a waiver of either liability or the right to litigate. Let us begin with the systemic strategies.

Employers' internal antidiscrimination policies and procedures take many forms, and they tend to be more elaborate in larger firms. But these programs typically share at least three basic elements: a more or less detailed prohibition of discrimination; complaint procedures by which employees can challenge alleged violations of the nondiscrimination policy; and the designation of one or more individuals, typically within the personnel or human relations department, with the responsibility of enforcing those policies and administering complaint procedures. The content of employers' internal antidiscrimination policies generally tracks the law in effect in whatever jurisdictions the company operates; for large companies, that tends to produce policies that reach beyond federal antidiscrimination law to include, for example, discrimination on the basis of sexual orientation.[46] Antiharassment policies generally prohibit a wide range of speech and conduct that some workers might find offensive on the basis of race, sex, religion, national origin, age, disability, or other criteria and that might give rise to harassment claims.[47] Those policies, too, often go beyond what the law requires. In a real though imperfect sense, these policies and the accompanying enforcement personnel and procedures, adopted in the wake of the employment rights revolution, have brought those external legal rights and social norms inside the workplace, and transformed them.[48]

Litigation has made its biggest mark on how firms deal with discipline, discharge, and other personnel disputes with employees. Employers, at the urging of lawyers and human relations professionals, have crafted grievance and dispute resolution mechanisms to try to stem the tide of legal claims and to reduce their cost.[49] Non-union grievance and dispute resolution procedures, which have proliferated in the past several decades, vary in their complexity from simple open-door policies to multi-step grievance procedures involving peer review, mediation, and arbitration. These systems are thought to enhance employee morale, longevity, and performance and to quell interest in unionization; they also allow management to rationalize discipline, monitor supervisors, and avoid mistakes. That being said, Lauren Edelman and others have shown that the threat of litigation—especially litigation over discharge and harassment claims under the antidiscrimination laws—has helped to spur the dramatic growth of these systems in medium and large-sized firms.[50] It has become near gospel among human relations professionals that corporate due process systems help to avoid litigation (as well as unionization) by resolving disputes within the firm and by flagging and permitting the correction of actions that may be found or plausibly claimed to be discriminatory.[51]

In effect, the equal protection clause of the workplace—antidiscrimination law—has helped to generate a modicum of due process for non-union employees in many large and medium-sized organizations. These corporate due process regimes typically afford "some kind of hearing," usually before a relatively impartial company official, not only for legally actionable claims but also for other complaints of unfair treatment.[52] At a minimum these procedures afford a sober second look and a check against the personal tyranny of low-level supervisors; they administer a dose of procedural regularity and soften the sharp edges of employment at will.

Antidiscrimination law has also reshaped hiring and promotional practices. In the first decade or so after Title VII was enacted in 1964, explicit and overt policies of segregation and discrimination that were endemic to many workplaces began to produce costly judgments and were largely dismantled. Less overt but still striking patterns of discrimination continued to generate costly lawsuits. Large employers—those that were most exposed to litigation and especially those that contracted with the federal government and were required to report on workforce demographics—recognized the need to take prophylactic measures in the form of both internal equal employment policies and "affirmative action" in various forms.[53] Some of these programs were adopted under the gun of litigation, either by direct court order or by consent decrees, but many more were adopted voluntarily in hopes of avoiding liability and the costs of litigation—financial, organizational, and reputational.

Some large firms are still adjusting to the antidiscrimination laws. Recall again Wal-Mart's announcement of sweeping new compliance and diversity programs—in particular its decision to link managers' compensation to their achievement of workforce diversity goals—in the midst of a massive sex discrimination lawsuit. In substance those measures look a lot like equal employment compliance efforts of firms subject to outside legal scrutiny. But the firm claims to be driven not by litigation or the fear of liability but by its own commitment to greater workforce diversity. Wal-Mart's diversity initiative, and its packaging for the public, is a reminder that some equal employment compliance regimes, especially in larger firms, have evolved into or contributed to more ambitious workforce diversity and inclusion programs.

Workforce diversity efforts often have an organizational existence that is separate from legal compliance activities and often aspire to a more profound transformation of workplace culture.[54] Clearly litigation avoidance and legal compliance are not the only factors in the growth of workforce diversity initiatives and in the affirmative pursuit by many large firms of a more diverse workforce. Proponents cite the sheer demographic imperatives behind these programs, as well as what they call the "business case for diversity."[55] But it is striking that high-profile discrimination lawsuits are often followed by public pronouncements about new and improved diversity initiatives, as they were at Wal-Mart, Coca-Cola, and Texaco, for example.[56] Clearly those programs, if they are successful, can help to avoid the kind of statistical disparities that got Wal-Mart into trouble and that are the single most damning body of evidence in the case.[57] No major company wants to be the next Wal-Mart, the next Coca-Cola, or the next Texaco on that score. Fear of litigation and the attendant bad publicity has helped to change patterns of hiring and promotions, at least in large, brand-conscious firms, even without actual litigation.

Internal grievance procedures and diversity programs alike have been criticized for their failure to fully realize employee rights or to transform workplace demographics. Internal grievance processes, for example, may tend to assimilate complaints of discrimination to other complaints of unfair treatment or to the ordinary run of personnel conflicts.[58] They may tame external law, bending it to fit organizational needs. One might see that process of domestication as a weakening of the antidiscrimination mandate. Or one might see it as part of the process of internalizing antidiscrimination norms, a process that gives those norms greater resonance and impact than they would have had as unadulterated impositions from outside the organization. Unfortunately, there is little solid evidence about how well these internal enforcement systems actually perform and whether they succeed in protecting employee rights.[59] Some scholars see great promise, while others see costly but largely symbolic gestures.[60]

So long as internal policies and grievance procedures played no direct role in the adjudication of formal legal complaints, their tendency to domesticate and perhaps distort external law to suit organizational needs was of limited significance to the enforcement of legal rights. These internal systems might avoid some discrimination or correct it, or they might dissuade individuals from pursuing legal claims by assuaging their sense of grievance or reconstructing their understanding of events. But as long as they afforded no immunity from liability, a formal complaint would still follow the course charted by external law and proceed to some kind of resolution (or not), without regard to its fate within the corporate hierarchy. That changed with the Supreme Court's 1998 decisions in *Burlington Industries v. Ellerth*[61] and *Faragher v. City of Boca Raton*,[62] which established standards by which employers could be liable under Title VII for sexual harassment committed by supervisors.[63]

In *Faragher* and *Ellerth,* the Court reaffirmed employers' liability for supervisors' unlawful discrimination—including discriminatory harassment—regardless of whether high-level managers knew or approved of the unlawful conduct. However, with respect to one category of discrimination—the creation of a discriminatory hostile environment without any tangible adverse employment action—the Court afforded the employer an affirmative defense. The employer could escape liability by showing that it "exercised reasonable care to prevent and correct promptly any sexually harassing behavior" and that the employee "unreasonably failed to take advantage of any preventive or corrective opportunities provided by the employer or to avoid harm otherwise."[64] While the Court did not explicitly require employers to adopt internal anti-harassment policies and procedures, its decisions certified those policies as the surest path to the partial immunity offered by the affirmative defense—by what we might call the "self-regulation defense." After *Faragher* and *Ellerth*, it would be managerial malpractice for any sizable employer to fail to maintain such policies.

Faragher and *Ellerth* were explicitly limited to the case of supervisor harassment; they left open the problem of co-worker harassment. As there is no automatic vicarious employer liability for co-worker harassment, there is no need for a *Faragher*-type affirmative defense to that liability. Instead, the standard is negligence; the plaintiff must show that the employer, through its managerial hierarchy, knew or reasonably should have known of the hostile environment that co-workers had created and had failed to respond in a reasonable manner.[65] But the shadow of *Faragher* and *Ellerth* is bound to fall over those claims as well. As antiharassment policies and complaint procedures become standard practice, it will become more difficult for employers to claim that they acted reasonably if they lacked such procedures.[66]

The logic of affording employers any defense in *Faragher* and *Ellerth* was rooted in the fact that employers did not delegate authority to supervisors to harass employees. That logic seemed to discourage the extension of the self-regulation defense to discrimination claims involving tangible adverse action—action that necessarily requires employer-delegated authority—such as discharge, denial of promotion or demotion, pay disparities, or the like. But the Supreme Court took a step down that road just one year later. In *Kolstad v. American Dental Association*, the Court held that "good faith efforts to comply with Title VII," in the form of antidiscrimination policies and procedures, would bar punitive damages against the employer for intentional discrimination in promotions and presumably discharges.[67] Insofar as much of employers' litigation anxiety focuses on the (very small) risk of very large jury verdicts, *Kolstad* magnified the significance of internal antidiscrimination policies across the gamut of discrimination claims.

With these few decisions, the Supreme Court transformed employers' diversity programs and internal compliance and grievance procedures into front-line mechanisms for enforcing antidiscrimination law and avoiding liability. This is not wholesale self-regulation, in which firms are left alone to find ways to avoid discrimination, free from external scrutiny. Nor is the law merely casting a "shadow" beneath which firms devise whatever procedures they believe will best avoid liability. This is something new: the law is now directing and regulating the process of self-regulation. Under *Faragher*, the employer's antiharassment policies and practices must be "reasonable" in the eyes of the law to bar liability (and the employer bears the burden of proving that), and under *Kolstad*, the employer's internal antidiscrimination practices must demonstrate good faith to bar punitive damages. The courts are thus charged with distinguishing sham processes from effective ones. Employers in turn have to look to external legal standards to assess the adequacy of their own internal antidiscrimination policies.

If courts do their job well, judging employers against a "best practices" standard while keeping an eye on results, these doctrines should promote organizational practices that reduce the incidence of discrimination and harassment and afford a quicker, more accessible, and fair avenue of recourse to aggrieved employees. But if judicial oversight is cursory, and litigation ends up being barred by a mere pretense of self-regulation, then employers may be able to insulate themselves from the litigation threat that has driven much internal workplace reform. The chorus of judicial complaints about the volume of employment litigation gives reason to fear that judges may be predisposed to sign off on these internal procedures without close scrutiny.[68] The result may be a disguised form of deregulation under the guise of self-regulation.[69] That is a serious risk with a doctrine that rewards employers not just for successfully preventing discrimination and harassment but also for convincing a court that they tried to prevent it or would have tried if the plaintiff had come forward.

Managing the Litigation Threat by Contract: Waivers, Mandatory Arbitration, and the Privatization of Public Law Enforcement

Employers have also used contract as a shield against employment litigation and liability, including under the discrimination laws. Employers cannot contract out of liability for future discrimination claims; employees' right to be free from discrimination is nonwaivable.[70] But employers can and do use contract to manage their liabilities in two ways: they can contract out of liability for existing claims through a waiver executed at the time of the employee's departure, and they can contract out of the threat of civil litigation of future claims by demanding that employees sign mandatory arbitration agreements.

Existing legal claims, unlike future claims, are settlable and generally waivable.

The vast majority of employment litigation is brought by former employees, and much of it concerns the circumstances surrounding the employee's separation from the company, whether formally a quit, a layoff, or a discharge.[71] The economic insecurity that many employees face at that point gives employers a potential opportunity to preempt litigation by inducing departing employees to waive any claims that may have accrued during their employment as a condition of severance pay or increased severance pay. Many employers have seized that opportunity, managing their litigation risks in part by buying up potential claims from employees on their way out of the company.[72] We might consider this practice to be another form of self-regulation by contract, though it is once again a form of self-regulation that is at least partially regulated: if an employee has second thoughts and brings suit, then courts (or arbitrators, as we will see) will have to judge the adequacy of the waiver. They will have to decide, for example, whether the waiver was "knowing and voluntary."[73]

Congress stepped in to further regulate the waiver process when it became concerned that employers were undermining the Age Discrimination in Employment Act (ADEA) by conditioning retirement benefits on waiver of ADEA claims. Under the Older Workers' Benefits Protection Act (OWBPA), a valid waiver of an existing ADEA claim must be for consideration "in addition to anything of value to which the [employee] is already entitled," such as normal severance pay, and it must be preceded by disclosure of information about the triggering event and time to consult with an attorney.[74] The OWBPA seeks to ensure that employees have some idea of what they might be giving up and that they get something in exchange. The OWBPA is effectively regulating the waiver of other employment claims as well: because ADEA claims may be included in the single broad waiver that employers often seek from employees at the time of severance, employers are well advised to, and often do, follow the relatively stringent statutory standards of the OWBPA.[75]

So employers can contract out of liability for claims that have already arisen through a well-crafted waiver. As for future claims, employers cannot contract out of liability altogether, but they can contract out of the threat of civil litigation by demanding that employees sign mandatory arbitration agreements. In a pair of decisions a decade apart—*Gilmer v. Interstate/Johnson Lane Corp.*[76] and *Circuit City Stores, Inc. v. Adams*[77]—the Supreme Court upheld the enforceability of employees' agreements to submit future legal claims against the employer, including statutory discrimination claims, to an arbitrator rather than to a court.[78] Since *Gilmer,* many employers, especially larger employers, have turned to pre-dispute mandatory arbitration agreements as a way to take employment disputes out of the courts and into the more private, predictable, and party-controlled arbitral forum.[79]

The rise of mandatory arbitration represents a further step toward privatizing the enforcement of employees' legal rights and toward subjecting those rights to employer self-regulation. Both the rise of mandatory arbitration and the proliferation of internal grievance procedures and antidiscrimination policies represent organizations' efforts to tame the threat of litigation. Both seek to ameliorate the tension between outside legal norms and internal organizational needs, partly by bringing the organization into closer conformance with the outside norms and partly by domesticating those outside norms and the means of their enforcement. Both represent nascent forms of self-regulation in the enforcement of employee rights.

One might quibble with the characterization of arbitration as a form of self-regulation. Indeed, the objections might come from two directions. Some critics have characterized the use of mandatory arbitration as a form of "self-deregulation."[80] That is indeed a risk with which we will grapple here. But from the other direction, proponents of arbitration might argue that it is too inconsequential a departure from the prior system of rights enforcement to merit the moniker of self-regulation.[81] They point out that in principle, these agreements merely substitute one neutral outside forum for another; to be valid, they must preserve statutory rights and remedies.[82] The truth lies in between, for mandatory arbitration is another example of regulated self-regulation: employers write arbitration agreements, and they dictate how the process works and how arbitrators are chosen; yet they do so subject to the power of courts to reject or redact unfair or legally invalid provisions.[83]

Whether this form of self-regulation is sufficiently well regulated is another question. Judicial supervision is episodic, and it often takes a form that does little to discourage employers from overreaching. A court faced with an invalid clause—say, one that bars the award of attorneys' fees to prevailing Title VII plaintiffs—might simply strike the clause while enforcing the rest of the agreement, in which case employers who include such invalid clauses risk nothing and may gain by deterring some litigation. Or a court might enforce the agreement to arbitrate, leaving the contested issue to the arbitrator and post-arbitration judicial review (which is traditionally very limited), in which case prospective plaintiffs and their attorneys bear a burden of uncertainty that may deter them from proceeding at all.[84] The upshot is that employers, by securing arbitration agreements, gain considerable control over the adjudicatory process. Their control and their incentive to exercise it effectively is enhanced by their posture as likely "repeat players"; they foresee repeated resort to the arbitration process in a range of legal disputes.[85] So it is fair to describe arbitration as a form of employer self-regulation—not wholesale self-regulation but more or less regulated self-regulation.

It is precisely the self-regulatory aspect of mandatory arbitration that troubles many scholars and employee advocates. Even apart from employers' ability to skew particular terms of the agreement in their favor, arbitration subjects public law rights to interpretation and adjudication by private decision makers, subject to only limited judicial review.[86] There is no guarantee that arbitrators will follow precedent, nor will they necessarily produce precedent of their own for other arbitrators to follow. Precedent is a "positive externality" of the judicial process—a public good—that arbitration tends to underproduce. Moreover, arbitration proceedings are generally private, and awards are not necessarily explained or published. (Indeed, those are among its chief attractions to publicity-averse employers.)

In principle, individual employees choose whether to enter into arbitration agreements and can decide for themselves whether the agreement offers a fair trade-off. In fact, there is little reason to believe that employees who are put to a choice between signing the agreement and losing or foregoing employment have any real choice in the matter. Employers typically adopt these agreements unilaterally and impose them on employees with no pretense of negotiation.[87] In principle, the fairness of the arbitration bargain is subject to judicial oversight. In fact the courts are reduced to a largely reactive role of approving or disapproving (or deferring to arbitral judgment) the provisions that employers devise, and only when those provisions do not deter employees or their lawyers from litigating. Neither employee "choice" nor judicial supervision may be enough to deter or detect employer overreaching.

Much of the heat in the debate over mandatory arbitration is generated by the belief that arbitration reduces expected recoveries for plaintiffs. Studies suggest that awards to employee plaintiffs are generally lower in arbitration than in traditional court proceedings, but some studies also suggest that employees win more often in arbitration than in court.[88] Some arbitration proponents contend that arbitration is less costly and more accessible than litigation and may put a fair hearing and some form of relief within the reach of many claimants who could not file a lawsuit, much less get a judicial hearing.[89] That leads some observers to question the conventional wisdom that arbitration favors employers.[90] Much will turn on how these arbitration procedures work. And that, again, will be determined in the first instance by employers.

So employers are effectively engaged in a process of self-regulation in the matter of rights enforcement—not wholesale self-regulation but more or less regulated self-regulation. The picture would be bleaker were it not for another kind of self-regulation that is playing a major role in employment arbitration.[91] In 1995, major arbitration organizations, including the American Arbitration Association and the American Academy of Arbitrators, along with organizations representing both employers and employees—the American Bar Association's Section on Labor and Employment Law, the AFL-CIO, the National Employment Lawyers' Association (an organization of plaintiffs' attorneys), and the Chamber of Commerce, among others—devised a "Due Process Protocol" for employment arbitration. The Due Process Protocol, which establishes basic standards of procedural fairness, is effectively binding on all reputable arbitrators, insofar as the major arbitration providers and arbitrator associations are all signatories. Unfortunately, the Protocol is not legally binding on employers.[92] That fact, together with the episodic and limited nature of judicial scrutiny, has led some arbitration skeptics to suspect that there may be a vast netherworld of employer-dominated arbitration schemes that would fail any reasonable test of fair process.[93] It does appear, however, that self-regulatory efforts such as the Due Process Protocol have helped to tame the "wild West" of employment arbitration and have improved the fairness of the arbitrations that take place.

The emergence of regulated self-regulation in the enforcement of employee rights, especially in the antidiscrimination arena, has transformed both workplaces and the law. It has helped to shape internal compliance habits and structures in the corporate compliance field generally, including the enforcement of labor standards. Or at least it has done so in the larger firms, which are most exposed to both litigation and publicity and which have the largest investment in their reputation and their brand. Both the threat of litigation and liability under employment laws and the corporate self-regulatory mechanisms that have grown up under the shadow of that threat have largely failed to reach workplaces and workers at the bottom of the labor market. There, employee rights under the employment laws are often freely ignored. That turns out to be a recurring theme in the story so far and is a knotty challenge for the more prescriptive parts of this project that are yet to come. But let us dwell a bit longer among the major firms that have set the pace on corporate compliance regimes, for some of what is happening at the top may begin to address the challenge of reaching workers at the bottom of the labor market.

CORPORATE SOCIAL RESPONSIBILITY AS
REGULATED SELF-REGULATION?

Among large brand-conscious firms, the movement toward corporate compliance appears to be greater than the sum of its parts and greater than the sum of the ordinary economic incentives that one can discern behind it. As suggested by our brief survey of Fortune 500 corporate Web sites in the introduction, large firms vow publicly not just to comply with legal standards but to exceed them—to be not just law-abiding corporate citizens but model citizens.[94] Corporate compliance programs have evolved from ordinary precautions taken under the shadow of the law into a form of regulated self-regulation that is orchestrated by the law. Along the way, however, corporate compliance has also morphed into a vocal embrace of "corporate social responsibility."[95] To understand how that came about, we must look at how corporations responded not only to the demands of external law, but also to the demands of other external and internal constituencies—worker and consumer advocates, community and civil rights groups, environmental and human rights activists, and their allies in the investor community—using a variety of levers to pressure corporations to commit to going above and beyond what the law requires.

Ordinary domestic labor and employment laws play very little part in this story. But law appears in several roles. International human rights instruments and institutions may bear on firms' domestic labor practices and may be part of a publicity campaign even absent mechanisms for enforcement, as in the case of the Human Rights Watch report on Wal-Mart.[96] Constitutional free speech rights may protect advocates' publicity campaigns (for example, from defamation claims). And the law of corporate governance and shareholder rights gives activists a procedural wedge into corporate decision making.

The Growth of Corporate Social
Responsibility Programs

There is an episodically lively debate over the extent to which corporate officers and managers may or should respond to the interests of shareholders only or of other "stakeholders" as well—workers, consumers, communities, for example.[97] Since the 1980s, most corporate law scholars have hewed to the "shareholder primacy" line, and executive compensation packages have been jiggered to ensure managers' incentive to maintain high share prices.[98] In the meantime, however, other stakeholders have managed to amplify their own voices within corporations, partly by altering the calculus affecting share price and partly by becoming shareholders or influencing shareholders and using shareholder rights within corporate governance. Through both an "outside game" and an "inside game," stakeholder advocates have induced corporations to take greater responsibility for worker rights, human rights, and environmental sustainability—greater than the law demands and greater than the single-minded pursuit of profit would seem to call for.

The "outside game" seeks to galvanize public and consumer sentiment against (or sometimes in favor of) the corporation's reputation, brand, and products on the basis of conditions or practices within the corporation's operations or supply chain.[99] Activists seek, in short, to promote a "market for virtue," as David Vogel calls it.[100] Illegal or inhumane working conditions, flagrant discrimination, persecution of labor activists, uncontrolled toxic emissions in suppliers' factories, or clearcutting of ancient forests may arouse public outrage, bruise the corporate brand, dampen consumer support, or trigger a boycott. By the same token, exemplary programs for promoting diversity, family-friendly personnel policies, or decent labor and environmental standards may earn a "Best Companies" badge or a "Sweat-Free" or "Fair Trade" label, as well as the favor of advertisers, customers, and prospective employees. Hence the "business case" for corporate social responsibility.

For firms with an investment in their brand and reputation, these external pressures can magnify the impact of the law and of penalties that are paltry and infrequent, for a firm's bottom line may be threatened not only by criminal prosecutions or civil lawsuits, but also by the bad publicity and blow to reputation that may attend lawbreaking.[101] But these external pressures can also extend the reach of the social norms underlying the law—whether norms of decent working conditions, freedom of association, sustainability, or diversity and inclusion. Firms can be induced to go above and beyond the substance of the law's demands (for example, to offer paid parental leave or domestic partner benefits that the law does not require) or to take voluntary responsibility for working conditions of workers for whom the firm is not legally liable as employer or in places where there is no effective regulatory authority (for example, working conditions in the Cambodian factories of suppliers).[102] Activists have had considerable success in linking firms' reputations, and potentially the value of their brands, to socially responsible practices.

The outside game often works in conjunction with an "inside game" by which shareholders themselves, large and small, press firms to adopt socially responsible positions and programs. Some of the key actors are large investors—

public pension funds such as the California Public Employee Retirement System (CalPERS) and the Norwegian Government Pension Fund—and socially responsible investment (SRI) mutual funds that screen for various social responsibility criteria.[103] The securities laws play an important role behind the scenes here: the Securities and Exchange Commission (SEC) in its rules has taken a rather broad view of the shareholder resolutions that must be included in the corporation's proxy statement. Under those rules, even smaller shareholders can submit shareholder resolutions that pressure corporate boards to make concessions and commitments to protect the interests of workers, communities, and the environment.

David Vogel takes a balanced look at the corporate social responsibility movement in his book *The Market for Virtue: The Potential and Limits of Corporate Social Responsibility* and finds both potential and limits.[104] But the "market for virtue," and with it the potential of corporate social responsibility, is still growing. SRI funds rose from $639 billion in 1995 to $2.71 trillion in 2007.[105] In the realm of shareholder advocacy alone, the number of proposals for public interest proxy resolutions rose from 236 in 2001 to 367 in 2006, and shareholder support for these resolutions rose from 7.9 percent in 2001 to 15.4 percent in 2007.[106] Although these public interest proposals are rarely adopted, they sometimes secure improvements nonetheless: between 2001 and 2003, for example, "256 socially inspired resolutions were withdrawn after the targeted firms made concessions."[107]

Advocates' outside strategies and shareholders' inside strategies are intertwined; it is partly the threat of bad publicity (or the promise of good) that motivates corporate directors and managers to accede to shareholder proposals for expanded social responsibility. The programs that firms have adopted in response to these outside and inside pressures go beyond the mere profession of social responsibility. Much as the law has induced firms to establish "effective compliance programs" to back up the commitment to comply, the external and internal proponents of corporate social responsibility commitments may demand private enforcement procedures—especially monitoring and reporting procedures—to back up those commitments.[108] Corporations may initially sign on to a fairly superficial commitment to human rights or sustainability and then find themselves propelled—by advocates' skillful deployment of inside and outside pressures—down a path toward serious regulatory investments. The progression of the anti-sweatshop movement, discussed below, provides a case in point.

Controversies abound within and about the movement for corporate social responsibility. One set of controversies is over whether corporations' pursuit of social responsibility is consistent or in conflict with profit-maximization and the financial interests of shareholders.[109] Some observers hold that corporate fiduciaries are *permitted* to pursue social goals only if they are consistent with long-term profit maximization; some argue that corporations and their fiduciaries are *motivated* to pursue social goals only if they are consistent with long-term profit maximization.[110] Either or both of these beliefs have led proponents to emphasize "the business case for social responsibility."[111] Others contend for a less constrained view of corporate social responsibility.[112] Einer Elhauge, for example, argues that corporate fiduciaries do have the legal discretion, under the venerable "business judgment rule," to pursue social goals that do not maximize profits and that such discretion serves the interests of both the public (because legal standards and sanctions fall short of optimal deterrence) *and shareholders* (because the cost of policing a strict profit-maximization mandate would outweigh shareholder gains and because market pressures adequately constrain nonprofit-maximizing pursuit of social goals).[113]

One thing is not controversial: Big corporations are ever more vocally and visibly proclaiming their commitment not only to compliance with legal demands, but also to worker rights, diversity and inclusiveness, and family friendliness, as well as human rights, community development, and environmental sustainability. If we were simply to take at face value these proclamations, we would be wildly optimistic about the extent to which corporations themselves have internalized social norms and embraced the responsibility of enforcing them. To be sure, there would still be the problem of the low-wage sector, in which labor and employment law violations are chronic and clustered and where the law in action is far less vigorous than the law on the books. But at the top of the labor market, among the leading firms, the law's aura appears to emanate well beyond its formal boundaries.

Of course, appearances may be deceiving. First, some of the firms in the upper echelons of the economy have historically been among the chronic lawbreakers. For example, Wal-Mart, at least in its pre-2005 incarnation, became notorious for its low (though not illegal) hourly wages and employee benefits, its widespread (and decidedly illegal) demands for off-the-clock work, and its allegedly discriminatory promotional policies. Its current public embrace of corporate ethics and responsibility may signal new ways of doing business, but critics cannot be blamed for suspecting that the changes may be only superficial.[114] In general, it is simply very hard to know whether corporate compliance and corporate responsibility programs actually work to achieve compliance (or better) or mainly to fend off criticism and regulatory scrutiny.

Second, the firms at the top are often the direct beneficiaries and the indirect promoters of the low-wage work done for firms at the bottom of the market, where legal violations are endemic. A good deal of that work was once performed in-house by the full-time employees of the big companies but has been contracted out to less visible and less established contractors, who race to underbid each other by cutting labor costs (and who diffuse or eliminate the big companies' responsibility for labor standards). Another big chunk of that low-wage work is performed in the lower rungs of a manufacturing supply chain— much of it overseas but some of it in the U.S., where firms are similarly driven to compete on the basis of lower labor costs. Once again, Wal-Mart may serve as an example, with its use of maintenance contractors employing undocumented immigrants and its famously fanatical supply-chain management.[115] We will return below to the links between the large and well-heeled firms that tout their corporate social responsibility to burnish their brand and the small and marginal firms that do much of the dirty work on which the former depend, for those links will play a critical part in pushing current developments in a productive and progressive direction.

So the corporate social responsibility phenomenon should not blind us to the widespread social irresponsibility and even hypocrisy that may lie underneath the Fortune 500's gleaming brands. But neither should the latter blind us to the possibilities that lie in the former. As foolish as it would be to take corporations' own word for the depth and breadth of their commitment to compliance and social responsibility, it would be equally foolish to discount the importance of that commitment—both the public proclamations themselves and the organizational resources that stand behind them. We will return in Chapter 6 to the theories and experiences that should inform our assessment of these corporate compliance and social responsibility programs. For now let us turn to the anti-sweatshop movement, which may serve as a case study in the origins and consequences of corporate social responsibility programs.

Corporate Codes of Conduct and the Anti-Sweatshop Movement

The global anti-sweatshop movement has mounted a decades-long effort to hold the big multinational footwear and garment brands accountable for the improvement of labor standards in the factories of the developing world in which the vast bulk of their products are manufactured.[116] In particular, it has sought to make corporate codes of conduct meaningful instruments for improving labor standards and for filling the regulatory vacuum that multinational corporations and their suppliers were taking advantage of in developing regions of the world.

The codes are grounded in two crucial features of the big global garment brands. First, the brands were compelled to develop the capacity to monitor the quantity and quality of goods produced in far-flung factories; that made more credible efforts to hold them accountable for labor conditions in those distant operations. Second, the brands were extremely sensitive to consumer perceptions, which worker advocates were able to link partly to working conditions in those distant factories. Worker advocates succeeded in pricking the conscience of some Western consumers and in turning their indignation toward the brands through a series of shocking exposés of the child labor, forced labor, subsistence wages, and horrendous working conditions that went into producing their expensive sneakers and jeans.

The anti-sweatshop activists pursued both an outside and an inside strategy. The outside strategy—the exposés, publicity campaigns, boycotts—sought to make corporations like Gap, Nike, and Wal-Mart what I will call "super-employers" of their suppliers' workers: regardless of whether they were legally liable as employers, they were held politically liable.[117] The political liability of these super-employers is based on their economic and organizational capacity to monitor and influence those workers' terms and conditions of employment; on their use of contracting practices that, however rational, drive suppliers to compete on the basis of low labor costs; on the economic benefits they gain from those lower labor costs; and on the ability of advocates to stir public and consumer sentiment on the basis of these facts. Advocates' outside strategy set the stage for sympathetic shareholders and investors to deploy inside strategies to pressure corporate fiduciaries to cultivate a "sweat-free" reputation by promulgating supplier codes requiring suppliers to comply with basic labor standards.

The early private, voluntary schemes varied greatly, both in the content of corporate codes and in the nature and quality of monitoring. Commitments were often vague; workers' freedom of association (a "core" international labor right) was generally ignored; and little effort was made to inform workers of the code's provisions. Even when monitors were nominally independent, critics pointed to inspection protocols that allowed cheating to go undetected and reporting practices that indulged firms' preference for secrecy, thus blocking the crucial flow of information to advocates and consumers.[118]

A textbook illustration of the weaknesses in these first-generation supplier codes is supplied by the ubiquitous Wal-Mart, Inc. Since 1992, Wal-Mart has maintained its own supplier code: "Standards for Suppliers."[119] Before 2005, the code required suppliers to comply with certain local and international labor standards—no mention of workers' freedom of association—and subjected them to monitoring by Wal-Mart or its agents.[120] Monitoring was not independent, visits were rarely unannounced, and results were not made public. In 2005, the International Labor Rights Fund filed a class-action lawsuit on behalf of workers in China, Bangladesh, Indonesia, Swaziland, and Nicaragua. The suit alleged that violations of Wal-Mart's supplier code were rampant and that Wal-Mart not only tolerated those violations but also "reign[ed] over a sweatshop gulag that condemns workers around the world to provide forced and uncompensated labor."[121] Wal-Mart's legal response was revealing: it contended that the "Standards for Suppliers" created no duty on Wal-Mart's part to inspect factories and no contractual duty at all toward workers at supplier factories, but at most a contractual right on Wal-Mart's part to monitor the factories. The district court's decision dismissing the lawsuit on these and other grounds was affirmed on appeal.[122]

But Wal-Mart's response outside of the litigation was even more revealing. In 2005, the same year the lawsuit was filed and the same year the company revised its "Global Statement of Ethics" for its own employees, Wal-Mart revised its "Standards for Suppliers" and its monitoring program. Wal-Mart added several provisions, including recognition of workers' freedom of association (although much of Wal-Mart's supply chain is in China, where independent unions are prohibited by law), and it increased monitoring. According to its 2005 Report on Ethical Sourcing:

> Wal-Mart added several significant provisions to our Standards for Suppliers encompassing health and safety practices, freedom of association, and the rights of foreign contract workers. . . . We have one of the most active Ethical Standards programs in the retail industry. In 2005, we audited more factories than any other company in the world, performing more than 13,600 audits of 7,200 factories. We increased the number of unannounced audits by 100 percent. When violations are found, our first priority is to work with our suppliers to ensure their factories achieve compliance. We are confident that this collaborative approach is the best way to help our suppliers understand the business benefits of operating factories meeting labor, environmental, and health and safety standards.[123]

With these measures, Wal-Mart has sought to climb from its position as notorious laggard to one of leadership in the monitoring of suppliers.

Wal-Mart's actions show how far activists have succeeded in extending the basic ethos of corporate responsibility, corporate compliance, and self-regulation to corporations' supply chains. Even aside from questions of efficacy, this is a remarkable accomplishment. It is particularly remarkable in that there is often little hard law for the corporations to comply with in much of their global operations. Corporations typically face no threat of liability for suppliers' labor practices, especially when those suppliers are in developing countries, and suppliers themselves often face little legal pressure to comply with local labor standards, given the weakness of local regulatory institutions. Yet many major American and European corporations—especially those that market directly to consumers—have felt compelled to extend their public commitments to corporate compliance and social responsibility, and to develop their managerial and monitoring capabilities, to reach far-flung factories for which they bear no legal responsibility.

These supplier codes can thus be seen as an extension of the internal corporate compliance schemes examined above, with all the strengths and potential weakness of those schemes. They potentially activate corporate regulatory resources that, in the aggregate, swamp those of the relevant government bodies; yet they may be more show than substance. Just as with internal corporate compliance systems, we have to ask whether these supplier codes actually work or merely present a façade of social responsibility. Worker advocates—operating both inside and outside the big firms—have pressed firms for stronger codes, greater attention to workers' freedom of association, greater transparency, and more rigorous monitoring of factory compliance. They have sought to ensure that monitors are independent of employers, have access to complete information about factory locations, make unannounced visits, and conduct confidential interviews with workers; and they have sought to make workers aware of code provisions and to protect them against retaliation. Wal-Mart's post-2005 program appears designed to meet some of these demands.[124]

Reforms such as these put structures and resources behind the façade of the early corporate supplier codes. Still unclear is whether monitoring works for workers. Consider a recent assessment of Nike's factory-monitoring program, which is one of the most extensive and sophisticated in existence. A visitor to Nike's corporate Web site, Nike.com, will readily locate with a few mouse clicks Nike's supplier code of conduct, a description of factory-monitoring protocols, and a list of all active factories producing Nike goods.[125] Yet a recent study commissioned by Nike found only modest improvements in the wages and working conditions of factory workers as a result of monitoring alone: "Notwithstanding the significant efforts and investments by Nike and its staff to improve working conditions among its suppliers, monitoring alone appears to produce only limited results. Instead, our research indicates that when monitoring efforts are combined with other interventions focused on tackling some of the root causes of poor working conditions —by improving the ability of suppliers to better schedule their work and improve their quality and efficiency—working conditions appear to significantly improve."[126] In particular, the frequency and intensity of interaction between suppliers and Nike staff—not necessarily compliance staff but production staff— was associated with significant improvements.

The message is sobering. By themselves, factory monitoring programs, even as they are becoming more sophisticated and demanding, may often be serving as fig leafs for big corporations while delivering little improvement for workers. Factory monitoring risks becoming a form of "cosmetic compliance" with demands for supply-chain accountability. Apart from the uneven quality of monitoring, there are two main criticisms. First, monitoring programs typically neglect, and in fact may "crowd out," other regulatory efforts with greater long-term promise—specifically, workers' own organizations and local regulatory institutions. Second, most programs fail to address the economics of supply chains. Even while demanding compliance with supplier codes, most brands continue to play dozens or hundreds of suppliers off against one another, forcing them to extract too much work for too little money to keep their contracts and abandoning them when problems arose or costs increased, even if these were a result of monitoring.[127]

Some advocates have sought to meet these concerns with new approaches to supply-chain accountability. The Worker Rights Consortium (WRC), which harnesses the purchasing power of universities to pressure the brands that supply their "logo" products, has been at the forefront of these efforts. From its founding, the WRC declined to certify factories' compliance (which it viewed as misleading given existing monitoring capabilities) but rather investigated workers' complaints, usually in factories where workers had achieved some level of collective mobilization. The WRC aspired to empower workers themselves and to help build local regulatory competency rather than to ignore or supplant it. The WRC's investigations were models of thoroughness and independence, and its alternative strategy was hailed by worker advocates for its integrity and democratic aspirations.[128] But the investigative process was so labor-intensive that the WRC was able to investigate only a handful of factories each year.[129] And some of those factories then lost their contracts. The

WRC responded with a new monitoring model that sought to address some of the problems that stem from the sheer size and fluidity of brands' supply chains. The WRC's Designated Supplier Program (DSP) would require brands to close the set of supplier factories and to build closer relationships with suppliers based on a contract price that covered the cost of decent wages and labor conditions, rather than forcing suppliers into fierce competition with each other to minimize labor costs.[130] The DSP would dramatically reshape supply chains, but it has not yet secured enough support from the universities to take effect.

On the face of it, Wal-Mart's most recent revision of its supply-chain management strategy purports to move in a similar direction, "away from intermittent transactions with many suppliers toward longer-term arrangements with a smaller group of manufacturers." As to those manufacturers, it claims to be tightening ethical and environmental standards, including labor standards, and expanding both internal and external monitoring.[131] CEO Lee Scott explained: "I firmly believe that a company that cheats on overtime and on the age of its labor, that dumps its scraps and its chemicals in our rivers, that does not pay its taxes or honor its contracts, will ultimately cheat on the quality of its products. And cheating on the quality of products is the same as cheating on customers."[132]

By linking labor and environmental concerns to core operational concerns, Wal-Mart echoes a strong version of the "business case for social responsibility": it is not just that outside activists can *make* social irresponsibility costly by damaging the firm's reputation, but also that social irresponsibility *is* costly, in that suppliers' abusive labor and environmental practices contribute to, or are evidence of, or go hand in hand with, problems of quality, product safety, and productivity. The link between social concerns and operational concerns is important for another reason: To the extent that the brands do engage with their suppliers more intensively over operational as well as social concerns, that is precisely the sort of engagement that the Nike study found to have the greatest tendency to improve labor conditions.

Scott's statement also suggests that these changes at Wal-Mart did not come about, and may never have come about, on the strength of concerns about workers' rights alone. Wal-Mart announced its new program in Beijing at what it called the "Sustainability Summit," and its emphasis was more on the environment than on workers' rights. Chinese factories, which supply most of Wal-Mart's products, have been under the public spotlight for rampant environmental abuses, not to mention poisonous consumer products. Consumer demands for more environmentally sustainable manufacturing practices and, above all, stronger guarantees of product safety have made it imperative for Wal-Mart and other large Western brands and retailers to tighten control over production processes. Workers may become the incidental beneficiaries.

The jury is still out on whether supplier codes and new supply-chain management practices will significantly improve labor standards at the bottom of global production chains. We will return to this body of experience in the next chapter, for factory monitoring and corporate codes of conduct have been widely studied and have given rise to some broader lessons about monitoring and effective self-regulation. Certainly the state of the art of global factory monitoring has improved, and every set of improvements teaches new lessons about what it takes for monitoring to work. And there is no quibbling with the success of the anti-sweatshop movement in bringing attention to the conditions endured by poor and anonymous workers in faraway factories and in putting pressure on corporations to do something about abuses for which they bear no legal responsibility.

We may reserve for now the question whether these corporate social responsibility programs qualify as "regulated self-regulation." Compared to traditional corporate compliance programs, these programs respond more to social pressures than to legal pressures. They take their shape from a rolling process of private experimentation and an evolving notion of "best practices," and from the demands of internal and external advocates of stakeholder interests, rather than from the demands of courts and regulators. Yet these two developments in corporate governance have become closely intertwined in firms' organizational charts and in their self-promotional efforts.

Government regulation of terms and conditions of employment is a blunt instrument that cannot capture the range and variety of either workers' interests or firms' capabilities; uniform minimum standards inevitably demand too little of some firms and too much of others while suffering from chronic underenforcement, especially in the sizable low-wage sector. Litigation, though it has stimulated some real workplace reforms, is too costly and time-consuming to serve as an adequate mechanism for resolving most workplace disputes, especially, again, among low-wage workers. And neither litigation nor regulation gives workers a voice in shaping their own working conditions. The decline of collective bargaining, and the absence of any alternative form of employee representation, has left a yawning democratic deficit that is not addressed by workplace rights and regulations and that indeed undermines those rights and regulations.

On the other hand, we have seen that many employers have responded to the multiplying threats of employment liabilities by creating self-regulatory systems—internal compliance and complaint structures that implicitly recognize employees' central role both as informants and as rights-bearers—and in many cases more ambitious corporate social responsibility programs. And we have seen that regulatory practice and legal doctrine have veered in the direction of "regulated self-regulation"—toward explicitly evaluating, encouraging, rewarding, and relying upon firms' self-regulatory systems. In these developments we are seeing the rise of a new paradigm of workplace governance that, whatever its merits, almost certainly reaches more workplaces and workers than the New Deal's preferred system of collective bargaining now does.

The rise of employer self-regulation—more or less well regulated—is no mere flash in the pan. As we will see in Chapter 6, that development is in keeping with trends in both the theory and practice of regulation across the globe.[133] In many of these settings, there is still too little research that rigorously evaluates the efficacy of the internal compliance regimes that are gaining legal recognition (though that is changing).[134] And there remains much skepticism from organized labor and worker allies about the efficacy of corporate self-regulation and the meaningfulness of corporate social responsibility claims.[135] But a preference on the part of many employee advocates for stronger adversarial enforcement is increasingly tempered by a realization that workplaces are too numerous and too varied, and production is too mobile and too global, to hope for traditional regulatory methods to do the whole job. There will simply never be enough inspectors to rely on public enforcement alone. The question is no longer whether to rely on self-regulatory mechanisms at all, but how to ensure that those mechanisms are effective in improving labor standards and enforcing employee rights rather than being a cover for deregulation.

Before turning to that task in Chapter 6, however, we must complete the emerging picture of regulated self-regulation. Thus far we have examined the developments that have grown out of the interaction between regulators and courts, on the one hand, and corporate managers, on the other hand. We have seen how top-down legal regulation has led to corporate self-regulation and how corporate self-regulation is becoming incorporated into new strategies of governmental and legal regulation. But what this picture leaves out is the rise of bottom-up, grassroots experiments in "self-regulation by contract," with workers' organizations playing the leading roles. It is to those stories that we now turn.

Chapter 5 Self-Regulation
from the Bottom Up

The trend toward self-regulation, and the regulation of self-regulation, may well be the right trajectory, even the inevitable trajectory, for development of the law and governance of the workplace. But serious internal compliance efforts are largely confined to larger firms with long time horizons and significant investments in reputation, while the low-wage workforce and the problems of substandard and illegal employment practices are concentrated in smaller, less visible, and less rooted enterprises. Those enterprises have neither the means nor the motivation to invest in serious internal compliance structures, and they are often able to operate under the regulatory radar. That, in turn, is partly because low-wage workers—especially the immigrant and undocumented workers who populate these workplaces—are less likely to contact public agencies as individuals and typically have no collective representatives to demand regulatory attention on their behalf. Low-wage workers in these marginal enterprises come up short on all fronts: they usually lack union representation, recourse to internal complaint or compliance structures, and access to the courts; and they often have difficulty drawing the attention of regulatory agencies.

So what is to be done? We might begin by looking at what is being done already by low-wage workers who are struggling to secure an effective voice in their working lives. For workers and their advocates, sometimes with the help of public regulators, are undertaking their own experiments in "self-regulation," by which they confront the inadequacies of ordinary forms of public regulation with constructive forms of self-help.

THE RISE OF SELF-REGULATION BY CONTRACT

One important development, discussed in Chapter 2, is the rise of neutrality and card-check agreements—which are sometimes called "codes of conduct" but which I will call "neutrality agreements" here. Fed up with the antiquated and ineffectual law of union representation campaigns, unions are working whatever levers they have at their disposal to pressure and persuade employers to opt out of the standard NLRB election campaign process and accept alternative ground rules for representation campaigns.[1] Through neutrality agreements, unions are seeking to straighten and shorten the path to more-or-less traditional union representation and collective bargaining in the face of an ineffectual and delay-ridden NLRB regime for securing representation.

Unions' efforts to use private contract to improve upon public policy are intriguing in part because of their parallels with the rise of negotiated codes of conduct and monitoring schemes by which some worker advocacy groups—worker centers, with or without union support—are seeking to improve labor standards in low-wage workplaces. There, too, workers use various forms of pressure to induce employers to agree to higher standards of conduct and more rigorous private monitoring of compliance than exists under the background public law. Some of these agreements (which I will call here "monitoring agreements") provide for arbitration or mediation of disputes. And some of these agreements bind not the low-wage employers themselves but the larger, more visible, and more capable organizations on which those low-wage employers depend for business. For it turns out that many low-wage employers and their workers supply goods and services to larger organizations—the "super-employers" mentioned in Chapter 4—that have the capacity, if not the legal obligation, to regulate their suppliers.

Formal monitoring agreements are not the sole province of worker centers, nor are they the only tools by which worker centers seek to improve the lives of low-wage workers. But these agreements and the campaigns behind them are among the most promising developments within low-wage labor markets. The nascent rise of monitoring agreements in the U.S. builds on the successes and learns from the failures of the global anti-sweatshop movement and its efforts to improve labor standards in factories outside the U.S. Monitoring agreements, like neutrality agreements, respond to the inadequacies of public policy and public enforcement by turning to the framework of contract. Through both monitoring agreements and neutrality agreements, worker advocacy organizations contract with private employers for higher standards of workplace conduct and more effective and efficient enforcement mechanisms than public law provides. Both represent a kind of "self-regulation by contract."

At the same time, both monitoring agreements and neutrality agreements—and indeed the very idea of "self-regulation by contract"—call to mind the system of collective bargaining itself, whose New Deal proponents envisioned a system of quasi-private self-governance based on collective freedom of contract. But there the two newer forms of "self-regulation by contract" diverge. Neutrality agreements are meant to serve as a stepping stone toward what is usually a full-fledged collective bargaining regime, while monitoring agreements do not necessarily do so and may even substitute for collective bargaining. That will eventually bring us to the question of whether monitoring agreements are or can become mechanisms for effective workplace governance and effective worker participation in governance—whether these new forms of "self-regulation by contract" can thrive where collective bargaining has not and whether they can do for workers what collective bargaining did and still does within its shrinking ambit.

As observed above, domestic monitoring agreements build on the experience of the global anti-sweatshop movement. I want to focus here not on the global anti-sweatshop codes themselves (which do cover U.S. factories that supply the global brands),[2] but rather on the more homegrown experiments by which low-wage workers themselves, and sometimes regulators, seek to secure better wages and working conditions, not through traditional collective bargaining but through other models of representation and self-help. The anti-sweatshop movement's efforts to gain regulatory traction over workplaces in developing countries with neither effective local regulatory agencies nor viable independent labor unions have been instructive because, as we have seen, low-wage workers in the U.S. face their own problems of chronic underenforcement and a lack of union representation. On the other hand, U.S. workers have access to tools and resources well beyond those of most developing countries. Here there is a functioning though inadequate regulatory regime; an extensive array of formal legal rights, including some privately enforceable labor standards, rights against employer retaliation, and a right to unionize; an independent court system; a private bar that represents employees; and an array of independent worker advocacy organizations, including unions as well as "worker centers." By injecting some of those additional resources into the basic contractual strategy of the anti-sweatshop movement, some low-wage workers and their allies inside and outside government have pioneered new ways to address the enforcement deficit, and potentially the democratic deficit, that they face in their workplaces.

These new monitoring schemes follow the basic pattern of the anti-sweatshop codes: an organization acting on behalf of workers exerts some kind of leverage against employers (or against "super-employers" higher up the supply chain) to induce them to enter into an agreement to improve labor standards and to submit to more or less formal monitoring of compliance with the agreement. The schemes vary along several dimensions. They vary in the type and potency of the leverage—legal, reputational, economic, or some combination—that advocates deploy both to secure and to help enforce the agreement. They vary in their reliance upon a background threat of public enforcement; indeed, I will start with two monitoring schemes in which public enforcement agencies play leading roles. They also vary in their focus on legal entitlements as opposed to other improvements sought by workers; their reliance upon union support or other outside financial support such as foundation grants; the form and formality of monitoring; and the extent of active and organized involvement by employees themselves.

Most of the agreements arise primarily out of controversies over wages, hours, and overtime pay. We have seen that where the bare economics tempt employers to underpay their workers, public law typically does too little to outweigh that temptation and too little to induce employers to undertake serious self-regulatory efforts. On the other hand, several features of wage and hour laws multiply the possibilities for creative approaches to enforcement (as compared to both OSHA and the NLRA, for example). First, both liability and damages under the FLSA and parallel state wage statutes are often straightforward and readily provable, and in a labor-intensive business they may be quite substantial given the sheer number of hours and workers at issue. If the detection problem can be overcome, then the relative simplicity of proof and the large liabilities in some of these cases may give enforcement agencies leverage that OSHA, for example, lacks to induce participation in novel forms of wage and hour enforcement. Such leverage is wholly lacking under the NLRA for the enforcement of labor rights.

Second, some features of the FLSA may help to induce larger, more visible, and better-capitalized employers to regulate the wage and hour practices of their smaller and less visible contractors. Among labor and employment laws, the FLSA contains an unusually broad definition of "employer," which may make a firm liable as a "joint employer" for the unlawful wage and hour practices of contractors a step or two down the supply chain.[3] Even when the larger firm is not liable for those practices as an employer, the Department of Labor (DOL) has the power under the FLSA's hot-goods provision to embargo goods produced in violation of the Act.[4] That can give the larger firms an incentive —at least when goods are time-sensitive—to avoid or correct violations down the supply chain. Both provisions of the FLSA help to put legal muscle behind at least some efforts to hold super-employers responsible for working conditions within their supply chain.

Third, states have wider latitude to regulate in the wage and hour arena than in health and safety or labor relations.[5] There is no federal oversight or preemption of state wage and hour enforcement; states can impose higher minimum wage and overtime requirements and can deploy their own enforcement strategies and resources. Even cities may become regulators under a growing number of "living wage" laws.

Fourth, both federal and state wage and hour laws allow for private civil remedies, with provisions for attorney fees and aggregate forms of action.[6] Private rights of action enable individual employees, groups of employees, and their advocates to supplement government enforcement efforts and to provide added leverage and the possibility for prospective relief aimed at long-term corrective action. By contrast to the wage and hour laws, there are no private rights of action for employees under the NLRA or under either OSHA or state occupational and health laws. State tort law might have supplied some private rights of action where safety violations lead to injury, but the workers' compensation laws largely foreclose creative use of tort law in support of workplace safety.

These features of wage and hour regulation empower more regulatory actors, give them more potential points of leverage, and create more room for experimentation than exists under OSHA. One direction in which experimentation has proceeded is through the use of explicit codes and monitoring agreements. The strategy of "self-regulation by contract" is not yet widespread. It is a promising but precarious strategy, for reasons that will begin to emerge in the stories that follow. None of these schemes has been in operation long enough or successfully enough to demonstrate its sustainability as an alternative model of workplace regulation or governance. Indeed, some of the schemes described here have already lapsed, and others may have lapsed by the time this book is read. At the same time, however, similar schemes may well have cropped up, for the basic strategy of self-regulation and monitoring by contract is both powerful and flexible.

PUBLIC EXPERIMENTS IN
SELF-REGULATION BY CONTRACT

I begin with two examples of novel public enforcement strategies that follow the basic model of self-regulation by contract. One targets "super-employers" in a classic supply-chain context; the other targets small independent retailers.

The DOL Program of Monitoring
in Garment Manufacturing

The garment industry is a low-wage sector with notoriously high rates of non-compliance with minimum wage and overtime pay requirements, as well as with other labor laws.[7] Larger and more visible "manufacturers" (who supply finished apparel, with their own labels, to retailers), or sometimes large retailers themselves, contract out garment production to a network of smaller, low-visibility, and minimally capitalized contractors. We have seen this problem on a global scale, where the sewing is done well beyond the reach of U.S. regulators. But even for the small share of garment production that takes place within the U.S., enforcement is spotty and sweatshops persist. These low-wage workplaces at the bottom of the production chain rely heavily on undocumented immigrant labor, among whom the fear of deportation exacerbates the usual fear of reprisals that silences many low-wage employees.

As noted, the FLSA's definition of "employ" — "to suffer or permit to work" — is the broadest in American law.[8] That definition can make employers responsible as joint employers for the wages paid to workers who, under other legal frameworks, would not be deemed their employees. After nearly seventy years of judicial interpretation, the scope of employer liability continues to puzzle and divide the courts.[9] So in the garment sector, for example, whether manufacturers are liable for the wage and hour violations that are often endemic among their contractors may depend on how and how regularly manufacturers monitor the quality, quantity, or speed of production in the contractors' shops.[10] The prospect of liability would lead manufacturers to expand their monitoring of contractors to include wage and hour practices for which they may be held liable. But the incentive to monitor is doubly discounted by the low probability of inspection (of the contractors) and uncertainty about the manufacturer's liability as a "joint employer." That uncertainty is multiplied where the workers are, as they often are, more than one step removed from the manufacturer.

In an effort to improve FLSA compliance in the garment sector, the DOL in the early 1990s turned to the long-neglected "hot-goods" provision of the FLSA, which allows the Secretary of Labor to petition to embargo goods produced in violation of the law.[11] The interdiction of goods, unlike traditional sanctions, hits the large manufacturers at the top of the supply chain, at least in time-sensitive retail markets like fashion apparel, without regard to the niceties of joint employer liability.[12] By targeting the goods themselves, the remedy cuts through contracting arrangements that may insulate manufacturers from liability for the substandard wages of workers at the bottom of the production chain; it gives manufacturers an incentive to discover and fix those compliance problems to avoid costly interruptions in the supply of garments. The manufacturers' *capacity* to discover and fix such problems grows out of imperatives of production itself, which require manufacturers and contractors, or "jobbers," to work together closely to produce high-quality goods in very short and fast production runs.[13] Capitalizing on these features of the apparel industry, DOL in the early 1990s began to deploy the threat of a hot-goods embargo to induce manufacturers to agree to monitor the wage and hour practices of their contractors.[14] The manufacturers in turn entered into agreements with their supplier contractors to abide by wage and hour laws, keep records, and submit to inspections by representatives of the manufacturers or outside monitors.

The DOL "hot goods" program leverages limited public enforcement powers to generate a system of private enforcement that is potentially more vigilant than a public agency could possibly be.[15] This is a form of self-regulation in which the regulated "self " is expanded to include the entire chain of interconnected, albeit nominally independent, entities in the supply chain. The program recognizes that manufacturers already have an economic incentive and the operational capability to monitor the quality and quantity of what their suppliers produce; it encourages them to extend that monitoring to ensure compliance with labor standards. The program should also induce manufacturers to pay the higher contract prices that may be necessary to pay lawful wages.

The now familiar question is whether the DOL monitoring program is an *effective* system of self-regulation. Empirical evidence on the efficacy of the program presents a glass half full: compliance has improved significantly but is far from complete, even among monitored contractors.[16] Critics of the program, echoing common critiques of global supply-chain monitoring, have questioned the independence and inspection protocols of the monitors, which are typically private profit-making entities chosen and paid by the manufacturers and which may be too inclined to find compliance as long as they do not fear public inspections.[17] They have little reason to conduct unannounced inspections, for example, unless required to do so by the DOL. And DOL requirements are not very demanding in this or other respects. Clearly there is much room for improvement, but there was little pressure to make those improvements during the Bush administration.

State Enforcement through Self-Regulation:
The Greengrocer Code of Conduct

Federalism is often touted as a cauldron of innovation.[18] A striking example of creative state enforcement of wage and hour laws—one that suggests the potentialities of both federalism and self-regulation—can be found in New York City's greengrocer markets, the small retail produce markets that sprang up in the city in the 1980s.[19] The story began with a union organizing drive among the overwhelmingly Mexican and Mexican-American greengrocery workers. Although the union organizing drive stalled, the union and its allies in the community had found rampant wage and hour violations. They started bringing evidence of violations to the Labor Bureau of the state Office of the Attorney General (OAG), where Elliot Spitzer, then Attorney General, and Patricia Smith, then head of the OAG's Labor Bureau (later President Obama's nominee for Solicitor of Labor in the federal DOL), had put a high priority on enforcement of labor standards in low-wage work. State investigations showed a pattern of very similar violations: workers were paid $200–$300 a week for seventy-two-hour weeks—well below minimum wage, not to mention the legally required overtime premium. Cases were pretty open and shut. But case-by-case investigations and settlements were not going to solve the problem, given the OAG's limited resources and the large number of greengrocers in the city. Moreover, the resulting back-pay liability was often ruinous for these small businesses; closing them down would do little good for the workers, the produce-consuming public, or the community.

Once having gained the attention of employers with its initial burst of enforcement actions, the OAG brought representatives of employers and labor to the bargaining table.[20] The greengroceries—all independent small businesses

—were operated almost entirely by Koreans and Korean-Americans and were effectively represented by the Korean Produce Association. The workers, for their part, were represented by the state AFL-CIO and Casa Mexico, a worker advocacy group for Mexican immigrants. Together with the OAG, they devised a Greengrocer Code of Conduct (GGCC).[21] A merchant's submission to and compliance with the GGCC secured a kind of provisional amnesty with respect to past violations of wage and hour laws.[22]

The GGCC bound signatory employers to comply with wage and hour laws and other labor and employment laws, to keep payroll records, to undergo training and to allow their employees to do so, and to post notices advising employees of their rights. The GGCC also contained some provisions that went beyond legal mandates—for example, to provide some paid sick days and paid vacation days. In a separate section containing more aspirational provisions, signatory employers "recognize[d] that it is good business practice not to discharge an employee unless there is a reason for discharge which is related to that employee's job performance."

Most important, employers agreed to submit to regular inspections by independent labor standards monitors appointed by the OAG. Monitors made unannounced visits to the workplaces, inspected employers' payroll records, spoke privately with employees, assisted employers in compliance, and reported on violations to the OAG and to a Code of Conduct Committee. The three-member Committee, which oversaw the Code, dealt with disputes, and certified new signatories, included appointees of the OAG, Casa Mexico, and the employers.[23] Notably, the GGCC provided for a rudimentary form of employee representation: for shops with more than ten employees, the monitor should appoint an employee spokesperson after consultation with employees.[24] Unfortunately, the provision was largely symbolic, as almost no greengrocers employ that many workers.[25] Employers adamantly resisted any real provision for direct employee representation.[26]

The GGCC appeared to significantly improve rates of compliance with wage and hour laws, especially among the 20 percent of merchants who were signatories of the Code, but even among those who were not.[27] Monitors found that workers at signatory shops were generally paid at least the minimum wage plus time-and-a-half for any hours beyond forty in each week. Some technical and record-keeping violations remained common in these small businesses, but the improvement was dramatic.[28] Unfortunately, the original GGCC expired in February 2005. It appears, not surprisingly, that "many of the merchants [were] happy for the code to expire because they dislike[d] having their stores inspected by the outside monitors."[29] In hopes of reinstilling the fear of enforcement that brought the GGCC into being, the OAG in 2006 began to file new enforcement actions.

While the DOL's garment-monitoring program is an example of state-driven "self-regulation by contract," the GGCC is a hybrid of bottom-up and top-down self-regulation. The story of the GGCC began with a union organizing drive. The drive sputtered, and the local union itself played no direct role in the negotiation or administration of the GGCC, in part because merchants refused to deal with it. Yet representatives of the state AFL-CIO did participate in the negotiations. Casa Mexico participated in negotiations for the creation of the Code and, as noted, appointed one member to the tripartite Code of Conduct Committee. The involvement of Casa Mexico meant that employees had a potential organizational voice and ally to whom they could turn with complaints without risking reprisals; whether Casa Mexico has the power, and the staying power, to carry out that role is an open question, however.[30]

The weakness of worker representation is one of several sobering aspects of the GGCC. Even with the state OAG at the table, and even in the face of a credible threat of public enforcement and back-pay liability that could drive any targeted merchant out of business, the merchants managed successfully to resist both direct union involvement in code enforcement and direct employee representation in the monitoring process. They did agree to unannounced inspections of shops and payroll records and to the training of employees—important concessions. But union involvement and employee representation were deal breakers, according to Patricia Smith, who conducted negotiations for the state.

Moreover, the GGCC was short-lived, at least as a formal matter. It was short-lived for a reason that will recur throughout this survey of monitoring experiments: it is difficult and costly to maintain the pressure that induces employers to submit to agreements, and especially monitoring provisions, that they do not like. In this case, it was the threat of ruinous back-pay liability that had induced employers to sign onto the Code. But that threat had a limited shelf life, for the statute of limitations on past violations began to run out, and monitoring had succeeded in dramatically reducing the most blatant and easily provable violations among signatory employers. Without a new wave of costly prosecutions against industry laggards, the immediate impetus for this regime of monitored self-regulation dropped out, and the Code formally lapsed.

There were other possible sources of leverage in support of the Code. For example, Code signatories were awarded a GGCC "seal of approval" that they could display in their shop windows, in hopes of drawing consumer favor. But cultivating that consumer favor—a kind of reverse boycott—would have required a major public campaign that would itself have been costly, and it did not materialize. Alternatively, a union or Casa Mexico might have organized workers and community members to put pressure on merchants, through pickets and other publicity, to sign up or remain signed up. But that did not happen either.

Even after its apparent demise as a formal matter, it seems likely that the GGCC had some continuing positive legacy among greengrocers. The memory of prosecutions, and the education that merchants gained in the law and how to comply with it, may well have some continuing residual impact on wage and hour practices and may forestall a return to the pre-Code pattern of complete disregard for the law. The law may now cast a shadow in the greengrocer business that it did not before the OAG became involved. But for the GGCC to serve as a model for wage and hour enforcement through state-driven, community-based monitoring agreements, policymakers and advocates will have to learn lessons from its failure as well as from its successes.

Both the garment-monitoring program and the GGCC are examples of what traditional regulatory agencies can do if they focus their attention temporarily on a particular group of employers, locate their vulnerabilities, wield a credible threat of enforcement that would do serious damage to the employers, and convert that threat into leverage to induce the firms to regulate themselves or their contractors. Both of these programs involved monitors from outside the firms whose workers' wages were at issue; indeed, the GGCC monitors were drawn largely from the pool of workplace monitors that had grown up around the DOL's garment industry monitoring program. Still, the monitoring arrangements between the two programs, and within the DOL program, ran a wide gamut in independence, expertise, and accountability.

A recent episode in New York underscored the problems that remain in monitoring—as well as the importance of continued public enforcement. In July 2008, the New York State Department of Labor (NY DOL) and its Fair Wages Task Force targeted a large sweatshop in Queens, where they found that the employer, Jin Shun, Inc., had forced employees to work twelve-hour days and six or seven days a week at subminimum wages and had then falsified records and elaborately coached employees to lie to both public investigators and private monitors. The NY DOL assessed over $5 million in back wages and damages and tagged ten thousand pieces of clothing under the state hot-goods law. Patricia Smith, the Labor Commissioner, explained in the accompanying press release that "cursory inspection in monitoring factories is not enough. . . . While you may require your suppliers to abide by strict codes of conduct, these codes do workers no good if they are not aggressively enforced."[31]

There is a big cautionary tale here regarding corporate monitoring schemes. The Queens sweatshop produced garments for the Gap, Banana Republic, Victoria's Secret, and the Limited, all of which maintain private monitoring systems as part of their corporate responsibility programs. The Gap, for example, proclaims the following:

> We believe that all individuals who work in garment factories deserve to be treated with dignity and respect, and are entitled to safe and fair working conditions. Our team of more than 90 full-time employees is dedicated to improving conditions in the factories that make our clothes, and the lives of garment workers. . . .
>
> Because we don't own the factories where our clothes are made, we regularly inspect them to ensure that working conditions meet our standards. But our efforts don't stop there. We recognize that we have a responsibility to work in partnership with factories, as well as other apparel companies and concerned organizations, to improve working conditions across the industry. Together, we are striving to make garment factories around the world safe and fair places to work.[32]

On the one hand, this recent episode underscores the gap that sometimes still exists between the increasingly prominent espousals of corporate social responsibility and the reality for workers. (One suspects the gap is even larger in the more numerous and remote factories around the world that face even less chance of public inspection than does a factory in Queens.) On the other hand, actions like that of the NY DOL may induce the large brands to improve their programs—they may spur The Gap to narrow the gap! We will return to this lesson in Chapter 6.

SELF-REGULATION BY "PRIVATE" CONTRACT

Given chronic shortfalls in systematic public enforcement, workers and their advocates have sometimes taken things into their own hands. They have often resorted to legal actions, both administrative claims before public enforcement agencies and private litigation, to do what liability rules are supposed to do: compensate aggrieved workers and encourage employers to clean up illegal practices. But these legal complaints are often just part of a larger campaign of publicity, education, and organizing that aims to induce employers (or super-employers) to commit themselves to new forms of self-regulation and enforcement.

The MCTF and Monitoring
in Janitorial Services

Janitorial services is a chronically low-wage sector that relies heavily upon un-documented immigrant labor; many contractors operate as virtual outlaws in violation of immigration laws, tax laws, wage and hour laws, and other labor protections.[33] But much as garment workers supply goods through contractors to large and publicly visible manufacturers and retailers, janitors occupy the bottom rung of a supply chain that is often headed by large and visible corporations with some investment in their name and reputation. Some large maintenance companies themselves fit that bill, for the maintenance industry has undergone a fair degree of consolidation at the top while continuing to contract out much of the work to small, marginal contractors. But the supply chain for maintenance work might run all the way up to a bank, a retailer, or a real estate developer for which the janitors perform essential maintenance services.

By contracting out janitorial services to low-wage contractors, those larger and more publicly accountable firms may lower their maintenance costs without directly violating the law. Building owners or retailers may in fact be legally liable as joint employers for wage and hour violations.[34] In one high-profile case, retail grocers Albertsons, Vons (part of Safeway), and Ralphs (part of Kroger) agreed to a $22.4 million settlement of wage and hour claims by janitors working directly for contractors.[35] Apart from any legal liability, however, the larger firms may find themselves politically liable for serious wage and hour violations among their janitorial contractors. Both Target and Wal-Mart have learned in recent years that building owners can become super-employers whom the public holds accountable for janitors' wages and working conditions.[36]

The link between low-wage janitors and high-profile building owners has been a critical strategic element of organizing campaigns conducted since 1985 by SEIU under the banner of "Justice for Janitors." As a result of these campaigns, the sector is now partially unionized in major cities in California, as well as in Washington, D.C., and Houston, for example. Unionized janitors receive at least minimum wages and overtime in accordance with the law and usually health and other benefits, for a total cost at least 40 percent higher than the labor costs of the worst outlaws among non-union contractors.[37] Recognizing that the non-union, low-wage sector threatened to undercut them both, the SEIU and unionized employers created and funded a nonprofit watchdog organization, the Maintenance Cooperation Trust Fund (MCTF), to identify and challenge labor standards violations among janitorial contractors.

The MCTF, a unique kind of worker center established through collective bargaining, seeks to identify and publicize lawbreakers and to educate workers about their rights. Sometimes—and, from MCTF's standpoint, ideally—worker education leads to union organizing. But whether or not that happens, MCTF encourages and assists workers in demanding lawful payment of wages from employers. As such, the everyday operations of MCTF make it an informal monitor of compliance and an informal representative of janitorial workers in the unorganized part of this partially organized sector.[38]

Sometimes MCTF pursues private litigation on behalf of workers for labor violations; it was MCTF, along with SEIU, that won the $22.4 million settlement on behalf of California janitors at three grocery chains. Sometimes MCTF pursues public enforcement, bringing evidence of violations to state or federal regulators and urging them to bring enforcement actions.[39] The MCTF took the latter course upon discovering rampant wage and hour violations on the part of Global Building Services, which performed maintenance services for Target Stores in California and much of the West. The case was complicated by the fact that most of the affected workers were undocumented immigrants —many of them no longer employed by Global, hard to locate, and reluctant to speak—and by the fact that Global had itself contracted out much of the janitorial work to smaller contractors who often paid in cash and kept no payroll or time records.[40] But investigations revealed widespread violations for which Global was clearly liable, either directly or as a joint employer.[41] The DOL sued Global and secured a settlement in which Global agreed to pay $1.9 million in back wages to 775 employees.[42]

The settlement did not exhaust Global's past liabilities, nor did it, in the view of MCTF, ensure future compliance or improved conditions for Global's workers. Global, for its part, recognized that its wage and hour practices, and those of its subcontractors, were "out of control" and a continuing source of potential liability. MCTF's then pending litigation against California grocers clearly darkened the "shadow of the law" under which Global bargained with MCTF. Seeking to avoid further costly litigation, as well as a damaging publicity campaign that could threaten Global's contracting relationships, Global entered into a separate agreement with MCTF to clean up its payroll practices and submit to MCTF's monitoring of future compliance with wage and hour laws. Under the agreement, MCTF inspected records and job sites and met with workers to determine employer compliance with labor standards. As long as MCTF played this monitoring role and had access to Global's records, it agreed to file no complaints against Global; it could, however, report noncompliance to the DOL and state labor officials. Early returns on the MCTF/ Global agreement and its impact on compliance were promising.[43]

Unfortunately the agreement lapsed within a year because Global lost its largest contract (with Target). It is unclear whether Global's loss of its contract was related to the DOL enforcement action or the subsequent MCTF agreement. It would not be hard to imagine Target's abandoning Global in favor of another low-road contractor that could offer up the 40 percent labor cost savings that Global had lost. On the other hand, Target might have wished to avoid the taint of another rogue janitorial contractor. After the original settlement between the DOL and Global, Target released a statement that it "does not tolerate unethical business practices in any form, including on the part of our vendors" and "will be taking appropriate action."[44] In any event, the MCTF experience teaches other lessons as well.

The first lesson lies in MCTF's ability to leverage public and private enforcement efforts. The Global agreement piggybacked on a federal DOL enforcement action. MCTF relies more often and more extensively on state enforcement, which is stronger in California than in most other states. MCTF was also able to exercise considerable leverage over Global on its own by credibly threatening costly private litigation and publicity against violators.[45] Without a strong background threat of public or private enforcement, however, MCTF would lose much of the leverage it has against employers.

Another related lesson is about the limits of liability as leverage, and it echoes the lessons of the GGCC. If the Global agreement had secured compliance going forward and had outlasted the several-year limitations period on the past back-pay liabilities that induced Global to enter the agreement, it is unclear what would have kept Global from turning its back on the monitoring agreement and sliding back into noncompliance. Would MCTF have to start over in accumulating enough evidence of liability to induce another agreement? The answer might lie in community organizing and grassroots pressure and publicity; but if militancy and community activism must continue indefinitely in order to maintain a monitoring agreement, one might well question its sustainability over time. Another answer might lie in collective bargaining; once Global was under the spotlight and its workers educated about their rights, a return to its old low-road ways might make it a ripe target for SEIU's organizing. But if that is the answer, then it would suggest that monitoring agreements are not an alternative to collective bargaining—something that could succeed where collective bargaining has not—but only a temporary stopgap strategy.

That leads to the third lesson, or set of lessons, concerning financial support for monitoring efforts (a problem that the GGCC avoided by its state sponsorship). Formal monitoring requires staff and money, which are in short supply among many worker organizations other than unions, with their dues base. Global itself, under the shadow of an entirely legitimate threat of additional liability from a private lawsuit, was paying a fee for MCTF's monitoring of its own payroll records and those of its subcontractors. Moreover, MCTF, unlike many worker centers, had a source of financial support to undertake its monitoring work: SEIU and its unionized contractors set up and funded MCTF under the auspices of federal labor law to underwrite its monitoring work and to limit the ability of scofflaw contractors to undercut them both. So MCTF seems to have devised a "business model" for its monitoring efforts that has eluded many worker centers.

But problems with this model remain. One is not a problem for MCTF but for the generalizability of its strategy: to the extent that its financial viability is dependent on a major union's success in organizing and on the resulting collective bargaining relationships, MCTF is a reminder that even nontraditional worker advocacy organizations and campaigns may be dependent on traditional unions rather than an alternative to them. The continuing decline of unions will bring down organizations like MCTF as well. (On the other hand, the MCTF may serve as a model for innovative union strategies that extend their support for workers beyond the current reach of collective bargaining and that help them defend organizing gains against low-road competition.) Another problem with MCTF's business model is that it did not generate enough funds after all. MCTF is heavily dependent on the dedication of its full-time director, Lilia Garcia, who sometimes has gone without a paycheck to continue the work, and on the unpaid efforts of workers themselves. It is unclear whether an organization and monitoring effort that runs largely on volunteer energies is sustainable in the long run and across a wide range of settings. (On the other hand, it is unlikely that an organization that does not keep up a high level of worker and community energy and commitment can cultivate the trust and communication with workers on which its monitoring—formal or informal—depends.)

A more serious problem from the standpoint of some MCTF and union officials was not the lack of funds but their source. In their view, MCTF's dependence on employer support—the support of Global, that is—potentially threatened its integrity and the trust of workers that was so essential to its ability to serve workers. It took extraordinary organizing efforts by MCTF to gain the trust of workers, whose ability to blow the whistle on their employers is in-

hibited by both fear (of employer reprisals, of immigration problems) and ignorance of the law. Could MCTF maintain its integrity as the ear and voice of
those workers when it was financially dependent on the employers being monitored? The potential for a conflict of interest was neither realized nor resolved
in the short time the Global agreement was in effect. But the concern is one
that plagues any worker center that succeeds in securing employer funding for
monitoring efforts. (On the other hand, reliance on state funding or union
funding—the only real alternatives on the horizon—would tie the fate of the
monitoring model to the very institutions whose waning role is motivating the
search for alternatives.)

Even with all these unanswered questions, the MCTF is an important innovation. It reminds us, among other things, that once some employers within
an industry are induced somehow to take the high road of better labor standards, they have an economic incentive to support efforts to put pressure on
low-road competitors. That lesson has not been lost on worker advocates, as the
next example illustrates.

ROC-NY and Manhattan's
Restaurant Workers

ROC-NY, introduced in Chapter 1, is an advocate for mostly immigrant restaurant workers in Manhattan. From the outset, it focused on complaints of unpaid and subminimum wages and overtime, misappropriation of tips, discrimination, and harassment—all the subjects of formal legal rights and
regulations. The group has pursued these complaints through both lawsuits
and lawful self-help—picketing, leafletting, street theater (and sometimes off-
street theater inside restaurants)—but even the latter tactics tend to put the
spotlight on legal complaints.

Beginning with its January 2005 settlement agreement with the Smith and
Wollensky Restaurant Group (S&W), the group has made it increasingly clear
that its aims extend beyond restaurant workers' legal entitlements. The settlement agreement reached beyond the twenty-three plaintiffs and beyond their
specific legal complaints. S&W promised not only to reform wage and hour
practices and to train managers on workers' legal rights, but also to institute
paid vacations and sick days, progressive discipline policies, and an orderly promotion policy. None of the additional policy changes were required by law, yet
they became legally enforceable once incorporated into the settlement agreement. Informal monitoring and troubleshooting by ROC-NY has thus far
made legal enforcement against S&W unnecessary, however. According to

ROC-NY founder and co-director Saru Jayaraman, few workers have reported violations of the agreement, and for those who have, ROC-NY has been able to resolve the issues promptly.

Success breeds success. ROC-NY has mounted eight successful campaigns in five years against major restaurateurs, including Fireman Hospitality Group, which settled after a long battle. As in the case of the unionized janitorial contractors that funded MCTF, the major employers who were first induced to sign on to labor standards improvements became potential allies in the effort to extend similar improvements to competitors. ROC-NY has spearheaded the formation of the Restaurant Industry Roundtable, a nonprofit association of "high-road" restaurateurs that is seeking to brand its members, with ROC-NY's support, as the industry's good citizens. The Roundtable is in its infancy still but might become a vehicle for more ambitious reform efforts.

ROC-NY's settlement agreements and the successful campaigns that produced them show how private enforcement litigation—even without the background of public enforcement as in the MCTF-Global agreement—can be deployed as leverage to secure wider and more lasting improvements for workers and even a limited form of collective voice. Workers at S&W and Fireman restaurants in Manhattan can now call upon ROC-NY to pursue complaints of unfair treatment; based on the settlement agreement, ROC-NY has some leverage to pursue those complaints.

The experience of ROC-NY has brought to light one further sign of trouble for the worker center movement. During its long conflict with ROC-NY, Fireman filed NLRB charges claiming that ROC-NY was a "labor organization" under the broad terms of Section 2(5) of the NLRA and that its picketing constituted an illegal attempt to compel Fireman to recognize it as the employees' bargaining agent. The NLRB's General Counsel rejected the charges, concluding that, based on the record at the time, ROC-NY was not a labor organization (and that even if it were, its activities would not violate the NLRA as it had no recognitional objective).[46] This was not the first time an employer had argued that ROC-NY was a labor organization and therefore subject to an array of duties and liabilities under federal labor laws. In 2004, an employer argued unsuccessfully to the DOL that ROC-NY was a labor organization and as such was required to comply with the extensive reporting requirements of the Labor-Management Reporting and Disclosure Act of 1959.[47] Both challenges to ROC-NY were rejected. But both determinations were based on a particular record of ROC-NY's activities at a particular time, and the question may recur. We will return to it in Chapter 7 below.

The Coalition of Immokalee Workers

One of the most impressive examples of bottom-up self-regulation through monitoring comes from the tomato fields of Florida, where workers face low pay and appalling working conditions—sometimes including modern forms of slavery.[48] Florida's migrant farm laborers would seem to be among the most powerless of workers. They are virtual orphans of the labor laws, excluded from the coverage of the NLRA, excluded from the FLSA's overtime requirements, and largely ignored by state law in most heavily agricultural (and Southern) jurisdictions, including Florida. And these workers and their direct employers are usually invisible to the public. Yet migrant farm workers share with some janitors and garment workers the potential advantage of being at the bottom of a supply chain that leads to large and powerful companies that are vulnerable to public and consumer pressures. Fast-food chains, which purchase a very large share of the tomatoes picked in Florida and the Southeast, are not even arguably joint employers of the tomato pickers under the law. Yet it turns out that they can be made politically liable for the farmworkers' plight.

The Coalition of Immokalee Workers (CIW) is "a community-based worker organization" that represents tomato pickers and other agricultural workers centered in Immokalee, Florida, near Ft. Myers.[49] The CIW's members are largely Mexican, Guatemalan, and Haitian immigrants who follow the tomato and citrus harvest from Florida up the East Coast. The organization began in 1993 in a church basement in response to the falling piece-rate wages of tomato pickers. Several years of organizing enabled the group to conduct a series of general strikes and a well-publicized hunger strike that succeeded in raising wages by 13–25 percent and in gaining attention and allies throughout the country. The group then formed the Anti-Slavery Campaign to combat the reemergence of involuntary servitude—in the form of debt bondage—in Florida's farm fields. Several major prosecutions followed from the CIW's organizing and investigations. The CIW gained nationwide respect and publicity as a grassroots human rights organization.

Taking advantage of that public attention, the CIW in 2001 launched a nationwide boycott against Taco Bell and its parent company, Yum! Brands (Yum), for supporting forced labor. With the help of student, religious, labor, human rights, and community groups across the country, the CIW spearheaded rallies and cross-country tours and a ten-day hunger strike outside of Taco Bell headquarters involving seventy-five farmworkers and students. "During that strike," says CIW, "we posed Taco Bell's executives one question: 'Can

Taco Bell guarantee its customers that the tomatoes in its tacos were not picked by forced labor?' The company had no answer." Finally in March 2005, the boycott was ended with Yum's agreement to "work with the CIW to improve working and pay conditions for farmworkers in the Florida tomato fields."[50]

The agreement provides for Taco Bell to pay a penny per pound more for tomatoes and to ensure that the increase is passed on to workers, nearly doubling their pay. Taco Bell agreed to provide records of all Florida tomato purchases, and to require growers to provide all their wage records, to the CIW so that it could monitor compliance with the penny-per-pound pass-through to workers. Implementation of this and other improvements in working conditions is through "the first-ever enforceable Code of Conduct for agricultural suppliers in the fast-food industry," with CIW itself making up part of the monitoring body. Through the Code, Yum requires suppliers to abide by the few applicable laws regarding wages and hours, equal opportunity, and safety, including a strict prohibition on involuntary servitude. And Yum "strongly encourages Florida growers in the tomato industry to provide working terms and conditions similar to those provided by suppliers outside of the agricultural industry." Yum represents that it "will conduct business with those tomato growers that demonstrate consistent adherence to these higher standards."

The Code provides for unannounced inspections of suppliers. But for those commitments that cannot be monitored by an examination of payroll and purchase records, it relies mainly on a complaint procedure: "In the event YUM and/or the [CIW] receives a credible complaint from a tomato picker alleging conduct by a Florida tomato grower that violates any applicable laws, codes or regulations as specified above, YUM and CIW will work together to investigate the complaint with no undue delay, and if it is determined that there are reasonable grounds to believe that a violation has occurred, YUM may revoke a supplier's approved status."[51] Complaints may also be referred to public enforcement agencies. If the agency finds a violation and it is "serious or systematic," YUM agrees that it "will revoke a supplier's approved status." A complaint procedure might be a shaky foundation for monitoring in many settings, where workers may not know their rights or may fear reprisals, but CIW leaders were confident that it would work within their well-organized community of workers. The CIW has worked so long and hard to educate workers, and is so much a part of their lives, that its leaders believe they are bound to learn of any complaints workers have.

Even as it scrambled to set up monitoring procedures under the Taco Bell agreement, the CIW immediately began preparations to extend the boycott, and eventually the code of conduct, to McDonald's and other fast-food companies through the newly-formed Alliance for Fair Food.[52] In the case of McDonald's, the single largest purchaser of tomatoes in the Southeast, those preparations bore fruit. In April 2007, after two years of CIW's publicity campaign and on the eve of its commencing a boycott, McDonald's and the CIW came to an agreement.[53] The landmark accord included the penny-per-pound pass-through, but it also improved upon the Taco Bell agreement in several respects. It provided for a stronger code of conduct that aims to "increase farmworker participation in monitoring supplier compliance," and it committed McDonald's to collaborate with the CIW "in developing and implementing a credible third-party verification system" that aims for industry-wide participation and coverage.[54]

Immediately the CIW turned the spotlight on Burger King Corp. (BKC) and began preparing its next campaign. Burger King pushed back more aggressively than its competitors, calling the existing penny-per-pound pass-through agreements of Taco Bell and McDonald's "un-American." Initially, BKC not only refused to discuss an agreement with the CIW, but it also joined with a conservative tomato growers' organization to attempt to defeat existing agreements by imposing $100,000 fines on growers that signed onto those agreements. But the CIW prevailed again. In May 2008, the CIW and BKC came to terms on an even stronger code of conduct. BKC agreed not only to the penny-per-pound pass-through, but to an additional 1.5 cents per pound to fund added payroll and administrative costs. The BKC agreement went beyond earlier agreements in other ways, establishing "zero tolerance guidelines for certain unlawful activities that require immediate termination of any grower from the BURGER KING® supply chain" and explicitly providing for "farmworker participation in the monitoring of growers' compliance with the company's vendor code of conduct." In a nod to its recalcitrant past, the CEO of BKC observed: "We are pleased to now be working together with the CIW to further the common goal of improving Florida tomato farmworkers' wages, working conditions and lives. The CIW has been at the forefront of efforts to improve farm labor conditions, exposing abuses and driving socially responsible purchasing and work practices in the Florida tomato fields. We apologize for any negative statements about the CIW or its motives previously attributed to BKC or its employees and now realize that those statements were wrong. Today we turn a new page in our relationship and begin a new chapter of real progress for Florida farmworkers."[55]

The CIW promptly turned its sights on Subway, Chipotle, Whole Foods, and other major food retailers.

The CIW's success with Taco Bell, McDonald's, and Burger King is especially remarkable because it relied on virtually no background threat of state or private enforcement. The slavery prosecutions were almost the only point at which domestic law entered the picture. While farmworkers are now "employees" covered by the FLSA's minimum wage (but not overtime) requirements, the FLSA's joint employer doctrine would not reach retailers. Nor was the CIW able to draw upon union support or the prospect of traditional union organizing or collective bargaining, for its workers have no legal organizing or collective bargaining rights under either federal or state law. The CIW hopes eventually to bring its farmworker constituents out of the legal wilderness, and its agreements with the fast-food chains speak in rather diffuse terms of joint lobbying for greater legal rights for farmworkers. But that is a long-term goal. One lesson from the CIW experience is an echo of the early labor and civil rights movements: positive law may be one important source of leverage in a struggle for justice and decency, but it is not always an essential one or even the most effective one.

On the other hand, positive law played a behind-the-scenes role that harkens back to the corporate social responsibility story chronicled in Chapter 4: as part of CIW's multifaceted campaign against Yum, McDonald's, and BKC, sympathetic shareholders presented resolutions, for inclusion in corporate proxy statements, proposing action on behalf of the tomato pickers and citing principles of international law in support of the workers' goals. McDonald's, for example, argued to the SEC that the resolution could be excluded from the proxy statement on five separate grounds under SEC rules, but in March 2007 the SEC rejected all five arguments and required McDonald's to include the resolution. McDonald's reached its settlement with CIW the next month. A similar behind-the-scenes drama took place at BKC.[56] CIW's ability through the securities laws to carry its publicity campaign into corporate boardrooms shows how the law may provide important support for the *means* by which worker advocates press their aims even when the law (at least domestic law) does little to back up the aims themselves.

Still, the CIW's reliance on organizing, publicity, and coalition building raises questions. The CIW has been extraordinarily successful in organizing both its own community of farmworkers and a growing coalition of supportive foundations and advocacy organizations. It gained crucial assistance, including financial support, from the Robert F. Kennedy Memorial Foundation for Human

Rights in Washington, D.C., and from the Carter Center in Atlanta, as well as from smaller organizations across the country. But the CIW's reliance—and possible dependence—on foundation support raises some questions about the sustainability and replicability of its strategy. Other questions follow from the sheer intensity of the organizing effort that was required to bring about the Taco Bell, McDonald's, and Burger King agreements. A nationwide boycott is an extraordinary undertaking and cannot be regenerated easily in case of noncompliance. Gradual extension of the agreements across the industry may soften each firm's incentive to defect from the agreement. But what will happen if defections do happen? Without the ability to trigger public or private enforcement actions, the CIW may need to maintain indefinitely its very high level of community organizing and coalition-building activities, as well as its extraordinary leadership. How many groups of workers can do that?

The picture that emerges from the last four chapters is complicated and still changing; it contains a mix of discouraging and encouraging elements (and it is not always clear which is which). On the one hand, we find that traditional industrial self-governance through collective bargaining—still the only legally sanctioned form of collective employee representation in the U.S.—has declined to the point where it has ceased to be a real option for many employees seeking an effective voice at work. In the meantime, the law of the workplace has expanded to fill part of the vacuum left by the decline of collective bargaining. The growth of employment law—the proliferation of employee rights (and lawsuits) and of minimum labor standards (and regulations)—has encouraged employers to self-regulate and to create more or less elaborate internal compliance structures. More recently and controversially, the law has taken that encouragement a step further by allowing employers to partially substitute internal enforcement procedures for public enforcement, provided they meet certain standards of efficacy.

In some ways, the move toward regulated self-regulation in employment law may appear to echo the New Deal embrace of self-governance over public regulation as the primary mode of protecting workers and improving wages and working conditions. We are once again moving toward internal "lawmaking" and "law enforcement" within a public law framework and away from direct public regulation or judicial resolution of workplace disputes. In the New Deal, the embrace of workplace self-governance went hand in hand with the endorsement, empowerment, and massive expansion of institutions for worker representation. This time around, however, workers have been largely cut out of the internal governance schemes, for the current trend toward self-regulation is taking hold at the same time that the system of self-governance through collective representation and bargaining is so diminished, and still diminishing, in scope. As a result, the "self" that is increasingly claiming the prerogative to regulate itself is less likely than ever to encompass employees other than as individuals, who face familiar and daunting impediments to effective bargaining or intervention on their own behalf. It is also troubling that the low-wage workers who are most in need of legal rights and improved labor standards are the least likely to work in organizations with sophisticated self-regulatory schemes.

It is for these reasons that the still small and scattered experiments in bottom-up self-regulation, and the extension of accountability for working conditions to super-employers up the supply chain, are so important. Employers at the bottom of the labor market bear little resemblance to the self-proclaimed beacons of corporate responsibility in the Fortune 500. Their low-wage employees have benefited least from the rise of corporate compliance schemes and suffered most from the decline of unions and the shortfall of public enforcement. Yet they too have sometimes turned to forms of self-regulation. Partly inspired by the high-profile global anti-sweatshop movement and its continuously improving monitoring strategies, worker centers, as well as public officials, unions, and other worker advocates, have used the eminently flexible framework of contract to create new self-regulatory mechanisms for improving labor standards.

These experiments in self-regulation by contract still occupy only a very small part of the landscape of labor standards regulation in the U.S. And there is much skepticism among unions and worker advocates about the efficacy of corporate codes of conduct and monitoring agreements. Yet their importance is bolstered by the rise of parallel developments elsewhere in the law of work and beyond: the growth and legal encouragement of corporate compliance programs across a range of regulatory arenas, the decades-long efforts to gain regulatory traction over conditions in the factories of the developing world, and even the labor movement's use of voluntary contractual regulation of the representation process through "neutrality agreements." Something important is afoot here, and understanding it is a big step toward shaping it.

Part Two **Toward Co-Regulation**

in the Workplace

Chapter 6 Principles of Self-Regulation
for the U.S. Workplace

The continuing decline of union representation, the lack of alternative mechanisms of employee voice and empowerment, the loosening grip of the state on private employers, and rising economic inequality have fostered a sense of anxiety, even crisis, among worker advocates and scholars of labor relations and the law of the workplace. But while the crisis of workplace governance has its particular shape and pathos, it is only one dimension of a broader set of challenges to public efforts throughout the world to exercise effective social control over the increasingly footloose, flexible, fast-changing organizations and networks through which most goods and services are produced.

The market is now unrivaled as a basic way to organize the economy. The financial meltdown of 2008 vividly exposed some of the vulnerabilities of globalized markets and the need for more intelligent and vigilant regulation. But even when markets are working as expected, they produce externalities; underproduce public goods; and reproduce and magnify the advantages of those with wealth, scarce skills, and information. The developed nations and regions of the world are all struggling to develop institutions and tools that can regulate externalities, promote public goods, and abate inequalities without smothering or driving away the capitalist engines of wealth and growth. At the same time, the proponents of public regulation cannot help but notice that those capitalist engines themselves—especially the large multinational corporations—have developed sophisticated regulatory systems of their own in order to minimize legal and political frictions and to ensure a reliable flow of goods, services, and information both upstream and downstream within their sprawling networks of suppliers, contractors, and customers.

In response to these forces, regulators in the U.S. and abroad have gravitated toward new approaches to regulation—new ways to control the socially undesirable dimensions of corporate conduct and to promote public values within an increasingly fluid and boundariless economic environment. Much of what is new about these approaches to social control is their reliance on the regulatory resources within regulated entities. Summarizing the conclusions of a wide-ranging study of business regulation across the world, John Braithwaite and Peter Drahos observe, "[t]he last two decades of the twentieth century saw the rise of a 'new regulatory state,' where states do not so much run things as regulate them or monitor self-regulation."[1] Experiments in regulated self-regulation can be found across a range of fields in the U.S.[2]

This chapter takes a step back from the particulars of the existing regime of workplace regulation in the U.S. and begins to chart a path for the future. It recognizes that the problem of regulating labor standards and employee rights is one facet of the larger problem of regulating the conduct of business enterprises generally, and it looks to the wealth of literature on that larger problem to begin identifying principles for well-regulated self-regulation in the workplace.

COMMON CONCERNS IN DIFFERENT LANGUAGES: NEW GOVERNANCE AND THE ECONOMICS OF CORPORATE COMPLIANCE

Most of the recent literature on regulating corporate behavior falls into two seemingly antagonistic camps: traditional economic analysis and what we may call "New Governance." But differences in tone, tools, and terminology may mask some important areas of agreement on the question of how to structure law so as to encourage organizations to advance public values and comply with public norms even when those public values and norms may be in tension with the private interests of (and within) the organization. Those on both sides of the divide who take both organizations and incentives seriously reach some surprisingly convergent conclusions on the basic structure of the regulatory enterprise.

Fine-Tuning the Incentives: The Economics of Corporate Compliance

The problem of corporate compliance has conventionally been approached in the U.S. with the tools and assumptions of law and economics—incentives, externalities, agency and information costs. Individuals within organizations are presumed to be "rational actors": they seek to advance their own interests, and they respond predictably to regulatory carrots and sticks. We may call this the "deterrence model" of corporate compliance, and it has been applied to tort law, criminal law, and administrative law and across the substantive areas governed by each—environmental, consumer safety, antitrust, and securities law, for example. Adherents of the deterrence model are not all of one mind on these matters; they vary, for example, in their inclination to introduce behavioral and organizational complications into the models and in their receptivity to empirical evidence.

One question that runs through these debates is whether to look inside the organizational "black box" or only at what comes out—whether to look at internal processes or only at outcomes.[3] A pure "black box" approach would hold the firm fully accountable for harms that result from its operations, thereby inducing owners and managers (putting aside for now any slippage between the two) to put in place controls or precautions within the organization that would reduce those harms.[4] Alternatively, liability may be "duty-based," or dependent on whether the firm has the right sort of internal controls or precautions in place; the firm may not be liable for harmful outcomes that occur in spite of such controls.

The "black box" approach reflects in part skepticism about the ability of courts or regulators, as compared to firms and their managers, to identify effective precautions against wrongdoing or injury. At the broadest level, the "black box" approach and the skepticism that underlies it map onto arguments for regulation through *ex post* liability regimes versus command-and-control regulatory strategies that prescribe specific appropriate practices *ex ante*.[5] Consider the problem of tainted meat. A tort regime might simply hold meatpackers liable for injuries from tainted meat and let them figure out how best to avoid those injuries and attendant liabilities. By contrast, a command-and-control regulation would prescribe not only quality standards but also specific meat inspection protocols; that would require regulators to know what protocols will be effective and to inspect not only the quality of what leaves the meat-packing plant but also what happens inside the plant. The right answer might be a finely tuned mix of *ex post* and *ex ante* approaches, as each may have strengths that offset the other's vulnerabilities.[6] Still, there is tension between the two approaches and a debate at least over the emphasis to be placed on each.

The basic question whether to look inside the "black box" or only at outputs recurs within debates about competing *ex post* and *ex ante* regimes respectively. Within the *ex post* regime of tort law, the "black box" approach maps onto arguments for strict liability (versus negligence) and for entity-level liability (versus individual agent liability). Strict liability at the entity level is supposed to induce the organization and its managers to adopt the appropriate technological and organizational precautions and to manage and discipline individuals accordingly. By contrast, liability rules that give firms credit for taking precautions—like negligence or like the *Faragher-Ellerth* defense under Title VII—require courts to look inside the organization to judge the adequacy of those procedures. And within *ex ante* regulatory regimes, traditional enforcement takes more of a "black box" approach, whereas regulated self-regulation looks inside the box. Traditionally, if the firm violates substantive *ex ante* rules of conduct —for example, by failing to use required safety devices—then it is penalized without regard to whether it had in place internal controls that sought to prevent this failing or alternate safety precautions that were equally effective. Of course, *ex ante* rules like this require regulators to look inside the firm in a physical sense, dictating certain precautions and punishing their absence. But traditional regulators did not look behind the results of inspections at the firm's workplace safety systems; they treated the *organization* as a "black box." A system of regulated self-regulation, by contrast, requires some assessment of the organization's internal rules and practices in deciding how to respond to the results of inspections (or in deciding whether or how often to inspect, a decision that raises further complications that are taken up below).

A "black box" approach that holds firms fully accountable for outputs, and leaves them to figure out the most efficient technological and organizational controls, may seem sensible in the face of galloping technological change and increasing organizational complexity, both of which make it harder for regulators to see what is going on inside firms, much less to judge what processes and precautions are likely to be effective in controlling wrongdoing. Judges and regulators may be better equipped and more willing to judge outputs than to delve into and assess the efficacy of internal controls (especially when those controls have failed).[7]

Unfortunately, the "black box" approach in its starkest form has its own vulnerabilities. We may put aside for now the risk that firms may be able to escape *ex post* liabilities through insolvency or dissolution. And let us put aside for the moment evidence that human beings' responses to regulatory sticks and carrots diverge from the economists' notion of rationality. There is another more basic problem with relying on strict entity-level liability to deter wrongdoing and produce good outcomes: firms may be able to reduce their liabilities not only by improving outcomes but by concealing bad ones. Strict entity-level liability may actually *discourage* firms from instituting policing measures or complaint procedures that bring wrongdoing to light.[8] That is a risk with relying solely on the external policing of corporate conduct and punishment of bad outcomes and an important argument in favor of duty-based regimes that explicitly reward internal reporting and policing procedures.

On the other hand, if we do not know what to look for in an internal compliance system or whether we can reliably recognize it, then rewarding firms for having such a system (by reducing either liability or outside scrutiny) may invite deregulation behind the pretense of compliance activity. The move toward regulated self-regulation has often proceeded with too little regard for those concerns and allowed firms to get by with "cosmetic compliance"—paper policies that fail to vindicate public norms and fail to improve outcomes.[9] For example, a firm that maintains an official policy of encouraging employees to report wrongdoing internally but covertly discourages such reporting may conceal most wrongdoing while earning reduced penalties for any wrongdoing that is uncovered. So the problem of firms reducing their liability by concealing wrongdoing does not disappear and may even be exacerbated under a regime that rewards compliance policies without ensuring that they actually work.

Deepening Democracy: New Governance and Reflexive Law

The deterrence model does not depend on human behavior corresponding precisely to the "rational actor" model as long as deviations are minor or random. But mounting evidence of broadly predictable deviations from the rational actor model is more disruptive.[10] For example, it seems that treating "good citizens" as would-be lawbreakers to be motivated by carrots and sticks, as the deterrence model does, may suppress civic impulses and foster resistance.[11] If individuals and organizations can actually internalize public values—if some individuals have consciences and civic impulses and some organizations have civic cultures that counter base self-interested calculations—then a great deal rides on discovering whether and how a regulatory regime can be structured to help foster those tendencies (while still deterring the basely self-interested). More broadly, the sheer size and complexity of modern organizations cast doubt on the ability of regulators to steer them through simple deterrence-based strategies.

Responding to concerns such as these, a growing number of scholars have become convinced of the need to energize and motivate regulated actors themselves to collaborate in shaping and enforcing regulatory norms.[12] The proponents of "New Governance" aim to replace rigid, uniform, centralized, and adversarial approaches that grew up in and after the New Deal with more flexible, responsive, cooperative, decentralized, and democratic forms of social control over market actors.[13] (The New Governance posture toward *ex post* liability regimes is less developed and more ambivalent.) Within this emerging cluster of ideas, two interlocking themes are central: the idea of "decentering the state" and elevating the regulatory role of other nongovernmental actors, including regulated entities themselves; and the idea of "reflexivity" in law—of replacing direct regulatory commands with efforts to shape self-regulation and self-governance within organizations.[14] New Governance scholars also share a belief that regulated actors—both individuals and organizations—are not simple rational utility maximizers and are not motivated solely by carrots and sticks. Individuals have consciences and organizations have cultures, and both can be shaped and steered by intelligent regulators and regulatory regimes.

New Governance ideas have only recently begun to gain adherents among American labor and employment law scholars.[15] That is surprising, for New Governance thinking itself has drawn heavily from regulatory experience within the workplace—mainly in occupational safety and health—here and abroad.[16] Moreover, its unifying themes should sound familiar to those versed in the American law of the workplace, especially in the system of collective bargaining. Collective bargaining is decentralized and non-state-centered, and it is potentially flexible, responsive to local conditions and to changing needs, cooperative, and democratic. The New Deal proponents of collective bargaining proclaimed its superiority to centralized regulation of terms of employment, and they took for granted its superiority to litigation of workplace disputes. Now that the post–New Deal regime of regulation and litigation is wearing thin, it is worth taking a new look at unions and collective bargaining. But it is also worth looking elsewhere, for even under a reformed labor law regime it is unlikely, for reasons explored in the next chapter, that collective bargaining will reach more than a fraction of the workers who need and want better ways of resolving workplace disputes and greater collective influence at work. What is needed is a new paradigm of workplace governance that is compatible with and even conducive to unionization and collective bargaining but that is not wholly dependent on those institutions.

The forms of regulated self-regulation that are already emerging in the U.S., and that are chronicled in Chapters 4 and 5, exemplify forms of "reflexive law": both contractual code of conduct and monitoring strategies and the law that fosters internal corporate compliance regimes operate by "encourag[ing] actors within subsystems to internalize the general norm."[17] The "general norms" emanate from outside the organization—from the society and usually the democratic political process; the goal of regulated self-regulation is to induce firms to internalize, tailor, and realize those norms within their own organizations. Unilateral and negotiated codes of conduct and monitoring arrangements, as well as internal compliance and complaint structures, all purport to do just that: not just to deter violations of workers' rights and labor standards but to commit the regulated organization itself to those rights and standards. The organization becomes not just a target or object of the government's commands but a locus of governance. The rules that the organization itself takes on board and implements should accordingly fit better and more seamlessly into the organization's operations.

The biggest risk of relying too heavily on internal compliance regimes is that they will fit *too* comfortably within the institution, its reigning management, and its institutional culture. Internal compliance structures may reflect rather than combat internal norms of silence and conformity. They may sacrifice externally derived public norms when those clash with internal demands for higher profits and lower costs. They may be a sham, garnering insulation from public oversight that amounts to a kind of "self-deregulation." Forms of self-regulation in which the state retreats too far from its oversight function risk replicating inequalities between the parties and deflecting pressure that might otherwise lead to more effective forms of public regulation. These are the very questions that most concern both skeptics and thoughtful proponents of New Governance and "reflexive law" generally. Reflexive approaches to regulation, it is said, risk deferring too much to the autonomy of self-regulating institutions and perpetuating existing patterns and hierarchies that need disrupting from outside, specifically from the democratically accountable state.[18] These are also the questions that will occupy much of the remainder of this book.

But we must grapple with those questions without the comforting assumption that it is possible simply to reject the move toward self-regulation and to strengthen traditional top-down public enforcement (even with increased union representation). Workplace organizations are too numerous, too varied, and too complex, and production is too mobile and too global, to hope for traditional regulatory methods to do the whole job. There will simply never be enough inspectors to rely on public enforcement alone. Private litigation can pick up part of the slack, but only if liability rules are crafted to encourage the right kind of internal self-regulatory structures. The question is no longer whether to invest in self-regulatory mechanisms but how to make those mechanisms effective in improving labor standards and work lives.

So whether the object is compliance with employment law or environmental law or securities law and whether we use the lens of deterrence or the lens of "New Governance," it appears that efforts to get firms to comply with external law face a general challenge: how can society encourage effective self-regulation and cultivate corporate responsibility without being fooled by the pretense of self-regulation? Can the public tap into the prodigious regulatory resources inside private firms and channel them toward the advancement of public values while guarding against cheating or "cosmetic compliance"? If we can discover reliable principles and mechanisms for effective self-regulation that cannot be feigned, then we have the makings of not only New Governance but better governance. If not, then it may make sense to marshall limited public regulatory resources toward the better detection and punishment of bad outcomes.

In any event, the law-and-economics-inspired deterrence model should not be cast aside. As a descriptive matter, that model is not much concerned with organizational culture or individual conscience and psychology. And as a normative matter, issues of democratic participation and accountability, central to New Governance scholarship and to this project, still lie largely outside the deterrence model's field of vision. But within its field of vision, the law-and-economics scholarship brings sharpness and acuity that may complement the insights of New Governance scholarship. In particular, it may help to generate some usefully cold calculations about what it takes to deter the basely self-interested individuals and organizations that still populate the regulatory landscape. Fortunately, there is growing evidence of mutual recognition between these formerly remote, if not hostile, camps.[19] Among the chief mediators are the apostles of behavioral economics, who complicate the standard economic assumptions about human motivations and open the door to considerations of culture, norms, trust, and reciprocity.[20] Democracy and participation may not be far behind.

RESPONSIVE REGULATION AND U.S. REALITIES

Among the analytical frameworks that aim to illuminate and shape the mega-trend toward self-regulation, that of Responsive Regulation is perhaps the most powerful. Responsive Regulation, as elucidated chiefly by Professor John Braithwaite and his collaborators, takes due account of "rational actor" models of behavior but is animated primarily by more complex human psychological and organizational dynamics that have been observed in many different regulatory domains and national settings.[21] The Responsive Regulation framework is also particularly well suited to addressing the problem of labor regulation.

Responsive Regulation and Meta-Regulation

A fundamental problem for regulators stems from the variety and complexity of human motivations among regulated actors.[22] In short, there are both "good guys" and "bad guys" among regulated actors, and there are many who could go either way, depending partly on the workings of the regulatory scheme. The good guys are inclined to do the right thing, in keeping with public values and standards, at least as long as it is economically viable to do so; the bad guys are inclined to exploit any opportunity to increase profits at the expense of public values and will respond only to regulatory sticks and carrots. But most regulated actors are somewhere in between: they may go either way, depending in part on how regulators treat them and whether good behavior is rewarded and bad behavior is punished. In other words, dispositions toward compliance with regulatory norms are both *heterogeneous* and *endogenous*: they are varied, and they respond to the regulatory environment. Both variety and responsiveness to the regulatory environment can be observed within industries as well as within firms. Some firms foster a culture of corporate citizenship; others defect from public standards whenever it profits them. Within firms, some individuals are more committed to doing the right thing than others. Even individuals may find that their consciences speak to them in more than one voice.[23] And both firms and individuals may shift their disposition one way or the other depending on how the regulatory winds blow.

These dynamics pose a challenge for regulators, particularly in a world of scarce enforcement resources. A system of regulation that assumes that all regulated actors are self-interested opportunists who will respond only to carrots and sticks will waste resources on those who seek to do the right thing, and it may provoke a backlash of resistance and squander the goodwill and the vast regulatory resources within those actors. Good citizens want to be treated like good citizens and may retreat into a more grudging mode of compliance, or even resistance, if they are treated like potential cheaters. Yet a system that assumes instead that regulated actors are well intentioned and seek to abide by the law—such as a system of wholesale self-regulation—invites the more opportunistic actors to cheat. That puts competitive pressure on would-be law abiders, breeds resentment, and erodes trust and norms of good citizenship.[24]

The regulatory solution proposed by Braithwaite is the establishment of a pyramid of enforcement mechanisms, from the least interventionist form of self-regulation and self-reporting at the bottom of the pyramid to the most punitive sanctions—the "benign big gun"—at the top.[25] The choice of enforcement mechanism is based on the behavior of the regulated entity and is subject to change based on new experience: Compliance is rewarded with less adversarial and more cooperative, firm-based enforcement strategies. Noncompliance or cheating is met with the escalation of regulatory scrutiny and sanctions, followed by either further escalation in response to chronic noncompliance or a return to cooperative strategies in response to improved compliance.[26] The pyramid should contain several incremental steps, for a system with just a few regulatory tracks—for example, one cooperative and one punitive—risks locking actors into adversarial patterns or allowing them to coast on an outdated record of cooperation because a switch in regulatory modes appears too drastic. And the pyramid should have a high peak, for the more onerous the highest penalty, the more pressure there is on regulated actors to cooperate and the more infrequently that penalty will have to be used. Braithwaite and co-author Ian Ayres describe the appropriate regulatory strategy as a version of the "tit-for-tat" strategy that game theorists have found to produce a cooperative equilibrium among repeat players in prisoner's dilemma–type games.[27]

A system that relies heavily on self-regulation and that encourages cooperation between regulators and regulated actors seeks to tap into a wealth of knowledge, experience, creativity, goodwill, and organizational efficacy within the firm. If those resources can be brought to bear on the enforcement of legal norms, then scarce public regulatory resources can be targeted at bad actors and leveraged into more thorough accomplishment of the public's regulatory aims. But such a system is also vulnerable both to cheating by reputedly compliant actors and to capture of regulators, who may indulge a preference for cooperation when it is not warranted.[28] That is where stakeholders—in the case of workplace rights and standards, employees—enter the picture.

Responsive Regulation seeks to guard against both cheating and capture in part by empowering third-party watchdogs that are independent of both regulators and the regulated and that represent the public interests that the particular regulatory scheme seeks to advance. It is a tripartite model of regulation.[29] Where the chief beneficiaries of regulation are outside the firm—as in the case of environmental or consumer safety regulation—public interest groups (PIGs) must represent those interests, mostly from the outside. But "[t]he simplest arena to understand how tripartite regulation would work is with occupational health and safety."[30] In that setting, a union and its "elected union health and safety representatives" participate in inspections, receive information, and initiate enforcement.[31] Ayres and Braithwaite suggest that "one could usefully grant the same rights to a nonunion safety representative elected at a nonunionized workplace," provided that one could ensure access to technical and legal assistance; for "[w]here there is no power base and no information base for the weaker party, tripartism will not work."[32]

Since the theory of Responsive Regulation was first fully set forth, Braithwaite and others have tested and elaborated its basic insights and prescriptions. Braithwaite has recently restated and refined the theory in response both to critics and to subsequent empirical research and developments.[33] First, Braithwaite recognizes that regulated actors vary radically not only in their disposition to comply with regulations, but also in their capacity to do so, and that small and marginally viable firms pose a serious challenge to any regulatory system, but especially to any system that relies heavily on firms' own self-regulatory capabilities. He suggests that the answer lies in the links between those small, marginal firms and the leading firms on which they are often economically dependent.[34] Second, Braithwaite recognizes that public enforcement often needs supplementing and that private litigation can play a useful regulatory role, especially if it can "mobilize two things that public enforcement fails to elicit: inside information and entrepreneurial legal talent."[35] He sees a potential model in American-style *qui tam* litigation, in which private citizens— usually employee (or ex-employee) whistleblowers who help identify and redress corporate misconduct against the government—and their attorneys can secure a portion of the large recoveries that sometimes result. By tapping both the organizational resources within supply chains and the enforcement resources inside firms and the private bar, the model of Responsive Regulation can extend the penetration of public norms in a world of scarce public enforcement resources.

Other scholars have also built on the lessons of Responsive Regulation. Based on her own and others' subsequent research, Professor Christine Parker strongly affirms the propositions that democratic control of corporate behavior depends on fostering effective corporate self-regulation and social responsibility, and that these depend in turn on the participation and empowerment of stakeholders.[36] Parker and others find strong evidence that deterrence and enforcement remain necessary components of a system of self-regulation.[37] Yet simple economic models of "deterrence" fail to capture the complexity of organizational motivations and give up too easily on the possibility of corporate virtue and good citizenship.[38] Focusing on the latter, Parker asks how well-intentioned managers, with the support of regulators, can create "the open corporation—the company that democratically self-regulates."[39] Democratic self-regulation at its highest stage requires what she calls "meta-regulation": corporations must "evaluate and learn from their own self-regulation performance and failures," and regulators must "test companies' self-evaluations, and learn from them how to improve law and regulatory practice."[40]

Self-regulation as it is conceived in Responsive Regulation (as well as meta-regulation) is not a substitute for public regulation. It bears little resemblance to the bland invocations of "voluntary compliance" of some employer advocates and allies.[41] Rather, it embeds self-regulation in a system of external and internal accountability—external accountability to public regulators with the power to impose coercive sanctions and internal accountability to the workers whose interests are at issue. And it situates self-regulation in a broader scheme in which traditional inspections, enforcement, and punitive sanctions continue to operate for the less scrupulous or less capable actors at the bottom of the labor market. Responsive Regulation and its conceptual cousins aspire to cultivating a culture of *responsibility* and respect for public norms inside regulated entities' public norms, but they do not neglect the need for deterrence. The question remains, however, whether Responsive Regulation is a viable model for workplace regulation in the United States.

Responsive Regulation of Workplace Rights and Standards

The problem of corporate compliance with workplace rights and labor standards is complicated—even more than Responsive Regulation theorists have recognized—by the fact that those laws protect employees who are inside the firm. We have already observed that employees play crucial and multiple roles in all internal compliance regimes. They are indispensable monitors of compliance, whether it is compliance with environmental or consumer safety or minimum wage laws. They are in a position to observe wrongdoing and are potential whistleblowers, both within and outside the firm.[42] Unfortunately, employees are vulnerable to pressure and retaliation from managers and supervisors.[43] Such reprisals are especially likely in regard to hazards or violations that are part of a firm's low-cost strategy of competition. So the law must be engineered both to induce firms to encourage and respond to employee reports instead of suppressing them and to protect employees who do report wrongdoing against reprisals.[44] Those challenges are endemic to the problem of corporate compliance.

But in the case of employment laws, employees play an additional role: they are the law's *beneficiaries* and the victims of noncompliance—the ones who face workplace hazards or discrimination or are denied overtime pay. That can make employees more effective monitors of compliance with employment laws than they are in the case of other laws. Workers are not only on the scene and well informed about workplace conditions, but they are also motivated to represent their own interests within the firm. Of course, employees still face collective action problems. For the most part, the law of the workplace secures "public goods" within the workforce or some subset of it. Employees as a group share in the benefits of compliance, and the benefits of compliance to employees as a group, as well as the costs of compliance to employers, are much larger than the benefit to any one employee.[45] No one employee can realize the full benefits of his or her individual efforts to improve labor standards, and so such efforts are likely to be inefficiently low. That is most obviously true with regard to the mitigation of health and safety hazards, but it is also true of wage and hour practices, leave policies, and even equal employment policies. When working conditions are dealt with by policies, any worker's effort to bargain for better conditions is encumbered by the expectation that improvements may have to be extended to others as well, while those others may stand by in hopes of free-riding on their co-worker's enforcement efforts. If that collective action problem can be overcome, however, activating employees within internal compliance systems has an even greater potential payoff for employment laws than for other laws.

Responsive Regulation thus appropriately insists on organized, institutional stakeholder representation. Within the internal self-regulatory regime, a union or other representative of employees functions not only as an independent third party but also as an integral constituent of the "self" that is charged with self-regulation. So employee representatives not only monitor self-regulation; they also participate directly within the self-regulatory process, helping to devise rules and standards, implement them, monitor compliance, take complaints, train employees, and the like.[46]

Unfortunately, the presence of employees inside the firm, and their consequent vulnerability to reprisals, raises the concern that employee representatives —if they, too, are entirely internal to the firm—might not be sufficiently independent of the firm to play their role as checks against cheating and capture. That suggests the need for a form of employee representation with a foot outside the workplace as well as inside. Unions fit the tripartite bill particularly well, for they are designed to capture the advantages of employees' inside position while meeting the challenges posed by both the "public goods" nature of workplace conditions and the problem of worker dependency and fear.[47] Unions supplant the need for individual workers to step forward with complaints and can protect workers against unwarranted discipline or discharge. They have, through their members, information about working conditions on the ground, and they can represent members' aggregate interest in improving them. They almost invariably bring job security—protection against arbitrary discipline and discharge, and thus against reprisals—as part of their package of contractual benefits.[48] Ayres and Braithwaite suggest non-union safety committees as an alternative, but they do not dwell on what that would mean and how it would work. Whether a non-union employee committee can serve these functions remains an open question to which we will return.

Employees' presence inside firms, and their vulnerability to reprisals, complicates the Responsive Regulation of labor and employment laws in another way as well. Our legal system relies heavily on the ability of a law's beneficiaries—injured consumers or aggrieved shareholders—to hold firms accountable for wrongdoing by complaining to regulators or filing lawsuits. As Braithwaite has recently recognized, the ability of victims, individually or collectively, to seek recourse through litigation is especially important in a system of self-regulation because it provides an additional outside check—beyond what overmatched public regulators can do—against internal compliance processes that do not work. But in the case of employment laws, there are no outside "private attorneys general." The laws' beneficiaries are employees, who are subject to the employer's authority and economic leverage (and are usually terminable at will). Employees may have a private right of action that is not formally subject to employer control, but it is no surprise that employees rarely sue their current employers. (Ex-employees sometimes sue, but their incentive to sue is skewed toward wrongful discharge–type laws and against laws that secure public goods. And, as discussed in Chapter 4, departing employees are often pressured to waive any legal claims as a condition of severance pay.) By and large, the victims of employer misconduct are a firm's current employees, over whom the employer exercises significant power. The vulnerability of employee complainants to employer reprisals is thus an even greater threat to effective self-regulation in the case of employment laws than with other laws.

Responsive Regulatory Theory Meets U.S. Regulatory Reality

The application of Responsive Regulation to labor regulation in the U.S. faces several hurdles: Can Responsive Regulation work in an environment of chronic underinvestment in the enforcement of labor standards? Can it work in the overwhelmingly non-union American workplace and in the face of the vehement anti-unionism of most American employers? Or would an effort to apply Responsive Regulation to U.S. reality founder on the shoals of underenforcement, union decline and anti-union animus, and the insecurity of employees terminable at will? Responsive Regulation turns out to be a useful starting point, but not the ending point, in the search for a framework for effective self-regulation.

THE ENFORCEMENT GAP AND THE LOW-WAGE SECTOR

While Responsive Regulation aims to make more efficient use of scarce enforcement resources, it still demands greater regulatory oversight and resources than are, or are perhaps ever likely to be, available to a regulatory agency like OSHA.[49] Many of the regulatory experiences on which Braithwaite draws are from a time and place (his home country of Australia) in which regulation was taken rather more seriously, at least as measured by resources and human capital, than in most of the U.S. labor standards arena. Ironically, some of the fieldwork on which Braithwaite based his Responsive Regulatory theory was done in the U.S. Mine Safety and Health Administration (MSHA).[50] But MSHA has traditionally maintained both a much higher density of inspectors and a bigger arsenal of penalties than does OSHA for the workplaces under its jurisdiction.[51] For example, unlike OSHA, MSHA is allowed to shut down an unreasonably dangerous workplace or mine. That is the quintessential "big gun" that can help steer employers onto the path of cooperation.

The low rate and modest cost of enforcement under both OSHA and other labor standards regimes in the U.S. defy one of the key prescriptions that Responsive Regulation shares with the deterrence model: the cost of noncooperation or "defection," primarily in the form of enforcement and sanctions, must be great enough to deter willful defectors and thus to protect cooperators against that demoralizing and injurious competition from the defectors. In other words, an effective system of self-regulation relies on an effective system of public regulation to catch the laggards, the defectors, and the cheaters. Ideally, "[n]on-compliance comes to be seen (accurately) as a slippery slope that will inexorably lead to a sticky end."[52] But without a serious escalation in labor standards enforcement—one that increases both the probability that violations will be detected and the penalties for serious violations—an effort to apply the tenets of Responsive Regulation might end up masking what amounts to a process of deregulation.

As discussed in Chapter 3, underenforcement (as well as low union density) has allowed employers in many sectors to pursue a low-wage, low-cost strategy and to put competitive pressure on more responsible firms. The linchpin of this strategy in many low-wage sectors is the employment of undocumented immigrants, who have few market alternatives and can be intimidated into silence. The size and persistence of the low-wage sector in the U.S. on the periphery of the formal economy, and typically in chronic violation of employment, immigration, and taxation laws, is striking in comparison with most other developed and wealthy economies.[53] Many of the firms in this sector have not even the pretense of "corporate compliance" programs; they are not walking the walk or talking the talk but are simply hiding in the dark and neglected corners of the labor market. These firms thus pose the most frontal challenge to efforts to increase reliance on self-regulation in the labor standards arena.

All is not hopeless. A renewed commitment to enforcement at the federal level and a resurgence of union organizing among low-wage workers would improve compliance and fortify the foundations for Responsive Regulation as well. We have also seen the emergence of novel initiatives by state regulators and worker organizations, sometimes in tandem, that target precisely these low-road firms. Further possibilities lie in the many economic linkages between large, visible, and organizationally competent firms and the smaller, marginal, low-road firms that often supply them. We began to glimpse in Chapters 4 and 5 the possibilities of expanding accountability—social and legal—down the supply chain and of tapping the regulatory resources within large firms to police smaller firms within their supply chains. Braithwaite has absorbed these possibilities into his own vision of Responsive Regulation, and we will return to them below.[54]

The problem of underenforcement might also be mitigated by the expanded use of private litigation. Until recently, private litigation was a distinctly American wild card that tended to be neglected by most regulatory theory—or at least that which emanated from outside the U.S. But the rest of the world has recently discovered the use of private litigation, especially aggregate litigation, to serve regulatory objectives.[55] Braithwaite has focused upon the even more distinctly American device of *qui tam* litigation—a kind of formalized bounty-hunting by internal whistleblowers—as ripe with regulatory possibilities. The U.S. remains particularly well equipped to pursue private enforcement litigation, as it is well staffed with the entrepreneurial lawyers who play a crucial supporting role.

But public enforcement is still crucial. That is especially true in the low-wage sector, where private litigation is least lucrative and is bound to be rare. Public enforcement is especially essential in health and safety, where there are virtually no private rights of action in sight, at least for now. (Recall that OSHA does not authorize, and in fact preempts, private litigation to enforce health and safety standards and that workers' compensation laws almost completely displace personal injury tort actions.) Public resources could be more effectively aimed at sectors and employers whose noncompliance is most chronic or serious.[56] But better targeting of existing public enforcement activity would not eliminate the problem of underenforcement. Unless regulators' sights are to remain permanently fixed on the targeted sectors and employers, they need to come up with strategies to secure compliance that do not depend on intensive continuing oversight—something to leave behind as they move on to a different set of targets. Those structures will need to draw on nongovernmental regulatory resources, both within and outside the regulated firms. The theory of Responsive Regulation suggests that targeted enforcement may be best deployed as leverage to induce firms to accept otherwise unacceptable conditions that aim to ensure future compliance.

THE REPRESENTATION GAP: NON-UNION WORKPLACES
AND ANTI-UNION EMPLOYERS

Beyond the challenge of driving and managing a system of effective self-regulation in a context of chronic underenforcement, another challenge is how to adapt tripartism to predominantly non-union American workplaces. In workplaces in which unions exist, theory predicts and experience shows that their participation in self-regulatory programs makes such programs more effective.[57] Where unions exist, their meaningful participation in self-regulatory programs should be one condition for a firm's gaining whatever regulatory concessions follow from effective self-regulatory programs. Unions' participation is indeed required, where they exist, in OSHA's Voluntary Protection Program (VPP), described in Chapter 4.

Therein lies the rub, however. Unions exist in too few workplaces in the U.S. to serve as the only vehicle of employee representation. It would be possible to say that the only internal compliance programs that should be accorded any legal recognition—any more cooperative enforcement procedures, any relief from the harshest penalties—are those in which unions participate as the exclusive collective bargaining representative of employees. But the trend toward regulation of self-regulation has too much momentum, and already reaches too far, to be confined to the 8 percent or so of the private-sector workforce that is unionized, or even to the larger percentage that might gain union representation with a reformed labor law and a reinvigorated labor movement. Unless we find ways to make self-regulation effective beyond the small union sector, we are more likely to end up with ineffective forms of self-regulation than to curtail the spread of self-regulation altogether. The challenge is to find mechanisms of effective self-regulation for the non-union workplace that facilitate, or at least do not impede, the emergence of unions and union-like forms of self-organization.

The simplest way to implement tripartism in a non-union setting, and the suggestion of Ayres and Braithwaite, is to require the creation and participation of non-union employee committees. But that answer confronts several problems, at least in the American context. In short, internal employee committees that are not scrupulously independent of the employer (and that do anything more than funnel "suggestions" to the employer) are generally unlawful under the NLRA's "company union" ban (described in Chapter 2) and are unlikely in any case to be adequate employee representatives within a self-regulatory framework. Yet employee committees that are scrupulously independent of the employer will be vehemently resisted by employers who fear anything that might resemble or lead to unionization. The pivotal and complex question of how to assure effective employee representation within a system of self-regulation in the U.S. is the subject of the next chapter.

Unfortunately, the problem of employer aversion to independent employee representation interacts with the problem of chronic underenforcement in a way that is potentially fatal to the central thesis of this book. The thesis is that effective self-regulation requires effective employee representation and that the law should therefore condition the legal benefits of self-regulation on the existence of genuine employee representation. That is how the trend toward regulated self-regulation can become both an effective regulatory system and a vehicle for new forms of workplace governance that empower workers. At its core, a system of self-regulation proposes a *quid pro quo* in which the advantages of a cooperative self-regulatory approach are held out as a reward for and an inducement to good behavior. But the conditions for entry into the self-regulatory arena can be only as demanding or as costly as the tangible and intangible rewards of self-regulation. A requirement of independent employee representation would sharply raise the perceived cost of opting into the self-regulatory system; the resulting costs might well outweigh the rewards of self-regulation as long as the default regulatory regime entails such a low risk and cost of enforcement. For most U.S. employers most of the time, the expected cost of public enforcement may be too low to justify taking the risk that they associate with independent employee representation. Without a greater background threat of enforcement and sanctions, it will therefore be difficult to induce most employers to take meaningful steps toward independent employee representation within a system of self-regulation.

One lesson is that employees' access to independent representation cannot be left to the discretion of employers, even with the extra inducement of a more cooperative regulatory regime. This is another reminder of the need for labor law reform that enables employees who want independent union representation to overcome employer resistance and demand a role in workplace governance. Still, the ideal of genuine tripartism—in which strong and independent unions represent employees vis-à-vis both their employers and regulatory agencies—is an elusive aspiration in the current political and labor relations climate in the U.S. We need to consider alternative mechanisms for making self-regulation work and alternative ways to secure an effective employee voice within a system of self-regulation. These are the issues to which we will return in Chapter 7.

EMPLOYMENT AT WILL

The idea of self-regulation depends on insiders speaking up—monitoring compliance, pointing out problems, and seeking improvements. Yet those insiders, as employees of the monitored firm, may fear that speaking up will put their jobs in peril. In most of the developed world, employees enjoy a measure of job security, and of legal protection against unjustified discharge, even without whatever added protections a union may bring.[58] But of course the background rule in the U.S. is the opposite: absent either contractual job security or some specific legal prohibition on particular grounds for discharge, employment is terminable at will, for any reason or no reason at all. Union representation and collectively bargained job security help to mitigate employees' fear that speaking up will lead to reprisals; that is one reason that the "representation gap" poses a problem for a system of effective self-regulation.

The background rule of employment at will has important implications for applying Responsive Regulation, or any general theory of effective self-regulation, to the U.S. Indeed, the background expectation of job security enjoyed by employees in most of the developed world may be one of the unspoken assumptions behind Responsive Regulation. Crafting a system of self-regulation in the U.S. requires, at a minimum, greater attention to protecting employees who speak up from employer reprisals. That problem calls to mind—at least to the American mind—the solution of whistleblower protections. But crafting effective whistleblower protections—that is, ex post remedies for whistle-blowers who suffer reprisals—is neither simple nor sufficient to open up channels of internal and external communication about wrongdoing. We will return to the problem briefly below and again in Chapter 8. For now it is enough to note that making self-regulation work in the U.S. workplace will require special attention to the problem of affording individual employees the security they need to play their crucial roles as day-to-day monitors of compliance.

The prescriptions of Responsive Regulation risk running aground on the shoals of some troubling U.S. realities—the enforcement gap, the representation gap, and the job security gap. In that light, let us turn to some alternative perspectives on regulation that might offer lessons on how to retrofit Responsive Regulation to the U.S. setting.

REGULATING IN A REGULATORY VACUUM: RATCHETING LABOR STANDARDS

As discussed in Chapters 4 and 5, the global anti-sweatshop movement has confronted the problem of regulating some of the lowest of low-wage workers in the virtual absence of both local state enforcement and employee representation. That movement and its very partial success have drawn the interest of Braithwaite and other theorists who are seeking to generate models of regulation for a post-command-and-control world.[59] Archon Fung, Dara O'Rourke, and Charles Sabel have made that experience the foundation for a new approach to regulation of labor standards that they call "Ratcheting Labor Standards" (RLS).[60] Like Responsive Regulation, RLS relies on both the internal regulatory capacity of firms themselves and third-party nongovernmental organizations (NGOs). But unlike Responsive Regulation, RLS does not count on the state to monitor, inspect, or sanction employers or to regulate their self-regulation; nor does it depend on independent representation of the employees whose working conditions are at stake. Those may turn out to be problems for the theory of RLS; but at the same time, RLS may suggest ways to improve domestic enforcement of employee rights and labor standards in the face of chronically inadequate regulatory oversight and a severe representation gap.[61]

Ratcheting Labor Standards
in Global Sweatshops

RLS is founded on the recognition that the large transnational enterprises at the top of the manufacturing pyramid—the brands and branded retailers—have prodigious regulatory capabilities with regard to their chain of suppliers, including those at the bottom rungs of the global production hierarchy. Those regulatory capabilities can be tapped and channeled toward the goal of improving labor standards by creating mechanisms of transparency and exploiting the large enterprises' vulnerability to public and consumer pressure. Firms can be induced to compete with each other on the basis of their labor standards while monitoring organizations compete with each other on the basis of the quality of their monitoring.[62] The goal is not "compliance" with fixed labor standards but "continuous improvement."[63]

As with Responsive Regulation, a focal point of regulatory activity is within firms themselves, specifically within transnational corporations. But in this case, the firms regulate not just themselves but also their suppliers. Those corporations have, by necessity, developed effective systems to monitor and coordinate the activities of far-flung contractors and subcontractors.[64] They have done so in pursuit of the optimal trade-off between quality and cost. It is of course the cost side of that equation that may tend to produce a race to the bottom in labor standards. But to the extent that improved labor standards can go hand in hand with higher quality, greater agility, and ultimately productivity, the same competitive imperatives can help generate improvement, if not quite a race to the top, in labor standards.[65]

A crucial driver within RLS, however, is consumer solidarity with workers and repugnance toward exploitative practices. Transnational corporations have enormous investments in their brands, making them highly sensitive to the negative publicity that can follow the exposure of exploitative labor practices among their suppliers.[66] To brand-conscious corporations, bad publicity—and the loss of prestige, sales, and share price that can follow—can be more potent sanctions than those wielded by regulatory agencies. These pressures can induce corporations to enter into codes of conduct that commit them to enforce international and domestic labor rights and to improve labor standards beyond what either body of law mandates and to submit to a system of outside monitoring that would both verify progress and permit comparison of labor standards with the highest-performing firms operating under similar conditions.[67]

A central element of RLS is transparency—that is, the transmission of reliable information about labor practices and conditions from the bottom layers of the supply chain (located mostly in remote, poor, developing nations with weak regulatory institutions) to the public and the customers of the multinational corporation in the developed world. The reliability of that information depends, in turn, on the transparency of monitoring regimes and protocols, so that consumers and watchdog organizations can compare the performance of monitors.[68] Transparency enables comparison, and comparison engenders competition and improvement.

So the crucial actors in RLS, apart from the multinational firms themselves, are consumers, a critical mass of whom must be mobilized to punish brands associated with unusually poor labor practices and to support brands associated with decent labor practices; and NGOs, which serve both as monitors, inspecting and certifying labor conditions with the cooperation of firms, and as advocates, publicizing good and especially bad labor practices. According to Fung, O'Rourke, and Sabel, together these actors can drive a race to the top—a competition in improved labor standards—among brand-conscious multinational corporations. The prodigious internal resources of the multinationals, together with the power of publicity and consumer pressure, largely supplant governmental oversight and compulsion in an economy that moves faster and reaches further than any government can.

RLS has powerful virtues. It explicitly engages the complexities of modern global manufacturing supply chains and seeks to harness the resources of the largest, most visible, and most competent (if not always civically virtuous) corporate actors to regulate the less competent and less visible entities through which they get most of the labor that goes into their products. It is a scheme of self-regulation in which the "self" encompasses the network of firms that make up the supply chain in much of the manufacturing sector. Engaging those networks and the economic interdependencies that suffuse them allows for the expansion of self-regulation from the good corporate citizens (who qualify for self-regulation under Responsive Regulation) to the smaller and more marginal firms at the bottom of the labor market, where labor standards are usually most degraded.[69]

One vulnerability of the scheme lies in its dependence on the sympathy of Western consumers and their potentially fickle sense of outrage and complicity over sweatshop conditions.[70] One problem is that consumer sympathies are most readily engaged with regard to goods that they or their children consume directly, like shoes, apparel, and toys; only a subset of the world's worst factories produce such goods. Even then, many consumers may prefer to ignore the conditions under which their sneakers and T-shirts are produced. The system's dependence on consumer sentiment is due in turn to the lack of coercive state authority to reliably discipline the outlaws and opportunists (as well as the virtual absence of independent union representation in the producer countries themselves).

Of course, where there is no viable regulatory alternative, an RLS-like system may not have to work very well to be worth supporting. But where there is a reasonably competent regulatory regime, as there is within the United States, it does not make sense to sidestep it altogether in favor of a private monitoring regime. Agencies like OSHA and the DOL's Wage and Hour Division are potentially capable, when they set their sights on an employer, of undertaking investigations, imposing sanctions, and enforcing judgments. The problem within the U.S. is underenforcement: inadequate density of enforcement activity and sometimes inadequate remedial or punitive tools. So let us consider the lessons of RLS and the global factory-monitoring regimes for the U.S. labor standards regime.

RLS and Responsive Regulation: Points of Convergence and Divergence

There are important points of convergence between Responsive Regulation and RLS. Both recognize and seek to mobilize the vast regulatory resources that lie within the modern firm. Both diverge from the "command" feature of command and control, adopting instead a quasi-contractual approach to regulation: firms agree, under certain constraints, to submit to standards of conduct and self-regulatory protocols that go beyond the law's minimum standards and its enforcement regime. Both Responsive Regulation and RLS represent efforts to make self-regulation effective, in part by designating nongovernmental actors to play crucial roles safeguarding the interests of workers and the public. The two models diverge, however, on the roles of the state, outside monitors, and worker representation.

Public enforcement through government coercion, rarely used but always on call, plays a pivotal role in Responsive Regulation, while it is absent from RLS.[71] Indeed, the private and stateless code of conduct approach to regulating working conditions in developing countries has been criticized on the ground that it not only ignores but also circumvents and potentially undermines local governmental regulators.[72] At a minimum, governmental powers and institutions, where they exist, can be brought into the RLS equation in helpful ways, while NGOs might help to fill the partial regulatory vacuum that frustrates the full implementation of Responsive Regulation in the United States (and elsewhere). A hybrid approach might thus expand the role of outside, nongovernmental actors to the extent that both the role and efficacy of government diminish.

A related point of divergence between the two models is the nature of the monitoring entity that both would require. Responsive Regulation would have stakeholder (employee) representatives such as unions monitor the firm's self-regulation, while RLS implicitly assumes employees have no collective representation and appoints outside entities to perform the monitoring. Experience under factory codes, as we have seen in Chapter 4, makes it clear that outside monitoring is no panacea. It is no substitute for a strong and institutionalized culture of compliance within the regulated entity. But in a regulatory environment in which public oversight and enforcement are in short supply and wrongdoing may be easily concealed behind the trappings of compliance, outside monitoring is an enormously promising institution, albeit one that needs scrutiny and reform.

One reason outside monitoring has often proven ineffectual in the labor standards setting is that it has operated without the active involvement of workers themselves. Effective monitoring requires the participation of workers. But the converse may also be true: participation of workers, at least in the non-union setting, may require the support of outside monitors. Outside monitors may be able to supply some of the independence and expertise that unions supply within Responsive Regulation's tripartism but that are missing from the non-union and anti-union workplaces that predominate within the United States. Indeed, if done right, monitoring may help to liberate employee voice, individual and collective, where there is no independent organized representative with a foot outside the workplace. I will return to this possibility in Chapter 8.

The two models also diverge with respect to the identity and role of the stakeholder representatives. Responsive Regulation insists on empowering representatives of the primary regulatory beneficiaries—workers in the case of labor standards laws. While RLS seeks to engage a variety of nongovernmental actors as monitors and advocates, it is more hazy and less insistent about the role of the workers whose working conditions are at issue. Trade unions figure among possible advocates of RLS, monitors and proponents of improvement, and beneficiaries of its regime of transparency. But the workers whose working conditions are at stake do not play a central role in the scheme.[73] The inattention to worker involvement is a weakness not only of RLS in theory but also of private code of conduct schemes in practice.[74] In developing countries with little or no governmental enforcement capacity or protection for workers' right to organize and speak for themselves, it may seem more realistic to turn instead to outside NGOs, which have the advantages of independence and the ear of wealthy consumers. Of course, outside groups lack the direct knowledge that workers themselves have about working conditions. So RLS relies on both advocacy organizations (who can supply independence and economic leverage) and monitoring organizations (who inspect workplaces and supply information to advocacy groups and consumers) to perform the functions that Responsive Regulation assigns to employees' own organizations.

But a consensus is emerging among participants in global anti-sweatshop schemes, including the proponents of RLS, that monitoring is not a substitute for employee voice. Monitoring can work effectively only if employees can speak for themselves, not just during but in between outside inspections. As one set of commentators put it, "Workers are the only people who can really know the everyday realities of the workplace so without their genuine involvement any system of monitoring has limited value."[75] The point was also made by a corporate director of human rights programs in China: "We have inspections of factories, both announced and unannounced. But you just don't have the assurance that things will be the same the next day. . . . The best monitors are the workers themselves."[76] Increasingly, global anti-sweatshop regimes seek to incorporate a role for worker voice and respect for workers' freedom of association into codes of conduct and monitoring protocols.[77] An effective labor standards regime in the U.S. will have to do this as well.

SHORING UP A SYSTEM OF AUDITED
SELF-REGULATION: LESSONS FROM
CORPORATE LAW

Some of the special difficulties in applying Responsive Regulation and RLS to the American law of the workplace arise from the peculiarities of the workplace, but others arise from peculiarities of the American legal context. As such, we may learn additional lessons from one American system of monitored self-regulation that is well established and, of late, widely debated: the system of financial reporting and audited self-regulation in publicly traded corporations.

While the analogy may seem strained at first, the problem of securities fraud and corporate self-dealing is parallel in some ways to the problem of disregard for labor standards: the pressure to maximize profits (or apparent profits) tempts managers to cut corners, hide problems, and disregard legal constraints. Knowledge of legal transgressions is hidden from public view and mostly confined to insiders within complex organizations. The employees who have that knowledge and might be moved to expose illegal conduct may be economically dependent on the transgressors within the organization and vulnerable to reprisals. And public enforcement of the law is episodic at best.

Of course, at that level of generality, the problem is roughly that of organizational compliance with legal constraints generally. We have already identified some distinctive aspects of the problem of organizational compliance with laws that protect employees, and there are distinctive aspects of the problem of organizational compliance with laws that protect shareholders as well. Still, the traditional system of safeguards against corporate fraud and insider self-dealing, and recent legislative efforts to strengthen that system, may suggest some useful elements of an American system of effective self-regulation that we have missed to this point.

Since the early New Deal, the law's basic solution to the problem of hidden corporate self-dealing and securities fraud has been a system of mandatory disclosure and self-regulation.[78] Accurate information, properly digested and analyzed, should inform the market transactions that determine share prices and the corporation's ability to raise capital. Corporations will thereby be disciplined, investor confidence maintained, and shareholders protected. But the tasks of ensuring the accuracy of information and digesting and analyzing it are not left to the diffuse collection of shareholders and investors who are the main beneficiaries of the underlying laws and mandatory disclosures. Those tasks are divvied up among a variety of private actors who, together, largely supplant direct public enforcement.

The task of monitoring the accuracy of corporate reporting is assigned mainly to independent, publicly licensed auditors (themselves subject to a system of professional self-regulation) who must certify a firm's compliance with relevant standards of accounting and disclosure.[79] The task of interpreting and acting on the information that firms disclose and that auditors certify is effectively assigned by the market to large institutional investors and securities analysts with the incentive and ability to analyze the information.[80] And when things go wrong—when disclosures are false or misleading and investors are harmed—the law allows for private litigation. In particular, aggregate litigation on behalf of shareholders as a group is expected to help remedy and deter misconduct.[81]

In securities regulation as in the law of the workplace, the role of direct state regulation is minimal (by design or default), and the ability of individual beneficiaries to protect their own interests is beset by collective action problems. The integrity of this system of self-regulation thus depends on tapping into the incentives and capabilities of a variety of private actors and organizations outside the corporation; each plays some role in monitoring ongoing compliance or in holding the corporation accountable for noncompliance after the fact.

A wave of corporate scandals, epitomized by Enron, dealt a blow to the proponents of corporate self-regulation. But the primary legal response to those scandals, the Sarbanes-Oxley Act, relied less on new forms of public regulatory oversight than on refinements to the system of self-regulation. Sarbanes-Oxley sought to buttress the system of outside auditing and to combat the capture of auditors by imposing measures designed to ensure the professional independence of the auditors from the regulated firms.[82] It strengthened the oversight of auditors and imposed new constraints and liabilities on those auditors.[83] At the same time, legislators sought to tap into the enormous regulatory potential that resides within corporations themselves by encouraging employees to disclose wrongdoing. To that end, the law required companies to establish a system of internal reporting and mandated internal reporting by some high-level officers.[84] The law also prohibited reprisals against employee whistleblowers and backed that prohibition with both criminal sanctions and a private right of action with the full panoply of tort and equitable remedies: compensatory damages, back pay, reinstatement, attorneys' fees, and litigation costs.[85]

Sarbanes-Oxley thus sought to fortify an existing system of regulated self-regulation by combatting the capture of outside monitors and protecting and institutionalizing whistleblowing by employees—that is, by ensuring the independence and accountability of the outsiders looking in and by encouraging insiders to speak out. Congress backed up these measures with beefed-up criminal and civil penalties administered by the Securities and Exchange Commission (SEC).[86] But much as in the labor standards context, the perennial mismatch between agency resources and the number and complexity of the regulated actors ensures that the SEC and public prosecutors can play only the most episodic role in enforcement. While even an occasional criminal prosecution of a company or a top executive can pack a surprising deterrent punch, enforcement is assumed to come primarily from private securities litigation. Hence one potent criticism of the resulting scheme: Sarbanes-Oxley left intact the hurdles to private enforcement that were imposed by the Private Securities Litigation Reform Act of 1995 (PSLRA) and Supreme Court case law, and that weakened one of the important sticks that deterred both corporate insiders and gatekeepers from engaging in or tolerating abuse.[87]

Other critics of Sarbanes-Oxley criticize not its weakness but its strength, or rather the burdens of compliance, which have led some companies to opt out of the disclosure regime (and others to threaten doing so) by "going private" and tailoring their disclosures and audit practices to whatever private capital markets demand.[88] The option of self-deregulation through privatization may seem to disrupt the basic analogy to labor and employment laws, for employers have no comparable choice of opting out of those laws. But many firms do have the option of abjuring serious internal compliance efforts and taking their chances with a hit-or-miss default regime of traditional enforcement; some marginal firms may go off the books, and others may contract out some of their labor needs to firms that go off the books or have little exposure to detection and enforcement. The labor standards of those workers would then be governed by the labor market—by whatever it took to get the workers they needed—subject to the risk of getting caught.

In both cases, then, the relevant legal regimes are conventionally regarded as mandatory; yet firms may have some latitude to opt out of each regime if market forces permit and if the law's favored regime is seen as onerous. To whatever degree firms are able to opt for effective deregulation, both legal regimes are constrained in what they can demand of firms. In that respect, too, the two legal regimes of securities regulation and employment law run roughly parallel—and counter to the logic of Responsive Regulation, which encourages voluntary self-regulation in part by making the less cooperative path *more* onerous, and progressively more so as noncompliance becomes more egregious. It may be that the need for access to U.S. capital markets will keep the vast majority of corporations within the system of audited self-regulation (or that Congress will cut back on some of its requirements).[89] In the case of employment law, however, the "enforcement gap" might prove to be the Achilles' heel of efforts to construct a system of effective self-regulation for the workplace.

So with eyes wide open to the potential pitfalls ahead, let us draw from the experience with audited self-regulation in the securities context some tentative lessons for the development of an effective system of self-regulation of workplace rights and standards—for filling some of the gaps between the prescriptions of Responsive Regulation and the realities of the U.S. law of the workplace.

First, where public resources for inspections and oversight fall short—whether by design or by default—independent private monitors can help to fill that gap and to secure compliance with laws that firms and their managers are economically tempted to violate. Second, in view of that temptation, safeguards will be needed to prevent the capture of monitors by the monitored firms themselves. The safeguards adopted in the labor context may be quite different from those in the securities context, where billions of dollars may be at stake and where auditing is itself a multi-billion-dollar business. But the importance of independence, obvious as it might seem, requires close attention. Of course, this same lesson has been learned through experience with global supplier codes and factory monitoring; what the Sarbanes-Oxley example adds is a highly publicized, homegrown American illustration of the value of independent monitors and how the law can help secure their genuine independence from the monitored entity.

Third, because outside monitoring is inevitably only partial and episodic, employees themselves are essential day-to-day inside monitors. Yet individual employees who report misconduct are up against the distinctively American rule of employment at will. Sarbanes-Oxley takes a two-pronged approach to the problem by both requiring internal reporting mechanisms and reports by some high-level employees and protecting employee whistleblowers with strong overlapping remedies that are designed to deter retaliation. On paper, Sarbanes-Oxley represents the gold standard in protection of employee whistleblowers, with not only administrative enforcement but also criminal sanctions and fully compensatory private civil remedies against reprisals. Unfortunately, early returns suggest that administrative enforcement of the whistleblower provision (lodged, oddly, in OSHA because of its experience with whistleblower claims under the OSH statute) has been largely illusory.[90] Given this experience, as well as the limited resources of public agencies in the labor context, the Sarbanes-Oxley model of private rights of action for whistleblowers seems especially worthy of exploration.[91]

Employees function not only as monitors but also as beneficiaries of employment rights. Hence the fourth lesson from the homegrown American model of corporate self-regulation: liability rules and private litigation on behalf of both employee whistleblowers and victims of misconduct can supply some of the enforcement energy and motivation that is supposed to emanate from the state in Responsive Regulation but that chronically falls short in the

American law of the workplace. Private litigation may sometimes serve as a "big gun," the fear of which induces companies to take the path of cooperation and compliance. Litigation can fill that role only where there are both private rights of action and practical ways to pursue them. As in the securities context, that may require aggregate litigation. If the hurdles to private enforcement or aggregation are too high, as some observers believe is the case with shareholder litigation under the PSLRA, then so may be the expected gains from noncompliance.

Finally, the corporate self-regulation experience reinforces another main lesson of Responsive Regulatory theory: where the benefits of compliance are shared among a large number of beneficiaries, there must be some mechanism or institution that aggregates individual incentives to both monitor and enforce compliance. That might take place *ex post* through aggregate litigation, but it is also important for the beneficiaries to have some kind of organized or institutional presence in monitoring compliance *ex ante*. In the securities context that role has been assigned to independent members of the board of directors (other directors may be compromised by alliance with management and controlling shareholders) as well as to institutional investors—major institutions with a significant but not controlling stake in the company, whose interests are seen as largely aligned with those of individual small investors.[92] In the context of employment law, the workers are already inside the organization, but they need some mechanism for aggregating their individual voices and incentives to help secure the public good of compliance with labor and employment laws.

The trend toward regulated self-regulation already has a momentum and a scope—across areas of regulation and across regions of the world—that make it well nigh inexorable. We can shape it, but it is too late, and in any case misguided, to stop it. That, in any case, is the belief animating the proponents of New Governance and this book. The well-founded fear is that the trend toward regulated self-regulation will become, at least in the American workplace, a thinly disguised form of self-deregulation. The hope—bolstered and informed by several bodies of theory and experience surveyed here—is that it can be shaped into a workable regime for advancing public policy and workers' interests. The U.S. regime of workplace regulation is neither the well-staffed and vigilant regulatory regime that Responsive Regulation assumes as its starting point, nor the regulatory vacuum assumed by RLS and confronted by the global anti-sweatshop movement. Nor, obviously, do the problems of workplace regulation map precisely onto the problems that gave rise to the system of audited self-regulation under the securities laws. But all of these approaches teach useful lessons about how to tap into the regulatory resources inside private firms, and how to stimulate and channel self-regulatory activity toward the advancement of public values, without routine public regulatory oversight.

We will turn first to the need for institutions of collective representation of employees. A wealth of experience and theory from various quarters points to the conclusion that effective self-regulation of labor and employment laws requires effective representation of employees in the process of self-regulation. What is needed in the law and governance of the workplace is what I will call "co-regulation." The term is not original; it has been used before to describe collaborate processes of self-regulation in which stakeholders are integrally engaged.[93] Co-regulation in the present context means a process of self-regulation of labor standards and employee rights, at the firm or workplace level, in which the workers whose rights and labor standards are at issue themselves participate in the self-regulatory process through some form of independent collective representation. But what form can that realistically take? That is the question to which we now turn.

Chapter 7 Employee Representation: Old and New Ways of Aggregating and Amplifying Employees' Voices

The workers whose rights and working conditions are governed by labor and employment law need an effective, independent, collective voice both to empower them within the self-regulatory processes on which courts and regulators are increasingly inclined to rely and to invoke the support of regulators, courts, and the public when self-regulatory processes fail. The yawning representation gap and shrinking union membership in the U.S. thus pose perhaps the greatest challenges to efforts to shape trends toward self-regulation into an effective regulatory regime. At the same time, the trend toward regulated self-regulation offers a potential strategy for addressing that representation gap. The basic strategy is to offer employers valuable self-regulatory privileges and defenses, as well as reputational benefits, in exchange for their maintenance of internal compliance structures that the law deems adequate, including effective employee representation. The movement toward self-regulation may offer a new source of traction in efforts to afford workers a meaningful voice in the workplace and may open the door to new forms of self-governance.

What is needed is a representational structure that overcomes the two major impediments to effective monitoring of compliance by individual employees: the fear of employer reprisals, subtle and overt, that deters employees from reporting deficiencies and seeking to address them, and the collective action hurdles to securing the "public good" of compliance with employment laws. Institutionally speaking, such representation calls for a vehicle that has a foot both inside and outside the workplace—inside the workplace to know what employees know, to aggregate their incentives to act, and to contribute to the firm's own internal processes of self-regulation; and outside the workplace to avoid employer pressure and reprisals, to expose the workplace to external scrutiny if necessary, and to provide a check against defective internal procedures. This chapter aims to give more concrete form to these abstract requirements.

Three basic institutions present themselves as candidates for the representation of employees within a system of regulated self-regulation: (1) union representation in the context of a traditional collective bargaining relationship; (2) internal workplace committees; and (3) worker centers or other worker advocacy organizations with an organizational locus outside the workplace. We have begun to glimpse some of the practical challenges facing each of these institutions of worker representation. In addition, American labor law poses challenges to the viability and efficacy of each of these institutions as an integral component of a system of regulated self-regulation.

UNION REPRESENTATION:
BARRIERS TO ORGANIZING AND
EXCLUSIVE COLLECTIVE BARGAINING

Under the twentieth-century paradigm of workplace governance, workers choose whether to be represented by a union by a majority vote within an "appropriate bargaining unit," usually within the confines of a single firm and a single facility. If the majority chooses union representation, that representation is "exclusive"—exclusive of bargaining by other labor organizations and by individuals on their own behalf. Union representation leads to collective bargaining, backed by economic pressure tactics by both sides, and is ordinarily expected to culminate in a collective bargaining agreement. The collective bargaining agreement governs the terms and conditions of the workers' employment and various aspects of workplace management and provides for the resolution of disputes under the agreement through a grievance-arbitration system. In a well-functioning collective bargaining relationship, formal contractual rights, remedies, and processes lead to the development of informal cooperation and union influence within the enterprise.

Traditional union representation within this framework, when and where it still exists, gives workers precisely the sort of independent collective representation that they need to hold up the third leg of an effective tripartite system of regulated self-regulation. With a presence and power base both inside and outside the particular workplace, with the resources and expertise that major unions have at their disposal, and with collectively bargained protections of job security and fair treatment, unions can overcome both the fear of reprisals and the collective action problems that impede employees' monitoring of compliance with laws enacted for their benefit.[1] Unions have been shown to improve employer compliance with health and safety requirements and to make self-regulatory innovations within the health and safety laws, such as mandatory employee safety committees, more meaningful and effective.[2] By incorporating legal entitlements such as workplace safety, nondiscrimination, and overtime pay into the collective bargaining agreement, unions afford an internal—and much more expeditious—procedure for enforcing those legal entitlements. Unions' role in improving compliance with employment laws is largely incidental to their collective bargaining functions, through which unions seek and achieve for employees more than compliance with minimum standards. They secure higher wages, nonmandatory employment benefits like pensions and health insurance, and job security, as well as a mechanism for resolving workplace disputes and a measure of collective influence within workplace governance. That is why so many workers—about one-third to one-half of the nonmanagerial, nonsupervisory workers who do not have a union, as well as nearly all of those who do—say that they would choose union representation if they had the chance.[3]

So how is it that unions now represent just 8.5 percent of the private-sector nonagricultural workforce?[4] And what are the prospects for revival? There is a vast literature on those questions.[5] While the fate of organized labor is not the primary concern here, it is worth a brief detour. As noted above, labor unions operating within a collective bargaining relationship are the ideal third leg of a tripartite system of regulated self-regulation. If unions can perform that role for most workers—say, under a reformed labor law—then exploring alternative institutions for employee representation may be a distracting sideshow. But if unions are unlikely, even with labor law reform, to reach more than a fraction of the workers who want and need representation, then it is critical to identify or construct alternative institutions of employee representation. That is not to take away from the pressing need for labor law reform but only to suggest that more is needed. With that in mind, let us turn to the question of what explains union decline, for the answer to that question will tell us much about the prospects for union growth.

Causes of Union Decline,
Clues to Unions' Future

One reason union membership is so low is that many of those who want union representation face the intimidating prospect of employer resistance, in legal and illegal forms.[6] Bruce Kaufman observes that the increasing intensity of employer resistance "was remarked upon by management specialists in the 1980s and has continued as 'union-free' status has become both more acceptable and attainable."[7] Quantifying the extent of employer intimidation and retaliation—even apart from measuring its impact on representation contests —has proven to be difficult and controversial. But statistical studies generally indicate that employer retaliation against union supporters has increased.[8] Kaufman contends that those studies "significantly understate the upward trend in the breadth, depth, and effectiveness of management opposition."[9]

Employer resistance, including retaliation and threats of retaliation, defeats many union organizing drives that do get off the ground, often at an early stage of organizing, long before any election. But the frustration of actual union organizing efforts is only the beginning of how employer resistance discourages unionization. Employees' recognition of their employers' intense opposition to unions discourages many from seeking or perhaps even desiring union representation in the first place. Even apart from a fear of reprisals against union supporters and even apart from the low probability of success in the face of intense employer opposition, employees may see too little upside to unionization under those circumstances. Employees may reasonably believe that even a successful union drive is less likely to yield significant gains and more likely to lead to conflict, animosity, and job losses if management is determinedly anti-union.[10] Union representation gives only the right to bargain and to exert economic pressure in support of bargaining demands, but the right to bargain with an employer that does not want, and is not required, to reach any agreement whatsoever may not seem worth the risks of a long and bitter battle for representation. So employer resistance to unions helps to explain not only the limited success of active organizing drives but also the limited enthusiasm that some employees feel toward union representation.

But what explains growing employer resistance? Much of the answer lies in economic factors, to which we will turn in a moment. But part of the reason employers resist unionization so aggressively is that they can. The labor laws do too little to regulate and deter aggressive and illegal forms of employer resistance. Chapter 2 flagged a number of persistent criticisms of the NLRA from the union side—in particular, the lawfulness of some inevitably coercive employer tactics, union organizers' banishment from the workplace, and the long delays and weak remedies with which the law meets illegal forms of coercion. Some observers dispute the role of both employer resistance and weak labor laws in explaining union decline.[11] But a careful recent review of the empirical literature on employer resistance and union decline suggests otherwise. According to Bruce Kaufman, "[a]nyone familiar with the world of work recognizes that the forces of weak labor law, determined employer opposition, and sometimes weak enforcement make successful organizing and winning first contracts a very difficult task" and have contributed to "the significant long-term decline in new workers organized and represented by unions."[12] There is thus a dire need for labor law reforms that make it easier for employees who want to form a union to do so and to bargain collectively for improvements in their working lives.

The current reform proposal, the Employee Free Choice Act (EFCA), contains three elements that would improve the prospects for employees who want union representation.[13] First, it would allow employees to express their choice by signing union authorization cards, without going through the formal election campaign that employers have used as an occasion for high-pressure anti-union propaganda and veiled or overt threats of job loss. Second, it would expand remedies and add penalties for the worst forms of anti-union coercion, especially for the discriminatory discharge of union supporters. Third, it would create a mechanism for mediation and binding arbitration of first contracts when collective bargaining fails to produce an agreement within a reasonable time.

This is not the place for a thorough examination of EFCA and its likely impact.[14] The main protagonists have made their views clear. Both organized labor and big business have invested heavily on the basis of their shared prediction that EFCA would lead to a significant upsurge in successful union organizing and first contracts.[15] Yet even if EFCA or some version of it does break through the political logjam that has blocked labor law reform for many decades, it is unlikely to unleash enough organizing activity in the foreseeable future to reach many of the workers who want and need collective representation in the workplace. Consider unions' own estimates of the impact of EFCA, according to Steven Greenhouse: "Some labor leaders predict that if the bill is passed, unions, which have 16 million members nationwide, would add at least five million workers to their rolls over the next few years."[16] Even if all of those new members were in the private sector, that would increase private-sector union density from under 8 percent to about 12 percent. Indeed, even a tripling of union membership would leave three-quarters of the private-sector labor force unrepresented. So labor law reform is the beginning, not the end, of a serious effort to address the "representation gap" in U.S. workplaces.

Perhaps the most important constraints on union density are economic. For many commentators, increased economic competition is a dominant cause of declining unionization and constraint on potential union growth.[17] Unionization is generally associated with higher costs and modestly lower profits.[18] That is largely due to the union wage premium—the higher wages and benefits—that are a major draw for would-be union members but also a major impetus for employer opposition.[19] Employees seek union representation, and employers oppose unions, for more than economic reasons: employees seek a stronger voice and a measure of security and liberty in their work lives; employers resist giving up unilateral managerial prerogatives; and both do so for reasons that go beyond the compensation package. But higher wages and benefits are still at the heart of the case both for and against unionization, and are, for some commentators, the single most important explanation for union decline. In an increasingly competitive market economy, they say, the union wage premium and its impact on profits will lead to stronger employer resistance, the failure or shrinkage of union firms, and the flow of capital to the non-union sector.[20]

Increased product market competition is not an alternative to employer resistance as a cause of union decline; it is said to largely *explain* employer resistance. In Michael Wachter's words, "[a]s long as unions raise labor costs in competitive sectors of the economy, unionized firms will continue to lose market share, managers in the nonunion sectors will continue to strongly resist unionization, and labor law reforms that facilitate unionization will remain unpopular."[21] According to Wachter, the upshot is that unions, if they seek a wage premium without "other offsetting economic advantages," are doomed to become a "niche movement," one that is confined to the public sector and to marginal sectors of the economy, "where individual firms or industries take advantage of either uninformed or immobile workers to enforce below competitive pay packages."[22]

The Wachter argument suggests a bleak forecast not only for union growth but also for any institution that seeks to enable workers in any particular workplace to seek higher wages and benefits. To be sure, the argument rests on some debatable premises and tractable policy components that, once revealed, may open a larger role for unions.[23] In particular, unions face a brighter future in locally bound service sectors and wherever they are able to generate "offsetting economic advantages" in the form of improvements in productivity and quality. Still, one finds no predictions of union growth that will be nearly large enough to fill the representation gap that both frustrates employee desires and impedes the development of effective forms of co-regulation in the workplace.

There is also the matter of employee preferences. Not all employees who want some form of collective representation at work want "union representation." The best available data suggest that many workers prefer a form of collective representation that is less adversarial, and less independent of the employer, than the NLRA contemplates.[24] Again, that is at least partly an adaptive preference—a by-product of employer resistance. But employer resistance is sure to continue and to discourage many workers from forming independent unions, even under a reformed labor law. And some employees appear simply to prefer a more collaborative form of participation than the law now allows. We will return to this issue in the next section.

Beyond Exclusive Representation: New Roles for Unions

Unions, operating within an exclusive collective bargaining framework, can and should play a significant role in representing employees, including within a system of regulated self-regulation. Beyond that, however, creative unions may be able to extend their reach by representing workers outside that framework on a nonexclusive basis.[25] One innovative strategy for existing unions would be to seek collective bargaining itself on a nonexclusive, members-only basis. Some unions, taking their cue from Professor Charles Morris, have sought to open that avenue.[26] Morris has argued that the NLRA originally contemplated (and, properly interpreted, still accommodates) union representation and collective bargaining on a members-only basis.[27] Whether or not that is a viable road to collective bargaining—and critics have questioned both the legality and practicality of members-only collective bargaining under the Act[28]—it may be worth another look as a form of worker representation within a system of self-regulation. So, for example, might a union, on behalf of its members within a particular workplace, have the right to demand payroll information or to participate in safety inspections? Not under a conventional understanding of existing labor law, for those rights turn on the union's status as a recognized exclusive bargaining representative of the workers.[29] Under even a trimmed-down version of Morris's thesis, however, those might be open questions.

Unions might also take on new roles as employee advocates at large. In a model they call "open-source unionism," Professors Richard Freeman and Joel Rogers propose that unions affiliate with workers as individuals or as less-than-majority groups of workers and offer services—including information, expertise, and even representation in the enforcement of workplace rights—outside the exclusive collective bargaining setting.[30] Freeman and Rogers put much emphasis on the ability to offer many of these services, and to create a network of union-friendly workers, at very low cost over the Internet. The idea of "open-source unionism," partially realized in the AFL-CIO's Working America project, recognizes that unions are well equipped to educate workers about their rights, assist workers in identifying violations, provide legal representation to employees seeking to vindicate their rights, alert public agencies to the existence of violations and pressure them to prosecute, publicize violations, and generate public and consumer pressure on violators. Through those activities, even outside a collective bargaining relationship, unions can serve as or oversee monitors within a system of co-regulation, as indeed they did in both the Greengrocer Code in New York and the Global Building Services settlement in California.[31] These activities may or may not lead to a traditional union organizing campaign for exclusive bargaining rights.

Nonexclusive union representation within self-regulatory systems might take a variety of other forms. Unions and union lawyers have launched private litigation to enforce workplace mandates in non-union firms and to induce firms to take prospective self-regulatory measures, as we will see in Chapter 9 below. Some unions are actively pursuing alliances with worker centers, or even creating worker centers, as we have seen in Chapter 5. Professor Matthew Finkin has suggested that unions might play a role within the employee health and safety committees that have proliferated in non-union firms, as discussed below.[32] There are, in short, a variety of ways in which existing unions might represent workers within self-regulatory systems both through and outside of exclusive collective bargaining relationships. (Whether they can find a way to support those activities outside the standard union dues structure is still an open question.) Still, we need to consider whether there are other institutions for worker representation that can help ensure the efficacy of the systems of self-regulation that are proliferating and are likely to continue to do so.

INTERNAL WORKPLACE COMMITTEES:
QUESTIONS OF LEGALITY AND EFFICACY

The simplest way to implement co-regulation in a non-union setting, and the suggestion of Ayres and Braithwaite in *Responsive Regulation* and others, is to require the formation and participation of non-union employee committees.[33] Whether that takes the form of mandatory "works councils" of the sort now required throughout Europe or of employer-established workplace committees, legislation would be required in the U.S. I will focus primarily on nonmandatory workplace committees, which have an indigenous presence on the U.S. scene. But the works council alternative merits a brief detour, for it might seem in principle to supply just the sort of representation that non-union workers want and need within a system of co-regulation.

Works Councils: Panacea or Chimera?

U.S. scholars of labor law and labor relations have often looked across the Atlantic with envy at the European institution of works councils.[34] Works councils are elected bodies of employees who meet regularly with management to discuss workplace issues. Works council mandates originated in Germany, spread through much of Western Europe, and have since become the law throughout the European Union (EU). A series of EU directives now requires companies to maintain works councils for establishments above a certain minimum size.[35] The works council directives establish ground rules that govern the selection of representatives and the scope of consultation rights and rights to receive information. The more robust German works council laws go further and require "co-determination" on a number of topics such as safety and job restructuring.

The works councils operate alongside and often in coordination with unions, not as a substitute for them; they cannot bargain over wages (which are typically negotiated at a sectoral or regional level, not at the establishment or firm level), and they cannot strike. The works councils are designed, both in what they can do and in what they cannot, to foster greater cooperation between workers and management on topics for which cooperation seems most possible and productive. Wolfgang Streeck has argued that European works councils "may sustain a 'cooperative culture' within which experimentation with decentralized organizational structures can flourish."[36]

Works councils would seem to be a ready answer to the "representation gap" in the U.S., especially given workers' expressed desire for more cooperative institutions of collective voice. Paul Weiler was an early proponent of a works council law for the U.S.[37] But others have followed. Stephen Befort has proposed an "American Works Councils Act" with the following features:

(1) Employees would have the automatic right to call for the creation of a works council in an enterprise or facility above a certain minimum size.

(2) Employees would be empowered to elect representatives periodically, with hourly and salaried employees represented on a proportional basis.

(3) The works council would be entitled to receive information periodically from the employer with respect to personnel policies, financial conditions, and plans for future undertakings that may impact the performance and organization of work.

(4) The works council would be entitled to consult periodically with the employer on a broad range of subjects [including]

  (a) the manner of work performance and organization;

  (b) the hiring, transfer, and termination of employees;

  (c) compliance with pertinent laws and regulations; and

  (d) entrepreneurial decisions that may impact the performance and organization of work.

(5) The works council should not have the right to bargain with respect to employee compensation in the absence of an employer's consent.[38]

Challenges remain in integrating a works council scheme into the distinct structure of collective bargaining and union representation in the U.S.[39]

In principle, works councils would seem to be the next-best alternative to independent union representation in giving employees a voice in the workplace. Such an alternative comports with what most employees say they want, and it avoids some of the features of unions that most arouse employer resistance.[40] Works councils would also appear to be an ideal institution for giving nonunion employees a voice within a system of co-regulation and helping to ensure compliance with the panoply of external laws regulating the workplace. So I would gladly join my fellow labor law and labor relations scholars in calling for the establishment of works councils in the U.S.

Unfortunately, outside the academy, there appears to be virtually no constituency in the U.S. for mandatory works councils. The labor movement, which is the only organized voice for employees in the political process, views such institutions with great suspicion as a substitute for unions, and a poor substitute at that. Employers view such institutions as entailing many of the burdens and frictions that unions bring and, worse yet, as a gateway for union organizing. One might imagine that, especially as union density falls, some unions might be willing to gamble that the employers are right and take a chance on works councils as an organizing opportunity, but that would only stoke employer fears. The same dilemma plagues proposals for more modest reforms of Section 8(a)(2) of the NLRA as well, as we will see below. But in the case of mandatory works councils, the opposition of both organized labor and management seems to put this proposed reform in the category of "pleasant pipe dream."[41]

A more modest proposal would not mandate works councils but would prescribe them as one condition for participating in a system of co-regulation. The same kinds of legal ground rules for periodic elections, information disclosure, and consultation would apply, but only for employers that decided to participate in the co-regulatory enterprise. This is reminiscent of David Levine's proposal for "conditional deregulation," recently reintroduced by Jeffrey Hirsch and Barry Hirsch as a potential alternative to collective bargaining.[42] That proposal comes quite close to what is suggested here. But in keeping with the conviction that a new regime of workplace governance is most likely to take hold if it is rooted in the tools, resources, and institutions that we have, let us first examine an indigenous American institution of employee representation: internal workplace committees established by employer initiative.

Internal Workplace Committees

Recall that Ayres and Braithwaite suggest internal workplace committees as a way of realizing tripartism in the non-union workplace. If that is an answer to the representation gap and a way of achieving co-regulation, then we are on our way to a solution, at least in the health and safety context. Among larger companies, such committees are standard operating procedure; they are considered essential elements of a workplace health and safety program.[43] Health and safety committees are one explicitly recommended way of fulfilling the requirement of "employee participation" under OSHA's Voluntary Protection Program (VPP).[44] Indeed, workplace health and safety committees are required by state law in eleven states.[45]

Internal workplace committees appear to fit what most employees say they want by way of representation. As noted in Chapter 2, the most thorough survey of employee attitudes and preferences regarding voice and representation in the workplace found that over 80 percent of nonmanagerial employees said that they preferred an employee organization that was "run jointly" by employees and management. Nearly 60 percent preferred "joint employee-management committees that discuss and resolve workplace problems,"[46] a form of representation that, as we have already learned, is illegal under the NLRA. As observed above, those employee preferences are at least partly adaptive. Employees' awareness of managerial opposition to independent union representation may generate fear of reprisals, low expectations for successful bargaining, and anxiety about conflict and confrontation.[47] Still, employees' express desire for "cooperative" and "jointly run" mechanisms of collective employee influence surely counts in favor of allowing this approach.

But achieving co-regulation through internal workplace committees confronts several problems. To begin with, internal workplace committees are unlikely to include the growing number of contingent workers who are not members of a stable and cohesive workplace community. But even within a traditional workplace setting, internal workplace committees face challenges, some of which are unique to the U.S. First, as we have seen, employee committees that are not scrupulously independent of the employer are generally unlawful under the NLRA's "company union" ban. Second, such committees are unlikely in any event to be able to play their part in a self-regulatory regime.[48] Third, employee committees that *are* scrupulously independent of the employer will confront some of the same employer resistance as unions do, for employers are loathe to allow any form of employee representation that might resemble or lead to unionization. Even after reckoning with each of these problems, we may conclude that internal employee committees do have a role to play in a system of regulated self-regulation.

The first set of problems for internal workplace committees lies in the peculiarities of U.S. labor law, discussed briefly above in Chapter 2. Section 8(a)(2) of the NLRA makes it unlawful for an employer "to dominate or interfere with the formation or administration of any labor organization." Section 2(5), in turn, defines "labor organizations" broadly to include "any organization of any kind, or any agency or employee representation committee or plan, in which employees participate and which exists for the purpose, in whole or in part, of dealing with employers concerning grievances, labor disputes, wages, rates of pay, hours of employment, or conditions of work." In seeking to banish the scourge of "company unions," Congress effectively banned not only organizations that purported to bargain collectively, or that masqueraded as unions, or that were used by employers to evade the duty to bargain with the employees' own chosen representative; it also banned some employee representation plans that were favored by employees and that worked well, by all accounts, within the particular organization. In effect, the NLRA rules out a range of intermediate options between purely individual bargaining and full-fledged union-like representation and limits the range of potential experimentation with alternative forms of employee representation within a tripartite scheme for labor standards regulation.[49]

The case of workplace health and safety committees is both exemplary and unusual. It is exemplary in showing the scope of the legal ban and its potential for inhibiting experimentation.[50] Health and safety are obviously "conditions of work"; that means that any "employee representation committee . . . in which employees participate and which exists for the purpose, in whole or in part, of dealing with employers" on health and safety is a "labor organization." "Dealing with" employers is not limited to collective bargaining. If the committee is so impotent that it is equivalent to a "suggestion box" or "one-way communication device," then it does not "deal with" employers and does not trigger any special scrutiny. Such a committee is likely to be of little use. But if the committee does anything meaningful—if it serves as a regular site for "give and take" or "bilateral exchange" between employees and employers— then it is "dealing with" the employer, and qualifies as a "labor organization."[51] Of course, there is nothing illegal in being a labor organization or in dealing with one. But the NLRA makes it unlawful for employers to "dominate or interfere with the formation or administration . . . or contribute financial or other support" to a labor organization. So if the committee is a labor organization, then the employer cannot place managers on the committee or influence the committee's membership or structure or support its operations financially.

It is surely possible to have a health and safety committee in a non-union workplace that meets the law's requirements of independence. Both OSHA's VPP regulations, which recommend the use of such committees, and the NLRB's judgment that state laws mandating workplace health and safety committees are not preempted by the NLRA are premised on that possibility.[52] Both are careful to confine their approval to committees that are lawful under the NLRA—that is, committees that are either too powerless to come within Section 2(5)'s broad definition of "labor organization" or sufficiently independent of the employer to steer clear of Section 8(a)(2).

Employers are not always so careful, however. Thousands of workplace health and safety committees that currently exist in non-union workplaces are very likely operating in violation of Section 8(a)(2): they "deal with" employers but operate under managerial control.[53] This is possible partly because it is rarely in anyone's interest to pursue these violations. Perhaps the utility of workplace health and safety committees is clear enough to most employers, employees, and employee advocates. In any event, outside the context of an active organizing campaign, the threat of an unfair labor practice charge is remote enough that federal law on this point is widely ignored. Even in the unlikely event that someone files an unfair labor practice charge based on maintenance of a safety committee, the most onerous remedy that could result would be an order to disband the committee; as elsewhere under the NLRA, there are no fines or penalties for this violation of the law.[54] In this one context it may be fortunate for employees that NLRB remedies are so toothless and the risk of an unfair labor practice is worth taking for many employers. The result is that employees in many firms do have at least a limited form of collective (though not independent) representation on health and safety issues through these committees.

For other terms and conditions of work covered by labor standards laws, employee committees appear to be less common. The legal hurdles are equally clear and equally lacking in deterrent force, but there seems to be no comparable pattern of widespread disregard for the law and thus no organized mechanism of collective employee voice on these matters in the non-union workplace. We will return in a moment to the question of why that might be so. But let us first consider whether, as a policy matter, the widespread existence of internal health and safety committees in the workplace is something to welcome and to build on. Can these internal employee committees adequately represent employee interests and guard against employer cheating within a system of regulated self-regulation?

It may be helpful to recall why employee committees that operate under managerial control were banned back in 1935. Proponents of the Wagner Act in the early 1930s saw "company unions," including employer-dominated workplace committees, as potent tools of union avoidance and as subservient and ineffectual vehicles of employee empowerment.[55] One might argue that once the Taft-Hartley amendments of 1947 abandoned the policy of encouraging union representation in favor of a policy protecting employee "free choice," Section 8(a)(2) became an anachronism. If employees are free to choose no representation at all, why should they be barred from choosing a weak and ineffectual form of representation? Both "choices" may be equally suspect given the heavy hand of managerial power. But why was the law neutral toward the former while prohibiting the latter? It is tempting to regard Section 8(a)(2) as a vestige of New Deal preoccupations and an artifact of labor law's ossification —of the political gridlock that has obstructed sensible labor law reform.[56]

But even if a labor law regime devoted to employee free choice might tolerate employees' choice of a weak and ineffectual form of representation, a regime of self-regulation cannot afford to do so. For if we are looking to fill the role of watchdog against employer cheating and reprisals within a system of regulated self-regulation, weakness and ineffectuality are fatal flaws, and employee free choice does nothing to cure them. The rights and labor standards at issue in a system of regulated self-regulation are not, after all, matters of choice for particular workers; they are nonwaivable mandates based on public policies and values.

Therein lies the second major problem with employee committees that exist only inside firms. With no outside power base, resources, or organizational structure, they are too vulnerable to cooptation or intimidation by employers to serve as the chief guardians against cheating by employers. Internal employee committees have no more power and no more protection against reprisals than the employees who serve on them, and those employees are almost invariably terminable at will. In many of the worst workplaces, many of the employees are immigrants, often undocumented, who fear not only discharge but also deportation.[57] Of course, health and safety committees, like other internal corporate compliance structures, are largely absent in those worst workplaces; that is part of the problem we are seeking to address. The point is that internal employee committees are unlikely to do much of anything to enable vulnerable employees to serve as monitors of their own terms and conditions of employment.

Part of what makes unions effective as watchdogs is that they exist both inside and outside the workplace. As organizations of insider employees, unions aggregate and channel the workers' own knowledge and interest in enforcement. Yet unions' organizational base outside the workplace gives them greater expertise, resources, independence from the employer, and insulation from reprisals than any group of employees alone could have. The existence of a union does not necessarily banish the fear of reprisals and job loss that might dampen the pursuit of regulatory objectives. But a union's organizational independence from the employer, as well as the contractual job security that a union usually secures for employees, provides crucial protection against reprisals that an internal committee does not.

What would it take to enable internal workplace committees to play a broader and stronger role, including a role in wage and hour enforcement and in protecting health and safety even when it is costly to do so? David Levine's proposal for "conditional deregulation," which has much in common with my proposed scheme of co-regulation, is premised on the voluntary establishment of internal employee committees with safeguards against employer domination. Employees must be protected against discrimination or reprisals based on their participation (or not) in the employee representation system; representatives would be "chosen freely and fairly" by employees, by election or otherwise, without interference from management; and establishment or disestablishment of the committee would be by majority vote of the employees. (Moreover, an employer "would not be permitted to set up a committee when it knows a union organizing campaign is taking place.")[58] The proposed safeguards would probably not provide a sufficient guarantee of independence from the employer to pass muster under Section 8(a)(2) and would require an amendment of the statute (which is what Levine proposes). At the same time, the proposed employee committees would probably look too independent for most employers to voluntarily adopt them.

That brings us to one final impediment to relying on non-union forms of employee representation within a system of self-regulation: employee committees that are strong and independent enough to meet both the requirements of federal labor law and the imperatives of an effective self-regulatory system are likely to run into the deep-seated opposition to unions that is virtually endemic among American managers, at least in non-union workplaces. If participation in a system of self-regulation were conditioned on the existence of an elected and independent employee council or committee, many employers would simply take a pass; they would see such entities as proto-unions, the risks of which would outweigh the benefits of a self-regulatory regime. This is a practical and political impediment, not a legal one. If the benefits of participation, or the costs of nonparticipation, are great enough, employers would overcome such misgivings. That is an issue to which we will return in Chapter 9.

In the meantime, thousands of non-union health and safety committees are currently operating within firms' internal compliance programs. In casting doubt on the ability of such committees to stand up to employers within a system of self-regulation, I do not mean to suggest that health and safety committees accomplish nothing. Empirical studies indicate that non-union safety committees do tend to improve workplace health and safety (though less than such committees do in the union setting).[59] They may do so by overcoming some of the public goods problems of labor standards enforcement and by aggregating the information, energies, and incentives of individual employees to engage in enforcement activity. Employee committees presumably play a useful role in improving safety within a firm that is genuinely committed to doing so; there is little reason to think that they can do much to counteract management that is consciously risking workers' safety. Similarly, internal safety committees are likely to be useful in addressing safety hazards that are inadvertent or incidental to the production process, especially those that cost the employer as much (in lost work time, for example) as it would cost to abate the hazard. What internal committees are unlikely to do is to effectively address workplace hazards that are integral to the production process and that serve the employer's bottom line—for example, a poultry-processing line whose speed produces repetitive motion injuries while lowering per-unit labor costs. When health and safety improvements come with a significant price tag, an independent organizational existence and power base outside as well as inside the workplace is essential for an employee organization to serve as the third leg of a tripartite system of regulated self-regulation—that is, as a guarantor against cheating (or the pursuit of profit at the expense of public values).

This suggests that internal workplace committees alone may play a rather limited role outside the health and safety arena, particularly in improving compliance with wage and hour laws, where noncompliance often reflects a deliberate cost-saving strategy and not a lack of information. Off-the-clock work and misclassification of workers to avoid overtime requirements, for example, are economically equivalent to a dangerously fast production line. Eliminating those violations would cut directly into the firm's bottom line. Just as health and safety committees in the non-union workplace are generally too weak to push back against unsafe practices that directly lower labor costs, internal non-union employee committees are unlikely to be of much value in avoiding deliberate cost-saving wage and hour violations.

On the other hand, what is deliberate and transparent within the workplace may not be equally deliberate and transparent at the top of the firm, where managers do not always have (or may avoid having) direct knowledge of wages and work schedules. That may be true within large and dispersed organizations, such as major retailers, or within networks of contractors in which liability for violations runs up the supply chain. To the extent that firms at the top of the ladder are liable for unlawful practices down the ladder (and to the extent that liability is large enough and likely enough to be worth avoiding), top managers have reason to inform themselves about those practices and to exercise their latent control over them. Internal employee committees may enable employees to channel information about low-visibility violations up the ladder to those who are liable for such violations.

What non-union employee committees might be able to do is to aggregate and articulate what employees know. Their ability to do that effectively might be bolstered by the sort of safeguards against employer domination that Levine suggests. What internal committees would still lack, even with those safeguards, is the necessary footing outside the workplace. That suggests that internal employee committees should operate in conjunction with some outside entity or actor that can supply power, independence, and protection against reprisals. Outside independent monitors might play that role. By themselves, outside monitors lack the presence inside the workplace that is essential to effective monitoring of labor standards. But together with internal employee committees, they might hold up the third leg of the tripartite stool quite well. We will examine the role of monitors further in the next chapter.

As suggested above, unions might also be able to serve as an outside resource for internal workplace committees in non-union workplaces. Professor Finkin has proposed that unions could supply much-needed independence and expertise to in-house health and safety committees—such as those that are mandatory in some states—even in workplaces in which they do not represent the majority of employees.[60] Of course, employers in non-union workplaces are unlikely to welcome their employees' consultation with unions on health and safety matters; the risk of reprisals remains. But a union would have the knowledge of the law and potential resources to challenge any illegal reprisals.

Non-union employee committees may also be able to play a role in the remedial or enforcement setting. For example, if an employer is found liable for serious or systemic violations of wage and hour laws in public or private enforcement proceedings, establishment of an independently elected worker committee might be a useful part of a prospective remedy for such violations. In that context, a court or agency might afford enough outside oversight—either directly or by way of independent monitoring—to protect employee members of such a committee against reprisals. A remedial decree that imposed such employee representation should include antiretaliation protections, including an expedited complaint process and a preliminary reinstatement remedy, for employees who play this post-enforcement monitoring role.

In-house committees, standing alone, are unlikely to be strong enough and independent enough to guard against employer cheating within a system of self-regulation whenever cheating brings significant savings. At the same time, they may create useful channels of information from employees to managers when lack of information is part of the problem, and they may do more than that when they operate in conjunction with other actors—independent monitors, unions or other independent worker organizations, or courts or regulators. They are in any case useful enough within a scheme of regulated self-regulation to warrant drawing them out from under the shadow of illegality that is cast by the NLRA's broad definition of "labor organization" and its ban on employer support or domination of labor organizations. As long as that statutory ban remains in place, any internal employee compliance committee—whether it is a condition of participation in a cooperative compliance program, mandated by state statute or remedial decree, or created voluntarily by an employer seeking to improve compliance—must be scrupulously independent of the employer. Political climate permitting, however, an amendment of Section 8(a)(2) may be in order.[61]

An amendment might take the form of a statutory "safe harbor" for employee committees that were not created in the context of, or with the motive of discouraging, union organizing activity; a safe harbor might be drawn to impose additional safeguards against employer domination, along the lines that Levine proposes.[62] A more drastic approach would be to revise the law's broad definition of "labor organization" and key it to the distinguishing feature of ordinary unions: the exclusive representation of employees in collective bargaining.[63] Before deciding what reform makes sense, we will want to consider the implications for worker centers, to which we will shortly turn. But consider that even if Section 8(a)(2) were simply repealed, the law would still prohibit employers from discriminating on the basis of union activity; from interfering, coercing, or restraining employees in the exercise of their Section 7 rights of self-organization and concerted activity; and from circumventing or refusing to bargain with a union chosen by a majority of employees. So it would still be unlawful to *use* internal employee committees to discourage independent concerted activity—to favor compliant employees over those pressing employee complaints more aggressively, to monitor employees' own discussions of their grievances, or to fend off a demand for recognition by a union with demonstrated majority support. The solid and sensible core of Section 8(a)(2) merely reinforces those independent prohibitions.

What Section 8(a)(2) adds is a prohibition on employee committees that are *not* demonstrably being used to frustrate independent organizing activity or union representation, that might deliver rather little to employees but that might help employees and employers to overcome some collective action and information problems and perhaps improve compliance with external law. That extra margin of interference with labor-management relations is difficult to justify in current conditions. At the same time, it is possible that Section 8(a)(2) discourages some sophisticated anti-union strategies that might not demonstrably run afoul of the NLRA's remaining prohibitions. As things now stand, any statutory change that could conceivably strengthen employers' hand against independent union organizing should await other labor law reforms that strengthen the right of employees to form an independent union.

WORKER CENTERS: NEW VEHICLES FOR
INDEPENDENT WORKER VOICE

The most promising new institutions for the representation of workers, including representation within self-regulatory structures, are "worker centers."[64] We have seen worker centers engaged in a range of informal monitoring activities, as well as formal monitoring under agreements they have managed to secure on behalf of workers. Worker centers are behind many of the most innovative experiments in what I have called "self-regulation by contract," especially at the bottom of the labor market.

Worker centers share some of the features of unions that enable them to overcome both the collective action problems and the fear of reprisals that face their members. They are based outside of any particular workplace, affording them a measure of independence from employers, while their members give them a presence and direct knowledge of working conditions inside the relevant workplaces. Indeed, many worker centers serve workers who do not work in any stable workplace, such as day laborers, and others serve workers of a particular ethnic group, occupation, or community without regard to the employer for which the workers happen to be working.[65] Worker centers have sometimes succeeded where traditional unions have failed and have managed to generate extraordinary organizational energy and collective human resources. The unions and major labor federations have taken notice and have begun to form alliances with worker centers, or even form worker centers, in some areas. An important example is the Maintenance Cooperation Trust Fund (MCTF), a worker center that was formed and is financed through collective bargaining agreements between the SEIU and unionized janitorial contractors in California.[66]

On the other hand, worker centers face serious practical difficulties, some of which were described in Chapter 5. Worker centers cannot be the primary linchpin of a nationwide system of co-regulation, for they are too scarce and too dependent on the "spontaneous combustion" of grassroots organizing energies in particular communities. At present, few have the resources and expertise to engage in the kind of systematic monitoring that may be required within a system of effective self-regulation in many sectors and workplaces. Few have found a "business model," or sustainable source of financial support, for those activities. Financial support from employers, pursuant to monitoring agreements, has proven both elusive and, for some worker advocates, troubling.

Worker centers also face potential legal risks. Depending on their activities, worker centers might become ensnared in the federal labor laws by falling within the definition of "labor organizations" under those laws.[67] That is not a risk for those organizations that represent only workers who are outside of the NLRA, such as the Coalition of Immokalee Workers, which represents fruit and vegetable pickers centered in south Florida. But most worker centers do represent "employees" within the scope of the NLRA. Depending on their activities, worker centers might be thrown into the same legal category, with some of the same legal obligations and restrictions, as the United Steelworkers Union or the Communication Workers of America. That could be devastating for these low-budget, highly informal organizations.

Recall the broad definition of labor organization in Section 2(5) of the NLRA: "any organization of any kind, or any agency or employee representation committee or plan, in which employees participate and which exists for the purpose, in whole or in part, of dealing with employers concerning grievances, labor disputes, wages, rates of pay, hours of employment, or conditions of work."[68] The breadth of the definition was intended by Congress to dovetail with Section 8(a)(2) to make a clean sweep of company unions. But the same definition potentially sweeps into the labor law domain many small and highly informal organizations. Worker centers are organizations in which employees participate, and they typically target terms and conditions of work encompassed by Section 2(5). The only question is whether those organizations "deal with" employers. Venerable case law establishes that "dealing with" is not limited to collective bargaining.[69] Interacting with employers on an occasional basis, or only in the context of a lawsuit against the employer for employment law violations, does not constitute "dealing" under Section 2(5).[70] But the more active worker centers become in seeking to secure or enforce codes of conduct or the like, the more readily they might be characterized as "labor organizations."

The problem is that status as a "labor organization" would potentially subject these entities—mostly upstart, shoestring organizations—to a large body of legal restrictions and burdens that have been piled onto labor unions over the past seventy-plus years. Whether or not those burdens make sense for large, full-fledged traditional trade unions, with their thousands of members and millions of dollars in membership dues, they would cripple the small and often highly informal organizations at issue here. For example, Section 8(a)(2) and the Taft-Hartley Act both prohibit a labor organization from receiving financial support from an employer. That prohibition may prove problematic for worker centers seeking to fund monitoring activities through employer contributions (though it might be avoided by the creation of a separate, and separately funded, monitoring entity that does not itself meet the definition of Section 2[5]). Status as a labor organization would also bring into play the restrictions in Section 8(b) of the NLRA. So, for example, under the law's ban on peaceful "secondary" picketing—that is, picketing of an employer the law deems neutral in the particular dispute—worker centers might be prohibited from picketing the customers, building owners, or other employers that ultimately use the workers' labor. Of greater concern—for the time being, more potential than actual—are the provisions of the Labor-Management Reporting and Disclosure Act (LMRDA), which impose a rash of reporting and other requirements on "labor organizations."[71] Fortunately, the LMRDA's definition of "labor organization" has been interpreted so as to leave worker centers in the clear.[72]

Even the NLRA's restrictions have thus far been confined largely to conventional labor unions and to internal workplace organizations that raise the spectre of "company unions" under Section 8(a)(2). The NLRB has deflected the few efforts by employers to entangle worker centers in the web of labor law. So, for example, ROC-NY was found not to be a labor organization based on its efforts to pressure a restaurant to settle a lawsuit on behalf of employees.[73] Those "dealings" with the employer were not enough to make ROC-NY a labor organization because of both their nature (efforts to press for settlement of litigation) and their limited extent.

So worker centers have thus far avoided entanglements with the labor laws. That may be largely because, thus far, they operate on the periphery of the labor market from a position of relative weakness. Few worker centers have wielded enough power to pose a serious threat to employers who are in a position to seek legal recourse against them—that is, employers that are not themselves virtual outlaws. If worker centers become significant actors in the labor relations landscape, as their proponents hope, and especially if they continue to experiment with codes of conduct and monitoring agreements that bring them into more regular dealings with employers, they might well become targets of Taft-Hartley complaints. How might worker centers avoid that dubious fate?

The problem that worker centers face here is arguably a mere glitch in the labor laws. The very broad definition of labor organization was first enacted in 1935 to give the greatest possible breadth to Section 8(a)(2)'s ban on company unions. The same definition then became applicable to the Taft-Hartley Act's restrictions on union activity. "Labor organization" had become the operative term for labor unions, and everyone knew what labor unions were. But the term "labor organization" now defines the reach of labor law provisions with two different, even opposite, purposes: one of those provisions sought to ban organizations that were too weak and dependent to represent employees effectively, while others sought to curb perceived abuses by organizations with potentially coercive powers. But worker centers have neither the particular vulnerabilities addressed by Section 8(a)(2) nor the potentially coercive powers addressed by Taft-Hartley. They are not as weak—or at least not as vulnerable to employer domination—as internal workplace committees because they originate and have their organizational locus outside the employer and the workplace. And they lack the coercive potential of unions because they do not seek exclusive representation of a group of employees on the basis of majority rule, nor do they seek through collective bargaining to compel the payment of dues (or agency fees) from all of the employees they represent, including nonmembers. It is those state-conferred powers that arguably justify the manifold restrictions the law places on unions (if they are justified at all), both in the interest of employees and, more controversially, in the interest of employers.

Without the powers of exclusive representation and mandatory dues exaction that unions have or seek, worker centers are simply unincorporated associations of workers pursuing their shared interests through various forms of constitutionally protected association and expression—education, peaceful advocacy, and sometimes litigation—much as other voluntary associations do. Indeed, without those additional powers, worker centers ought to enjoy the same constitutional freedom of expression and association and the same freedom from burdensome regulation of their internal affairs that other voluntary associations do. Worker centers that are engaged entirely or primarily in constitutionally protected forms of expression, advocacy, education, and association have a strong argument for avoiding a broad construction of the law that would suppress those activities or even doom these organizations altogether. The doctrine of constitutional avoidance, which has been given a good workout by the Supreme Court in its decisions under the NLRA,[74] makes good sense here.

The relatively short lifespan of the worker center movement makes it uncommonly difficult to predict its future. Much may turn on the role that traditional labor unions, with their vastly greater resources and considerable expertise, are willing and able to play in supporting and allying with the worker centers. Some worker centers were founded in the wake of frustrating efforts to draw the mainstream labor movement into the organizing of poor and mostly immigrant worker communities.[75] But nowadays one sees the active hand of unions within or behind many of the most vibrant worker center organizations and experiments.[76] For those who envision worker centers as an alternative or even a potential successor to traditional unions, that is unsettling. If labor unions continue to shrink in size and power, the worker center movement may lose an essential source of financial and organizational support.

A NOTE ON COLLECTIVE REPRESENTATION
AND MINORITY RIGHTS

The analysis so far has largely sidestepped the problem of how to ensure that collective representation—which is likely, even designed, to reflect median or majority preferences—does not neglect or submerge the legal rights and interests of minority groups within the workforce. Some of what minority groups need to protect their rights is relatively well guarded by majoritarian institutions. In particular, workers have a shared interest in the fairness and integrity of internal dispute resolution mechanisms. The large and growing collection of antidiscrimination laws effectively recognizes multiple overlapping subgroups within the workforce—each one of which is usually a minority of the workforce, even if most workers fall within one or more protected subgroups.

That last fact is not inconsequential. It is an unusual workforce in which a majority of workers are white male nonveterans under forty years of age without any disabilities or disfavored genetic traits. And that is without recognizing the additional protected categories created by state and local antidiscrimination laws, most important of which are those prohibiting discrimination based on sexual orientation. (That is also without reckoning with potential "reverse discrimination" claims by white or male employees.) On one hand, the proliferation of antidiscrimination laws may have helped to cultivate a growing societal consensus about the importance of combating discriminatory and arbitrary treatment. On the other hand, in any one workplace, women or minorities or disabled workers or some other subgroup of workers, or individuals within those subgroups, may nonetheless be subject to discrimination or harassment. It would be naïve to simply assume that institutions of collective worker representation could be counted on to champion the rights of those workers. While the concern for minority rights is a general one for institutions of collective (majoritarian) representation, the three potential institutions for worker representation considered here stand differently in relation to this concern.

With regard to labor unions, the concern for minority rights within these majoritarian institutions has a long history and has generated a lot of law. Some of that history is dismal indeed. Some unions fought long and hard, well into the 1970s, to maintain patterns of exclusion and segregation of women and especially nonwhite workers, and labor federation leadership generally did too little to combat racism within its component unions.[77] In response, courts and legislators imposed new legal duties on unions. Indeed, twenty years before Congress prohibited discrimination by unions and employers in 1964, the Supreme Court read into the federal labor laws a duty of fair representation on the part of unions toward all employees they represented.[78]

Union discrimination did not disappear in either 1944 or 1964. Once the most blatant forms of discrimination were abandoned, discrimination became hard to prove. In particular, the law makes it quite difficult, by design, for employees to show a breach of the duty of fair representation.[79] Unions are granted wide latitude in seeking to mediate among the competing interests of workers while advancing the shared interests of the workforce as a whole. The primary protection that minority groups have against majoritarian oppression in the union context is the union's need for group cohesion and its understanding that divisions among workers undermine the collective strength that is needed for effective bargaining. The law, especially Title VII and the duty of fair representation, provides important checks against majoritarian oppression. But it is largely the politics of organizing and collective bargaining within increasingly diverse workforces that have pushed the labor movement to invest heavily in the promotion of interracial solidarity.

Worker centers are too new and perhaps too weak to have accumulated any particular legal duties in this regard. In particular, worker centers do not have the statutory power of exclusive representation that was thought to necessitate the duty of fair representation for labor unions. Moreover, worker centers have tended to arise at the bottom of the labor market and in sectors in which minority and especially immigrant workers predominated. Worker centers have frequently championed claims of discrimination, which is often rampant in low-wage workplaces. Thus far, few concerns about the capacity or willingness of worker centers to deal with the discrimination claims of minority groups have yet surfaced.

Internal workplace committees, given their ephemeral existence under the shadow of Section 8(a)(2) of the NLRA, have no real record with regard to representation of minority groups within the workforce. There is no law governing them because the law barely recognizes them. As a result, we are left to ponder the abstract (but far from hypothetical) tension between majority sentiment and minority interests. That abstract tension does not disable these internal workplace committees from playing a useful role in much of what matters for individuals facing potential discrimination. Most important, workers have a shared interest in the quality and fairness of internal dispute resolution systems, including arbitration.[80] But there remains an inescapable risk that institutions for collective worker representation might be partial in their oversight of employer policies and unreliable guardians of the rights of disadvantaged subgroups within the workforce. That is what the duty of fair representation guards against in the union context, where the risk may be exacerbated by the unions' power of exclusive representation. To the extent that a system of co-regulation relies upon, and effectively empowers, internal workplace committees to help ensure compliance, it must also guard against the guardians' neglect of minority interests.

The solution to this problem may come from many directions. Part of the solution may lie in independent monitors whose role remains to be elaborated. Outside monitors are supposed to supply the requisite footing outside the workplace, and the insulation from employer power, that internal workplace committees lack. While outside monitors have thus far been seen as an answer to the vulnerability of individual employees and internal workplace committees, they may also supply a counterweight to the majoritarian tendencies of such committees.

Part of the answer may lie, too, in a more pluralistic conception of the internal workplace committee structure. Identity-based "caucuses" or affinity groups within the workplace can certainly coexist, and play a useful role, alongside more inclusive institutions of employee representation. Indeed, while workforce-wide employee representation is rare, affinity groups of racial, ethnic, or gender subgroups are a fairly common feature of the diversity programs of large corporations.[81] That may not be simply a product of the legal shadow cast by the NLRA (which would fall equally over such affinity groups to the extent that they "deal with" employers). It seems that collective representation of workers along lines of gender, race, and ethnicity does not arouse the same anxiety among employers as does the prospect of workforce-wide employee representation. It may be well to recall the not-entirely-past history of employers deliberately dividing workers along racial lines to defeat workforce-wide solidarity.[82] Separate affinity groups for minority workers may be most useful and least divisive when they operate alongside or inside of, and not instead of, institutions of collective representation that reflect the broad range of interests, and especially the overlapping and shared interests, of workers generally. That goes for unions as well as internal union committees.[83]

The prevailing solution to the problem of minority rights within majoritarian workplace institutions has been to allow individual litigation under the discrimination laws. That will continue to be necessary. To be sure, the efficacy of private rights of action may be affected, under *Faragher/Ellerth* and the law of mandatory arbitration, by internal self-regulatory mechanisms. And under the proposed scheme of co-regulation, employees would exercise some collective control over those dispute resolution procedures to ensure their responsiveness to employee concerns. But the risk of majoritarian neglect of minority concerns seems small in that setting, given the interest that all employees share in the fairness of those processes. The right to seek independent judicial or arbitral adjudication of one's rights under antidiscrimination law in case internal processes fail, free from the control of the employer or any group of employees, is a significant brake on abuse or neglect by both employer and employees' collective institutions.

The task of reimagining and rebuilding institutions of collective representation for employees, especially in the most competitive sectors of the economy, is perhaps the most challenging part of constructing a system of effective co-regulation. But it is imperative. For continuing the trend toward self-regulation of employment rights and standards without effective employee representation is a prescription for failure—for deregulation under the guise of self-regulation. It is the imperative of effective employee representation that I mean to capture with the term "co-regulation." Let us turn now to the remaining elements of a system of co-regulation.

Chapter 8 Architecture and Elements of Co-Regulation

If all workers suddenly had effective, independent collective representation within the workplace, that alone would launch a new era of shared governance and, almost incidentally, co-regulation of workplace rights and labor standards. But that is not the world we live in, nor the world we are likely to see in the future. Even with all hands on deck in support of labor law reform and labor organizing, we are very unlikely to see more than one-quarter of the workforce represented by unions in collective bargaining agreements in the foreseeable future. Nor are we likely to turn back the tide of self-regulation in favor of traditional top-down, command-and-control approaches to regulation and rights enforcement. What is more likely is a world in which firms' own internal self-regulatory systems play a major role in pursuing society's regulatory objectives; in which many employees are represented within those systems, at best, through an internal employee committee of some kind; and in which many of the worst workplaces have neither functioning self-regulatory systems nor any institutions of employee representation. In short, we must plan for a world in which employees will need outside support—in the form of both monitoring and enforcement—to sustain an effective system of self-regulation. Here we will examine the monitoring role of both independent outside monitors and insider employees in their role as would-be "whistleblowers." We will defer until Chapter 9 the role of stronger external sanctions, both public and private, in motivating firms to enter into and conscientiously pursue a program of self-regulation.

There remain, however, two questions about the basic architecture and content of this system of workplace self-regulation: what are the rights and standards that are the subject of self-regulation, and what is the entity whose self-regulation is being promoted and regulated? The answer to both questions may seem obvious: the law should promote and regulate the *employer's* self-regulation of the employee rights and labor standards established by *external law*. But the better answer to each question turns out to be more complicated. This chapter will begin with these basic questions about the nature of the self-regulating firm, or "promisor," and the nature of its promises. It will then turn to the roles of individual workers and independent monitors in ensuring the efficacy of self-regulation and guarding against "cosmetic compliance" under the guise of self-regulation. Chapter 9 will take up the question of how to move toward effective systems of co-regulation, both through public reforms, legislative and nonlegislative, and through private strategies, litigation-based and otherwise.

Throughout these two chapters, the discussion will remain at an intermediate level of generality. The general principles and elements outlined here are meant to allow for a good deal of variety at the level of particular workplaces. Behind those principles and elements are a basic commitment to experimentation and a recognition that the actors themselves have to construct many of the particulars to fit the industry, local labor-market conditions, and the workplace. It would be ironic if a book about the demise of command-and-control regulation in favor of more workplace-centered and responsive self-regulation ended with a detailed prescription of what every system of self-regulation should contain.

THE ROLE OF CONTRACT IN A WORLD OF
MANDATES: GOING ABOVE AND BEYOND

What are the substantive standards that are the object of self-regulation, and where do they come from? On one hand, all the talk of compliance and enforcement throughout this book seems to imply that we are aiming to hold employers to the law's mandatory employee rights and minimum standards. On the other hand, we have seen that employers engaged in self-regulation often promise more than mere compliance, whether their undertakings are negotiated or unilateral. How and where do contracts and voluntary promises fit within a world of employment mandates, especially within a system of self-regulation?

The law creates a patchwork of employment mandates—employee rights and minimum terms and conditions of employment that all or nearly all employers are bound to provide. Those mandates are backed by processes of public enforcement, private rights of action, or both. Atop this system of mandates, nearly all of the self-regulatory instruments and measures that are already part of the American law of the workplace have a quasi-voluntary or contractual character. Firms are not required to implement self-regulatory measures but are induced to commit themselves voluntarily, either unilaterally or by contract, to additional procedures and sometimes to higher substantive standards of conduct than the law requires. They may do so in order to avoid bad publicity or reputational harms that some constellation of public or private actors might otherwise be able to impose or to avoid certain onerous aspects of the default system of public or private enforcement, such as punitive damages or unannounced public inspections, or to live up to their own sense of social responsibility.

This quasi-voluntary or contractual feature is present in the corporate compliance regimes described in Chapter 4, both those that arose as simple liability-avoidance precautions and those that responded to the more explicit incentives proffered by courts and regulators, as under the Federal Sentencing Guidelines for Organizations or Title VII or OSHA's Voluntary Protection Program. The voluntary element is more obvious with the more ambitious corporate social responsibility programs and with the bottom-up experiments in self-regulation by contract reviewed in Chapter 5, such as the neutrality agreements and codes of conduct negotiated by U.S. worker organizations in recent years.

The adoption of additional and more rigorous internal compliance procedures is the most obvious way in which these voluntary or contractual programs have pushed standards above the operative legal floor. But these programs have often pushed substantive standards above the legal floor as well. Sometimes it is the inadequacy of the law's substantive standards (rather than mere underenforcement) that impels workers and their advocates to pressure firms to commit to higher standards. That was the case with the Coalition of

Immokalee Workers' (CIW) campaign on behalf of tomato pickers, who are excluded from many labor and employment laws, and that is the case with neutrality agreements that seek to constrain employers' anti-union campaigns more strictly than the labor laws do. But even when the pressure toward self-regulation is supplied primarily by a public or private threat to enforce minimum legal standards, the codes that are adopted in response to that threat frequently commit or at least aspire to higher standards of conduct than the law requires —higher wages, work breaks or vacation time, or additional benefits. The Manhattan greengrocers who signed onto the Greengrocer Code of Conduct (GGCC) in order to avoid ruinous back pay liability agreed not only to pay minimum wages and mandatory overtime, but also to provide sick days and vacation time that the law did not require. And the internal corporate codes of conduct that have proliferated under the shadow of criminal laws and the Sentencing Guidelines frequently pledge to reach beyond legal mandates toward higher standards of ethics and social responsibility.

So the rise of regulated self-regulation is a potential vehicle not only for improving enforcement of minimum legal standards but also for raising standards above the legal minimum. I say "potential" because many questions remain about the viability and efficacy of existing self-regulatory undertakings, both unilateral and negotiated. But realizing that potential is vital for reasons that may be obvious but that bear emphasizing. First, that feature of regulated self-regulation responds to some of the failings of the system of command-and-control regulation that it is supposed to supplant. Two of the inherent weaknesses of uniform minimum standards are their rigidity in the face of change and their uniformity in the face of widely varying capabilities among firms. Uniform minimum standards invariably demand too little of some firms that can do better, especially when political and legal processes are strewn with obstacles to reform. That has been a chronic problem in the case of the federal minimum wage, for example.

Of course, that is what contract is for. The advent of minimum federal labor standards in the New Deal was always meant to create a floor from which workers, as individuals or through unions, could bargain up. But with the decline of collective bargaining, it is crucial to find new mechanisms by which workers—including those who lack scarce skills and individual bargaining power— can secure improvements in their wages and working conditions above the legal minima. That is the second reason for pressing to realize the potential to improve upon substantive minimum standards: If regulated self-regulation could promise no more than better enforcement of minimum standards, then it would still have a place in the regulatory landscape, but it could hardly masquerade as a new form of workplace self-governance alongside the system of collective bargaining that preceded it.

If the aim is to make possible a process of continuing and varying improvements above mandatory minimum standards, then there will have to be an element of voluntariness in the content of the standards that are subject to self-regulation. For while it may make sense in some contexts to mandate self-regulatory procedures—Cal-OSHA does that, for example, in the health and safety context[1]—it is a bit nonsensical to talk of mandating substantive standards above mandatory minima. As with the twentieth-century paradigm of collective bargaining, the basic architecture of contract, atop a foundation of mandates, still appears to offer the best way forward. So we are looking for ways to induce firms to voluntarily commit themselves to both substantive standards of conduct and internal self-regulatory measures that go beyond what the external law mandates.

To say that commitments should be "voluntary" does not mean that there should be no pressure on firms to make those commitments. On the contrary, the law can and does encourage effective self-regulation by a combination of hard and soft rewards and penalties. Public agencies and worker advocates can deploy a range of positive and negative pressures—withholding of onerous penalties, less adversarial enforcement tracks, access to government contracts, cessation of a boycott or publicity campaign, certification as a model corporate citizen—to induce firms to promise more than the law requires of them. Lots of voluntary contracts throughout the society are made under economic, social, or legal pressures.

Nor does the endorsement of voluntariness here necessarily mean that a firm's fulfillment of its voluntary commitments, including those that go beyond legal requirements, should itself be merely voluntary. It is a normal feature of contract—both ordinary individual contracts and collective bargaining contracts—that commitments or promises are made voluntarily (albeit often under some kind of pressure) but are then binding and legally enforceable. There is normally some mechanism, either prescribed in the contract or supplied by the background legal regime, for adjudicating and remedying a breach of the contract.

This brings us to a crucial issue, for many of the unilateral corporate codes of conduct and many of the negotiated codes of conduct that have been surveyed here are not legally binding; if the firm reneges on its commitments, there is often no formal, direct enforcement mechanism.[2] The firm may risk a resumption of the pressures or a withdrawal of the inducements that led it to make the commitments in the first place—a renewed boycott, bad publicity, an enforcement of claims that had been held back—but no direct legal enforcement of the commitments themselves. That is more or less of a problem, depending on what the original inducements or pressures were. If the pressure was a boycott or a major publicity campaign, that may be a very difficult enterprise to resuscitate. If the pressure comes from the threat to prosecute or litigate legal claims, those claims are again limited to legal minima and in any case may have a limited shelf life (as with the wage claims behind the GGCC in New York). If the pressure is something like the Sentencing Guidelines or Title VII doctrine, which instruct courts on how to deal with criminal or civilly actionable conduct, then we are again back to enforcing only legal minima, and only as reliably and harshly as the background system of public enforcement, with all its shortcomings, permits.

Ideally, then, in exchange for conferring whatever benefits or withdrawing whatever pressures they have at their disposal, workers and regulators should aim for an enforceable contract with some process for adjudicating and remedying infractions. That process might be civil litigation, or it might be arbitration, as is standard both in collective bargaining agreements and in neutrality agreements between unions and employers that set the ground rules for organizing contests.

But that does not mean that voluntary commitments must necessarily be legally enforceable contracts to count as effective self-regulation. Obviously, if voluntary commitments are to be enforceable, they will be much harder to get. One guesses that Wal-Mart and other major garment brands may not have "committed" to improving wages and working conditions in their supplier factories if their commitments could be enforced like ordinary contracts by or on behalf of workers. But even aspirational commitments by a firm might be meaningful steps in the right direction. They may raise a firm's sights and lead to the creation of an internal constituency for improved conditions. Their breach may trigger reputational sanctions and may become fodder for a campaign of political and social pressures. Even ordinary contracts may have some provisions that are explicitly aspirational and not legally binding. In both contexts, the value of these aspirational provisions depends on the parties' relationship and the trust and expectations it has created—trust on the part of workers and their advocates that aspirational promises foretell good-faith efforts toward fulfillment and expectations on the other side that lack of such good-faith efforts will trigger consequences that are worth avoiding.

So the traditional vehicle of contract allows for a customized and variable mix of enforceable and unenforceable provisions of rules and standards and of coercive and reputational sanctions, depending on the circumstances. Some firms may be trusted more than others; some, by virtue of their lawbreaking past, may be vulnerable to particularly strong and immediate pressures, legal and nonlegal; and some worker advocacy groups under some circumstances may be confident of their ability to bring nonlegal sanctions to bear on defecting firms if necessary. The possibility of contractual sanctions, as well as whatever sanctions are available under market conditions and the background public law, expands the repertoire of workers and regulators and allows for some ratcheting up of labor standards beyond what the law requires of employers across the board.[3]

With regard to bottom-up self-regulation by contract, the resulting injunction to worker advocates may sound like "Take what you can get" and may seem to open the door to treating everything here as optional. To some extent that may be inevitable, at least for now. The trend toward self-regulation by contract is being shaped by many different actors—regulatory officials, attorneys, unions, worker centers, and other advocacy organizations—juggling many different sources of leverage—regulatory penalties and public and private legal claims, public and private business arrangements, publicity, boycotts, and strikes—and seeking to induce firms to enter into varying commitments that go beyond what the law can effectively command. They should aim to secure commitments in the form of enforceable contracts, but that will not always be possible, and it is not the only way to make progress.

The same may be said of unilateral corporate codes of conduct or the like, which are not usually legally enforceable by employees.[4] One might argue that an employer's unilateral, nonbinding commitments regarding working conditions should be insufficient to earn any of the legal benefits dealt out within a system of regulated self-regulation—reduced scrutiny or liabilities; for example, perhaps the Sentencing Guidelines or the *Faragher-Ellerth-Kolstad* standards should be recast so that firms seeking shelter under such frameworks must make their substantive commitments—their codes of conduct—directly enforceable by or on behalf of employees. I believe that would be counterproductive. Employers should be encouraged to aspire to going above and beyond legal mandates, but they need not make those above-and-beyond aspirations legally binding in order to gain privileges of self-regulation with respect to legal mandates. As long as the legal mandates themselves—the rights and labor standards required by law—are enforceable and as long as firms maintain the requisite structural and procedural safeguards of compliance with those legal mandates (including employee representation), they should qualify in the law's eyes as effective self-regulators. Firms' willingness (or not) to make binding substantive commitments that go beyond the law's requirements should be subject to the softer constraints of reputation, along with whatever peaceful economic pressures worker and consumer advocates can bring to bear.

The discussion here echoes familiar debates about "hard law" versus "soft law," with the partisans of New Governance generally standing up for the potential and sometimes surprising efficacy of soft law sanctions.[5] Here, a soft law approach to firms' above-and-beyond commitments seems more likely to foster a dynamic of continuing improvement than does a demand for legal enforceability. One contribution that external law could usefully make to the promotion of continuing improvement of employee rights and labor standards above legal mandates—and one that is entirely in keeping with the ethos of New Governance—is greater transparency with respect to the matter of legal enforceability. Firms might be required to disclose whether and how their code of conduct and other social responsibility undertakings are, in their view, legally enforceable. That would enable advocates to fine-tune their campaigns and to encourage firms to make their fine-sounding commitments to workers binding.

So the basic vehicle for self-regulation in the workplace is an express set of commitments by an employer to employees—a code of conduct or the like—the substance of which embraces at least relevant legal mandates, along with whatever additional substantive commitments or aspirations the employer is willing to include. The code must be backed up with internal self-regulatory processes to ensure compliance with its provisions, including some form of effective representation for employees (and, as developed below, independent monitoring where employee representation does not take an independent, union-like form).

But who is the responsible employer and for whom is the employer responsible? These are the questions to which we now turn.

WHAT IS THE LOCUS OF SELF-REGULATION?
HOLDING SUPER-EMPLOYERS ACCOUNTABLE

The very term "self-regulation" tends to imply that firms are regulating their own conduct and, in the case of the law of the workplace, the rights and labor standards of their own employees. But that underestimates the potential that lies in activating firms' own regulatory resources. We have already seen that some of the most encouraging existing experiments in self-regulation of labor standards extend the locus of self-regulation to include not only the direct employer of the workers whose conditions are of concern, but also the larger, richer, more stable, and organizationally sophisticated firms that gain the benefit of those workers' labor. Government agencies or worker advocates may put pressure—legal or nonlegal or both—not on the direct legal employers but on those larger entities, seeking to induce them to expand their already considerable oversight capabilities to the realm of labor standards. The problem, again, is that labor standards are often worst at the bottom of the labor market, where firms have little investment in reputation or capital and may be hard to hold accountable or even to locate. The solution has sometimes been found in inducing the firms higher up the supply chain to take responsibility for monitoring and improving conditions down the line. To a surprising degree, the law *can, should,* and arguably *does* do just that.

Let us begin with feasibility. As we have seen, employers at the top of these contracting ladders have developed extraordinary internal regulatory resources. Not only have they developed the sophisticated internal corporate compliance systems discussed above, but also, for purely operational reasons, firms have had to develop systems for monitoring the quality of the goods or services their contractors provide. Often that requires monitoring not just outputs but also processes of production.[6] To be sure, these two systems of control—control of internal compliance and operational control of suppliers—might currently be lodged in different parts of the corporate hierarchy. To the extent user firms are held liable for contractors' labor and employment violations, they may have to merge or link the two systems—to extend oversight of contractors to include not only the quality of goods and services but also the conditions under which they are produced and to extend their corporate compliance programs to include contractors' compliance.

We have seen that such linkages are already happening for many large firms even without a threat of legal liability. Brand-conscious multinational firms, at least, have learned they may be scarred by scandalously poor labor conditions in their contractors' fields and factories where goods are produced, whether or not they could be held legally responsible for those conditions. The Florida tomato pickers and their allies managed to impose "moral liability" on fast-food retailers Taco Bell, McDonald's, and Burger King for the desperate conditions facing those workers, even though those workers were clearly not the employees of the retailers—or perhaps "employees" at all—within the meaning of some employment statutes. The global anti-sweatshop campaigns in particular have managed to make garment manufacturers and retailers morally liable in the eyes of some Western consumers, without regard to their legal liability, for the oppressive conditions facing workers who sew their shoes and garments. And many firms have taken serious steps to avoid such scandals. Nike, for example, once scorned for its reliance on exploitative sweatshop labor, has developed an elaborate system of monitoring to improve working conditions among its almost seven hundred suppliers in fifty-two countries. The results are far from perfect, as Nike's own reports acknowledge. But conditions have improved from the days before monitoring began.[7] If Nike can monitor its hundreds of far-flung overseas suppliers, then it should be possible for other companies to monitor and take responsibility for their contractors within the U.S. that perform work that is integral to those companies' business, especially those that perform work within the companies' business premises.

Unfortunately, without the pressure of legal liability, these monitoring programs are both too weak and too limited in scope. First, many supply-chain monitoring programs are designed more to fend off public criticism than to improve labor standards and are quite ineffective. Everything we have learned about the pitfalls of "cosmetic compliance" and the need for effective employee voice and independent monitoring applies to supply-chain monitoring too. Second, these programs are concentrated in a few sectors like apparel, footwear, and toys. That is not because those are the sectors in which it is *feasible* for corporations to monitor contractors and suppliers; it is because those are the sectors that are most sensitive to consumer activism and outrage—especially activism by college students—and that have been successfully targeted by worker advocates. In the global supply-chain context, for now, there is not much leverage beyond organized consumer outrage and public pressure. But in the domestic context, the law can supply legal incentives for firms to monitor suppliers and contractors.

Of course monitoring is not costless. But the cost of firms' monitoring of their own contractors' labor practices is likely to be much lower than the cost of effective public enforcement, and the more a firm is already monitoring contractors' operations in the interest of quality, speed, and reliability of production, the less it should cost to extend monitoring to include wages and working conditions. The biggest cost to user firms is likely to be the increased contract price to cover wages and working conditions that meet minimum legal standards, but that must be counted not as a social cost but a benefit, for it strengthens the legal floor that is supposed to support individual and collective efforts by workers at the bottom of the labor market to bargain for better wages and working conditions.

So it is often feasible and cost effective to hold large user firms liable for the labor violations of their contractors. It is also justified. These large firms are susceptible to pressure and have in fact been induced in some cases to take on responsibility for conditions at the bottom of the supply chain because there is a plausible moral and economic case for holding them responsible. User firms both benefit economically from and predictably contribute to the erosion of labor standards by their growing practice of contracting out, or outsourcing, low-skill, labor-intensive parts of their business.

The basic theory of the firm has it that a firm's boundaries are defined by a series of decisions about whether to "make or buy"—to produce needed goods or services in-house through the firm's own employees or rather to purchase those goods or services from another firm or entity.[8] Firms in recent decades have been "making" less and "buying" more.[9] Firms might choose to contract out certain functions to gain economies of scale or specialized expertise that allow outside contractors to better perform services. But the trend toward contracting out is particularly pronounced for discrete activities that are labor intensive and require little capital or specialized skill, such as building cleaning and maintenance.[10] And the primary reason firms cite for contracting out labor-intensive services or processes such as maintenance is that it lowers costs.[11] Where do those cost savings come from?

Cost savings come in part from cutting workers off from the higher wages and benefits that prevail within the user employer's own workforce. The informal dynamics of internal labor markets tend to compress wage differentials and to push up wages at the bottom of the internal market above what workers with the relevant skills may command on the external labor market.[12] Those tendencies may be formalized in unionized firms by a collective bargaining agreement; unionization tends to have the greatest impact on the lowest wages in a bargaining unit.[13] And those tendencies may be reinforced by federal tax laws that strongly discourage firms from discriminating against their own lower-paid employees in benefits such as health insurance and pensions.[14] All of these constraints can be avoided by contracting out low-skilled work to a legally separate entity. Escaping a union wage scale, for example, is a major impetus for unionized firms to contract out work.[15] In essence, contracting out low-skilled work allows a firm to fill its labor needs at the lower wages that the external market will bear. There is nothing illegal in that, though it contributes to falling wages at the bottom of the labor market.

Other aspects of contracting out, however, contribute predictably to the proliferation of illegal labor practices. First, contracting out allows user firms to put contractors into competition with each other for the low bid. In sectors in which there are few barriers to entry or capital requirements and in which labor is the main cost item, contractors inevitably compete by pressing down wages to whatever the market (and the regulatory framework) will allow.[16] Second, these contractors pose a chronic challenge to the regulatory framework because they are typically much smaller and less visible and have little capital or reputation invested in their business.[17] They may be able to fly below the regulatory radar and may be judgment proof or prone to disappear in the event of enforcement. And because immigration enforcement, like labor standards enforcement, poses a fairly remote threat to these businesses, they often rely heavily on immigrant, and especially undocumented, workers who are particularly unlikely to complain about substandard wages or working conditions.[18] The upshot is that many less-skilled jobs that used to be performed within larger and more integrated firms, and that were part of those firms' internal labor markets, are now performed within a more thoroughly low-wage environment, often in a race to the bottom of the wage scale and outside the gaze of the public and regulators. The practice of contracting out thus puts downward pressure on wages and labor standards that is predictable and profitable, if not intentional.[19] That is the basic logic of holding those at the top accountable for the illegalities that flourish at the bottom of the labor market.

In fact, the single most important law in the low-wage landscape, the Fair Labor Standards Act (FLSA), aimed to do just that.[20] The practice of contracting out labor-intensive parts of a business to small, minimally capitalized contractors to cut labor costs was well known to New Deal reformers. In the early twentieth century, this was known as the "sweating system": middlemen sweated out their profits from workers under oppressive and illegal conditions, out of the public eye. The system was especially familiar in garment manufacturing; hence, the term "sweatshops." It was precisely to reach through those contracting arrangements that the drafters of the FLSA in 1938 defined employer liability very broadly. Following a pattern set by federal and state child labor laws, the FLSA defined the term "employ" to include "suffer or permit to work."[21]

The express purpose of this very broad formulation was to hold employers liable for substandard working conditions of their contractors' employees even when the common law would not have done so. Under the common law, an "employment" relationship is established by indices of control over the work of the individual worker, as well as by formalities of the relationship, such as who pays the worker. As a result, by delegating direct control of certain components of the business to a contractor, the larger company might escape legal responsibility for the employees' substandard wages and working conditions.[22] Under the "suffer or permit to work" standard, however, the user employer would be liable for wage and overtime violations, provided that the work was an integral part of the user employer's business (especially if it was performed on the user employer's premises) and if the employer had the means to learn that the work was being done and the economic power to prevent it. The goal behind this very broad standard of employer liability was to eliminate substandard wages and working conditions. But it was also to eliminate the competitive advantage of employers who used abusive contracting arrangements to lower labor costs and to protect responsible employers from that unfair competition.[23]

The original meaning of the phrase "suffer or permit to work," and the history and legislative intent behind Congress's use of the phrase, have been exhaustively documented by legal scholars.[24] But the courts have tended to ignore or misconstrue this broad phrase and have often gravitated back toward the common law "control" test. The Supreme Court, for its part, has recognized that the meaning of "employ" under the FLSA is the broadest of any federal labor and employment statutes.[25] The Court has helpfully directed inquiry away from issues of direct physical control and the formalities of the employment contract and toward "economic realit[ies]."[26] But by failing to explain which "economic realities" are important and why, the Court has left the door open to lower courts' use of absurdly indeterminate multifactor tests that often allow employers to avoid liability by delegating day-to-day control over work, and the direct payment of wages, to contractors.[27] Many lower courts seem convinced that Congress could not have meant to deprive employers of the ability to structure their contracting arrangements however they wished to compete effectively. That assumption is half right and half wrong: Congress did not prohibit any contracting-out arrangements; but it did seek to eliminate employers' ability to use them in a way that fostered substandard labor conditions and undercut responsible employers.

It would seem to be an uphill battle to excavate Congress's intent back in 1938 and restore the original meaning of "employ" under the FLSA on the basis of legislative history that much of the current Supreme Court categorically refuses to consider. On the other hand, an honest textual analysis of the phrase "suffer or permit to work" could lead to the same result; the legislative history serves mainly to show that Congress meant what it said here. For policymakers committed to improving enforcement of labor standards in low-wage labor markets, restoring the broad intended scope of employer liability under FLSA, and even extending it to other employment laws, would be a good start.

To the extent that the law looks through contracting arrangements and makes companies directly responsible as employers or joint employers of the workers whose labor they depend on, the law encourages the expansion of self-regulatory activity. Just as a matter of liability avoidance, firms that are sensitive to this expanded liability threat may have to extend their corporate compliance machinery beyond their own corporate boundaries (or else take the work itself back on board, performing the services or producing the goods in-house). Some firms may respond instead by recalibrating their contracting relationships to avoid being defined as employers—by further reducing their monitoring of suppliers' production, for example, or by outsourcing their contracts to lower-wage, less regulated countries. An expanded definition of "employer"—if it is backed by real enforcement, public or private—is likely to produce some of that kind of counterproductive liability avoidance. But it is likely to produce some of the right kind of liability avoidance, including improved monitoring of contractors, as well. For operational concerns may militate against increasing the geographic distance between firms and their contractors or decreasing firms' control of contractors or both. It is not always possible to outsource labor needs to other jurisdictions—maintenance is a prime example—and it is often economically desirable to supervise and control contractors' production of goods and services. So firms will often choose, rather than give up that operational control over quality and quantity of production, to extend that control to include labor standards for which they may be held legally answerable.

Expanding the law's definition of "employer" is not the only way for the law to induce firms to monitor their contractors' labor practices. The DOL's "hot-goods" program in garment manufacturing, flawed though it may be, suggests another existing mechanism that can be used to induce larger companies to monitor their low-wage, low-visibility contractors. Another tack was taken by a 2004 California law, called the "brother's keeper law" by some critics. It makes a firm liable to the employees of contractors in several chronic low-wage sectors (construction, farm labor, and janitorial and security guard services) if the firm "knows or should know that the contract . . . does not include funds sufficient to allow the contractor to comply with all applicable local, state, and federal laws or regulations governing the labor or services to be provided."[28] Like an expanded definition of "employer," the California law does not expressly require any particular monitoring or self-regulatory mechanisms, but it should induce firms to monitor their contractors' labor practices, and it gives regulators and advocates additional leverage to demand effective forms of self-regulation as the price of avoiding liability.

Even for those who are skeptical of the concept of regulated self-regulation and would prefer to rely on beefed up traditional enforcement, it makes sense to extend legal liabilities to super-employers for working conditions within the smaller, less visible, and less organizationally sophisticated employers through which they get their labor inputs. For those who do see the expansion of regulated self-regulation as promising, or in any case inevitable, broader super-employer liability would give regulators and worker advocates greater leverage in inducing those firms to self-regulate within the network of contractors on which they rely.

INDEPENDENT MONITORING
AND INFORMATION

All three approaches to self-regulation from which I have drawn—Responsive Regulation, ratcheted labor standards, and corporate self-regulation under the securities laws—recognize that for a system of self-regulation to be effective, it needs to be open to observation and criticism from without. "Transparency" may overstate the matter; "permeability" is closer to the mark.[29] At the heart of all three systems are channels of information disclosure. Each has some mechanism for gathering credible information from inside the firm—not just what the firm itself chooses to reveal—and for conveying that information to relevant outsiders. The latter include regulatory agencies (where they exist) as well as stakeholders or members of the public with an interest in the information: workers and their organizational advocates, pro-worker consumers, or, in the case of Sarbanes-Oxley, shareholders and securities analysts. While employers' own interest in self-regulation may be driven partly by a desire to insulate themselves from outside scrutiny, the key to making self-regulation effective is to resist that insulation.

To create those channels of information disclosure, regulators and theorists from a wide array of settings have converged upon the institution of independent outside monitoring.[30] Monitors come in many varieties, of course, and they do not always serve the role that theorists assign to them. Monitoring in the global sweatshop context, especially in the first generation of supplier codes, has often failed to ensure compliance; monitoring in the U.S. garment industry has had significant yet modest success in improving compliance with wage and hour laws. So what does it take to ensure that monitoring works?

To begin with, it takes genuine independence. That is, to effectively monitor compliance with public norms that may cost the firm money, monitors must be, at a minimum, independent of the firm they are monitoring. It probably should not require a lot of theory or research to make that point. But what may seem self-evident now—now that self-regulation is becoming a vehicle of public regulation—may not have seemed so clear when it seemed that auditors or monitors were simply helping firms to manage themselves under the shadow of the law. What it takes, in turn, to ensure monitors' independence presumably depends partly on what they are monitoring. It may be surprising, then, that we can learn something about how to ensure the independence of workplace monitors from Congress's effort in Sarbanes-Oxley to shore up the independence of the private accountants who serve as outside monitors of some aspects of compliance with securities laws.

In the wake of Enron and other scandals, those accounting firms were criticized for their willingness to defer to their corporate clients on the propriety of what later appeared to be highly suspect accounting and reporting practices. That excessive deference was traced in part to a conflict of interest between the accounting firms' role as auditors and gatekeepers on behalf of the public and their much more lucrative business consulting relationships with the firms they were auditing.[31] Ironically, some of those same accounting firms were also serving as factory monitors under corporate supplier codes, and they were criticized for a similar lack of zeal in uncovering potential wrongdoing and for monitoring protocols that seemed designed less to uncover code violations than to provide cover to their corporate clients against activist critics. Underlying the criticism was a conflict of interest that is strikingly parallel to that which Sarbanes-Oxley sought to fix in the securities context: the accounting firms' factory-monitoring activities were often only part of a much more lucrative business relationship with the monitored firms.[32]

So monitor independence, at a minimum, requires that the monitors not be economically beholden in this manner to the employers or super-employers that they are monitoring. That does not mean that the funding for monitoring itself cannot come from employers. Public funding might be ideal, but it is partly the scarcity of government resources that is driving the move toward self-regulation. Private foundations or charities may supply start-up funds, but a system of self-regulation that depends on foundation support does not seem sustainable in the long run. At least in the non-union workplace, it is not feasible for employees themselves to foot the bill. So the question is how to ensure monitors' independence even if employers are paying for monitoring.

To begin with, monitors' contracts should not be subject to termination at the whim of employers, even if employers are footing the bill. Selection and oversight should be done by an entity that is independent of the employer and that either is a bona fide worker organization—a union or community-based worker center—or includes such an organization, perhaps alongside representatives of the public and the employer on a tripartite body. Monitors' independence, and workers' trust in their independence, can also be assured in part by the procedures they follow. Inspection protocols should be well publicized, and inspections should not. Decades of experience have demonstrated the importance of unannounced inspections, as well as private meetings with employees. The point here, however, is not to prescribe inspection protocols but to ensure that they are subject to scrutiny and improvement based on evolving "best practices" and under the supervision of public or worker representatives or both.

The form that monitoring and inspections take depends, of course, on what is being monitored. In the case of pay practices, monitoring will generally include employer records—at least payroll and time records. In the case of workplace safety and health, it will include the physical premises as well as records, for example, of the employer's own safety inspections, of accidents or incidents, and of employee complaints. In some bottom-up experiments in self-regulation, monitoring is highly informal; it does not involve physical inspections or access to employer property or records but consists essentially of a worker organization's ability to pursue worker complaints of noncompliance. The CIW monitors the nonpay provisions of its codes of conduct (that is, provisions outside the penny-per-pound pass-through agreement) through a complaint process, combined with education of workers about their rights. That is also how ROC-NY monitors its existing agreements with major restaurateurs. Indeed, for the monitoring and enforcement of code of conduct provisions that guarantee individual employee rights against retaliation or discrimination, an individual complaint process is at least necessary, and perhaps sufficient in some cases. The key for informal monitoring to work is that workers must know their rights and know when they are being violated and, again, that workers know and trust the monitoring organization as a credible advocate for employees that is independent of the employer.

In some of the cases of bottom-up self-regulation chronicled above, a worker organization itself serves as the monitor. That is, of course, part of what unions do within a collective bargaining relationship. But the CIW and the MCTF have shown that unions are not the only worker organizations that have both the independence from employers and the ear and trust of the workers that are needed to play this watchdog role. Both organizations have strong community-based ties to the workers and function as worker centers. As monitors, they had access not only to employer payroll records but also to the ears and eyes of workers, who could report on abuses that may not be evident from the employer's own records. In other cases, monitors are not themselves worker organizations but are overseen in whole or in part by such organizations. The GGCC, for example, largely lacked mechanisms for direct employee representation, but employers under the GGCC submitted to unannounced inspections by monitors who were overseen by and accountable to employee organizations, as well as the state attorney general.

Monitor independence should be non-negotiable. Beyond that, the efficacy of monitors depends on what they can do in the event of noncompliance. That will depend in turn on a range of factors that will vary depending on the place (or jurisdiction), the industry, and the particular complaint. It will depend on the provisions of the agreement and its enforcement mechanisms, if any; on the vigor and efficacy of relevant public agencies to which complaints might be taken; and on the availability of private rights of action and the resources to pursue them. It will also depend on the monitoring organization's own resources, membership, and alliances and its capacity to put nonlegal pressure on violators, a variable to which we will return below. But independent monitors themselves, even if they are not worker organizations with those kinds of resources, are a crucial component of an effective system of regulated self-regulation.

If the monitoring of employers' self-regulation is genuinely independent, it can help to shore up the two weak legs of the tripartite stool in the U.S. law of the workplace: it can help to make up both for a shortfall of public inspections and enforcement and, to some extent, for a lack of independent union representation of employees. Monitors can help narrow the enforcement gap by putting more expert and independent eyes and ears in the workplace and boots on the ground than public agencies can do. Even without formal enforcement mechanisms under a monitoring agreement, monitors can gather information and direct complaints to public agencies, as the MCTF was explicitly authorized to do under its agreement with Global. Monitors can serve as a channel of information from employees to public regulators, leveraging the agencies' limited enforcement resources.

Monitoring itself can also work in some rather diffuse ways to advance workers' freedom of association and expression, for the presence of independent monitors cracks open the doors of the workplace to a degree of outside scrutiny beyond what rare governmental inspections could do; monitors demonstrate tangibly to employees that their rights matter and that someone is watching out for them. An employer's agreement to submit to outside monitoring represents the negotiated surrender of part of the sovereignty that employers still claim over the workplace. As it did before the New Deal, employer sovereignty over the physical workplace presents no small challenge, not only to the regulation of working conditions but also to competing principles of democracy and freedom of association within the workplace.[33] Breaching employer sovereignty by the physical intervention of third parties—parties accountable to workers and the public and independent of the employer—can advance those competing principles at least indirectly. Outside monitoring does not advance directly along the path toward full-fledged collective representation, but it may clear away some of the obstacles on that path by protecting individual employee voice and linking employees and outside worker advocates. Monitoring may thus enhance the prospects for employee representation and genuine co-regulation in the future.

Monitoring can also work in more concrete ways, in part by formalizing and protecting employee whistleblowing. Effective outside monitoring both depends on and helps to promote employees' ability to speak up for themselves without fear of reprisals. It does so in part by providing a conduit through which workers can speak anonymously, and in part by serving as a watchdog to whom workers can turn if they do suffer reprisals. The problem of employee fear in the non-union setting is an enormous hurdle to both self-organization and employee participation in enforcement. But if a system of outside monitoring helps to protect from retaliation individual employees who speak up— and it must do so to work at all—then it may help to lay the groundwork for employees to speak to each other as well and to associate for other shared workplace goals. If outside monitoring helps to alleviate the corrosive problem of employee fear, it may represent a step toward the liberation of employee voice more generally.

PROTECTING INDIVIDUAL EMPLOYEES' MONITORING ROLE

Workers themselves are the best monitors of most terms and conditions of employment and of compliance with employment mandates. We have seen that employees face two basic impediments to fulfilling their potential monitoring role: they are highly vulnerable to employer reprisals (unlike the private beneficiaries of most other regulatory regimes, who are outside the firm), and they typically face collective action problems given the "public goods" nature of compliance with most employment mandates. These are the problems that give rise to the need for both independent monitoring and collective representation. Both independent employee organizations, including unions and worker centers, and independent monitors can tap the wealth of information that employees have about their treatment and working conditions and channel it to those who can do something about it—public officials, employee organizations, or even managers. Both can serve as intermediaries, conferring the shield of anonymity and potentially circumventing the hurdles posed by fear of reprisals. Indeed, unions and worker centers may themselves serve as especially effective monitors because of their ability to aggregate and amplify employees' knowledge and interests and combat the fear of reprisals.

Even with institutions for employee representation and independent monitoring, however, individual employees need to play a part in monitoring compliance. What might be done, apart from the injection of independent outside monitors and employee organizations, to liberate individual employees to serve their own crucial monitoring role?

Reprisals against employees who report illegal or harmful conduct strike at the heart of a system of self-regulation. The most direct and conventional legal response to the fear of employer reprisals is simply to prohibit and punish reprisals through a *post hoc* employee remedy against reprisals. Antiretaliation provisions for employees who report violations have become near boilerplate in federal statutes regulating the conduct of private firms.[34] In particular, statutes establishing employee rights and labor standards often prohibit retaliation against employees who assert those rights.[35] And even when they do not do so explicitly, they may give rise to such protections by implication, either as a matter of statutory interpretation, as in the case of some antidiscrimination laws, or as a matter of common law through the tort of wrongful discharge in violation of public policy.[36] Notwithstanding the continuing force of employment at will in the U.S., courts and legislatures have widely recognized the absurdity, for both employees and the public, of permitting the discharge of employees for speaking out about legal wrongdoing.

At first glance, then, whistleblowers in the U.S. have the benefit of a more solicitous legal regime—one that is studded with special protections—than employees in the rest of the developed world.[37] But context is everything, and the context of U.S. whistleblower laws is the background rule of employment at will. The whistleblower laws are direct reactions, and exceptions, to the background rule of employment at will that would otherwise tolerate socially intolerable reprisals against those who disclose illegal or dangerous employer practices. Indeed, the very term "whistleblower" tends to reinforce the notion that speaking up about illegal or harmful conduct is an exceptional, dramatic, and dissident act. In the rest of the industrialized world, where the background rule requires good cause for discharge, whistleblowers do not obviously need the special protections of a whistleblower protection law, for they cannot lawfully be fired without a legitimate reason in any event.[38]

The background rule of employment at will helps to explain not only the proliferation of whistleblower protection laws but also their shortcomings. For the background rule of employment at will casts multiple burdens of proof, of process, and of delay on complainant employees who are seeking to fit within a whistleblower exception.[39] Many statutory whistleblower laws have been narrowly construed, or are backed by administrative procedures that swallow up many complaints without an adequate hearing, or offer limited remedies that have left them toothless.[40] Some, like OSHA's antiretaliation provision, suffer from all three of these problems. Even where employees have access to adequate remedies and a fair channel for pursuing their retaliation claim, they (or an agency on their behalf) bear the burden of proof, as well as the burden of delay, in that process. Unless and until the employee overcomes all of those hurdles, the default rule of employment at will prevails. As a result, *post hoc* whistleblower protection laws often fail to deliver the protections they promise.

A particularly disheartening illustration of these problems has played out under the whistleblower provisions of Sarbanes-Oxley. On paper, those provisions offer what I have described as the "gold standard" in whistleblower protections: they contain administrative, criminal, and private enforcement provisions.[41] But early experience under those provisions has been extremely disappointing, at least in the administrative process (lodged, ironically, in OSHA, based on its experience with whistleblower claims).[42] According to Professor Richard Moberly, "during its first three years, only 3.6% of Sarbanes-Oxley whistleblowers won relief through the initial administrative process that adjudicates such claims, and only 6.5% of whistleblowers won appeals through the process."[43] These numbers alone leave open the theoretical possibility that corporations have so internalized reforms that they have generated almost no meritorious whistleblower claims. But that would be a perilous assumption, and it is contradicted by Moberly's own assessments of the unwarranted hurdles faced by complainant employees.

Clearly whistleblower protections in the form of *post hoc* remedies against retaliation, while necessary, are not sufficient to open up internal channels of information about compliance. A linchpin of New Governance and regulated self-regulation is the effort to induce organizations to encourage and normalize internal disclosure and dissent, not just to refrain from punishing it.[44] But once those internal channels of information are folded into the picture, things get more complicated. Should the law protect internal whistleblowers or external whistleblowers or both? It is no simple matter to craft liability rules that simultaneously protect those who blow the whistle, encourage firms to create channels for internal disclosure, and encourage employees to use those internal channels.

One mistake would be to protect employees against reprisals *only* if they disclose wrongdoing to the public or the government and not if they report internally. Professor Orly Lobel has shown the particular perversity of that rule for a New Governance approach to controlling corporate misconduct, for it may both discourage employees from using reporting procedures set up by conscientious employers and encourage unscrupulous employers to take reprisals against employees who do report internally before they have the chance to go public.[45] Yet some state courts have so held under the common law of wrongful discharge in violation of public policy, on the theory that public policy is not served by internal reporting.[46] Similarly, the Supreme Court held in the *Garcetti* case that public employees who report wrongdoing internally as part of their jobs enjoy no First Amendment protection against employer reprisals.[47] Statutory whistleblower protections could fill that gap, but many replicate it by similarly denying protection to internal whistleblowers.[48]

A better solution would be broadly protecting employees who report wrongdoing, whether they do so inside or outside the firm, to the government or the public, and without regard to the existence of internal reporting channels. A genuinely responsive internal reporting process will almost always be a more appealing recourse for employees than the vagaries of going public, so an employee's decision to bypass an internal reporting process may itself send a strong signal that the internal process is not working as it should.[49] When we consider how crucial employee monitoring is to effective regulation—especially self-regulation—and how fatal the fear of reprisals is to employee monitoring, it might seem wise to err on the side of broad and accessible whistleblower protections that do not compel recourse to internal reporting procedures.

But the broadest protection for whistleblowers is not necessarily the best way to get information about wrongdoing to those who can do something about it. Employers that do maintain serious internal reporting procedures may be able to address problems more expeditiously if employees use those internal procedures. External whistleblowing has real costs—the disruption of legitimate corporate reporting procedures and of internal organizational cohesion within a genuine culture of compliance. Professor Lobel contends persuasively that a society can be too reliant on external whistleblowers and that loyalty has a legitimate place within organizations that embrace the mission of compliance and responsiveness to societal demands. Seeking to strike a balance between protecting employee dissent and supporting effective internal compliance systems, she has proposed a "sequenced" reporting system that requires employees to bring their concerns first to their immediate supervisors and then to internal grievance or reporting procedures, unless in either case those channels are shown to be ineffectual or risky.[50]

It is tempting to be cynical about appeals to organizational trust and loyalty in the context of employee disclosures of illegal or questionable conduct. But we should not reflexively assume good faith on the part of all whistleblowers or bad faith on the part of all organizations. Indeed, if we wholly discounted the possibility of a genuine culture of compliance, then the entire enterprise of regulated self-regulation would be a delusion and should be abandoned. The argument here is that it is possible to create and recognize a system of well-regulated self-regulation—one with built-in safeguards against bad-faith and cosmetic compliance. And we have begun to identify the necessary components of an effective self-regulatory system, including the participation of independent monitors and employee representatives within such a system. That leads me to suggest a variant of Lobel's sequenced reporting scheme.

Independent monitors and employee representatives ought to be natural avenues of reporting for employees who fear to complain directly to management; that is a major part of their role. Employers that take these major self-regulatory steps beyond the standard contours of existing corporate compliance programs should be rewarded with a shield against liability to whistleblowers who bypass this system to go public. In other words, one of the regulatory rewards that the law should afford to employers who meet public standards of effective co-regulation is a stronger claim on the loyalty of their employees and a defense against whistleblowers who bypass internal channels. Unless an employee can show that the co-regulatory system was a sham, notwithstanding the presence of purportedly independent monitors and employee representation, the firm should be entitled to insist that employees make their report first through internal channels and give employers a reasonable chance to fix reported problems.

Again, *post hoc* whistleblower protections will not do enough to encourage employees—at least non-union employees who want to keep their jobs—to speak up about illegal and abusive practices at work. But the combination of *post hoc* whistleblower remedies and internal reporting channels, together with independent monitoring and collective representation, would go far toward tapping the prodigious potential of employee monitoring of compliance with employment laws and liberating employees to speak up on their own behalf.

Having sketched the basic architecture and elements of an effective system of regulated self-regulation, let us turn to strategies for realizing this system. How do we get there from here?

Chapter 9 Getting There from Here:

Strategies for Promoting

Co-Regulation in the Workplace

The erstwhile paradigm of command-and-control regulation offered the comforting illusion that command entailed control—that we could achieve regulatory goals and change organizational behavior simply by enacting mandates. Although the era of mandates is hardly behind us, it has become increasingly clear over recent decades that there is a great deal of slippage between enacting mandates and achieving social objectives. The law has to reckon with powerful forces both inside firms and in the world in which firms function. There are the stubborn hydraulics of labor markets, product markets, and capital markets within which firms operate and the inescapable voluntariness of the contracts and investments that make up most of the economy. And there are the cultures and psychologies and logics that operate inside the organizations that are the objects of regulation and that make those organizations not impervious but difficult to penetrate and direct from the outside. These are some of the basic insights underlying the movement away from command-and-control and toward regulated self-regulation as a strategy of social control. Unfortunately, these same basic insights tell us that we cannot simply command the adoption of co-regulatory structures even if we are convinced that they represent the right future for workplace governance. Fortunately, we have seen that the movement toward self-regulation is already under way; in some respects, then, we are rowing downstream and with the current rather than upstream. It will nonetheless take some skillful steering to head in the right direction.

First, a word on terminology: the terms "co-regulation" and "effective self-regulation" will both be used here, in keeping with this book's thesis that they mean the same thing in the workplace context. Effective self-regulation of employee rights and labor standards requires effective employee involvement; it requires what I have called co-regulation. I hope to have made that case in principle. In what follows, I aim to sketch some potential reform strategies for steering existing trends toward self-regulation in the direction of co-regulation.

One crucial element of any program to improve labor standards and better enforce employee rights is labor law reform that makes it possible for employees who want union representation to get it. Labor law reform would do much to advance the cause of co-regulation by enabling workers to enforce their own rights, improve their own labor standards, and participate in workplace governance through collective bargaining. Not only union-represented employees would benefit. If employers seeking to avoid unionization were unable to use threats and coercion to that end, they might have to offer better terms and conditions of employment and better workplace governance instead. In other words, protecting employees' right to form a union would force employers to use "carrots" instead of "sticks" to avoid unionization. But labor law reform is not the only reform that is needed, and it is not my topic here. For with or without labor law reform, the movement toward self-regulation will almost certainly continue, and it needs to be steered in a productive, co-regulatory direction lest it end up deteriorating into disguised deregulation.

In the best of all political worlds, with all of the stars aligned and all of the key political actors persuaded of the virtues of co-regulation and shared workplace governance, it would be possible to enact federal laws that would help steer American workplaces toward that end. Even in that best of all worlds, it would be no simple matter to craft statutory interventions that would accomplish the desired ends, given the internal and external forces operating on firms. And that best of all worlds is probably not just around the corner. Still, the exercise of imagining an ideal national legal regime of co-regulation for the workplace is worthwhile, if only for the lessons it might offer both to state and local public officials and to individual agencies and private actors seeking to make the most of existing legal resources.

We are more likely, of course, to find ourselves in a second-best world, in which limited statutory reforms are possible and some regulatory agencies are on board, or even a third-best world, in which private actors—especially workers, worker advocates and organizations, and private lawyers who represent them—are left to do what they can with existing tools and resources. The virtue of the quasi-contractual architecture of regulated self-regulation as it has evolved so far is its versatility and usability by a range of actors, even without deliberate legislative intervention. Armed with sufficient leverage against a firm with self-regulatory capacity, both public regulators and worker advocates can induce firms to make co-regulatory commitments. If those advocates are persuaded of the virtues of co-regulation in the workplace, the question will be whether and how they can martial the requisite leverage, legal and nonlegal, to draw firms into making the necessary commitments and to make those commitments stick.

Perhaps paradoxically, the second- or third-best world in which we are likely to find ourselves may have some advantages over the seemingly first-best solution of comprehensive federal legislation. One lesson we may take from the ossification of labor law is that comprehensive federal statutory reform—at least if it preempts state or local or private experimentation—can become a straitjacket. It can be hijacked in one fell swoop when the political winds shift, as the Wagner Act was in part by the Taft-Hartley amendments, or it can become locked in against necessary modifications by cumbersome supermajoritarian hurdles within Congress, as labor law has been since the 1950s. By contrast, the emerging quasi-contractual architecture of regulated self-regulation is intrinsically friendly to experimentation and evolution over time; that is a strength or even a necessity in a globalized economy populated by fluid, flexible, and mobile organizations. Let us begin, then, by attempting to design a comprehensive federal statutory regime of co-regulation that builds on existing self-regulatory trends and that is itself friendly to experimentation and evolution.

A FEDERAL FRAMEWORK FOR CO-REGULATION

The basic existing architecture of regulated self-regulation is quasi-contractual; firms have put in place internal self-regulatory machinery "voluntarily" in response to various kinds of inducements. In particular, the Federal Sentencing Guidelines for Organizations have strongly shaped existing corporate compliance systems. Given the high stakes for corporations facing potential criminal liability, the Guidelines have put a lot of pressure on firms to put in place, at least on paper, the basic elements of an "effective compliance program": codes of conduct prescribing at least compliance with relevant law that are communicated effectively to employees and overseen by reputable, high-level company officials, along with systems to monitor compliance (including confidential reporting systems), appropriate incentives and sanctions to induce compliance, and an actual response by the firm if violations are discovered.[1]

The basic approach of the Guidelines—crafting an authoritative definition of effective self-regulation and making that the condition for valuable regulatory concessions—is promising. The Guidelines appear to serve a coordinating function, a template around which firms organize and assess their own compliance processes, even in the realm of employment law, where criminal punishments and prosecutions are rare. But the Guidelines and the internal compliance systems they have shaped have been fairly criticized for failing to guard against cosmetic compliance. Moreover, effective self-regulation in the context of the employment laws has some special features. So a starting point for reform would be to craft a definition of effective self-regulation in the employment context—that is, of co-regulation—that both leaves room for experimentation and firm-level variation and incorporates checks against cosmetic compliance. That definition should then be made a reference point for recalibrating enforcement regimes, penalties, and rewards under the employment laws.

We have seen that independent stakeholder representation is an essential element of effective self-regulation, whatever the area of concern; stakeholder representation is a missing feature of the Guidelines framework that ought to be reconsidered across the board. But stakeholder representation is particularly crucial and achievable in the context of employment laws, whose beneficiaries are already inside the firm. The value of employee representation includes but extends beyond the monitoring of compliance. A body that is elected by and representative of employees—whether it is a union or an internal employee committee—also has a role to play in shaping the code of conduct, communicating it to employees, designing incentives and disciplinary procedures, and responding to violations.

So an "effective compliance system" in the employment context requires participation of either an independent labor organization that represents employees pursuant to the federal labor laws or, for employees who lack such representation, an elected body of employee representatives within the workplace. The latter alternative will not always be possible to implement (especially in low-wage workforces with very high turnover); even when workplace-based employee representation is possible, there are questions about the level, scope, and form of representation, particularly in complex organizations in which employees are spread out over many sites. I leave those questions of implementation for another day. It would also raise concerns about employer domination of such committees, addressed in Chapter 7. The legal problem under the NLRA could be fixed, perhaps with a statutory "safe harbor" (as long as we are in our first-best world, in which all we have to decide is what legislation to enact). The practical problem of employer domination would remain. Beyond the requirement of employee selection, the primary safeguard against employer domination here is the coupling of internal employee committees with the institution of outside monitoring. That is the second element of co-regulation: where employees are not represented by an independent labor organization but only by an internal committee, there must also be an outside monitor that is independent of the employer and accountable in some manner to employees. The outside monitor helps along multiple dimensions to ensure compliance and to keep firms honest: by providing an independent outlet and means of communication and protection to vulnerable inside employees, who may be frustrated or silenced by internal self-regulatory processes, and by giving a window into those processes to outsiders—regulators, consumers, advocates—that have sanctions at their disposal.

So the centerpiece of a comprehensive co-regulatory reform is an authoritative definition of the basic elements of co-regulation under the employment laws. So much for the *quid;* what about the *quo?* What should firms get in exchange for maintaining an effective co-regulatory program thus defined?

To pose the question that way may seem to rest too heavily on a crude calculus of costs and benefits and to give short shrift to the norms of corporate responsibility and citizenship that might lead firms to conform to publicly articulated "best practices," or to improve upon those practices, without reference to any such calculus. I do not mean to neglect those virtuous dynamics. Much of the research on self-regulation across the world confirms a basic insight of Braithwaite and his collaborators regarding "responsive regulation": modern regulatory systems work better (or work at all) by tapping into and reinforcing the better civic and moral impulses within and among regulated organizations. But the research also confirms another of Braithwaite's basic insights: there must be mechanisms to detect and punish cheating by low-road competitors, for such cheating undermines impulses toward compliance and cooperation by demoralizing conscientious self-regulators and putting competitive pressure on them. We have to assume that some firms may seek a competitive edge by cutting corners on compliance and cannot be relied upon to respond to anything other than regulatory sticks and carrots. That is why it is so important to build in safeguards against cheating in the form of independent monitoring and representation of employees, and that is why it is important to ensure that effective self-regulation brings tangible, extrinsic rewards as well as whatever intangible and intrinsic rewards may come from corporate virtue.

There are two types of potential rewards for effective co-regulation: front-end rewards and back-end rewards. At the front end, co-regulators may be afforded a less onerous or adversarial public enforcement track (fewer inspections, for example); at the back end, they may be granted some immunity against liabilities or punishments when violations do occur. These rewards will vary across statutory schemes; wage and hour enforcement is different from occupational safety and health enforcement, and both are different from antidiscrimination law. This discussion will stay at the level of general principles. Let us begin with the back-end rewards.

The basic tenets of the deterrence model of corporate compliance would suggest that the existence of a co-regulatory defense will induce the prescribed precautions only if firms otherwise face a prospect of damages or fines or other costs that are large enough and likely enough to be worth avoiding. We have already observed that existing penalties and remedies under most employment laws (especially the wage and hour laws), when discounted to reflect the low probability of enforcement, are too weak to deter violations when market conditions invite such violations. By the same token, the existing enforcement pressures are too weak to induce firms to embark on the self-regulatory enterprise if it is not otherwise in their interest to do so. That will be even more true if we raise the cost of an effective self-regulatory program by incorporating a requirement of independent employee representation and monitoring. So it is clear that a beefed-up background threat of serious and escalating enforcement is a necessary component of a system of co-regulation.

Further specification of an ideal sanctions regime is suggested by Jennifer Arlen and Reinier Kraakman, whose complex analysis will be greatly simplified here.[2] Arlen and Kraakman contend that some form of "composite liability" — a composite between strict corporate liability for misconduct without regard to precautions taken and a duty-based regime that deals out sanctions based on precautions taken — creates the optimal incentives for self-regulation and self-policing within organizations.[3] They argue for a composite liability regime that would hold all firms liable for detected wrongs (the "residual sanction") but would impose an additional sanction on firms that fail to regulate themselves adequately.[4] The minimum "residual sanction" must cover the full social cost of the misconduct, enhanced to reflect the probability of nondetection; that is the strict liability dimension. (If a self-regulation defense enabled the firm to escape liability for actual harms to employees—especially harms such as underpayment of wages from which the firm profits—that would make it all too profitable for firms to create the appearance of self-regulation without the substance.) But self-regulators would escape the higher "default sanction," which must be high enough to induce firms to undertake self-policing and to discover and disclose wrongdoing when it occurs.

This analysis counsels the adoption of much larger default penalties than exist now under virtually any labor and employment laws. Indeed, existing monetary sanctions under the FLSA and OSHA, given existing enforcement levels, do not rise even to the level of the lower "residual sanctions" that Arlen and Kraakman deem necessary for all firms, including self-regulators. In the real world, monetary sanctions are effectively supplemented to some degree by "market sanctions," including the reputational hit that at least big firms suffer when they are labeled lawbreakers. Arlen and Kraakman assume those sanctions away for purposes of their analysis, but we know they exist for some firms. One might also hope that the problem of inadequate monetary penalties would be mitigated by the existence of individual and organizational proclivities toward compliance; a culture of compliance and individual conscience might effectively supplement external sanctions. But we have recognized that those proclivities are far from universal and that the available sanctions must be sufficient to deter those who do not share them. Recall the injunction of Responsive Regulation that regulators must have "big guns" in reserve for the most recalcitrant actors. "Big guns" are in rather short supply under the existing labor laws. In our first-best world, that would be remedied.

So part of what is needed to launch firms onto the high road of co-regulation is an adequate threat of publicly administered punishment for defectors. That threat, rarely deployed and judiciously withheld in the case of effective self-regulators, is one major driving force behind the self-regulatory enterprise. From a public budgetary perspective, raising potential penalties for violations, while committing to reduce them for virtuous self-regulators, is an inexpensive way to nudge firms in the direction of compliance and effective self-regulation. In theory that might suffice even without increasing regulatory vigilance and the probability that violations will be detected. Unfortunately, the most opportunistic employers may still be tempted to play the odds—to cut legal corners, intimidate employees into silence, and extract higher profits. The low-road, low-visibility employers with little reputational or other capital at stake may do so with impunity, counting on the option of insolvency or disappearance in case of detection. So in our first-best world, in which the political will to improve labor and employment standards through self-regulation is a given, we should also increase enforcement resources to increase the probability that wrongdoing will be detected. The aim is to ensure that virtuous self-regulators are not undercut and demoralized by competitors that do not invest in a self-regulatory program at all or that put up the pretense of self-regulation while covertly defecting.

Still, unless we are to posit a world of unlimited resources, the question is how to make optimal use of limited public enforcement resources. It seems obvious that inspection and enforcement resources should be targeted at sectors and actors where violations are expected to be most prevalent. If we have gotten things right on the other end—that is, if we have correctly identified the necessary elements of an effective self-regulatory program—then it is clear that effective self-regulators should be subject to a less adversarial, more trusting regulatory regime while others—non-self-regulators and those whose self-regulatory programs fall short—should encounter tougher and more intense regulatory scrutiny. In other words, effective self-regulating firms should get another kind of reward, in addition to the prospect of reduced penalties, in the form of a more cooperative and less onerous inspection regime.

This makes sense if regulators and courts can indeed distinguish genuine from cosmetic compliance programs up front, or if, in case of false positives at the front end, cheating is likely to be detected at the back end in spite of reduced regulatory scrutiny. That is precisely the point of requiring independent third-party involvement on behalf of the employee beneficiaries. Building a conduit for outside scrutiny, and a potential link to regulators, into self-regulatory structures is the best guarantee against cheating. It should enable regulators to place conscientious firms on a more cooperative, less intense enforcement track without too great a risk of evasion.

Both the front-end rewards of reduced scrutiny and the back-end rewards of reduced penalties are meant to induce firms that aspire to good citizenship to reshape their compliance structures in advance of—and in hopes of avoiding —legal entanglements. But some firms will resist the inducements to good citizenship, hoping either to avoid violations by other means or to skate by under the regulatory radar. We have already prescribed larger supercompensatory and punitive sanctions for firms that do run afoul of the law and that have failed to meet the prescribed standards of effective self-regulation. But those same sanctions might yet become leverage to demand or impose structural reforms. The elements of effective self-regulation should serve not only as a model for good corporate citizens seeking the high road, but also as a template for remedial action against bad corporate citizens caught taking the low road.

This is roughly the model followed by the DOL when it found endemic wage and hour violations among garment contractors. The "hot-goods" provisions of the FLSA gave the DOL leverage not only over the contractors themselves but also over the manufacturers whose goods might be caught in the "hot-goods" embargo, and it used that leverage to induce manufacturers to agree to monitor the wage and hour practices of their contractors. The program has been both lauded for the improvements it spurred and criticized for the noncompliance that remained. The program's failings lay not in the basic strategy but largely in the vague and inadequate guidelines for monitoring. Armed with a more exacting set of guidelines for effective monitoring—monitors that are genuinely independent and that work hand in hand with worker representatives within the affected workplaces—the DOL (or a state analog) might impose self-regulatory measures as the price for avoiding more onerous penalties.

Elsewhere I have referred to a "representation remedy" that captures elements of the present proposal.[5] And I have suggested that, given the ingrained aversion of U.S. employers toward any form of independent employee representation, the prospect of being hit with a "representation remedy" in case of serious violations may have as much deterrent effect as the usual threat of fines or damages. That is a bonus.

So a public commitment to encourage effective self-regulation, rigorously defined, coupled with an arsenal of seriously deterrent remedial responses to misconduct, can generate a number of strategies: at the front end, reduced regulatory scrutiny and a more cooperative regulatory relationship for effective self-regulators; at the back end, when misconduct is detected, lesser sanctions for effective self-regulators and heavier sanctions for non-self-regulators or, with the threat of those heavier sanctions as leverage, prospective self-regulatory reforms, including worker representation and independent monitoring.

Another component of the fully realized federal regime, previewed in Chapter 8, would be an expanded definition of "employer" that extends the liability of user firms for the employment violations of their contractors in cases where the user firms benefit from and should be aware of those violations. Whether the definition of "employer" remains statute-specific, as it is now, or is defined across regulatory regimes, an expanded definition would aim at least to eliminate one insidious incentive for contracting out production or services—the effort to avoid liability for illegal cost-saving employment practices. For contracting-out relations that remain, the objective would be to channel some of the prodigious regulatory resources within large firms toward the under- and unregulated lower tiers of the labor market. That should improve labor standards enforcement for the many low-wage workers whose labor accrues to the direct benefit of large, stable, organizationally sophisticated firms that invest in their reputation for social responsibility.

Of course, in some sectors the result of these reforms in the U.S. may be to redirect those contracts to less-regulated jurisdictions. For although we might redefine "employer" under U.S. labor standards laws to include, for example, the big garment brands that market goods manufactured in domestic sweatshops, basic principles of territoriality will prevent us from extending those laws to include workers in China or Bangladesh. For the goods and services that can be produced in low-wage, less-regulated regions of the world (and that are not already being produced there), the possibility of additional outsourcing is a risk that has to be factored into decisions about labor standards. But the place to make those calculations is in deciding what labor standards to put in place; once having set those standards, society should aim to make them stick throughout the domestic labor market—to prevent scofflaws from undercutting law-abiding employers and to discourage strategies of circumvention through contracting arrangements.

It is tempting to see the combination of increased penalties and enforcement resources and self-regulatory defenses and privileges as little more than a bigger pile of sticks and carrots with which to induce rational profit-maximizing firms to comply with public aims. And indeed, part of the objective is to ensure that those firms and those actors within firms that are motivated only by their private balance sheet of costs and benefits see a bottom line that favors compliance. But the objective is also to promote and reinforce the norms of corporate social responsibility that many firms, especially large firms, espouse and that many actually seek to live by. Firms that make good on commitments to exemplary citizenship should be treated differently—with less suspicion and more cooperation—than their competitors that cut every corner that is unguarded by regulators, and they should be protected against that sort of corrosive competition. A public regime of regulated self-regulation, backed by a strong system of traditional enforcement and penalties for noncompliance and cheating, can reward the good citizens, deter the cutthroat competitors, and help to persuade those who are wavering to choose a high-road over a low-road competitive strategy. And by defining good citizenship and effective self-regulation in a way that takes seriously the essential role, as well as the vulnerability, of employees themselves in promoting decent workplace practices, this regime of co-regulation can, at the same time, open new pathways for employee voice and influence at the workplace.

We set out to design a system of regulated self-regulation that was friendly to experimentation and capable of evolving without constant legislative tinkering. This calls for some mechanism that allows both regulators and stakeholder organizations to evaluate self-regulatory systems and their results, to identify "best practices," and to incorporate those lessons in the next round of innovations. Mechanisms that foster "continuous improvement" are central to the models of "democratic experimentalism" and to what Christine Parker and John Braithwaite call "metaregulation."[6] At a minimum, that requires reporting of self-regulatory innovations and results (for example, actual improvements in worker health and safety) so that regulators and stakeholders can see what works best. Moreover, a federal regime should allow a firm to gain self-regulatory privileges by persuading regulators and stakeholders that its own system of internal compliance is at least as effective as the legally prescribed regime, and it should allow states to substitute their own systems of regulated self-regulation on the basis of such a showing as well. Improvement requires experimentation, and experimentation requires flexibility and receptivity to varied approaches to self-regulation. But effective stakeholder participation is not one of those elements that should be up for grabs. Stakeholder participation—specifically employee participation—is the primary safeguard against cheating and cosmetic compliance, as well as regulatory capture, which is a real danger in ceding regulatory authority to the states.[7]

Worker advocates and worker-friendly policymakers should seek to enact federal legislation that launches a system of well-regulated self-regulation—a system of co-regulation—with workers' voices at the heart of such a system. The trend toward corporate self-regulation, and toward societal reliance on corporate self-regulation, is not going to be stopped, but it can be steered in a more worker-friendly direction. Supposing, however, that a comprehensive statutory scheme of regulated self-regulation might not be feasible or might take years to achieve, the question is what can be done by advocates and policymakers in the meantime?

PROCEEDING PIECEMEAL: PUBLIC REGULATORY STRATEGIES

One way of proceeding piecemeal is element by element. The various elements of a comprehensive federal scheme of regulated self-regulation include articulation of a "self-regulation" defense that incorporates the prescribed safeguards; stronger remedies and penalties and greater regulatory scrutiny for non-self-regulators and phony self-regulators; an expanded definition of employer liability that reaches further down supply chains; and labor law reform that makes it more feasible for workers to choose independent collective representation. Those elements are mutually reinforcing, but they are not entirely interdependent. In other words, given the forces that are already pushing firms to maintain internal compliance systems, any one of the foregoing reforms would help steer them in the right direction. For example, tweaking the existing legal definition of "effective compliance programs" to include employee representation, all by itself, would nudge some firms to adjust their internal programs in a co-regulatory direction. An expanded definition of employer liability, all by itself, would induce larger firms to reexamine their contracting practices, as well as their contractors' practices, with an eye to reducing that added exposure. Increasing the penalties for noncompliance, all by itself, would lead firms to make improvements in their internal systems that they believe would actually improve compliance.

Collective employee representation is one element, however, that calls most insistently for intervention. In theory, if the cost of noncompliance is great enough and if collective representation improves compliance, employers will welcome such representation. For example, increased enforcement and penalties might lead firms to get workers involved collectively in monitoring compliance. In fact, given the strong resistance to unionization (and anything like it) among American employers, that seems unlikely to happen without deliberate intervention. So reforms designed to promote effective institutions of employee representation would be a good place to start in a piecemeal approach to promoting effective self-regulation. Such reforms should include changes to the labor laws to better enable employees to form their own organizations and a statutory safe harbor for certain internal employee committees, as well as a redefinition of effective self-regulation, or "effective compliance programs," to require employee representation as one condition for gaining self-regulatory privileges or concessions.

Another way of proceeding piecemeal is agency by agency. Subject-specific legislation—for example, OSHA reform legislation—could obviously adopt a strategy of regulated self-regulation with some or all of the elements outlined above. Even without new legislation, there is a great deal that regulators could do within the confines of existing resources and statutory language. Regulators have considerable discretion within the enforcement process in deciding which firms and workplaces to target for inspection and scrutiny, whether to pursue violations, and what penalties to seek. A regulatory policy that embraced the idea of co-regulation in its choice of targets and remedies—even though it was operating within the constraints of the existing penalty structure and enforcement resources—would nudge firms down the right path. It would help define and reward good corporate behavior for those firms already aspiring to good citizenship, and it would adjust the deterrence calculus of costs and benefits that the low-road firms face.

Yet another way of proceeding piecemeal is jurisdiction by jurisdiction. At the state level, subject to the constraints of federal preemption, one might again pursue either a comprehensive statutory approach or another piecemeal strategy, element by element or agency by agency or both. The permutations are obviously multiplying before our eyes. But the kaleidoscopic possibilities for pursuing co-regulation should be welcomed—and indeed protected in any comprehensive federal approach. There is no need for policymakers and regulators to wait for comprehensive statutory reforms that might never materialize; reform can proceed in steps and along multiple pathways. As seen in Chapter 4, Maine and California are among the pioneers in promoting more cooperative and reflexive regulatory schemes in occupational safety and health regulation, while New York has promoted experiments in the wage and hour arena. Existing programs could be improved, and new ones launched more successfully, on the basis of a better apprehension of how self-regulation can be effectively regulated.

PROMOTING CO-REGULATION THROUGH
PRIVATE ACTION

There are many potential roadblocks—legal, political, and bureaucratic—to reform and experimentation by public agencies. So it is worth exploring other incremental strategies of bringing about co-regulation that are based not on capturing and recalibrating the machinery of government but on channeling the prodigious reform potential of private litigation and private shareholder activism.

Reform through Private Litigation
(and Litigation Avoidance)

I began by dividing the growing field of employment law into employee rights enforceable through litigation and workplace standards enforced by regulatory agencies. But that division turns out to be somewhat artificial, for employee rights, some of them backed with private rights of action, are embedded within many of the labor standards regimes and offer potential leverage to private-sector worker advocates. Private lawsuits can potentially help to fill the enforcement gap left by the undercommitment of public resources; indeed, they can sometimes supply "big guns" where the public agencies have too few in their arsenal. Private rights of action can function as "destabilization rights," helping to mobilize or simply bypass public regulators that become captured, hamstrung, sclerotic, or ideologically resistant to enforcing statutory rights and labor standards.[8]

Litigation by private parties has proven to be a potent stimulus to workplace reform in the U.S., especially under the civil rights laws. Recall the impact of discrimination and harassment lawsuits on employer practices and workplace culture. Patterns of segregation and discrimination that were endemic to many workplaces began to produce costly judgments. The response of employers ranged—and to some extent progressed—from elimination of overtly discriminatory practices to internal equal employment policies to affirmative action to the promotion of diversity and inclusion. Some equal employment programs were adopted under direct court order or under settlements or consent decrees; many more were adopted voluntarily by firms hoping to avoid liability and the many costs of litigation—financial, organizational, and reputational. Along the way, the law's formal recognition of internal compliance programs in cases like *Faragher, Ellerth,* and *Kolstad* shaped them and gave further impetus to their growth.

Contemporary corporate initiatives seeking diversity and inclusion eventually outgrew the compliance template, but they are its progeny. Corporate America's voluble commitment to diversity and inclusion has roots in antidiscrimination law much as the "culture of safety" touted by many firms has roots in OSHA: these programs purport to reach "beyond compliance," and they have their own internal constituencies and rationales that extend beyond liability avoidance, but their origins are partly in liability avoidance and corporate compliance. Private litigation under antidiscrimination law has effectively brought about a regime of regulated self-regulation.

I do not mean to be too sanguine here. Discrimination has hardly been banished. Some diversity programs are surely window dressing—the equivalent of "cosmetic compliance" in the post-compliance context. At least to the extent that employers put forward these programs as a basis for legal concessions, such as a partial defense to liability under *Faragher, Ellerth,* and *Kolstad,* they should be required to incorporate safeguards in the form of employee representation and outside monitoring. Workforce-wide employee representation is needed, especially to monitor the fairness of internal and arbitral dispute resolution schemes. But that basic form of employee representation might usefully be supplemented by additional identity-based subgroups for employees who fear that their particularized interests otherwise risk being submerged.

The present point is that the threat and reality of antidiscrimination litigation has stimulated a process of institutional reform that, albeit imperfect, appears to have improved the employment landscape and the working environment for many women and minorities, especially in the largest and most visible firms. And as the courts have started to articulate the shape of the institutional reforms that are needed to gain the law's favor (even if the courts have been too vague and superficial in doing so), employers have felt the need to reshape their internal structures accordingly. That experience has important lessons to teach as we consider how to extend and improve self-regulatory institutions in other areas of workplace law.[9] In particular, let us ask what private actors can do, especially through litigation under existing laws, to sidestep or supplement underequipped or inactive regulatory agencies to promote an effective system of self-regulation of labor standards. And let us focus here on wage and hour practices, where private litigation is a large and growing presence.

The question is complicated by the fact that such claims may fall within a mandatory arbitration clause and may not make it to court.[10] As discussed in Chapter 4, there is a good deal of controversy among employment law scholars over whether and under what conditions arbitration can be a fair and adequate forum for employment claims generally. In the past, mandatory arbitration agreements were rare among the lower-wage workers who feature in much wage and hour litigation; but that may be changing as the threat of aggregate wage and hour litigation has grown. Some wage and hour claims, especially for low-wage workers, are not viable on an individual basis, either in court or in arbitration, and can be vindicated only on an aggregate basis.[11] To the extent that employers are able to use mandatory arbitration agreements to exact from employees a waiver of the right to aggregate their claims, employers may be able to preclude some wage and hour claims altogether. That would be a serious blow to employment law enforcement, and especially to wage and hour enforcement, under any regulatory model. On the other hand, expanding private rights of action in the labor arena would open up additional avenues for the promotion of co-regulation. California took a big step in that direction with the enactment in 2004 (on the eve of Governor Arnold Schwarzenegger's inauguration) of the Labor Code Private Attorneys General Act (PAGA), tagged by employers as the "bounty hunter law."[12] PAGA permitted aggrieved employees to sue to enforce labor laws where the state did not do so—whether or not the underlying law provided for private enforcement—and to collect part of the civil fines that were assessed (as well as attorneys' fees). Alarmed employers sought repeal of the Act but succeeded only in amending it, limiting PAGA's reach to "serious violations" and interposing procedural prerequisites to litigation that are designed to give both regulators and employers a chance to remedy violations.[13] Even as amended, the law is an important tool for employees and their advocates seeking to improve enforcement, and it could be part of a strategy to pursue co-regulation.

The strategies available to private plaintiffs and their advocates loosely parallel the strategies available to public regulators: internal reform may be pursued one firm at a time under the highly focused pressure of litigation and potential or actual liability, or it may be promoted wholesale by establishing guidelines for firms seeking prophylactically to limit their liabilities or avoid litigation.

THE REMEDIAL STRATEGY

Let us put aside for present purposes the controversies surrounding arbitration and assume that an employer has been found to have engaged in widespread wage violations and faces liability in court. Beyond seeking redress for past violations, what can employees and their advocates do to bring about a regime of effective self-regulation for the future? Some private actors have already begun to show the way. The monitoring schemes under both the GGCC and the Global Building Services settlement with the MCTF, described in Chapter 5, came about as the result of investigatory footwork and bottom-up advocacy by unions and other worker advocates. At least in the case of MCTF, those worker advocates then went on to supply much needed expertise, credibility, and commitment to workers' interests within the monitoring schemes themselves. To be sure, in both cases, the threat of public enforcement supplied much of the impetus behind employers' participation in the monitoring schemes. But it is not clear that regulatory authorities are always essential players in the establishment of a scheme of monitoring and self-regulation. When labor standards regimes include private rights of action, they allow individuals and advocates to invoke the aid and eventually the coercive power of the judicial branch in support of their claims.

So one way in which private litigation can steer firms toward effective self-regulation is through prospective remedies in successful litigation. We may call this the "remedial strategy" for achieving institutional reform, and it has been pioneered in the employment discrimination context.[14] The remedial strategy is a resource-intensive approach that seeks reform one organization at a time. At the same time, the immediate prospect of big liabilities provides focused leverage and the ability to impose rather demanding conditions that firms would be unlikely to adopt outside that setting.

Suppose that a firm has been found liable for widespread off-the-clock work or "time-shaving"—doctoring of hourly employees' time sheets to reduce their pay. Whether these acts are the unauthorized acts of rogue supervisors, as employers typically claim, or the pervasive and tacitly encouraged cost-cutting strategies that many lawsuits allege, they call for prospective as well as retrospective relief as part of any remedy or settlement. That prospective relief might consist of organizational and technological reforms within a corporate compliance regime, and those reforms should include safeguards in the form of employee representation and independent monitoring of compliance. The pendency of litigation and the threat of megabucks liability may give employee advocates the kind of leverage over employers that government regulators used to secure monitoring in the apparel industry and the greengrocer context. While compensation is undoubtedly a major goal of these lawsuits—particularly where they are prosecuted by private attorneys on a contingency basis—some of the potential liability for past misconduct, and especially some of the supercompensatory liabilities, might be provisionally traded off in exchange for the firms' submission to a system of monitoring that promises to prevent future violations.

MCTF's monitoring agreement with Global Building Services—though now lapsed—illustrated the remedial strategy in action. Although the agreement came into being alongside a DOL enforcement action and without any actual private litigation, the impetus for the settlement was MCTF's ability to sue Global on behalf of the workers for the large liabilities that remained. Monitoring under the agreement was supplied by MCTF, a worker center that is both independent of the employer and accountable to workers, having been established through collective bargaining in the unionized segment of the janitorial business. MCTF, as a nonprofit watchdog organization, was more inclined than private attorneys might be to forego potential damages (and contingent attorney fees) in order to secure a prospective program for improving the employer's practices, and it was presumably less inclined to agree to conditions of secrecy or constraints on inspections that firms might seek. These considerations suggest the value of joint litigation ventures between nonprofit worker advocacy groups, including unions, and private attorneys. The Global agreement may serve as a useful template for extending the model of monitored self-regulation through private enforcement activity.

Even under the club of litigation and even when worker advocates, including unions, are at the table, prospective concessions may be hard to get. Employers may use whatever leverage they have to resist anything that smacks of collective employee representation or especially union involvement. This dynamic appeared in the GGCC negotiations, as we saw in Chapter 5: even under the threat of ruinous liability at the hands of the New York Attorney General's Office, the greengrocers adamantly and successfully resisted a provision for worker representation except, symbolically, in the rare store with ten or more workers. The workers did get better compliance and higher wages and a conduit from their small, marginal workplaces to outside scrutiny and assistance, but they did not get any formal vehicle for collective representation (which would have strengthened and perhaps extended monitoring of compliance).

The promise and limitations of private litigation may be discerned as well in the recent litigation in *Thomas v. Total Health Home Care Corp.*,[15] in which a class of home health care workers successfully challenged illegal wage practices —unpaid travel time, disciplinary wage cuts, and miscalculation of overtime pay. In addition to paying $2.2 million for back wages, the employer agreed to submit to monitoring of its payroll practices by "Monitoring Counsel," one of the plaintiffs' law firms. Monitoring Counsel was granted access to payroll and personnel records and the right to interview workers to monitor compliance. Notably, while attorneys for both the SEIU and the National Employment Law Project served along with private attorneys as class counsel, only the plaintiffs' private law firm was named as Monitoring Counsel. Moreover, the Monitoring Counsel agreed to maintain strict confidentiality of employees' contact information, "including not sharing any such information with . . . any labor or trade union or organizer thereof." Still, the *Total Health* settlement represents a breakthrough in its incorporation of formal independent monitoring into the settlement of a private wage and hour lawsuit. Even without a formal role for worker organizations, independent monitoring opens new channels of communication for shared workplace grievances and affords a safe vehicle for complaining about substandard conditions at work. Workers learned that taking action together, even through litigation, can lead to better working conditions. And giving workers a conduit to independent outside professionals committed to their interests, even on a narrow range of workplace issues, may give them a taste of, and a taste for, representation on a wider range of issues.

THE DOCTRINAL STRATEGY

So private advocates can promote effective self-regulation through a remedial strategy, using the club of litigation to induce employers to adopt self-regulatory measures that they would otherwise avoid. But if that were the only way private litigation could lead to reform—one defendant (or boycott target) at a time—then change would be slow indeed. Fortunately, the law casts a longer shadow than that. As in the antidiscrimination context, private litigation under the wage and hour laws can both extend the "shadow of the law" beyond that cast by an inadequate system of public enforcement and give more distinct shape to the legal shadow under which firms manage their operations. For every firm that is sued, many more want to minimize their exposure to litigation, liability, and the attendant reputational hit. If that requires self-regulatory precautions, then self-regulatory precautions (if they are not too costly) will follow. In other words, the mere prospect of litigation, together with the right kind of doctrine, can help bring about a regime of effective self-regulation. The linchpin of this "doctrinal strategy" for reform, as illustrated by the *Faragher-Ellerth-Kolstad* line of cases, is a partial defense for effective self-regulators, the contours of which guide the conduct of responsible firms seeking to reduce their legal exposure. The doctrinal strategy potentially leverages a few fully litigated cases into a lot of workplace reform.

The doctrinal strategy depends first of all on the existence of private rights of action that can generate substantial liabilities. The wage and hour laws fulfill those conditions in some cases: violations are often readily provable and the resulting liabilities serious, especially when illegal practices affect many employees over several years, given the prospect of attorneys' fees and liquidated damages.[16] The private bar has discovered that aggregate wage and hours claims —including some on behalf of low-wage workers—can be lucrative, and employers have begun to take notice of the resulting surge of lawsuits.[17] For firms that recognize their exposure to these lawsuits, the threat of private litigation might do what the threat of public enforcement has largely failed to do: deter violations and promote internal preventive measures.

Venerable Wal-Mart, Inc., again provides a case in point. In 2005, after years of criticism and litigation, Wal-Mart instituted a "Corporate Compliance team . . . to oversee Wal-Mart's compliance in a number of areas, including the company's obligations to associates in terms of pay, working hours and time for breaks."[18] The firm vowed to use its much-touted information technology systems to ensure that workers do not work more than the law permits or get paid for less than they work.[19] While it remains unclear how and whether these new systems will deter store managers, still under pressure to minimize labor costs, from demanding off-the-clock unrecorded work, it appears that Wal-Mart's new policies and procedures may have reduced the incidence of wage and hour violations.[20] In any event, those new policies are almost certain to feature in future litigation against the firm. Wal-Mart routinely defended off-the-clock claims by blaming rogue supervisors acting in violation of express company policy. Now that company policy has been beefed up and backed up with stronger compliance procedures, future lawsuits are likely to be met with a *Kolstad*-like argument: even if some Wal-Mart supervisors exacted off-the-clock work, the company's maintenance of preventive procedures should give it a defense against liability. How should a court respond?[21]

The answer that follows from the argument here should be one of qualified acceptance. The court should allow a *partial* defense—a defense against supercompensatory remedies, such as the liquidated damages otherwise available for willful violation of the FLSA—if and only if the firm's internal compliance program measures up to standards of effective self-regulation, including the required safeguards of employee representation and, where representation is not through an independent outside entity like a union, independent outside monitoring. Otherwise, the firm should be liable for the full measure of remedies and penalties, including liquidated damages.

The self-regulatory defense proposed here is obviously more exacting than that which exists under *Faragher-Ellerth-Kolstad;* nearly all existing compliance programs will fall short. If the proposed standard seems too exacting, consider that it is being applied here to firms that have already been found in violation of the law—and, in case of most wage and hour violations, to firms that have profited from their agents' violation of the law through lower wage costs. Whatever internal compliance programs they maintained failed to avoid the violations in question. The proposed co-regulatory defense is no straitjacket. Firms are not required to have a compliance program with all of the prescribed elements; they may opt for other procedures that they believe will prevent violations. But if violations do occur, then the firm's procedures will be measured against the law's standard for effective self-regulation, and if they do not measure up, the firm will get no break from the law's full sanctions.

Of course, neither the remedial strategy nor the doctrinal strategy for promoting effective self-regulation is guaranteed to succeed. In particular, neither is guaranteed to secure any form of employee representation. Other elements of effective self-regulation are becoming part of the zeitgeist, thanks in part to the Federal Sentencing Guidelines for Organizations and other legal inducements to self-regulation. Even independent monitoring is becoming an increasingly common recourse when corporate misconduct and scandal give reformers and regulators leverage to pursue corrective action. But the idea of giving an institutionalized voice to employees still runs into a wall of employer resistance. Stronger supercompensatory remedies might help overcome that resistance. Otherwise, employee advocates may need to augment the threat of litigation with an organized campaign of economic pressure—a damaging publicity campaign such as ROC-NY conducted against targeted restaurants or even a boycott such as the Coalition of Immokalee Workers mounted against leading fast-food chains—to secure a role for independent employee organizations. We will return to these nonlitigation strategies below.

THE UNFORTUNATE CASE OF OCCUPATIONAL SAFETY AND HEALTH LAW

In the crucial arena of workplace health and safety, there are virtually no footholds for private litigation. Unlike the FLSA, OSHA itself affords no private right of action to employees who are exposed to safety hazards or injured as a result. Even private rights of action for employee whistleblowers who are fired for reporting safety concerns are rare and endangered. OSHA's whistleblower protection provision, which affords no private right of action and no compensatory or exemplary damages, is notoriously ineffectual.[22] Nor can injured workers turn to tort law to promote health and safety reforms indirectly. Modern tort law would normally impose liabilities on firms that would effectively internalize the cost of injuries caused by workplace hazards and would stimulate precautions against accidents.[23] But state worker compensation laws channel workplace injury claims out of the tort system and into a low-profile, subcompensatory administrative system.[24] And for most employers, workers compensation insurance premiums are not experience-rated; they do not rise or fall with an employer's safety record.[25] As a result, the law fails to ensure that employers internalize anything like the full cost of occupational injuries and illnesses to workers and to society.

To be sure, employers do have some nonlegal incentives to regulate workplace hazards: the costs of lost-time accidents, of losing trained workers, and of paying whatever wage premium might be needed to fill manifestly dangerous jobs. But those incentives are not merely insufficient; they do not afford the kind of leverage for reform that civil liability might do. Within the present landscape of occupational safety and health law, there is neither a remedial strategy nor a doctrinal strategy by which employees and their advocates outside the government could pursue self-regulatory reform. Whatever creative reformist energies might have been unleashed by the threat of megabucks tort liability for workplace accidents remain well caged.

In the arena of workplace health and safety, there are only two openings for private litigation. First, under a narrow exception to workers compensation exclusivity, states generally allow tort litigation for some intentional harms.[26] Second, some state courts have recognized a tort remedy on behalf of workers discharged for complaining of safety violations (though some foreclose common law actions on the grounds that OSHA provides an "adequate remedy" for whistleblowers).[27]

The controversies over workers' compensation exclusivity and the availability of common law wrongful discharge claims for health and safety whistleblowers are small skirmishes in the larger battle to afford employees better ways to protect their interests in a safe and healthful workplace. As long as state and federal agencies continue to be sorely underequipped to ensure safety and health in the millions of workplaces under their jurisdiction—and that is likely to hold true even in an administration that is wholly committed to workplace safety —the public will depend on private regulatory resources. The most powerful and important private regulatory resources to activate are those inside firms themselves. But firms themselves face economic pressures, the balance of which sometimes points toward cutting corners and imperiling workers' lives and health. So activating the prodigious regulatory resources inside firms will require arming the primary beneficiaries of health and safety laws—workers themselves—with their own regulatory arsenal. Private rights of action for workplace injuries and diseases, for whistleblowers, and for enforcement of safety laws would supply needed leverage to that end. An understanding of the principles of effective self-regulation would then allow that leverage to be deployed so as to steer workplace organizations in the direction of effective reform.

Private Reform through Shareholder
Activism and Corporate Social Responsibility

Chapter 4 explored the rise in recent years of norms of corporate social responsibility by which firms embrace greater responsibility than the law im-
poses for the rights of workers and the well-being of communities and the environment that are affected by the firms' operations. The movement for
corporate social responsibility, incomplete though it surely is, has been largely
a product of external pressures—mostly negative pressures of litigation, boycotts, and publicity campaigns aimed at scandalous or illegal practices within
a firm's orbit, but also positive pressures in the form of "fair trade" and "sweat-
free" certifications, "best companies" reports, and the like. But those outside
pressures have helped to enable corporate shareholders to pursue an "inside
game" and to carry the torch of stakeholders like workers and environmental-
ists into corporate boardrooms. The combination of outside pressures and
shareholder activism may lead to the creation of internal structures and an internal constituency for actually living up to commitments that may have been
quite superficial at their inception.

   We have already noted that shareholder advocacy and socially responsible
investment criteria need not and do not end with general statements of good
corporate intentions. For example, monitoring practices for global supply
chains have improved through coordinated efforts of shareholder activists and
outside advocates. Much as the "remedial strategy" discussed above uses the
pressure of actual litigation and the threat of heavy-duty sanctions to induce
firms to adopt prospective reforms that they would otherwise resist, advocates
may be able to train the harsh glare of negative publicity on firms with scandalously bad labor practices within their supply chains and demand major reforms from inside and outside the corporation. That is roughly what happened
with Nike, and it led to its transformation "from pariah to pacesetter," in the
words of David Vogel.[28] And that is one way of understanding Wal-Mart's ongoing efforts to convert skeptics and become a leader rather than a laggard in
both its internal employment practices and its supply-chain management. But
for every Nike and Wal-Mart that is made a pariah and is driven into submission (or apparent submission) by a massive negative publicity campaign, there
are dozens or hundreds of firms that wish to avoid that fate. So much as the
"doctrinal strategy" can set standards of effective compliance that firms may
adopt in an effort to stay ahead of the litigation curve (as in *Faragher* and
Ellerth), outside advocates seek to establish "best practices" that firms can then

be pressured to adopt in order to earn a reputation as socially responsible corporate citizens and to avoid scandal.

In short, civil society actors—labor unions, worker centers, and their allies within the socially responsible investment community—have means of pressuring firms to commit to higher employment rights and standards and to adopt co-regulatory structures for realizing those rights and standards, even without government action or private litigation. If advocates are persuaded that "best practices" for the implementation of firms' own commitments to their workers (and suppliers' workers) track the tenets of co-regulation and include collective representation of workers and outside monitoring of compliance, they can attempt to promote those practices through a combination of inside and outside tactics. Just as standards for effective monitoring of supplier factories have been raised by the global anti-sweatshop movement, a domestic worker rights movement could seek to raise standards for effective compliance with labor standards—both those mandated by law and the higher standards adopted by firms themselves—in the direction of co-regulation.

There are many possible paths toward co-regulation—public and private; legislative, administrative, and judicial; federal, state, and local. And there are many possible protagonists in pursuing those paths—labor unions and other worker advocates; legislators, regulators, and other government officials; lawyers, scholars, and pundits. The simple message that unites all these efforts and actors is this: workers themselves need institutional mechanisms for defending and advancing their rights and interests at work. Unless employers recognize that principle and incorporate those mechanisms, they should not be entrusted with the enforcement of workers' rights and should not be entitled to self-regulatory privileges or immunities. In short: no self-regulation without worker representation.

Chapter 10 Conclusion:

No Self-Regulation without

Worker Representation

Among those who celebrated the 2008 election results, workers' organizations and allies were among the most elated and hopeful. After nearly a decade of neglect, the rights of workers were back on the front burner in Congress and in the administrative agencies, and real progress seemed possible. But what direction should reform take? Many of the demands and recommendations from workers' organizations have a familiar ring. Labor law reform that expands union organizing opportunities and the restoration and fortification of enforcement tools—stronger penalties, more inspections—have been on labor's agenda for several decades. Those reforms are undoubtedly necessary, but they are not sufficient.

A forward-looking agenda for labor should embrace and try to steer the movement toward regulated self-regulation—toward relying on, encouraging, and channeling the impulses and resources that lie within and among private firms toward public-regarding ends. The movement toward self-regulation is here to stay. It began to take root decades ago, and it now extends well beyond the law of the workplace, beyond the United States, and beyond the domain of domestic law. Its proponents are found not only in the corporate boardrooms, where public demands for deregulation have given way to the banner of corporate social responsibility, but also among the most stalwart defenders of the public imperative of regulation.

This book seeks to shape the movement toward self-regulation within the U.S. law of the workplace so that it protects the worker rights and working conditions that are its chief concerns. It seeks to do that in the face of some stubborn realities, including the dearth of institutions of collective representation in U.S. workplaces and a chronic enforcement deficit. With those realities in mind and with the guidance of a variety of experiences and theories of effective self-regulation, I have proposed a model of effective self-regulation that aims toward "co-regulation." The model seeks to deploy public and private enforcement resources to induce firms' entry into and faithful implementation of a system of self-regulation that is monitored by independent outside actors and that aims to free employees' own voices and monitoring capabilities. This proposal may seem far removed from both the lofty invocation of democratic values and the travails of Wal-Mart with which I began. So I will conclude by drawing those disparate threads together.

The Wagner Act of 1935 recognized both the intrinsic and the instrumental value of industrial democracy when it sought to secure workers' ability to participate in workplace decisions that vitally affected them. But today the very term "industrial democracy" sounds anachronistic, and its modern synonym, "workplace democracy," has never gained much popular currency. That is both a cause and a symptom of chronic political neglect—of the fact that Congress has not seriously revisited the issue of workplace governance since the 1950s. Over the past fifty years, the Wagner Act system has become distorted and dysfunctional, if not irrelevant, for most employees as the reach of unions and collective bargaining has declined steadily and seemingly inexorably. Just since 1995, that decline has produced two wrenching upheavals within organized labor's own ranks: the victory of insurgents, led by SEIU president John Sweeney, over the incumbent leadership of the AFL-CIO in 1995, and ten years later the departure from the Sweeney-led AFL-CIO of five major unions, again led by the SEIU, to form the Change To Win federation. Both Sweeney's backers in 1995 and the Change To Win unions in 2005 pled the urgency of new organizing as the heart of their cases for change. New organizing has indeed transpired, but not enough of it to reverse the slide in union density or to reduce the yawning "representation gap" between what workers want and what they have in terms of collective influence at work.

In the meantime, employment law has grown into a fearsome hydra head of liability for employers and a prolific fount of legal rights and entitlements, real or illusory, for employees. Employment laws now reach many aspects of employees' pay, hours, benefits, entitlement to leave, and work environment; the protean body of antidiscrimination law affects virtually all tangible and even intangible conditions of employment. Employment law's patchwork of mandates has become, by default, our nation's system of workplace governance. Of course, employment laws were never designed, either singly or together, as a system of governance, and they are a very poor substitute for the system of shared self-governance that was envisioned by the labor laws. Indeed, they are not really a substitute at all, for many of the rights and regulations that make up employment law are inevitably incomplete and underenforced without a complementary system of collective representation to back them up inside the workplace. The representation gap that faces American workers thus threatens not only workers' voice within workplace governance and their ability to bargain above the legal floor established by law; it threatens the floor itself.

Yet solutions to the representation gap may be more likely to grow out of the fertile ground of employment law, for all its shortcomings, rather than within the traditional realm of labor law. Employment law in general enjoys broader political support, or at least less monolithic political opposition, than does labor law. It also mobilizes a range of actors and institutional energies that labor law does not. It contains many more potential footholds for reform efforts and sources of leverage that might be turned to the cause of workplace democracy. Employment law—especially in the form of costly and embarrassing litigation—also packs a punch that labor law does not. It can lead and has led to some dramatic reforms in how workplaces are organized on the part of both employers who have experienced litigation and those who have observed its traumatic effect from afar. Even mighty Wal-Mart has been forced to institute major organizational and technological reforms to improve compliance with wage and hour laws and discrimination laws, among others. Partly as a result of these developments, employment law itself has circled back to the realization that "employers" are organizations with a vast potential for self-governance and self-regulation.

The rise of self-regulatory mechanisms for the enforcement of labor standards and employee rights presents a kaleidoscope of possibilities. On the one hand, there are undoubtedly vast regulatory resources—knowledge, expertise, and even some goodwill—within firms. A regulatory framework that activates those resources and channels them toward public goals promises to be far more effective than one that relies solely on traditional mechanisms of uniform standards, public inspections, fines, and enforcement. There will simply never be enough government inspectors to do the job alone. On the other hand, the movement toward self-regulation threatens to legitimate regulatory disengagement and to disguise a process of deregulation. A system of privatized enforcement that is detached from public oversight and that defuses the prospect of serious coercive sanctions for noncompliance may simply disguise a process of deregulation and the unleashing of market forces.

The movement toward self-regulation also casts a prismatic light back on the representation gap in the workplace. For one thing, it magnifies the dangers of still-declining levels of unionization. If responsibility for ensuring compliance with rights and labor standards is increasingly to be pushed inside the regulated firm itself, then it is deeply troubling that the employees whose rights and interests are at stake are increasingly unlikely to have an organized voice within the firm. At the very least, then, the movement toward self-regulation has the makings of a new argument for labor law reform that makes unionization possible for workers who want it.

Unfortunately, even if a worker-friendly constellation of political forces manages to produce real labor law reform for the first time in half a century, we are unlikely to see widespread union representation and collective bargaining in the foreseeable future. If all that were at stake were workers' ability to bargain above what the law guarantees, then the prospect of private-sector union density levels remaining below 20 percent might not be especially troubling; indeed, 20 percent union density would be cause for exultation among organized labor and its friends. But when we recognize the law's incapacity to enforce legal minima through conventional means and its growing tendency to delegate the main job of enforcement to firms themselves, we cannot be so sanguine. In an era of self-regulation, unrepresented workers are at risk of losing the legal protections—the minimum labor standards and employee rights—that the law means to make universal. Labor law reform that makes it possible for some workers to choose union representation will not solve that problem.

Fortunately, the movement toward self-regulation provides not only a justification for promoting broader employee representation but also potential leverage to that end. If the movement toward self-regulation is, as it should be, part of a regulatory scheme in which serious sanctions and liabilities also play a role, then the law can be used as leverage to induce both good corporate citizens and bad actors to meet public standards of effective self-regulation, either as prerequisites for the privileges of responsible self-regulators or as part of a remedy for noncompliance. The public, for its part, should recognize that effective self-regulation in the workplace requires both employee representation and, in most cases, independent monitoring. In short, the privileges and concessions that are increasingly dealt out to self-regulating employers should be reserved for those who maintain a system of co-regulation.

For an organization like Wal-Mart, a public commitment to co-regulation would leave the company free to institute any internal reforms and precautions it deemed wise. Those internal reforms may be worthwhile for the firm—even if external law completely ignored them—if they corrected or avoided practices that may otherwise trigger litigation, regulatory scrutiny, or scandal. Indeed, Wal-Mart has found it worthwhile to introduce significant internal reforms even in the absence of any direct regulatory rewards. However, if the company were seeking not only to avoid violating the law and to improve its battered reputation, but also to secure some immunity from public regulatory scrutiny or a partial defense against liability in case violations *did* take place, then its internal reforms would have to measure up against public standards of effective self-regulation. And those standards should require both institutions through which workers themselves participate in the enforcement of laws enacted for their benefit and, if those institutions were not unions with an independent existence outside the firm, independent monitors of compliance.

In spite of all that has been said here, we simply do not know enough to be sure that co-regulation will work as a regulatory model in the U.S. Uncertainties abound. In particular, it remains to be seen whether internal employee committees in non-union workplaces, even in conjunction with independent monitors, can guard against "cosmetic compliance" and covert deregulation. Much will turn on details of implementation and the vigor and creativity with which regulators and workers' institutions pursue these reforms. Reforms should be implemented in a spirit of experimentation, with a commitment to testing, evaluation, and revision in light of experience.

But we have set our sights still higher in portraying co-regulation as a potential pathway toward greater democracy and employee voice in workplace governance. One might well ask: What does any of this have to do with workplace democracy?

The aim here is two-sided: it is to allow employees to have a voice in, and to help enforce, those rights and regulatory regimes that exist for their benefit while at the same time using those regulatory regimes to create new channels for employee voice. But employee voice to what end? Liberating employee voice in the service of better compliance with employment laws seems a very modest step at best toward workplace democracy. Employment laws touch many terms and conditions of work, but the laws set only minimum standards, and still cover only a fraction of what employees care about at work—only a fraction of what collective bargaining, for example, might secure for them. Mere compliance with legal mandates, though it would be a big improvement for many workers, is hardly a worthy successor or alternative to collective bargaining.

On the other hand, employment law covers some of what employees care about in every workplace, and it covers more of what employees care about in low-wage workplaces, where workers are most in need of the law's aid. Moreover, the public seems to have an unquenched appetite for workplace mandates reaching additional terms and conditions of employment that workers care about. The minimality of the law's minimum standards can also be misleading, for we have seen that corporations' own standards of conduct and social responsibility commitments frequently aspire by their own terms to more than mere compliance and more than legal minima. A complicated and somewhat mysterious mix of motives—internal and external, organizational and psychological, legal and market-based—has led leading firms to explicitly embrace something like the values underlying many legal mandates.

The law should be reengineered to make the most of these self-regulatory regimes, in part by building into them institutions for worker representation. If a reengineered law of the workplace can induce firms to internalize the public values underlying legal mandates, or even just to live up to their own stated objectives—and injecting workers' voices into self-regulatory regimes will help to make that happen—then those regimes may grow into more robust forms of self-governance in which employees participate. Even if firms behave as the economists' deterrence model posits and aim no higher than the law effectively demands, employees themselves may be able push beyond that. For if employees can secure an effective voice in compliance—if they can overcome the collective action problems and fear of reprisals that undermine their role in enforcement of legal standards—then that voice may not be so easy to cabin. If employees become powerful enough to claim their full rights under the law, they may also become powerful enough to demand more of what else they want at work and perhaps to claim a broader role in firm governance.

Rejuvenating the idea of workplace democracy, and of the worker as a citizen of the workplace, aims both to improve workplaces and to deepen democracy. But the path to widespread workplace democracy in the United States is at best a long one, and its direction is uncertain and likely to change in coming decades as developments in the economy and the technology and organization of work continue to race along. Shoring up the law's long-unfulfilled promise of freedom of association and self-organization for workers is an essential first step, but it is not enough. Alongside the battle for labor law reform, pragmatic proponents of workplace democracy need to open up a new front in the campaign.

Perhaps the best that one can hope for in the current climate of change and uncertainty is to take a few steps in the right direction, advancing important substantive workplace goals to which the public is clearly committed while opening additional space for workers to speak for themselves and eventually to decide for themselves what forms of self-organization and participation will best serve their needs within their particular workplaces and their particular corners of the labor market. But to head in the right direction, we need to recognize the trajectory we are already on. We need to recognize the distinctive constellation of institutions and resources that are the legacy of past and present approaches to workplace governance in the U.S., and we need to recognize as well the powerful forces that are pushing regulatory actors across the globe toward forms of self-regulation, more or less well regulated and more or less accountable to the public. The idea of co-regulation aims to do that by harnessing trends toward self-regulation and channeling them into better forms of workplace governance in which workers have a genuine voice.

Notes

CHAPTER 1. INTRODUCTION

1. Kim Bobo, Wage Theft in America: Why Millions of Working Americans are not Getting Paid—and What We Can Do About It (2009); Steven Greenhouse, The Big Squeeze: Tough Times for the American Worker (2009); Annette Bernhardt, Heather Boushey, Laura Dresser, & Chris Tilly, The Gloves-off Economy: Workplace Standards at the Bottom of America's Labor Market (2008).

2. On wage and hour litigation against Wal-Mart, *see* Steven Greenhouse, *Wal-Mart Faces Fine in Minnesota Suit Involving Work Breaks,* N.Y. Times, July 2, 2008; Steven Greenhouse, *In-House Audit Says Wal-Mart Violated Labor Laws,* N.Y. Times, Jan. 13, 2004, at A16. On discrimination litigation, *see infra* Chapter 4. *See generally* Sanhita SinhaRoy, *Wal-Mart Shows a Pattern of Labor Violations,* Augusta Chronicle, July 1, 2004, at A05; Lewis L. Laska, *Wal-Mart Litigation Project, available at* http://www.wal-mart litigation.com (last visited Jan. 3, 2009).

3. *See* Stephen Kinzer, *Wal-Mart's Big-City Plans Stall Again,* N.Y. Times, May 6, 2004, at A27.

4. Human Rights Watch, *Discounting Rights: Wal-Mart's Violation of U.S. Workers' Right to Freedom of Association,* p. 4 (May 2007), *available at* http://hrw.org/reports/2007 /us0507/ [hereinafter Human Rights Watch, *Discounting Rights*].

5. Norwegian Ministry of Finance, press release, June 2006; quoted in *Human Rights Watch,* p. 58.

6. News release, *Wal-Mart Details Progress toward Becoming a Leader in Employment Practices* (June 4, 2004), *available at* http://walmartstores.com/FactsNews/NewsRoom /4645.aspx; last visited Jan. 3, 2009.

7. Wal-Mart Statement of Ethics (Jan. 1, 2005), *available at* http://www.walmartstores.com /GlobalWMStoresWeb/navigate.do?catg=9. The document contains a broad policy against discrimination that includes sexual orientation, marital status, "or any other legally-protected status"); a ban on harassment (which "is broadly defined and includes conduct which negatively interferes with work performance, diminishes the dignity of any person or which creates an intimidating, hostile or otherwise offensive work environment," apparently without regard to any link to discrimination); and a strong injunction against the performance or demand for work without compensation. For additional details, the statement refers to other policies—*e.g.*, on "harassment/inappropriate conduct" and "working off the clock"—that are available to employees but not to the public.

8. The Statement of Ethics also contains standard disclaimers: it "is not intended to create an express or implied contract of employment in and of itself"; it and other "policies of Wal-Mart may be modified at our sole discretion, without notice, at any time"; and "[e]mployment at Wal-Mart is on an at-will basis, where permitted by law, meaning Associates are free to resign at any time for any or for no reason and Wal-Mart may terminate an Associate at any time for any or for no reason."

9. The term "shadow of the law" is usually coupled with "bargaining" to describe the law's influence on private ordering. *See* Robert Mnookin & Lewis Kornhauser, *Bargaining in the Shadow of the Law: The Case of Divorce*, 88 YALE L.J. 950, 950–52 (1979). But it works as well to capture how managers manage in light of how their actions might be assessed in case of litigation or prosecution.

10. Interview with Saru Jayaraman, Feb. 15, 2007; Steven Greenhouse, *Two Restaurants to Pay Workers $164,000*, N.Y. TIMES, Jan. 12, 2005.

11. See Steven Greenhouse, *Judge Approves Deal to Settle Suit over Wage Violations*, N.Y. TIMES, June 19, 2008; Interview with Saru Jayaraman, *supra* note 10.

12. *See* ROC-United Web site, http://www.rocunited.org/what-we-do (last visited July 22, 2008).

13. The idea of the collective bargaining model as a system of industrial self-governance has been elucidated by industrial relations scholars (*see* JOHN COMMONS, INDUSTRIAL GOVERNMENT [1921]; Sumner Slichter, *The Changing Character of American Industrial Relations*, 29 AM. ECON. REV. 121–37 [1939]); by leading doctrinal scholars (*see* Archibald Cox, *The Legal Nature of Collective Bargaining Agreements*, 57 MICH. L. REV. 1, 2, 5–9 [1958]); by theorists (*see* PHILLIP SELZNICK, LAW, SOCIETY, and INDUSTRIAL JUSTICE [1969]); and by the Supreme Court. *See* United Steelworkers of Am. v. Warrior & Gulf Navigation Co., 363 U.S. 574, 580 (1960). For a leading critique of this conception of collective bargaining, *see* Katherine Van Wezel Stone, *The Post-War Paradigm in American Labor Law*, 90 YALE L.J. 1509, 1514–17 (1981).

14. *See* Cynthia Estlund, *The Ossification of American Labor Law*, 102 COLUM. L. REV. 1527 (2002), and Chapter 2 below.

15. *See* http://walmartstores.com (last visited June 28, 2008).

16. *See* http://www.exxonmobil.com/Corporate/community.aspx (last visited June 28, 2008).

17. *See* http://www.chevron.com/globalissues/corporateresponsibility/2008 (last visited May 6, 2009).

18. *See* http://www.gm.com/corporate/responsibility (last visited June 28, 2008).

19. *See* http://www.conocophillips.com/social/health_safety/index.htm (last visited June 28, 2008).

20. *See* http://www.ge.com/company/citizenship/employees/index.html (last visited June 28, 2008).

21. *See* http://www.ford.com/about-ford/company-information/public-policy/health-and-environmental-policy/environment-health-policies-807p (last visited June 28, 2008).

22. *See* http://www.citigroup.com/citigroup/citizen/humanrights/index.htm (last visited June 28, 2008).

23. U.S. Chamber of Commerce Web site, http://www.uschamber.com/issues/priorities/labor.htm (last visited July 22, 2008).

24. For an illuminating account of the history and abuse of demands for "cost-benefit analysis" and the toll on especially environmental and worker safety regulation, *see* RICHARD L. REVESZ & MICHAEL A. LIVERMORE, RETAKING RATIONALITY: HOW COST-BENEFIT ANALYSIS CAN BETTER PROTECT THE ENVIRONMENT AND OUR HEALTH (2008).

25. *See* Kevin M. Clermont & Stewart J. Schwab, *How Employment Discrimination Plaintiffs Fare in Federal Court,* 1 J. EMPIR. LEGAL STUDIES 429 (2004).

26. For critical accounts of employer responses to litigation and regulation, *see* Lauren B. Edelman et al., *Professional Construction of Law: The Inflated Threat of Wrongful Discharge,* 26 LAW & SOC'Y REV. 47 (1992); Thomas O. McGarity & Sidney A. Shapiro, *OSHA's Critics and Regulatory Reform,* 31 WAKE FOREST L. REV. 587, 590–609 (1996).

27. *See* STEPHEN G. BREYER, REGULATION AND ITS REFORM 131–55 (1982); Michael C. Dorf & Charles F. Sabel, *A Constitution of Democratic Experimentalism,* 98 COLUM. L. REV. 267, 278–79 (1998).

28. PAUL C. WEILER, GOVERNING THE WORKPLACE: THE FUTURE OF LABOR AND EMPLOYMENT LAW (1990).

29. *See* EUGENE BARDACH & ROBERT KAGAN, GOING BY THE BOOK: THE PROBLEM OF REGULATORY UNREASONABLENESS (1982).

30. *See* The Dunlop Commission on the Future of Worker-Management Relations, Final Report 59–60 (1995); Samuel Estreicher, *Saturns for Rickshaws: The Stakes in the Debate over Predispute Employment Arbitration Agreements,* 16 OHIO ST. J. ON DISP. RESOL. 559, 563 (2001); Wayne N. Outten, *Negotiations, ADR, and Severance/Settlement Agreements: An Employee's Lawyer's Perspective,* 604 PLI/Lit 235, 249–50 (1999); Jean R. Sternlight, *In Search of the Best Procedure for Enforcing Employment Discrimination Laws: A Comparative Analysis,* 78 TUL. L. REV. 1401, 1422–24 (2004).

31. *See infra* Chapter 6.

32. *See, e.g.,* Adelle Blackett, *Global Governance, Legal Pluralism and the Decentered State: A Labor Law Critique of Codes of Corporate Conduct,* 8 IND. J. GLOBAL LEGAL STUD. 401, 420 (2001); Kimberly D. Krawiec, *Cosmetic Compliance and the Failure of Negotiated Governance,* 81 WASH. U. L.Q. 487 (2003).

33. *See, e.g.*, Ian Ayres & John Braithwaite, Responsive Regulation: Transcending the Deregulation Debate 101 (1992); Bardach & Kagan, *supra* note 29, at 105–06.

34. *See, e.g.*, John Braithwaite, Regulatory Capitalism: How It Works, Ideas for Making It Work Better (2008); Ayres & Braithwaite, *supra* note 33.

35. The concept of tripartism in labor relations and labor regulation goes back at least to John Commons. *See* Bruce E. Kaufman, *John R. Commons and the Wisconsin School on Industrial Relations Strategy and Policy,* 57 Indus. & Lab. Rel. Rev. 3, 10 (2003).

36. On the role of unions in enforcing employment rights and labor standards, *see generally* Charles B. Craver, *Why Labor Unions Must [and Can] Survive,* 1 U. Pa. J. Lab. & Emp. L. 15 (1998); Robert J. Rabin, *The Role of Unions in the Rights-Based Workplace,* 25 U.S.F. L. Rev. 169 (1991).

37. Blackett, *supra* note 32. This critique was raised in the context of global labor regulation but is a concern within advanced industrial regimes as well.

38. *See* David I. Levine, Working in the Twenty-First Century: Policies for Economic Growth through Training, Opportunity, and Education ch. 8 (pp. 148–71) (1998). See also Jeffrey M. Hirsch & Barry T. Hirsch, *The Rise and Fall of Private Sector Unionism: What Next for the NLRA?,* 34 Florida St. U. L. Rev. 1133, 1140–45 (2007).

CHAPTER 2. OSSIFICATION OF LABOR LAW AND THE DECLINE OF INDUSTRIAL SELF-GOVERNANCE

1. This chapter is a condensed and revised version of Cynthia Estlund, *The Ossification of American Labor Law,* 102 Colum. L. Rev. 1527 (2002).

2. NLRB v. Jones & Laughlin Steel Corp., 301 U.S. 1, 30 (1937).

3. *See* Cynthia Estlund, Working Together: How Workplace Bonds Strengthen a Diverse Democracy 134–36, 169–73 (2003).

4. *See* Milton Derber, The American Idea of Industrial Democracy, 1865–1965, at 303–05 (1970); Mark Barenberg, *The Political Economy of the Wagner Act: Power, Symbol, and Workplace Cooperation,* 106 Harv. L. Rev. 1379, 1412–30 (1993); Clyde W. Summers, *The Privatization of Personal Freedoms and Enrichment of Democracy: Some Lessons from Labor Law,* 1986 U. Ill. L. Rev. 689, 697–99 (1986).

5. *See* The Developing Labor Law: The Board, the Courts, and the National Labor Relations Act, at 29–37 (Patrick Hardin et al., eds., 4th ed. 2001) [hereinafter DLL]; Nelson Lichtenstein, *Taft-Hartley: A Slave-Labor Law?,* 47 Cath. U. L. Rev. 763, 766–67 (1998); James Gray Pope, *The Thirteenth Amendment versus the Commerce Clause: Labor and the Shaping of American Constitutional Law, 1921–1957,* 102 Colum. L. Rev. 1, 105–12 (2002).

6. "Secondary" pressures target employers deemed legally "neutral" in a labor dispute. Taft-Hartley also prohibited unions from entangling employers in jurisdictional disputes, charging excessive dues, "featherbedding," or seeking payment for work not performed.

7. *See* Labor-Management Reporting and Disclosure (Landrum-Griffin) Act of 1959, Pub. L. No. 86–257, 73 Stat. 519 (codified as amended in scattered sections of 29 U.S.C.). The Landrum-Griffin amendments are explained in DLL, *supra* note 5, at 49–60.

8. Congress also banned "hot cargo" agreements, under which an employer agreed not to handle the products of another employer. 29 U.S.C. § 158(e).

9. *See* U.S. Department of Labor, Bureau of Labor Statistics, *Labor Force Statistics from the Current Population Survey, Union Affiliation Data* (chart 42, p. 252); *available at* http://www.bls.gov/cps/cpsaat42.pdf.

10. *See* RICHARD B. FREEMAN & JOEL ROGERS, WHAT WORKERS WANT (1999), finding that 63 percent of workers wanted more influence than they had at work, *id.* at 41; 56 percent would prefer to raise workplace problems through an employee association rather than on their own, *id.* at 55; and 32 percent of unrepresented workers (and 90 percent of union members) said they would vote for union representation if given the chance, *id.* at 69.

11. Collective bargaining thus has some features that Professors Dorf and Sabel associate with "democratic experimentalism." *See generally* Michael C. Dorf & Charles F. Sabel, *A Constitution of Democratic Experimentalism,* 98 COLUM. L. REV. 267 (1998).

12. *See* PAUL C. WEILER, GOVERNING THE WORKPLACE: THE FUTURE OF LABOR AND EMPLOYMENT LAW 7–8 (1990); Samuel Issacharoff, *Reconstructing Employment,* 104 HARV. L. REV. 607, 618 (1990) (book review of WEILER, GOVERNING); Clyde W. Summers, *The Privatization of Personal Freedoms and Enrichment of Democracy: Some Lessons from Labor Law,* 1986 U. ILL. L. REV. 689, 698.

13. For a few of the many discussions of organized labor's decline and its causes, *see* CHARLES B. CRAVER, CAN UNIONS SURVIVE? 34–55 (1993); MICHAEL GOLDFIELD, THE DECLINE OF ORGANIZED LABOR IN THE UNITED STATES 94–112 (1987).

14. *See* CRAVER, UNIONS, *supra* note 13, at 42–47; Samuel Estreicher, *Labor Law Reform in a World of Competitive Product Markets,* 69 CHI.-KENT L. REV. 3, 4–5 (1993); Leo Troy, *Is the U.S. Unique in the Decline of Private Sector Unionism?,* 11 J. LAB. RES. 111, 113–20 (1990).

15. Freeman and Rogers find evidence of this in employees' overwhelming preference for an employee organization that is "run jointly" by employees and management (85 percent) to one run "by employees alone" (10 percent). FREEMAN & ROGERS, *supra* note 10, at 56.

16. *See* Kate Bronfenbrenner et al., *Introduction* to ORGANIZING TO WIN: NEW RESEARCH ON UNION STRATEGIES 5–6 (Kate Bronfenbrenner et al. eds., 1998).

17. On the history of mob involvement in some unions, *see* JAMES JACOBS, MOBSTERS, UNIONS AND FEDS: THE MAFIA AND THE AMERICAN LABOR MOVEMENT (2006).

18. *See* CRAVER, UNIONS, *supra* note 13, at 47–51; WEILER, GOVERNING, *supra* note 12, at 105–33; Richard B. Freeman & Morris M. Kleiner, *Employer Behavior in the Face of Union Organizing Drives,* 43 INDUS. & LAB. REL. REV. 351, 351 (1990); Julius G. Getman, *Explaining the Fall of the Labor Movement,* 41 ST. LOUIS U. L.J. 575, 578–84 (1997); Michael H. Gottesman, *In Despair, Starting Over: Imagining a Labor Law for Unorganized Workers,* 69 CHI.-KENT L. REV. 59, 61–62 (1993); Paul C. Weiler, *Promises to Keep: Securing Workers' Rights to Self-Organization under the NLRA,* 96 HARV. L. REV. 1769, 1769–70 (1983).

19. *See* Karl E. Klare, *Judicial Deradicalization of the Wagner Act and the Origins of Modern Legal Consciousness, 1937–1941,* 62 MINN. L. REV. 265, 265–70 (1978); JAMES B. ATLESON, VALUES AND ASSUMPTIONS IN AMERICAN LABOR LAW 9–10 (1983).

20. *See* Craig Becker, *Democracy in the Workplace: Union Representation Elections and Federal Labor Law*, 77 MINN. L. REV. 495, 516–23 (1993).

21. *See id.* at 558–60.

22. *See* Roger C. Hartley, *Non-Legislative Labor Law Reform and Pre-Recognition Labor Neutrality Agreements: The Newest Civil Rights Movement*, 22 BERK. J. EMP. & LAB. L. 369, 381–82 n.66 (2001); Myron Roomkin & Richard N. Block, *Case Processing Time and the Outcome of Representation Elections*, 1981 ILL. L. REV. 75, 88.

23. *See* BRONFENBRENNER ET AL., *supra* note 16, at 4–5; Richard B. Freeman, *Why Are Unions Faring Poorly in NLRB Representation Elections?*, *in* CHALLENGES AND CHOICES FACING AMERICAN LABOR 45, 53 (Thomas A. Kochan ed., 1985); Weiler, *Promises, supra* note 18, at 1778–81.

24. The Supreme Court overturned Board decisions granting unions access to employer property in NLRB v. Babcock & Wilcox Co., 351 U.S. 105, 113–14 (1956), and Lechmere, Inc. v. NLRB, 502 U.S. 527, 536–37 (1992).

25. *See* Cynthia L. Estlund, *Labor, Property, and Sovereignty after Lechmere*, 46 STAN. L. REV. 305, 311–25 (1994).

26. *See* NLRB v. Mackay Radio & Tel. Co., 304 U.S. 333 (1938). Permanent replacement of strikers is distinguished from discharge, which is illegal, by the fact that replaced strikers are entitled to return to jobs that are unfilled at the end of the strike or that open later as a result of attrition, discharge, or expansion. Laidlaw Corp., 171 N.L.R.B. 1366, 1368–70 (1968), enforced, 414 F.2d 99 (7th Cir. 1969), cert. denied, 397 U.S. 920 (1970). "Unfair labor practice strikers," whose strike is provoked or prolonged by the employer's illegal conduct, are not subject to permanent replacement. *Id.* at 1472–78.

27. *See, e.g.*, ATLESON, *supra* note 19, at 19–34; CRAVER, UNIONS, *supra* note 13, at 29, 132–34, 143–46; JULIUS GETMAN, THE BETRAYAL OF LOCAL 14, at 224–28 (1998); WILLIAM B. GOULD IV, AGENDA FOR REFORM 185–88, 202–03 (1993); WEILER, GOVERNING, *supra* note 12, at 264–69; Michael H. Gottesman, *Union Summer: A Reawakened Interest in the Law of Labor?*, 1996 SUP. CT. REV. 285, 293–96; James J. Brudney, *To Strike or Not to Strike*, 1999 WIS. L. REV. 65, 71–72, 80–81 (reviewing GETMAN, BETRAYAL, *supra*).

28. For a sampling of scholarly criticism, *see* Mark Barenberg, *Democracy and Domination in the Law of Workplace Cooperation: From Bureaucratic to Flexible Production*, 94 COLUM. L. REV. 753, 879–983 (1994); Charles B. Craver, *The National Labor Relations Act Must Be Revised to Preserve Industrial Democracy*, 34 ARIZ. L. REV. 397, 429–31 (1992); Samuel Estreicher, *Employee Involvement and the "Company Union" Prohibition: The Case for Partial Repeal of Section 8(a)(2) of the NLRA*, 69 N.Y.U. L. REV. 125, 149–55 (1994); Gottesman, *In Despair, supra* note 18, at 86–87; Alan Hyde, *Employee Caucus: A Key Institution in the Emerging System of Employment Law*, 69 CHI.-KENT L. REV. 149, 187–90 (1993); Sanford M. Jacoby, *Current Prospects for Employee Representation in the U.S.: Old Wine in New Bottles?*, 16 J. LAB. RES. 387, 389–91 (1995); Michael H. LeRoy, *Employee Participation in the New Millennium: Redefining a Labor Organization under Section 8(a)(2) of the NLRA*, 72 S. CAL. L. REV. 1651, 1706–09 (1999); Clyde W. Summers, *Employee Voice and Employer Choice: A Structured Exception to Section 8(a)(2)*, 69 CHI.-KENT L. REV. 129, 141–48 (1993); Paul C. Weiler, *A Principled Reshaping of Labor Law for the Twenty-First Century*, 3 U. PA. J. LAB. & EMP. L. 177, 198–200 (2001).

29. On the constructive role that unions could play in the enforcement of public law, *see generally* Robert J. Rabin, *The Role of Unions in the Rights-Based Workplace,* 25 U.S.F. L. Rev. 169, 171–72, 199–218 (1991).

30. *See* James J. Brudney, *Reflections on Group Action and the Law of the Workplace,* 74 Tex. L. Rev. 1563, 1568–71 (1996).

31. *Id.* at 1571.

32. H.R. 8410, 95th Cong., 123 Cong. Rec. 23, 711–14 (1977); S. 1883, *id.* at 23, 738.

33. *See* DLL, *supra* note 5, at 67–68.

34. *See* 138 Cong. Rec. S8237 (daily ed. Sept. 24, 1992) (Senate cloture vote fails 57–42); 140 Cong. Rec. S8844 (daily ed. July 13, 1994) (Senate cloture vote fails 53–46); 140 Cong. Rec. S8524 (daily ed. July 12, 1994) (Senate cloture vote fails 53–47).

35. S. 295, 104th Cong. (1995). The TEAM Act would have allowed employers to establish employee participation programs "to address matters of mutual interest (including issues of quality, productivity, efficiency) and which [do] not have, claim, or seek authority to negotiate or enter into collective bargaining agreements [under this Act] with the employer." *Id.* §3.

36. *See* Teamwork for Employees and Managers Act of 1997: Hearings on S. 295 before the S. Comm. on Labor and Human Res., 105th Cong. 49 (1997) (testimony of Jonathan Hiatt, General Counsel, AFL-CIO).

37. *See Clinton Vetoes TEAM Act Despite Pleas from Business for Passage,* 152 Lab. Rel. Rep. (BNA) 417 at D-19 (Aug. 5, 1996).

38. Labor law is offered as a "prime example" of the ability of cohesive, well-organized groups to block legislation. *See* William N. Eskridge, Jr., & Philip P. Frickey, Legislation: Statutes and the Creation of Public Policy 52–57 (2d ed. 1995).

39. *See* Alan Hyde, *A Theory of Labor Legislation,* 38 Buff. L. Rev. 383, 445–46 (1990); Pope, *Thirteenth Amendment, supra* note 5, at 911–45.

40. Pope, *Thirteenth Amendment,* supra note 5, at 944–45. On the political power that business derives from its provision of essential goods and services and its mobility, *see* Charles E. Lindblom, Politics and Markets 175 (1977).

41. *See* Pope, *Thirteenth Amendment, supra* note 5, at 945.

42. *See* Barenberg, *Political Economy, supra* note 4, at 1443–46.

43. *See* Sanford M. Jacoby, *Reckoning with Company Unions: The Case of Thompson Products, 1934–1964,* 43 Indus. & Lab. Rel. Rev. 19, 19, 36–39 (1989); David Brody, *Section 8(a)(2) and the Origins of the Wagner Act, in* Restoring the Promise of American Labor Law 29, 41 (Sheldon Friedman et al. eds., 1994).

44. *See* Bruce E. Kaufman, *Does the NLRA Constrain Employee Involvement and Participation Programs in Nonunion Companies? A Reassessment,* 17 Yale L. & Pol'y Rev. 729, 735 (1999).

45. *See* Orly Lobel, *Agency and Coercion in Labor and Employment Relations: Four Dimensions of Power in Shifting Patterns of Work,* 4 U. Pa. J. Lab. & Emp. L. 121, 133–35 (2001).

46. *See, e.g.,* Simmons Indus., 321 NLRB 228, 254 (1996); Vons Grocery Co., 320 NLRB 53, 68–69 (1995); Sears, Roebuck & Co., 274 NLRB 230, 243–44 (1985).

47. *See, e.g.,* Polaroid Corp., 329 NLRB 424, 429 (1999); E. I. du Pont de Nemours & Co., 311 NLRB 893, 894–97 (1993).

48. *See* Crown Cork & Seal Co., 334 NLRB No. 92, slip op. at 3 (2001); General Foods Corp., 231 NLRB 1232, 1235 (1977).

49. From 1972 to 1993, the NLRB ordered the disestablishment of only fifty-eight illegal employer-dominated organizations. In 76 percent of those cases, charges were filed during an organizing campaign; most of these cases involved additional unfair labor practices. James Rundle, *Winning Hearts and Minds in the Era of Employee Involvement Programs, in* BRONFENBRENNER ET AL., *supra* note 16, at 213, 214.

50. *See* Ann G. Leibowitz, *The "Non-Union Union"?, in* EMPLOYEE REPRESENTATION IN THE EMERGING WORKPLACE: ALTERNATIVES/SUPPLEMENTS TO COLLECTIVE BARGAINING, Proceedings of the NYU 50th Annual Conference on Labor 235, 240–48 (Samuel Estreicher ed., 1998); Laura W. Stein, *What Can "Non-Unions" Do? A Response to Ms. Leibowitz and Professor Hyde, in* EMPLOYEE REPRESENTATION, *supra*, 267, 270.

51. *See* Kaufman, *supra* note 44, at 774–80.

52. *Id.* at 777–79; Stein, *supra* note 50, at 270, 273–75.

53. *See* FREEMAN & ROGERS, *supra* note 10, at 56–57, 142. Yet there was widespread support for independently elected employee representatives (preferred by 59 percent), resolution of disputes by outside arbitrators (59 percent), and some entitlement to confidential information (47 percent).

54. *Id.* at 152.

55. *Id.* at 60–63; Gottesman, *In Despair, supra* note 18, at 62–68.

56. *See* Larry Cohen & Richard W. Hurd, *Fear, Conflict, and Union Organizing, in* BRONFENBRENNER ET AL., *supra* note 16, at 181.

57. Employer-dominated unions in the 1930s may have had the unintended effect of stimulating collective action and cultivating worker leadership. *See* Barenberg, *Democracy and Domination, supra* note 28, at 831–35; Brody, *supra* note 43, at 36.

58. 29 U.S.C. §153(d) (2000). On the unreviewability of the General Counsel's prosecutorial discretion, *see* Detroit Edison Co. v. NLRB, 440 U.S. 301, 316 (1979); Vaca v. Sipes, 386 U.S. 171, 182 (1967).

59. *See* Michael Gottesman, *Rethinking Labor Law Preemption: State Laws Facilitating Unionization,* 7 YALE J. on REG. 355, 360–61, 408 (1990).

60. On the history of judicial antagonism toward labor activity, *see* WILLIAM FORBATH, LAW AND THE SHAPING OF THE AMERICAN LABOR MOVEMENT 59–66 (1998).

61. Due process was deemed to require judicial review, but trial courts were largely bypassed. Employers and their advocates had sought a larger role for courts in unfair labor practice proceedings. And when the Taft-Hartley Act banned certain union conduct, employers got access to the courts. Employers may sue directly under Section 303 of the Labor-Management Relations Act, 29 U.S.C. §187, for damages due to illegal secondary picketing. The Taft-Hartley Act's authorization of federal suits for enforcement of collective bargaining agreements, 29 U.S.C. §301, has in fact generated a federal common law of labor contracts with some vitality—for example, doctrines defining the deference due to labor arbitration and unions' "duty of fair representation." But these developments have left untouched the administrative scheme for the enforcement of basic employee rights under the NLRA.

62. *See* WEILER, GOVERNING, *supra* note 12, at 233–41.

63. 42 U.S.C. §§2000e–2000e17 (2000).

64. Expansion of litigation continued with the Age Discrimination in Employment Act, 29 U.S.C. 621–634, and the Americans with Disabilities Act, 42 U.S.C. §§12101–12213.

65. *See* Freeman & Kleiner, *supra* note 18, at 351–54; Weiler, *Promises, supra* note 18, at 1771–80. For an illuminating set of "case studies" of employers' anti-union campaigns and the law's inadequate response, *see* Richard W. Hurd & Joseph B. Uehlein, *Patterned Responses to Organizing: Case Studies of the Union-Busting Convention, in* FRIEDMAN ET AL., *supra* note 43, at 61.

66. New State Ice Co. v. Liebmann, 285 U.S. 262, 311 (1932) (Brandeis, J., dissenting). *See also* Dorf & Sabel, *supra* note 11, at 419–38; Michael W. McConnell, *Federalism: Evaluating the Founders' Design,* 54 U. CHI. L. REV. 1484, 1498 (1987).

67. For critical views of preemption doctrine, *see* Gottesman, *Preemption, supra* note 59, at 391; Eileen Silverstein, *Against Preemption in Labor Law,* 24 CONN. L. REV. 1, 11 (1991). The conventional view among labor law scholars favored broad federal preemption. *See, e.g.,* Archibald Cox, *Labor Law Preemption Revisited,* 85 HARV. L. REV. 1337, 1339 (1972); Bernard D. Meltzer, *The Supreme Court, Congress, and State Jurisdiction over Labor Relations: II,* 59 COLUM. L. REV. 269, 302 (1959).

68. Indeed, the act provides that the Board's power to prevent unfair labor practices "shall not be affected by any other means of adjustment or prevention that has been or may be established by agreement, law, or otherwise." 29 U.S.C. §160(a) (1994). This provision was once thought to foreclose the claim that Congress intended the Board's jurisdiction to be exclusive. *See* Gottesman, *Preemption, supra* note 59, at 386–87.

69. *See* Hill v. Florida, 325 U.S. 538, 548 (1945).

70. *See* Gottesman, *Preemption, supra* note 59, at 383–91.

71. San Diego Bldg. Trades Council v. Garmon, 359 U.S. 236 (1959). *Garmon* preemption is founded on the NLRB's "primary jurisdiction" to define protected and prohibited conduct under the Act.

72. *See* Sears, Roebuck & Co. v. San Diego Dist. Council of Carpenters, 436 U.S. 180, 198, 211–12 (1978). Professor Gottesman argues for a partial retreat from *Garmon. See* Gottesman, *Preemption, supra* note 59, at 359–61.

73. Lodge 76, Int'l Ass'n of Machinists v. Wis. Employment Relations Comm'n, 427 U.S. 132 (1976).

74. Wis. Dep't of Indus., Labor & Human Relations v. Gould, 475 U.S. 282, 283–89 (1986).

75. *See* Gottesman, *Preemption, supra* note 59, at 395.

76. That tort remedy resembles one of the classic "public policy" decisions upholding the wrongful discharge claim of an employee fired for filing a workers' compensation claim, Frampton v. Cent. Ind. Gas Co., 297 N.E.2d 425, 428 (Ind. 1973), and would likely be adopted by many state courts absent the preemption bar. *See* Gottesman, *Preemption, supra* note 59, at 369 n.59.

77. The states are permitted to reach labor activity incidentally in enforcing general state laws that protect core local interests—*e.g.,* laws against violence (UAW-CIO v. Russell, 356 U.S. 634 [1958]); threats of violence (United Constr. Workers v. Laburnum Constr. Corp., 347 U.S. 656 [1954]); trespass (Sears, Roebuck & Co. v. San Diego County Dist. Council of Carpenters, 436 U.S. 180 [1978]); intentional infliction of emotional distress

(Farmer v. United Bhd. of Carpenters, Local 25, 430 U.S. 290 [1977]); or, with some limitations, defamation (Linn v. United Plant Guard Workers Local 114, 383 U.S. 53 [1966]). But they may not target labor relations as such or punish protected activity under the guise of these laws.

78. *See Bldg. & Constr. Trades Council,* 507 U.S. at 227–32.

79. *See Gould,* 475 U.S. at 282.

80. Chamber of Commerce v. Brown, 128 S.Ct. 2408 (2008).

81. On the broader trend toward federalization through preemption, *see* Samuel Issacharoff & Catherine M. Sharkey, *Backdoor Federalization,* 53 UCLA L. Rev. 1353 (2006).

82. Jeffrey Hirsch has argued recently against the effort to expand states' regulatory author-ity in the labor arena on the grounds that it risks promoting a "race to the bottom" and in any case increases the labor law's complexity. Jeffrey M. Hirsch, *Taking States out of the Workplace* (December 6, 2008). Yale L. J. Pocket Part, Vol. 177, 2008; University of Tennessee Legal Studies Research Paper No. 53. Available at SSRN: http://ssrn.com /abstract=1312484.

83. The one statutory concession to regional variation is the Act's express immunization of state "right-to-work" laws—laws that bar contractual provisions requiring employees to join unions—which are widespread in the South. *See* 29 U.S.C. §164(b).

84. Gottesman, *Preemption, supra* note 59, at 358–61.

85. *See* Lochner v. New York, 198 U.S. 45 (1905); Adkins v. Children's Hosp. of D.C., 261 U.S. 525 (1923); Truax v. Corrigan, 257 U.S. 312 (1921); Adair v. United States, 208 U.S. 161 (1908).

86. In the Supreme Court, with a few exceptions cited below in note 93, constitutional ar-guments under NLRA have generally run against labor unions; all have been resolved by construing the statute to avoid constitutional concerns. The Court found "serious First Amendment concerns" in the NLRB's punishing an employer's retaliatory, though nonfrivolous, lawsuit against a union, BE & K Constr. Co. v. NLRB, 536 U.S. 516 (2002); in unions' use of contractually required dues to support political activity, Com-munications Workers of America v. Beck, 487 U.S. 735, 742–44 (1988); in extending NLRA coverage to teachers at church-operated schools, NLRB v. Catholic Bishop of Chicago, 440 U.S. 490 (1979); and in restricting employers' anti-union speech, NLRB v. Va. Elec. & Power Co., 314 U.S. 469 (1941). The Court construed the Railway Labor Act, and implicitly the NLRA, to require unions' fair representation without discrimi-nation on the basis of race to avoid a serious equal protection challenge to the statute's grant of exclusive representation. *See* Steele v. Louisville & Nashville R.R. Co., 323 U.S. 192, 203–04 (1944).

87. *See* William Forbath, *The Ambiguities of Free Labor: Labor and the Law in the Gilded Age,* 1985 Wis. L. Rev. 767, 797–801; Pope, *Thirteenth Amendment, supra* note 5, at 934–49; James Gray Pope, *The Three-Systems Ladder of First Amendment Values: Two Rungs and a Black Hole,* 11 Hastings Const. L.Q. 189, 197–98 (1984).

88. *See* John Hart Ely, Democracy & Distrust 75–77 (1980). According to Ely, the out-line of this new project was sketched in United States v. Carolene Products Co., 304 U.S. 144, 152 n.4 (1938).

89. Thornhill v. Alabama, 310 U.S. 88, 101–03 (1940). *See also* Marsh v. Alabama, 326 U.S.

501, 502–05 (1946); Thomas v. Collins, 323 U.S. 516, 532 (1945); Hague v. CIO, 307 U.S. 496, 515–16 (1939).

90. *See* Int'l Bhd. of Teamsters, Local 695 v. Vogt, Inc., 354 U.S. 284, 294 (1957).

91. *See, e.g.*, NAACP v. Claiborne Hardware Co., 458 U.S. 886, 886 (1982); Carey v. Brown, 447 U.S. 455, 466–67 (1980); Police Dep't of Chicago v. Mosley, 408 U.S. 92, 95–96 (1972); Shuttlesworth v. City of Birmingham, 394 U.S. 147, 155 (1969); Edwards v. South Carolina, 372 U.S. 229, 235 (1963).

92. *See* Michael J. Klarman, *Rethinking the Civil Rights and Civil Liberties Revolutions*, 82 Va. L. Rev. 1, 39–46 (1996).

93. In Edward J. DeBartolo Corp. v. Fla. Gulf Coast Bldg. & Constr. Trades Council, 485 U.S. 568 (1988), the Court construed the statute narrowly and allowed the peaceful distribution of leaflets to consumers, in recognition of serious constitutional concerns. *Id.* at 576. The Court recognized but avoided constitutional concerns about the ban on secondary consumer picketing in NLRB v. Fruit & Vegetable Packers & Warehousemen, Local 760 ("Tree Fruits"), 377 U.S. 58, 63 (1964) but then brushed aside those concerns in the Safeco case, NLRB v. Retail Store Employees Union, Local 1001, 447 U.S. 607, 616 (1980).

94. Thus was the regulability of labor boycotts, unlike "political" boycotts, explained in NAACP v. Claiborne Hardware Co., 458 U.S. 886, 912–13 (1982).

95. *See* James J. Brudney, *A Famous Victory: Collective Bargaining Protections and the Statutory Aging Process*, 74 N.C. L. Rev. 939, 1027–28 (1996). First Amendment objections to union security provisions were first noted, and avoided by statutory construction, in Int'l Ass'n of Machinists v. Street, 367 U.S. 740 (1961), under the Railway Labor Act. The contours of the permissible "agency fee" were elucidated in Ellis v. Bhd. of Ry., Airlines & Steamship Clerks, 466 U.S. 435 (1984) and carried over to the NLRA in Communications Workers of America v. Beck, 487 U.S. 735 (1988).

96. *See Beck*, 487 U.S. at 745; *Ellis*, 466 U.S. at 452–54.

97. *See International Labor Organization (ILO) Declaration on Fundamental Principles and Rights at Work* (1998), *available at* http://www.ilo.org/public/English/standards/decl/declaration/text/index.htm.

98. The International Covenant on Civil and Political Rights (ICCPR) declares: "[E]veryone shall have the right to freedom of association with others, including the right to form and join trade unions for the protection of his interests." *Id.* at 41–42 (quoting ICCPR, Dec. 16, 1966, art. 22, 999 U.N.T.S. 171). The ICCPR, which the U.S. ratified in 1992, requires ratifying states "to respect and to ensure to all individuals within its territory and subject to its jurisdiction the rights recognized in the present Covenant"; "to adopt such legislative or other measures as may be necessary to give effect to the rights recognized in the present Covenant"; and "to ensure that any person whose rights or freedoms as herein recognized are violated shall have an effective remedy." *Id.* at 41–42. http://www.hrw.org/reports/2000/uslabor/USLBR008–04.htm—P516_118763.

99. The U.S. sought unsuccessfully to impose a "state action" requirement and to protect the freedom of association only against "governmental interference." Manfred Nowak, U.N. Covenant on Civil and Political Rights: CCPR Commentary 387 & n.15 (1993).

100. Lance Compa, Unfair Advantage: Workers' Freedom of Association in the United States under International Human Rights Standards 8 (2000), *available at* http://www.hrw.org/reports/2000/uslabor/USLBR008–02.htm10.

101. *Id.* at 16.

102. *See* Catherine Powell, *Dialogic Federalism: Constitutional Possibilities for Incorporation of Human Rights Law in the United States,* 150 U. Pa. L. Rev. 245, 259–60 (2001).

103. Letter to Members of Congress from James Brudney, Cynthia Estlund et al., Dec. 12, 2007 (footnotes omitted). Footnotes in this passage cite Oakwood Healthcare, Inc., 348 NLRB No.37 (2006); Brown University, 342 NLRB No.42 (2004); Oakwood Care Center, 343 NLRB No.76 (2004); Brevard Achievement Center, 342 NLRB No.101 (2004); Delta Brands, Inc., 344 NLRB No.10 (2005); Waters of Orchard Park, 341 NLRB No.93 (2004); Holling Press, Inc., 343 NLRB No.45 (2004); IBM Corp, 341 NLRB No.148 (2004); Albertson's, Inc., 351 NLRB No.21 (2007); Desert Toyota, 346 NLRB No.3 (2005); and First Legal Support Services, 342 NLRB No.29 (2004).

104. In addition to Albertson's, Inc., Desert Toyota, and First Legal Support Services, cited in note 102, *see* St. George Warehouse, 351 NLRB No.42 (2007); Intermet Stevensville, 350 NLRB No.94 (2007); Abramson, LLC, 345 NLRB No.8 (2005); The Register-Guard, 344 NLRB No.150 (2005); The Grosvenor Resort, 350 NLRB No.86 (2007); Oil Capitol Sheet Metal, Inc., 349 NLRB No.118 (2007); and Toering Electric Co., 351 NLRB No.18 (2007).

105. Oakwood Healthcare, Inc., 348 NLRB No.37 (2006); Brown University, 342 NLRB No.42 (2004); Oakwood Care Center, 343 NLRB No.76 (2004); Brevard Achievement Center, 342 NLRB No.101 (2004).

106. The Guard Publishing Company, d/b/a The Register-Guard, 351 NLRB No. 70 (Dec. 16, 2007).

107. Dana Corp., 351 NLRB No.28 (2007).

108. James J. Brudney, *Neutrality Agreements and Card Check Recognition: Prospects for Changing Paradigms,* 90 Iowa L. Rev. 819 (2005).

109. *See id.* at 828–30.

110. *See id.* For empirical data on neutrality agreements, *see* Adrienne E. Eaton & Jill Kriesky, *Union Organizing under Neutrality and Card Check Agreements,* 55 Indus. & Lab. Rel. Rev. 42, 45 (2001).

111. James J. Brudney, *Isolated and Politicized: The NLRB's Uncertain Future,* 26 Comp. Lab. L. & Pol'y J. 221, 221–22 (2005); Matthew W. Finkin, *Employer Neutrality as Hot Cargo: Thoughts on the Making of Labor Policy,* 20 Notre Dame J.L. Ethics & Pub. Pol'y 541, 542 (2006).

112. *See* Labor-Management Relations Act of 1947, 301, codified at 29 U.S.C. §185. *See generally* Charles I. Cohen, Joseph E. Santucci, Jr., & Jonathan C. Fritts, *Resisting Its Own Obsolescence: How the National Labor Relations Board Is Questioning the Existing Law of Neutrality Agreements,* 20 Notre Dame J.L. Ethics & Pub. Pol'y 521, 524 (2006).

113. For example, does a union's effort to secure a neutrality agreement amount to a demand for recognition (which would trigger a thirty-day limit on picketing in support of that demand)? *See* Marriot Hartford Downtown Hotel, 347 NLRB No. 87 (2006).

114. Shaw's Supermarkets, 343 NLRB No. 105 (2004).

115. Dana Corp., JD–24–05 (NLRB Div. of Judges, Apr. 8, 2005) ("Dana II"). Dana II extends a much criticized doctrine in Majestic Weaving Co., 147 NLRB 859 (1964), enf. denied, 355 F.2d 854 (2d Cir. 1966).

116. Heartland Industrial Partners, LLC, JD(NY)–23–05 (NLRB Div. of Judges, June 16, 2005). For an illuminating analysis of the "hot cargo" issue, *see* Finkin, *supra* note 111, at 541.

117. Dana/Metaldyne Corp., 351 NLRB No. 28 (2007). ("Dana I," so-called because a second Dana case involving voluntary recognition agreements, *see supra* n. 115, is awaiting the NLRB's decision.)

CHAPTER 3. THE RISE OF EMPLOYMENT LAW

1. Adkins v. Children's Hospital, 261 U.S. 525 (1923); Adair v. United States, 208 U.S. 161, 174 (1908); Lochner v. New York, 198 U.S. 45 (1905).

2. *See, e.g.*, RICHARD A. POSNER, ECONOMIC ANALYSIS OF LAW 346–51 (6th ed. 2003).

3. *Id.*

4. The idea of compensating wage differentials was a major argument in defense of the old tort rules of assumption of the risk and the fellow servant rule, which foreclosed most personal injury tort actions by employees against their employers in the nineteenth century. *See, e.g.*, Farwell v. Boston & Worcester R.R. Corp., 45 Mass. (4 Met.) 49 (1842). "The general rule . . . is, that he who engages in the employment of another for the performance of specified duties and services, for compensation, takes upon himself the natural and ordinary risks and perils incident to the performance of such services, and in legal presumption, the compensation is adjusted accordingly." *Id.* at 57. For modern analogs of the argument, *see* Thomas A. Lambert, *Avoiding Regulatory Mismatch in the Workplace: An Informational Approach to Workplace Safety Regulation,* 82 NEB. L. REV. 1006, 1021–23 (2004); W. KIP VISCUSI, RISK BY CHOICE: REGULATING HEALTH AND SAFETY IN THE WORKPLACE (1983).

5. *See* RICHARD REVESZ & MICHAEL LIVERMORE, RETAKING RATIONALITY: HOW COST-BENEFIT ANALYSIS CAN BETTER PROTECT THE ENVIRONMENT AND OUR HEALTH (2008); SUSAN ROSE-ACKERMAN, RETHINKING THE PROGRESSIVE AGENDA: THE REFORM OF THE AMERICAN REGULATORY STATE 86–88 (1992).

6. *See* Cass R. Sunstein, *Constitutionalism after the New Deal,* 101 HARV. L. REV. 421, 439 (1987).

7. Michael L. Wachter, *Labor Unions: A Corporatist Institution in a Competitive World,* 155 U. PA. L. REV. 581 (2006).

8. *See* Orly Lobel, *The Renew Deal: The Fall of Regulation and the Rise of Governance in Contemporary Legal Thought,* 89 MINN. L. REV. 342, 379 (2004); Donald W. Stever, *Experience and Lessons of Twenty-Five Years of Environmental Law: Where We Have Been and Where We Are Headed,* 27 LOY. L.A. L. REV. 1105, 1109 n.7 (1994).

9. It is the kinship between collective bargaining and corporatism that is the linchpin of Professor Wachter's argument for why unionization first burgeoned in the New Deal and why it has since shrunk. Wachter, *supra* note 7.

10. 29 U.S.C. §§201–209 (2000).

11. The FLSA originally covered only about 20 percent of the workforce; it excluded agricultural, household, and retail workers, as well as the entire public sector. *See* Howard Wial, *Minimum-Wage Enforcement and the Low-Wage Labor Market* 15 (MIT Task Force on Reconstructing America's Labor Mkt. Inst., Working Paper No. WP11, Aug. 1, 1999), *available at* http://mitsloan.mit.edu/iwer/pdf/tfwial.pdf.

12. For an overview of FLSA enforcement, *see id.* at 6–9.

13. *See* Clyde W. Summers, *Labor Law as the Century Turns: A Changing of the Guard,* 67 NEB. L. REV. 7, 9 (1988).

14. Similarly, the Social Security Act established a minimal system of retirement security, leaving individuals and unions to bargain with employers for more generous retirement benefits. 42 U.S.C. §§301–1397jj (2000).

15. Living Wage Resource Ctr., *Living Wage Successes: A Compilation of Living Wage Policies on the Books,* http://www.livingwagecampaign.org/index.php?id=1958 (last visited Apr. 15, 2008).

16. *See generally* JOHN FABIAN WITT, THE ACCIDENTAL REPUBLIC: CRIPPLED WORKINGMEN, DESTITUTE WIDOWS, AND THE REMAKING OF AMERICAN LAW (2004). *See* Alfred W. Blumrosen et al., *Injunctions against Occupational Hazards: The Right to Work under Safe Conditions,* 64 CAL. L. REV. 702, 722–23 (1976).

17. WITT, *supra* note 16, at 190–94; N.Y. Cent. R.R. v. White, 243 U.S. 188 (1917).

18. *White,* 243 U.S. 188.

19. Mark L. Matulef, *On-the-Job Lead Poisoning: Early Judicial Treatment of Claims for Recovery from Exposure to Workplace Lead,* 10 U. BALT. J. ENVTL. L. 1, 20 (2002).

20. *See* Sidney A. Shapiro & Randy Rabinowitz, *Voluntary Regulatory Compliance in Theory and Practice: The Case of OSHA,* 52 ADMIN. L. REV. 97, 132 (2000).

21. *See* James J. Brudney, *Reflections on Group Action and the Law of the Workplace,* 74 TEX. L. REV. 1563, 1569 (1996).

22. 29 U.S.C. §651–78. *See* Thomas O. McGarity, *Reforming OSHA: Some Thoughts for the Current Legislative Agenda,* 31 HOUS. L. REV. 99, 100 (1994). *See also* S. REP. No. 91–1282, at 2–5 (1970); H.R. REP. No. 91–1291, at 14–16 (1970).

23. 29 U.S.C. §654.

24. THOMAS O. MCGARITY & SIDNEY A. SHAPIRO, WORKERS AT RISK: THE FAILED PROMISE OF THE OCCUPATIONAL SAFETY AND HEALTH ADMINISTRATION 37 (1993).

25. ROBERT A. KAGAN & EUGENE BARDACH, GOING BY THE BOOK: THE PROBLEM OF REGULATORY UNREASONABLENESS 4, 48, 113–116 (1982).

26. 29 U.S.C. §667.

27. Alison D. Morantz, *Has Devolution Injured American Workers? State and Federal Enforcement of Construction Safety,* 25 J. L. ECON. & ORG. 183 (2009); Alison D. Morantz, *Examining Regulatory Devolution from the Ground Up: A Comparison of State and Federal Enforcement of Construction Safety Regulations* 4–5 (Stanford Law & Econ. Olin Working Paper No. 308, January 2007), *available at* http://ssrn.com/abstract=755026.

28. *See* Morantz, *Examining, supra* note 27, at 31.

29. Employee Retirement Income Security Act of 1974 (ERISA), Pub. L. No. 93–406, 88 Stat. 829 (codified as amended at 29 U.S.C. §§1001–1461 [2000]).

30. Many of ERISA's provisions targeted the "defined benefit" pension plans that then were most prevalent; ERISA may in fact have contributed in a variety of ways to the dramatic shift toward "defined contribution" plans, which put greater risk—upside and downside —on employees. *See* Margaret M. Blair, *The Great Pension Grab: Comments on Richard Ippolito, Bankruptcy and Workers: Risks, Compensation and Pension Contracts,* 82 Wash. U. L.Q. 1305, 1307 (2004); Henry H. Drummonds, *The Aging of the Boomers and the Coming Crisis in America's Changing Retirement and Elder Care Systems,* 11 Lewis & Clark L. Rev. 267, 296 (2007).

31. 29 U.S.C. §§2101–2109.

32. 29 U.S.C. §§2601–2654.

33. H.R. 1542, 110th Cong. (2007).

34. *See generally* Brudney, *supra* note 21, at 1563.

35. Benjamin Sachs has shown that individual antiretaliation provisions of some statutory regimes, though they do not explicitly contemplate collective activity, can be used as a catalyst and an alternative form of protection for such activity. *See* Benjamin I. Sachs, *Employment Law as Labor Law,* 29 Cardozo L. Rev. 2685 (2008).

36. *See* H.R. 1280, 103d Cong. (1993); H.R. 3160, 102d Cong. (1991).

37. *See* Randy S. Rabinowitz & Mark M. Hager, *Designing Health and Safety: Workplace Hazard Regulation in the United States and Canada,* 33 Cornell Int'l L.J. 373, 431 (2000); Mark Seidenfeld, *Empowering Stakeholders: Limits on Collaboration as the Basis for Flexible Regulation,* 41 Wm. & Mary L. Rev. 411, 500 (2000); Kenneth A. Kovach et al., *OSHA and the Politics of Reform: An Analysis of OSHA Reform Initiatives before the 104th Congress,* 34 Harv. J. on Legis. 169, 175 (1997).

38. *See* James T. Bennett & Bruce E. Kaufman, *Conclusion: The Future of Private Sector Unionism in the U.S.—Assessment and Forecast, in* The Future of Private Sector Unionism in the United States 359 (James T. Bennett & Bruce E. Kaufman eds., 2002).

39. That problem was highlighted both by Freeman and Medoff in their classic assessment of unions, Richard B. Freeman & James L. Medoff, What Do Unions Do? (1984), and by Professor Paul Weiler in his important critique of labor and employment law, Paul C. Weiler, Governing the Workplace: The Future of Labor and Employment Law (1990).

40. Wial, *supra* note 11, at 9.

41. David Weil, *Regulating Noncompliance to Labor Standards: New Tools for an Old Problem,* 45 Challenge 47, 58 (2002); David Weil, *Compliance with the Minimum Wage: Can Government Make a Difference?* 8–11, *available at* http://ssrn.com/abstract =368340.

42. Weil, *Compliance, supra* note 41, at 10.

43. Wial, *supra* note 11, at 9; Weil, *Compliance, supra* note 41, at 9–13, 45.

44. *See* Weil, *Compliance, supra* note 41, at 10. *See generally* Samantha C. Halem, *Slaves to Fashion: A Thirteenth Amendment Litigation Strategy to Abolish Sweatshops in the Garment Industry,* 36 San Diego L. Rev. 397, 415 (1999).

45. *See* Katherine V. W. Stone, From Widgets to Digits: Employment Regulation for the Changing Workplace 78 (2004).

46. *See* Annette Bernhardt, Siobhán McGrath, & James DeFilippis, *Unregulated Work in the*

Global City: Employment and Labor Law Violations in New York City 28–29 (2007) (a report by the Brennan Ctr. for Justice at N.Y. U. Sch. of Law).

47. See Bernhardt et al., *supra* note 46; Kim Bobo, Wage Theft in America: Why Millions of Working Americans are not Getting Paid—and What We Can Do About It (2009); Steven Greenhouse, The Big Squeeze: Tough Times for the American Worker (2009).

48. *See* Bernhardt et al., *supra* note 46, at 12; Abel Valenzuela, Jr., et al., *On the Corner: Day Labor in the United States* 14 (2006), Ctr. for the Study of Urban Poverty report, *available at* http://www.sscnet.ucla.edu/issr/csup/uploaded_files/Natl_DayLabor-On_the_Corner1.pdf.

49. *See* Bernhardt et al., *supra* note 46, at 10–13; Make the Road by Walking, *Street of Shame: Retail Stores on Knickerbocker Avenue, Bushwick, Brooklyn, New York* (2005), *available at* http://www.maketheroad.org/pix_reports/2005MaySTREETofShame.pdf.

50. Greenhouse, The Big Squeeze, *supra* note 47, at 57–58.

51. *Id.* at 227.

52. *See* Steven Greenhouse, *Altering of Worker Time Cards Spurs Growing Number of Suits,* N.Y. Times, Apr. 4, 2004, at 11.

53. Greenhouse, The Big Squeeze, *supra* note 47, at 64.

54. *Id.* at 70.

55. Bernhardt et al., *supra* note 46, at 12.

56. *See* Steven Greenhouse, *Workers' Suit against Wal-Mart Granted Class Action Status in New Jersey,* N.Y. Times, June 1, 2007, at C7.

57. Greenhouse, The Big Squeeze, *supra* note 47, at 101–2.

58. *Id.* at 49. Wal-Mart says that it has changed its lock-in policy and now requires someone with a key to be on site, *id.* at 55, and that it is "cracking down" on managers' demanding off-the-clock work and altering time sheets. *Id.* at 153. It does not appear that these violations have completely disappeared, though they do seem to be less frequent. *See* Human Rights Watch, *Discounting Rights: Wal-Mart's Violation of U.S. Workers' Right to Freedom of Association,* 33–34 (May 2007), *available at* http://hrw.org/reports/2007/us0507/.

59. Greenhouse, The Big Squeeze, *supra* note 47, at 53.

60. *Id.* at 53–54.

61. Alvarez v. IBP, Inc., No. CT–98–5005–RHW, 2005 WL 3941313 (E.D. Wash. Dec. 20, 2005).

62. Greenhouse, The Big Squeeze, *supra* note 47, at 111–12.

63. *Id.* at 112.

64. *See* Bernhardt et al., *supra* note 46, at 17–18; Catherine Ruckelshaus & Bruce Goldstein, *From Orchards to the Internet: Confronting Contingent Work Abuse* (2002), National Employment Law Project, *available at* http://www.nelp.org/docUploads/pub 120.pdf.

65. Bernhardt et al., *supra* note 46, at 17–18; U. S. Gov t. Accounting Office, Employment Arrangements: Improved Outreach Could Help Ensure Proper Worker Classification, GAO 06–656 (2006); Françoise Carré & Randall Wilson, *The Social and Economic Costs of Employee Misclassification in Construction* (2004), Labor & Worklife Program at Harvard Law Sch., *available at* http://www.law.harvard.edu/programs

/lwp/Misclassification%20Report%20Mass.pdf; Lalith DeSilva et al., *Independent Contractors: Prevalence and Implications for Unemployment Insurance Programs* (Planmatic, Inc., for the United States Dep't of Labor, 2000), *available at* http://wdr.doleta.gov /owsdrr/00–5/00–5.pdf.

66. Greenhouse, The Big Squeeze, *supra* note 47, at 122–23.

67. *Id.* at 122–24.

68. *Id.* at 125.

69. *Id.* at 123.

70. *See* Bernhardt et al., *supra* note 46, at 16, 35–36; Michael J. Wishnie, *Emerging Issues for Undocumented Workers,* 6 U. Pa. J. Lab. & Emp. L. 497 (2004).

71. Bernhardt et al., *supra* note 46, at 32.

72. Conservative commentators argue, in fact, that the economic drivers (including workers' compensation laws) are doing all of the work in improving workplace safety. *See, e.g.,* John Hood, *OSHA's Trivial Pursuit: In Workplace Safety, Business Outperforms the Regulators,* Policy Review (Hoover Institution), No. 73 (1995).

73. *See* Bernhardt et al., *supra* note 46, at 12, 35–36.

74. 29 U.S.C. §666(a)–(b) (2000). Multiple violations can produce multiple fines, and in some cases quite large fines. However, OSHA's efforts to address egregious cases by multiplying the fine by the number of employees affected were curbed by Reich v. Arcadian Corp., 110 F.3d 1192, 1199 (5th Cir. 1997). *See* Stacy Cooper et al., *Employment-Related Crimes,* 40 Am. Crim. L. Rev. 367, 378–79 (2003).

75. *See* Shapiro & Rabinowitz, *supra* note 20, at 109.

76. *Id.* at 108–09.

77. AFL-CIO Safety & Health Dep't, AFL-CIO, *Death on the Job: The Toll of Neglect* 4 (11th ed. 2002), *available at* http://www.aflcio.org/mediacenter/resources/upload/deathon thejobthetollofneglectapril2002.pdf.

78. Bernhardt et al., *supra* note 46, at 32.

79. For a discussion of the incentives acting on a potential violator, *see* McGarity & Shapiro, *supra* note 24, at 212.

80. These figures are from OSHRC's Web site. *See* http://www.oshrc.gov/decisions /comm07.html.

81. McGarity & Shapiro, *supra* note 24, at 247.

82. Bureau of Labor Statistics, U. S. Dep't of Labor, *Fatal Occupational Injuries by Event or Exposure and Major Private Industry Sector* (2005) (showing that in 2005 mining resulted in 874 fatalities while construction resulted in 1,192 fatalities), *available at* http://www .bls.gov/iif/oshwc/cfoi/cftb0213.pdf; Bureau of Labor Statistics, U.S. Dep't of Labor, *Workplace Injuries and Illnesses in 2005,* at 16 (2005) (showing that in 2005 mining resulted in about 76,900 nonfatal injuries or illnesses while construction resulted in about 414,900 nonfatal injuries or illnesses), *available at* http://www.bls.gov/iif/oshwc/osh/os /osnr0025.pdf.

83. Greenhouse, The Big Squeeze, *supra* note 47, 18–20.

84. *Id.* at 25–26.

85. Polly Walker et al., *Public Health Implications of Meat Production and Consumption,* 8 Publ. Health Nutrition 348 (2005).

86. *See* DANIEL M. BERMAN, DEATH ON THE JOB: OCCUPATIONAL HEALTH AND SAFETY STRUGGLES IN THE UNITED STATES 9 (1978); McGarity, *supra* note 22, at 117.

87. Paul Taylor, *City Officials Urge Criminal Probe of Safety Lapses at Fatal Fire Scene,* WASH. POST, Sept. 7, 1991, at A3.

88. Michael S. Worrall, *Meatpacking Safety: Is OSHA Enforcement Adequate?,* 9 DRAKE J. AGRIC. L. 299 (2004).

89. Bernhardt et al., *supra* note 46, at 15.

90. *Id.* at 30.

91. *Id.* at 35.

92. *Id.* at 19; Devah Pager & Bruce Western, *Race at Work: Realities of Race and Criminal Record in the NYC Job Market* 9–12 (2005), *available at* http://www.princeton.edu/~pager/race_at_work.pdf.

93. *See* William E. Forbath, *Caste, Class, and Equal Citizenship,* 98 MICH. L. REV. 1, 18 (1999); PAUL FRYMER, BLACK AND BLUE: AFRICAN AMERICANS, THE LABOR MOVEMENT, AND THE DECLINE OF THE DEMOCRATIC PARTY (2008).

94. For perspectives on the roots of civil rights legislation, *see* Michael J. Klarman, *Brown, Racial Change, and the Civil Rights Movement,* 80 VA. L. REV. 7, 10 (1994); Daniel B. Rodriguez & Barry R. Weingast, *The Positive Political Theory of Legislative History: New Perspectives on the 1964 Civil Rights Act and Its Interpretation,* 151 U. PA. L. REV. 1417 (2003). Historical accounts are found *in* CHARLES WHALEN & BARBARA WHALEN, THE LONGEST DEBATE: A LEGISLATIVE HISTORY OF THE 1964 CIVIL RIGHTS ACT 155–56, 184–89 (1985); David B. Filvaroff & Raymond E. Wolfinger, *The Origin and Enactment of the Civil Rights Act of 1964, in* LEGACIES OF THE 1964 CIVIL RIGHTS ACT 9, 22–26 (Bernard Grofman ed., 2000)

95. *See* Civil Rights Act of 1964, Pub. L. No. 88–352, 703, 78 Stat. 241, 255 (codified as amended at 42 U.S.C. §2000e–2 [2000]).

96. *See* Age Discrimination in Employment Act of 1967, Pub. L. No. 90–202, 81 Stat. 602 (codified as amended at 29 U.S.C. §621–634); Pregnancy Discrimination Act, Pub. L. No. 95–555, 92 Stat. 2076 (1978) (codified at 42 U.S.C. §2000e); Americans with Disabilities Act of 1990, Pub. L. No. 101–336, 104 Stat. 327 (codified as amended at 42 U.S.C. §12101–12213 [2000]); Genetic Information Nondiscrimination Act of 2007, S. 358, H.R. 493, 110th Cong., 1st Sess. (2007); Civil Rights Act of 1991, Pub. L. No. 102–166, 105 (1991).

97. Before the Civil Rights Act of 1991, race discrimination plaintiffs could seek damages, and a jury trial, by using 42 U.S.C. §1981(a) alongside Title VII of the Civil Rights Act of 1964. After the 1991 amendments, a jury trial and damages (subject to caps) were available under Title VII itself.

98. *See* Griggs v. Duke Power Co., 401 U.S. 424, 431 (1971); Barnes v. Costle, 561 F.2d 983, 990 (1977); Meritor Savings Bank, FSB v. Vinson, 477 U.S. 57, 73 (1986).

99. For one description and powerful critique of the at-will rule, *see* Clyde W. Summers, *Employment at Will in the United States: The Divine Right of Employers,* 3 U. PA. J. LAB. & EMP. L. 65 (2000).

100. *See, e.g.,* Luedtke v. Nabors Alaska Drilling, Inc., 768 P.2d 1123, 1136–37 (Ala. 1989) (discharge for refusing random drug tests); Petermann v. Int'l Bhd. of Teamsters, Local

396, 344 P.2d 25, 27 (Cal. Ct. App. 1959) (discharge for refusing to give perjured testimony); Nees v. Hocks, 536 P.2d 512, 516 (Or. 1975) (discharge for serving jury duty).

101. The Supreme Court announced the concept of property rights in employment in Board of Regents v. Roth, 408 U.S. 564, 577–78 (1972), and filled in the outlines of what process is due before deprivation of such property in Cleveland Board of Education v. Loudermill, 470 U.S. 532 (1985). For an early and influential articulation of this concept, *see* Charles A. Reich, *The New Property,* 73 YALE L.J. 733 (1964).

102. *See, e.g.,* Ohanian v. Avis Rent A Car System, Inc., 779 F.2d 101 (2d Cir. 1985); Pugh v. See's Candies, Inc., 171 CAL. RPTR. 917 (Cal. Ct. App. 1981).

103. *See, e.g.,* Toussaint v. Blue Cross & Blue Shield of Mich., 292 N.W.2d 880 (Mich. 1980); Woolley v. Hoffmann-La Roche, Inc., 491 A.2d 1257, modified, 499 A.2d 515 (N.J. 1985).

104. *See* STONE, *supra* note 45.

105. For a survey of the conflicting case law in several branches of wrongful discharge law, *see* STEVEN L. WILBORN ET AL., EMPLOYMENT LAW: CASES AND MATERIALS (2007).

106. On economic obstacles to discrimination litigation and arbitration, *see* Lewis L. Maltby, *Employment Arbitration and Workplace Justice,* 38 U.S.F. L. REV. 105, 115–17 (2003).

107. *See* F. RAY MARSHALL, THE NEGRO AND ORGANIZED LABOR 113, 128–29 (1965); F. Ray Marshall, *The Negro in Southern Unions, in* THE NEGRO AND THE AMERICAN LABOR MOVEMENT 128, 145 (Julius Jacobson ed., 1968); Patricia Hill Collins, *African-American Women and Economic Justice: A Preliminary Analysis of Wealth, Family, and African-American Social Class,* 65 U. CIN. L. REV. 825, 846 (1997). The history of discrimination by craft unions was sufficiently notorious to be the subject of judicial notice by the Supreme Court. *See* United Steelworkers of Am. v. Weber, 443 U.S. 193, 198 n.1 (1979).

108. *See, e.g.,* Steele v. Louisville & Nashville R.R., 323 U.S. 192, 202–03 (1944). For a historical overview of the relationship between the labor unions and African American workers, *see* FRYMER, *supra* note 93.

109. *See, e.g.,* Pugh v. See's Candies, Inc., 171 CAL. RPTR. 917 (Cal. Ct. App. 1981).

110. *See* Deborah C. Malamud, *Engineering the Middle Classes: Class Line-Drawing in the New Deal Hours Legislation,* 96 MICH. L. REV. 2212 (1998).

111. *See, e.g.,* Woolley v. Hoffmann-La Roche, Inc., 491 A.2d 1257, 1264, modified, 499 A.2d 515 (N.J. 1985).

112. *See* Bruce E. Kaufman, *What Do Unions Do? Evaluation and Commentary, in* WHAT DO UNIONS DO? A TWENTY-YEAR PERSPECTIVE 520, 549–50 (James T. Bennett & Bruce Kaufman eds., 2007).

113. *See* NELSON LICHTENSTEIN, STATE OF THE UNION: A CENTURY OF AMERICAN LABOR (2002).

114. *See* Wachter, *supra* note 7.

CHAPTER 4. THE RISE OF REGULATED SELF-REGULATION IN THE WORKPLACE (AND BEYOND)

1. *See* Chapter 3.

2. *See* EUGENE BARDACH & ROBERT A. KAGAN, GOING BY THE BOOK: THE PROBLEM OF REGULATORY UNREASONABLENESS 32 (1982).

3. *See* Thomas O. McGarity & Sidney A. Shapiro, Workers at Risk: The Failed Promise of the Occupational Safety and Health Administration 43 (1993).

4. *See* Ian Ayres & John Braithwaite, Responsive Regulation: Transcending the Deregulation Debate 8 (1992). In the case of OSHA, however, lengthy processes of administrative and judicial review, procedural constraints on inspections and enforcement, and reduced funding all impaired the agency's effectiveness. *See* McGarity & Shapiro, *supra* note 3, at 139–45, 186–87, 229, 254.

5. *See* Bardach & Kagan, *supra* note 2; Michael C. Dorf & Charles F. Sabel, *A Constitution of Democratic Experimentalism,* 98 Colum. L. Rev. 267, 278–79 (1998); Daniel Yergin & Joseph Stanislaw, The Commanding Heights: The Battle for the World Economy 357–59 (2002).

6. The alternatives to command and control have many variations, including "responsive regulation" (*see* Ayres & Braithwaite, *supra* note 4) and "democratic experimentalism" (*see* Dorf & Sabel, *supra* note 5). For other contributions to this vein (and alternative terminology), *see* David A. Dana, *The New "Contractarian" Paradigm in Environmental Regulation,* 2000 U. Ill. L. Rev. 35, 36 (2000); Jody Freeman, *Collaborative Governance in the Administrative State,* 45 UCLA L. Rev. 1, 22 (1997); Marshall J. Breger, *Regulatory Flexibility and the Administrative State,* 32 Tulsa L.J. 325 (1996); Douglas C. Michael, *Cooperative Implementation of Federal Regulations,* 13 Yale J. on Reg. 535, 540–41 (1996); and Richard B. Stewart, *Reconstitutive Law,* 46 Md. L. Rev. 86, 108–09 (1986). There are important differences among these models, but all of them involve devolution of regulatory activity to the regulated entities themselves, all aim for greater flexibility, and all struggle with the tension between flexibility and accountability.

7. *See* Kimberly D. Krawiec, *Cosmetic Compliance and the Failure of Negotiated Governance,* 81 Wash. U. L.Q. 487, 488–90 (2003).

8. *See* Ayres & Braithwaite, *supra* note 4, at 7–10.

9. Harvey L. Pitt & Karl A. Groskaufmanis, *Minimizing Corporate Civil and Criminal Liability: A Second Look at Corporate Codes of Conduct,* 78 Geo. L.J. 1559, 1578–96 (1990).

10. U.S. Sentencing Commission, Guidelines Manual (Nov. 2004) [hereinafter USSG], §8C2.5.

11. USSG §8B2.1.

12. Memorandum from Larry D. Thompson, Deputy Att'y. Gen., to Heads of Dep't Components and U. S. Att'ys (Jan. 20, 2003), *available at* http://www.usdoj.gov/dag/cftf/corporate_guidelines.htm; Department of Justice Corporate Leniency Policy (1993), *available at* http://www.usdoj.gov/atr/public/guidelines/0091.htm.

13. *See Incentives for Self-Policing: Discovery, Disclosure, Correction and Prevention of Violations,* 65 Fed. Reg. 19,618 (2000); Publication of the OIG Compliance Program Guidance for Hospitals, 63 Fed. Reg. 8987 (1998); *Final Policy Concerning the Occupational Safety and Health Administration's Treatment of Voluntary Employer Safety and Health Self-Audits,* 65 Fed. Reg. 46,498, 46,502 (2000).

14. In re Caremark Int'l Inc. Derivative Litig., 698 A.2d 959 (Del. Ch. 1996).

15. Jeffrey M. Kaplan et al., Compliance Programs and the Corporate Sentencing Guidelines: Preventing Criminal and Civil Liability 24:1 (Jeffrey M. Kaplan et al. eds., West Group 2006) (1993).

16. For a generally favorable assessment of this approach to controlling corporate crime, *see* Jennifer Arlen & Reinier Kraakman, *Controlling Corporate Misconduct: An Analysis of Corporate Liability Regimes,* 72 N.Y.U. L. Rev. 687, 745–52 (1997). For a skeptical assessment based on the lack of empirical evidence of the efficacy of these regimes, *see* Krawiec, *supra* note 7, at 510–15.

17. One scholar argues that the self-regulatory requirements of both Caremark and Sarbanes-Oxley apply directly to laws that protect workers, consumers, or the environment. *See* Larry Cata Backer, *The Duty to Monitor: Emerging Obligations of Outside Lawyers and Auditors to Detect and Report Corporate Wrongdoing beyond the Securities Laws,* 77 St. John's L. Rev. 919 (2003).

18. For two early and encouraging studies of self-regulation and cooperative regulation of workplace health and safety, *see* John Braithwaite, To Punish or Persuade: Enforcement of Coal Mine Safety 120 (1985), and Joseph V. Rees, Reforming the Workplace: A Study of Self-Regulation in Occupational Safety 2 (1988).

19. David Weil, *If OSHA Is So Bad, Why Is Compliance So Good?,* 27 RAND J. Econ. 618, 619 (1996).

20. *See* Orly Lobel, *Interlocking Regulatory and Industrial Relations: The Governance of Workplace Safety,* 57 Admin. L. Rev. 1071, 1102 (2005).

21. *Id.* at 1103–04.

22. For earlier overviews of cooperative initiatives within OSHA enforcement, *see* Sidney A. Shapiro & Randy S. Rabinowitz, *Punishment versus Cooperation in Regulatory Enforcement: A Case Study of OSHA,* 49 Admin. L. Rev. 713 (1997); Breger, *supra* note 6, at 325, 329–31; Sidney A. Shapiro & Randy S. Rabinowitz, *Voluntary Regulatory Compliance in Theory and Practice: The Case of OSHA,* 52 Admin. L. Rev. 97 (2000).

23. The original 1982 regulations were revised in 2000. *See* Revisions to the Voluntary Protection Programs to Provide Safe and Healthful Working Conditions, 65 Fed. Reg. 45,650 (Dep't of Labor, July 24, 2000). On how these regulations have been implemented, *see* U.S. Dep't of Labor, *Voluntary Protection Programs (VPP): Policies and Procedures Manual* (Mar. 25, 2003), *available at* http://www.osha.gov/pls/oshaweb/owadisp.show_document?p_table=DIRECTIVES&p_id=2976 [hereinafter VPP Manual].

24. VPP Manual, *supra* note 23, ch. I X.B.

25. Lobel, *supra* note 20, at 1105.

26. *See* GAO, *Workplace Safety and Health: OSHA's Voluntary Compliance Strategies Show Promising Results, but Should Be Fully Evaluated before They Are Expanded,* GAO–04–378 (Mar. 2004), *available at* http://www.gao.gov/new.items/d04378.pdf (cited in Lobel, *supra* note 20, at 1109); Lobel, *supra* note 20, at 1108–11.

27. *See* Lobel, *supra* note 20, at 1118.

28. *See* Comprehensive Occupational Safety and Health Reform Act, H.R. 1280, 103d Cong. Title II (1993); Comprehensive Occupational Safety and Health Reform Act, H.R. 3160, 102d Cong. Title II (1991).

29. Gregory R. Watchman, *Safe and Sound: The Case for Safety and Health Committees under OSHA and the NLRA,* 4 Cornell J.L. & Pub. Pol'y 65, 82–89 (1994); Randy S. Rabinowitz & Mark M. Hager, *Designing Health and Safety: Workplace Hazard Regulation in the United States and Canada,* 33 Cornell Int'l L.J. 373, 431 (2000); Mark Seidenfeld, *Em-*

powering Stakeholders: Limits on Collaboration as the Basis for Flexible Regulation, 41 WM. & MARY L. REV. 411, 497–98 (2000).

30. On union fears, *see* Kenneth A. Kovach et al., *OSHA and the Politics of Reform: An Analysis of OSHA Reform Initiatives before the 104th Congress,* 34 HARV. J. ON LEGIS. 169, 175 (1997); Seidenfeld, *supra* note 29, at 500. On employer fears, *see id.*; Rabinowitz & Hager, *supra* note 29, at 431.

31. U.S. Dep't of Labor, *President Clinton, The New OSHA: Reinventing Safety and Health* (Feb. 21, 1995), *available at* http://govinfo.library.unt.edu/npr/initati/common/reinvent .htm.

32. Lobel, *supra* note 20, at 1119 (citing MALCOM K. SPARROW, THE REGULATORY CRAFT: CONTROLLING RISKS, SOLVING PROBLEMS, AND MANAGING PROBLEMS 86–87 (2000).

33. Lobel, *supra* note 20, at 1119 (citing SPARROW, *supra* note 32, at 252–53).

34. Chamber of Commerce v. Dep't of Labor, 174 F.3d 206 (1999).

35. *See* Lobel, *supra* note 29.

36. OSHA preempts state statutes that "directly, substantially, and specifically" concern worker safety, even if they set higher standards. Gade v. Nat'l. Solid Wastes Mgmt. Ass'n., 505 U.S. 88, 107 (1992). However, OSHA permits state regulation of workplace safety (1) pursuant to a state OSHA plan approved by the Secretary of Labor, 29 U.S.C. §667(b)– (c) (2000), *see Gade,* 505 U.S. at 102–04; (2) with respect to hazards that are not regulated by OSHA, *see* 29 U.S.C. §667(a), and *see Gade,* 505 U.S. at 100; (3) through common law duties of employers and workers' compensation statutes, 29 U.S.C. §653(b)(4); and (4) through laws of general application that do not specifically target workplace safety, *see Gade,* 505 U.S. at 107.

37. *See* Matthew W. Finkin, *Employee Representation outside the Labor Act: Thoughts on Arbitral Representation, Group Arbitration, and Workplace Committees,* 5 U. PA. J. LAB. & EMP. L. 75, 93–94, 95–100 (2002).

38. For a study examining the effects of mandated health and safety committees, *see* David Weil, *Are Mandated Health and Safety Committees Substitutes for or Supplements to Labor Unions?,* 52 INDUS. & LAB. REL. REV. 339, 358 (1998).

39. David Weil, *Mandating Safety and Health Committees: Lessons from the States, in* INDUSTRIAL RELATIONS RESEARCH ASSOCIATION 47TH ANNUAL PROCEEDINGS 273, at 277–78 (1995).

40. The program is described *in* Rees, *supra* note 18, at 11–12.

41. *See* Cal. Lab. Code §6401.7 (West 2004). A guide to the program can be found at Cal. Dep't of Industrial Relations, *Guide to Developing Your Workplace Injury and Illness Prevention Program* (Mar. 2002), at http://www.dir.ca.gov/dosh/dosh_publications/iipp .html. For a brief overview, *see* Shruti Rana, *Fulfilling Technology's Promise: Enforcing the Rights of Women Caught in the Global High-Tech Underclass,* 15 BERKELEY WOMEN'S L.J. 272, 301 (2000).

42. Specifically, employers with annual payrolls over $800,000 and a workers' compensation experience rating above 1.2 times the average in the industry. N.Y. Workers' Comp. Law §134 (McKinney, 2004); N.Y. Comp. Codes R. & Regs. tit.12, §59–1.5 (2004).

43. Amy Goldstein & Sarah Cohen, *Bush Forces a Shift in Regulatory Thrust: OSHA Made More Business-Friendly,* WASH. POST, Aug. 15, 2004, at A1.

44. *See, e.g.,* U.S. Chamber of Commerce, *Multi-Industry Letter Opposing the Onslaught of Anti-Arbitration Bills and Provisions That Have Been Introduced in This Congress,* May 1, 2008, *available at* http://www.uschamber.com/issues/letters/2008/080501_anti_arbitration.htm.

45. One prominent observer found the bill "fatally flawed" but important for its symbolism. *See* Mark A. Rothstein, *Is GINA Worth the Wait?,* 36 J.L. MED. & ETHICS 174 (2008).

46. As of 2008, 85 percent of the Fortune 500 companies had policies banning discrimination on the basis of sexual orientation. *See* HUMAN RIGHTS CAMPAIGN FOUNDATION, THE STATE OF THE WORKPLACE FOR LESBIAN, GAY, BISEXUAL AND TRANSGENDER AMERICANS 2007–2008, 24 (2009), available at http://www.hrc.org/documents/HRC_Foundation_State_of_the_Workplace_2007–2008.pdf (last viewed May 7, 2009).

47. *See* Cynthia L. Estlund, *Freedom of Expression in the Workplace and the Problem of Discriminatory Harassment,* 75 TEX. L. REV. 687, 690 (1997); Vicki Schultz, *The Sanitized Workplace,* 112 YALE L.J. 2061, 2191 (2003).

48. For a recent elaboration of the complex interactions between corporate human relations professionals, activists, and courts and regulators behind this process, see FRANK DOBBIN, INVENTING EQUAL OPPORTUNITY (2009). This rich, in-depth account is too recent to be reflected in these pages, but is roughly compatible with what follows here.

49. *See* Lauren B. Edelman et al., *The Endogeneity of Legal Regulation: Grievance Procedures as Rational Myth,* 105 AM. J. SOC. 406 (1999) [hereinafter Edelman et al., *Grievance Procedures*].

50. *Id.* at 408; Lauren B. Edelman et al., *Professional Construction of Law: The Inflated Threat of Wrongful Discharge,* 26 LAW & SOC'Y REV. 47, 74–79 (1992); DOBBIN, *supra* note 48.

51. In fact it is unclear whether an internal dispute resolution system reduces the incidence of litigation or outside complaints (for example, with the Equal Employment Opportunity Commission [EEOC]). *See* Edelman et al., *Grievance Procedures, supra* note 49, at 431–32. Some human resources (HR) advisers also claimed that the existence of these mechanisms could serve as a partial shield against liability by convincing adjudicators of the fairness of the employer's decision making. Until recently, there was little doctrinal basis for that proposition. However, the law has recently come to partially vindicate the HR advice. *Id.* at 435–36.

52. *See* Lauren B. Edelman, *Legal Environments and Organizational Governance: The Expansion of Due Process in the American Workplace,* 95 AM. J. SOC. 1401 (1990).

53. Lauren B. Edelman et al., *Internal Dispute Resolution: The Transformation of Civil Rights in the Workplace,* 27 LAW & SOC'Y REV. 497 (1993) [hereinafter Edelman et al., *Internal Dispute Resolution*].

54. For an account of how employment discrimination law is leading firms to find new ways to maintain and manage diverse workforces, *see* Susan Sturm, *Second Generation Employment Discrimination: A Structural Approach,* 101 COLUM. L. REV. 458 (2001).

55. David B. Wilkins, *From "Separate Is Inherently Unequal" to "Diversity Is Good for Business": The Rise of Market-Based Diversity Arguments and the Fate of the Black Corporate Bar,* 117 HARV. L. REV. 1548 (2004).

56. Henry Unger, *Coke Aims $1 Billion at Diversity Program,* ATLANTA JOURNAL-CONSTITUTION, May 16, 2000; Constance L. Hays, *New Chief Executive of Coke Says Diversity*

Is a High Priority, N.Y. TIMES, Mar. 10, 2000; Kurt Eichenwald, *Texaco Plans Wide Program for Minorities,* N.Y. TIMES, Dec. 19, 1996; Adam Bryant, *How Much Has Texaco Changed?,* N.Y. TIMES, Nov. 2, 1997.

57. *See* Dukes v. Wal-Mart, Inc., 222 F.R.D. 189 (N.D. Cal. 2004) (allowing use of statistical expert testimony in Title VII discrimination case).

58. *See* Lauren B. Edelman et al., *Diversity Rhetoric and the Managerialization of Law,* 106 Am. J. Soc. 1589, 1632–34 (2001) [hereinafter Edelman et al., *Diversity Rhetoric*]; Edelman et al., *Internal Dispute Resolution, supra* note 53, at 511; Krawiec, *supra* note 7, at 538.

59. *See* Krawiec, *supra* note 7, at 511–15; Anne Lawton, *Operating in an Empirical Vacuum: The* Ellerth *and* Faragher *Affirmative Defense,* 13 COLUM. J. GENDER & L. 197, 197–98 (2004).

60. Among the more skeptical accounts, *see, e.g.,* Samuel R. Bagenstos, *The Structural Turn and the Limits of Antidiscrimination Law,* 94 CAL. L. REV. 1, 28 (2006); Joanna L. Grossman, *The Culture of Compliance: The Final Triumph of Form over Substance in Sexual Harassment Law,* 26 HARV. WOMEN'S L. J. 3, 3 (2003); Michael Selmi, *Sex Discrimination in the Nineties, Seventies Style: Case Studies in the Preservation of Male Workplace Norms,* 9 EMP. RTS. & EMP. POL'Y J. 1, 46 (2005); Susan Bisom-Rapp, *An Ounce of Prevention Is a Poor Substitute for a Pound of Cure: Confronting the Developing Jurisprudence of Education and Prevention in Employment Discrimination Law,* 22 BERKELEY J. EMP. & LAB. L. 1, 3 (2001); Theresa M. Beiner, *Sex, Science and Social Knowledge: The Implications of Social Science Research on Imputing Liability to Employers for Sexual Harassment,* 7 WM. & MARY J. WOMEN & L. 273, 275 (2000); Linda Hamilton Krieger & Susan Fiske, *Behavioral Realism in Employment Discrimination Law,* 94 CAL. L. REV. 997, 1017–19 (2006). Among the more favorable assessments, *see, e.g.,* Tristin K. Green, *Discrimination in Workplace Dynamics: Toward a Structural Account of Disparate Treatment Theory,* 38 HARV. C.R.-C.L. L. REV. 91, 145 (2003); Sturm, *supra* note 54, at 491–92. Some commentators see potential as well as the need for safeguards not yet in place. *See* Susan D. Carle, *Acknowledging Informal Power Dynamics in the Workplace: A Proposal for Further Development of the Vicarious Liability Doctrine in Hostile Work Environment Sexual Harassment Cases,* 13 DUKE J. GENDER L. & POL'Y 85, 86–87 (2006); Melissa Hart, *The Possibility of Avoiding Discrimination: Considering Compliance and Liability,* 39 CONN. L. REV. 1623 (2007.

61. 524 U.S. 742 (1998).

62. 524 U.S. 775 (1998).

63. *Faragher* and *Ellerth* were foreshadowed by Meritor Savings Bank v. Vinson, 477 U.S. 57, 72–73 (1986), which indicated that an adequate grievance procedure might insulate an employer from some liability for harassment by supervisors.

64. *Faragher,* 524 U.S. at 807.

65. *See, e.g., Faragher,* 524 U.S. at 799; Burns v. McGregor Electronic Indus., Inc., 989 F.2d 959, 966 (8th Cir. 1993); Barrett v. Omaha Nat'l Bank, 726 F.2d 424, 427 (8th Cir. 1984); Katz v. Dole, 709 F.2d 251, 255 (4th Cir. 1983).

66. Glenn Kramer, *Reasonableness for Free: Why Buy Employment Practices Liability Insurance When EEOC.gov Gives Protection Away?,* 3 CARDOZO PUB. L. POL'Y & ETHICS J. 459, 484 (2005).

67. 527 U.S. 526, 544 (1999).

68. *See* Edelman et al., *Grievance Procedures, supra* note 49, at 432.

69. That is the concern of many skeptics. *See, e.g.,* Bagenstos, *supra* note 60.

70. *See* Cynthia Estlund, *Between Rights and Contract: Arbitration Agreements and Non-Compete Covenants as a Hybrid Form of Employment Law,* 155 U. PA. L. REV. 379, 409–11 (2007)

71. John J. Donohue & Peter Siegelman, *The Changing Nature of Employment Discrimination Litigation,* 43 STAN. L. REV. 983 (1991).

72. *See* Jonathan D. Glater, *For Last Paycheck, More Workers Cede Their Rights to Sue,* N.Y. TIMES, Feb. 24, 2001, at A1.

73. Alexander v. Gardner-Denver Co., 415 U.S. 36, 52 n. 15 (1974); Richardson v. Sugg, 448 F.3d 1046, 1054 (8th Cir. 2006).

74. Age Discrimination in Employment Act (ADEA), 29 U.S.C. §626(f)(1)(A)–(H).

75. *See* Glater, *supra* note 72.

76. 500 U.S. 20 (1991).

77. 532 U.S. 105 (2001).

78. The Ninth Circuit was the last of the circuits to so hold. *See* E.E.O.C. v. Luce, Forward, Hamilton & Scripps, LLP 345 F.3d 742, 744–45 (9th Cir. 2003) (en banc). Note, however, that some states, including California, hold that an arbitration agreement secured on a take-it-or-leave-it basis as a condition of employment is "procedurally unconscionable" and is invalid if it also contains provisions that are "substantively unconscionable," which is to say unduly harsh or oppressive. *See* Circuit City Stores, Inc. v. Adams, 279 F.3d 889, 893 (9th Cir. 2002); Armendariz v. Found. Health Psychcare Svcs., Inc., 6 P.3d 669, 690 (Cal. 2000).

79. Lewis L. Maltby, *Out of the Frying Pan, into the Fire: The Feasibility of Post-Dispute Employment Arbitration Agreements,* 30 WM. MITCHELL L. REV. 313, 319–21 (2003).

80. *See* Paul D. Carrington, *Self-Deregulation, the "National Policy" of the Supreme Court,* 3 NEV. L.J. 259, 259 (2002/2003). Carrington's focus is on mandatory arbitration of consumer claims. He portrays employment arbitration as comparatively even-handed as a result of judicial oversight and arbitral self-regulation in the form of the Due Process Protocol discussed below, but he still sees room for employer abuse. *Id.* at 284–85. Carrington's critique echoes that of Professor Stone. Katherine Van Wezel Stone, *Mandatory Arbitration of Individual Employment Rights: The Yellow Dog Contract of the 1990s,* 73 DENV. U. L. REV. 1017 (1996).

81. Samuel Estreicher, *Arbitration of Employment Disputes without Unions,* 66 CHI.-KENT L. REV. 753 (1990).

82. *See Gilmer,* 500 U.S. at 27–34.

83. *See id.* at 34.

84. The Supreme Court has mandated this result under the Federal Arbitration Act (FAA) in a number of non-employment disputes. *See, e.g.,* Green Tree Fin. Corp v. Randolph, 531 U.S. 79 (2000); PacifiCare Health Sys. v. Book, 538 U.S. 401 (2003); Green Tree Fin. Corp v. Bazzle, 539 U.S. 444 (2003); Buckeye Check Cashing, Inc. v. Cardegna, 546 U.S. 440 (2006).

85. The "repeat player effect" has been a large bone of contention between critics and de-

fenders of arbitration. Empirical evidence that arbitrators are biased in favor of employers as repeat players is equivocal. Lisa Bingham, *Is There a Bias in Arbitration of Non-Union Employment Disputes?*, 6 INT'L. J. CONFLICT MGMT. 369, 371 (1995); Elizabeth Hill, *AAA Employment Arbitration: A Fair Forum at a Low Cost*, DISP. RESOL. J., May–Jul. 2003 at 45. But the larger repeat player effect may be the greater incentive of the employer, which anticipates numerous employment disputes, to invest in devising an arbitration system that serves its interests. On the other side, employees undoubtedly face a collective action problem in deciding whether and how to challenge an arbitration agreement at the time it is presented to them.

86. *See* Stone, *Yellow Dog, supra* note 80, at 1018; Clyde W. Summers, *Mandatory Arbitration: Privatizing Public Rights, Compelling the Unwilling to Arbitrate*, 6 U. PA. J. LAB. & EMP. L. 685, 685–86 (2004).

87. For example, the Texas Supreme Court has held that the imposition of mandatory arbitration is like any other modification to an at-will employment contract: "[W]hen an employer notifies an employee of changes to the at-will employment contract and the employee continues working with knowledge of the changes, he has accepted the changes as a matter of law." *In re* Halliburton Co., 80 S.W.3d 566, 568 (Tex. 2002).

88. *See* Lewis L. Maltby, *Private Justice: Employment Arbitration and Civil Rights*, 30 COLUM. HUM. RTS. L. REV. 29, 46–47 (1998). Most litigated employment disputes are resolved on dispositive motions, not at trial, and the overwhelming majority of those motions is won by employers. *Id.* at 47. Arbitration traditionally has no dispositive motions but resolves cases on the merits. Alexander J. S. Colvin, *Empirical Research on Employment Arbitration: Clarity amidst the Sound and Fury?*, 11 EMP. RTS. & EMP. POL'Y J. 405 (2007).

89. *See* Samuel Estreicher, *Saturns for Rickshaws: The Stakes in the Debate over Predispute Employment Arbitration Agreements*, 16 OHIO ST. J. ON DISP. RESOL. 559, 564–65 (2001); Maltby, *Private Justice, supra* note 88, at 45–51; Theodore J. St. Antoine, *Mandatory Arbitration of Employee Discrimination Claims: Unmitigated Evil or Blessing in Disguise?*, 15 T.M. COOLEY L. REV. 1, 7–8 (1998). Yet with arbitrators' fees, which often reach five figures, some argue that arbitration can be as costly or more costly than litigation. *See, e.g.*, Jean R. Sternlight, *Forum Shopping for Arbitration Decisions: Federal Courts' Use of Antisuit Injunctions against Courts*, 147 U. PA. L. REV. 91, 126 & nn. 150–52 (1998); Katherine Van Wezel Stone, *Rustic Justice: Community and Coercion under the Federal Arbitration Act*, 77 N.C. L. REV. 931, 959 & nn.161–62 (1999); Henry S. Noyes, *If You (Re)build It They Will Come: Contracts to Remake the Rules of Litigation in Arbitration's Image*, 30 HARV. J. L. & PUB. POL'Y 579, 586–89 (2007).

90. *See* Michael Z. Green, *Debunking the Myth of Employer Advantage from Using Mandatory Arbitration for Discrimination Claims*, 31 RUTGERS L. REV. 399, 418 (2000).

91. *See* Martin H. Malin, *Due Process in Employment Arbitration: The State of the Law and the Need for Self-Regulation*, 11 EMP. RTS. & EMP. POL'Y J. 363 (2007).

92. Critics have argued that it should be. Jeffrey W. Stempel, *Mandating Minimum Quality in Mass Arbitration*, 76 U. CIN. L. REV. 383 (2008).

93. *Id.* Those fears may be exaggerated. One arbitration skeptic, Professor Arnold Zack, conducted an informal study of employment arbitration in practice and found to his

surprise that nearly all of the arbitration agreements he could identify provided for arbitration by reputable providers that adhered to the Protocol. E-mail from Arnold Zack to author (Oct. 21, 2006) (on file with author). On Zack's opposition to mandatory pre-dispute arbitration, *see* Arnold M. Zack, *Testimony before the Commission on the Future of Worker-Management Relations* (1994), *available at* http://digitalcommons .ilr.cornell.edu/key_workplace/387/

94. *See* Chapter 1.

95. For a comprehensive overview of "corporate social responsibility" (CSR), *see generally* David Vogel, The Market for Virtue: The Potential and Limits of Corporate Social Responsibility (2005); The New Corporate Accountability: Corporate Social Responsibility and the Law (Doreen McBarnet, Aurora Voiculscu & Tom Campbell eds., 2007); Corporate Social Responsibility: Readings and Cases in a Global Context (Andrew Crane, Dirk Matten & Laura Spence eds., 2007); Claire Moore Dickenson, *Human Rights: The Emerging Norm of Corporate Social Responsibility*, 76 Tul. L. Rev. 1431 (2002).

96. Human Rights Watch, *Discounting Rights: Wal-Mart's Violation of U.S. Workers' Right to Freedom of Association* (May 2007), *available at* http://hrw.org/reports/2007/us0507/.

97. *See, e.g.*, Stephen Bainbridge, *In Defense of the Shareholder Wealth Maximization Norm: A Reply to Professor Green*, 50 Wash. & Lee L. Rev. 1423, 1427–28 (1993); Einer Elhauge, *Sacrificing Corporate Profits in the Public Interest*, 80 N.Y.U. L. Rev. 733, 737 (2005); Margaret M. Blair and Lynn Stout, *A Team Production Theory of Corporate Law*, 85 Va. L. Rev. 247, 254 (1999).

98. *See* Frank H. Easterbrook & Daniel R. Fischel, The Economic Structure of Corporate Law 36–39 (1991); John Macey, *An Economic Analysis of the Various Rationales for Making Shareholders the Exclusive Beneficiaries of Corporate Fiduciary Duties*, 21 Stetson L. Rev. 23, 24–25 (1991); Bainbridge, *supra* note 97.

99. *See* Michael E. Porter and Mark R. Kramer, *Strategy and Society: The Link between Competitive Advantage and Corporate Social Responsibility*, 84 Harv. Bus. Rev. 78, 80 (2006); Vogel, *supra* note 95, at 77–82.

100. *See* Vogel, *supra* note 95.

101. Romen Shamir, *Mind the Gap: The Commodification of Corporate Social Responsibility*, 28 Symbolic Interaction 229, 231 (2005).

102. *See* Vogel, *supra* note 95, at 96–109.

103. *Id.* at 63–64; *see generally* CalPERS, *Core Principles of Accountable Corporate Governance* (2007), *available at* http://www.calpers-governance.org/principles/domestic /us/down loads/us-corpgov-principles.pdf.

104. Vogel, *supra* note 95.

105. *See* Social Investment Forum, *2007 Report on Socially Responsible Investing Trends in the United States* [hereinafter Social Investment Forum, 2007 Report on SRI], *available at* http://www.socialinvest.org/. That is about 25 percent greater than the growth of all assets under professional management during the same period.

106. Figures for 2001 are from Vogel, *supra* note 95, at 64, citing Social Investment Forum, 2003 Report on Socially Responsible Investing Trends in the United States. Figures for 2006 and 2007 are from Social Investment Forum, 2007 Report on SRI.

107. Vogel, *supra* note 95, at 64.

108. *See* Peter Utting, *Corporate Responsibility and the Movement of Business,* 15 DEVELOPMENT IN PRACTICE 375, 383–86 (2005).

109. *See* Elhauge, *supra* note 97; Antonio Vives, *Corporate Social Responsibility: The Role of Law and Markets and the Case of Developing Countries,* 83 CHI.-KENT L. REV. 199, 216–21 (2008).

110. *See* Vogel, *supra* note 95, at 12–13 (reviewing the debate). Milton Friedman famously said, "There is one and only one social responsibility of business—to use its resources and engage in activities designed to increase its profits so long as it stays within the rules of the game." MILTON FRIEDMAN, CAPITALISM AND FREEDOM 133 (1962). *See also* MICHAEL NOVAK, THE FUTURE OF THE CORPORATION 14–15 (1996).

111. *See* Vogel, *supra* note 95, at 16–45; Porter and Kramer, *supra* note 99.

112. *See* Vives, *supra* note 109, at 217; Blair and Stout, *supra* note 97; Elhauge, *supra* note 97.

113. Elhauge, *supra* note 97.

114. Human Rights Watch, in its report on Wal-Mart, found some evidence that new procedures were reducing the incidence of some labor violations, such as off-the-clock work, but its report reserved judgment on whether the changes were meaningful or lasting. *See* Human Rights Watch, *supra* note 96.

115. *See* Ellen Israel Rosen, *The Wal-Mart Effect: The World Trade Organization and the Race to the Bottom,* 8 CHAP. L. REV. 261, 263–64, 278 (2005).

116. For a discussion of those efforts, *see* KIMBERLY ANN ELLIOTT & RICHARD B. FREEMAN, CAN LABOR STANDARDS IMPROVE UNDER GLOBALIZATION? 49–72 (2003); Mark Barenberg, *Toward a Democratic Model of Transnational Labour Monitoring?, in* REGULATING LABOUR IN THE WAKE OF GLOBALISATION: NEW CHALLENGES, NEW INSTITUTIONS 37 (Brian Bercusson & Cynthia Estlund eds., 2007) [hereinafter Barenberg, *Toward a Democratic Model*]; Mark Barenberg, *Law and Labor in the New Global Economy: Through the Lens of United States Federalism,* 33 COLUM. J. TRANSNAT'L L. 445, 447–48 (1995).

117. The term "super-employer" is mine. But the idea of using supply chains—and the contractual links between poor, exploited workers and large corporations—as the linchpin of a regulatory strategy is not original. *See, e.g.,* Michael P. Vandenbergh, *The New Wal-Mart Effect: The Role of Private Contracting in Global Governance,* 54 UCLA L. REV. 913 (2007); ARCHON FUNG, DARA O'ROURKE, & CHARLES SABEL, CAN WE PUT AN END TO SWEATSHOPS? (2001).

118. For thoughtful assessments of corporate codes in practice, *see* Barenberg, *Toward a Democratic Model, supra* note 116; Adelle Blackett, *Global Governance, Legal Pluralism and the Decentered State: A Labor Law Critique of Codes of Corporate Conduct,* 8 IND. J. GLOBAL LEGAL STUD. 401, 416–17 (2001); Dara O'Rourke, *Outsourcing Regulation: Analyzing Nongovernmental Systems of Labor Standards and Monitoring,* 31 POL'Y STUD. J. 1, 20–25 (2003). For a highly revealing report on the practices of one prominent monitoring organization, *see* Dara O'Rourke, *Monitoring the Monitors: A Critique of Corporate Third-Party Labour Monitoring, in* CORPORATE RESPONSIBILITY AND LABOUR RIGHTS: CODES OF CONDUCT IN THE GLOBAL ECONOMY 196–207 (Rhys Jenkins, Ruth Pearson, & Gill Seyfang eds., 2002).

119. Wal-Mart Stores, Inc., *2005 Report on Ethical Sourcing* 8 (2005) (discussing the content and formation of the Standards for Suppliers), *available at* http://www.walmart stores.com/Sustainability/7951.aspx.

120. *See* http://www.laborrights.org/projects/corporate/walmart/Supplier-Standards-2005 .pdf.

121. The case is now being handled by International Rights Advocates. *See* http://www.ir advocates.org/walmartcase.html.

122. *See* Doe v. Wal-Mart Stores, Inc., 572 F.3d 677 (9th Cir. 2009).

123. *See* Wal-Mart Stores, Inc., *2005 Report on Ethical Sourcing, supra* note 119.

124. *Id.*

125. http://www.nike.com/nikebiz/nikebiz.jhtml?page=25.

126. *See* Richard M. Locke et al., *Does Monitoring Improve Labor Standards? Lessons from Nike,* MIT Sloan Research Paper No. 4612–06 (2006); *available at* http://papers.ssrn .com/sol3/papers.cfm?abstract_id=916771.

127. *See* Blackett, *supra* note 118; Barenberg, *Toward a Democrat Model, supra* note 116. Jill Esbenshade, Monitoring Sweatshops: Workers, Consumers, and the Global Apparel Industry (2004).

128. *See* Esbenshade, *supra* note 127, at 186–91; *see also* Barenberg, *Toward a Democratic Model.*

129. For a list of investigations, with reports, *see* the WRC Web site, http://www.workers rights.org/Freports/index.asp#freports.

130. For a description of the Designated Supplier Program (DSP), *see* http://www.workers rights.org/dsp.asp.

131. Stephanie Rosenbloom, *Wal-Mart to Toughen Standards,* N.Y. Times, Oct. 22, 2008, at B1.

132. *Id.*

133. *See* Jody Freeman, *Private Parties, Public Functions and the New Administrative Law,* 52 Admin. L. Rev. 813, 831–35 (2000); John Braithwaite & Peter Drahos, Global Business Regulation 28 (2000); Jodi L. Short & Michael W. Toffel, *Coerced Confessions: Self-Policing in the Shadow of the Regulator,* 24 J. L. Econ. & Org. 45 (2008).

134. Robert A. Kagan et al., *Explaining Corporate Environmental Performance: How Does Regulation Matter?,* 37 Law & Soc'y Rev. 51 (2003).

135. For critical perspectives, *see* Harry W. Arthurs, *Private Ordering and Workers' Rights in the Global Economy: Corporate Codes of Conduct as a Regime of Labour Market Regulation, in* Labour Law in an Era of Globalisation 471, 485–87 (Joanne Conaghan et al. eds., 2002); Blackett, *supra* note 118, at 406–18; Krawiec, *supra* note 7, at 510–43.

CHAPTER 5. SELF-REGULATION FROM THE BOTTOM UP

1. James J. Brudney, *Neutrality Agreements and Card Check Recognition: Prospects for Changing Paradigms,* 90 Iowa L. Rev. 819 (2005).

2. *See, e.g.,* Fair Labor Association, *2004 Annual Report* (summarizing monitoring activities, including at nine U.S. factories), *available at* http://www.fairlabor.org/2004report

/overview/monitoring.html. For specific examples of monitoring affecting U.S. operations, *see* Gap Inc., *2003 Social Responsibility Report* 12; *Reebok Human Rights Programs*
(Region Specific Actions), *available at* http://www.reebok.com/Static/global/initiatives
/rights/text-only/business/improving.html; Peter DeSimone & Investment Responsibility Research Center, *Wal-Mart Global Labor Standards* 3, *available at* http://www.irrc
.org/resources/03n_wmt.pdf. An actual monitoring report on a U.S. supplier for Nike,
Inc., can be viewed at http://www.fairlabor.org/all/transparency/charts_2003/0700
8218B_Nike_USA.pdf.

3. This issue is discussed further in Chapter 8 below.

4. Under 29 U.S.C. §217, the Secretary of Labor may bring an action to enjoin the sale or
transport of goods manufactured by individuals who were not legally compensated under
29 U.S.C. §215 (2004).

5. The FLSA ets only a floor on wage and hour standards and expressly permits states to
establish higher standards. 29 U.S.C. §218(a). OSHA preempts some state regulation of
workplace health and safety. *See supra* Chapter 4. The NLRA preempts nearly all state
regulation of labor relations.

6. 29 U.S.C. §216(b) (2004). Additionally, Congress's mandate to award attorneys' fees for
a successful FLSA action further encourages private parties to act as "private attorneys
general." Laffey v. Northwest Airlines, 746 F.2d 4, 11 (D.C. Cir. 1984).

7. David Weil, *Regulating Noncompliance to Labor Standards: New Tools for an Old Problem*,
45 CHALLENGE 47, 62–63 (2002) [hereinafter Weil, *Labor Standards*].

8. 29 U.S.C. §203(g) (2000). *See* Bruce Goldstein et al., *Enforcing Fair Labor Standards in
the Modern American Sweatshop: Rediscovering the Statutory Definition of Employment*,
46 UCLA L. REV. 983, 1003–05 (1999).

9. Some courts recognize the FLSA's breadth in finding joint employer liability. See Nan
Zheng v. Liberty Apparel Co., 355 F.3d 61, 66 (2d Cir. 2003); Baker v. Flint Eng'g &
Constr. Co., 137 F.3d 1436, 1440 (10th Cir. 1998); Antenor v. D & S Farms, 88 F.3d 925,
929 (11th Cir. 1996). Others still feel the pull of the narrower common law "right of control" test of employment status. *See, e.g.*, Aimable v. Long & Scott Farms, 20 F.3d 434,
440–41 (11th Cir. 1994); Zhao v. Bebe Stores, Inc., 247 F. Supp. 2d 1154, 1159–61 (C.D.
Cal. 2003). *See* Goldstein et al., *supra* note 8, at 1008–15.

10. *See, e.g.*, *Zheng*, 355 F.3d at 65, 79; Chao v. Ladies Apparel Group, Ltd., No. 01-Civ. 10724
(JGK), 2002 U.S. Dist. LEXIS 10078, at *20 (S.D.N.Y. May 28, 2002); Bureerong v.
Uvawas, 922 F. Supp. 1450, 1469 (C.D. Cal. 1996).

11. *See* Shirley Lung, *Exploiting the Joint Employer Doctrine: Providing a Break for Sweatshop
Garment Workers*, 34 LOY. U. CHI. L.J. 291, 312 n.166 (2003).

12. *See* Weil, *Labor Standards*, *supra* note 7, at 52–54; Lora Jo Foo, *The Informal Economy:
The Vulnerable and Exploitable Immigrant Workforce and the Need for Strengthening Worker
Protective Legislation*, 103 YALE L.J. 2179, 2204 (1994).

13. For a description of these arrangements in apparel, *see* Weil, *Labor Standards*, *supra* note
7, at 34–36.

14. *See* David Weil, *Compliance with the Minimum Wage: Can Government Make a Difference?* 18, *available at* http://ssrn.com/abstract=368340 [hereinafter Weil, *Compliance*].

For an official (Clinton-era) guide to the program for manufacturers, *see* Department of Labor, *Protecting America's Garment Workers: A Monitoring Guide, available at* http://permanent.access.gpo.gov/lps23481/www.dol.gov/esa/forum/monitor.htm.

15. This may be an example of what Lars Noah calls "administrative arm-twisting." *See* Lars Noah, *Administrative Arm-Twisting in the Shadow of Congressional Delegations of Authority,* 1997 Wis. L. Rev. 873, 874–75.

16. Weil, *Compliance, supra* note 14, at 22. Weil found that minimum wage compliance levels rose from 63 percent (with no monitoring) to 74 percent (with low monitoring) to 79 percent (with high monitoring) in New York City; from 33 percent to 56 percent to 72 percent respectively in Los Angeles; and from 71 percent to 94 percent to 95 percent respectively in San Francisco. *Id.*

17. *See* Laura Dubinsky, *The Fox Guarding the Chicken Coop: Garment Industry Monitoring in Los Angeles, in,* Corporate Responsibility and Labour Rights: Codes of Conduct in the Global Economy 161 (Rhys Jenkins, Ruth Pearson, & Gill Seyfang eds., 2002).

18. *See* Chapter 2.

19. *See* Matthew T. Bodie, *The Potential for State Labor Law: The New York Greengrocer Code of Conduct,* 21 Hofstra Lab. & Emp. L.J. 183 (2004) [hereinafter Bodie, *State Labor Law*]. For a firsthand account of the negotiation of the agreement, *see generally* Matthew T. Bodie, *The Story behind the New York City Greengrocer Code of Conduct: A Conversation with Patricia Smith,* 6 Regional Lab. Rev. 19 (2004) [hereinafter Bodie, *Smith Interview*].

20. *See* Bodie, *State Labor Law, supra* note 19, at 192. *See* Bodie, *Smith Interview, supra* note 19, at 22–23.

21. The text of the GGCC is *available at* http://www.oag.state.ny.us/labor/final_ggcode _english_long.pdf (last visited July 26, 2008) [hereinafter GGCC]. For a more detailed description of its provisions, *see* Bodie, *State Labor Law, supra* note 19, at 194–99.

22. *See* Bodie, *Smith Interview, supra* note 19, at 91; Steven Greenhouse & Seth Kugel, *Labor Truce Wearing Thin for Koreans and Mexicans,* N.Y. Times, Sept. 27, 2004, at B3.

23. *See* Bodie, *Smith Interview, supra* note 19, at 25.

24. GGCC, *supra* note 21, at III.6.

25. Communication from Patricia Smith, Associate Attorney General of New York, Labor Division (July 13, 2004) (on file with author).

26. *Id.*

27. *See* Greenhouse & Kugel, *supra* note 22.

28. Because of complexities in the computation of overtime premiums, many employers remain in technical violation of the laws. But the substantial compliance achieved thus far is a vast improvement over the rampant violations discovered initially. *Id.*

29. *Id.*

30. Alan Hyde casts serious doubt on Casa Mexico's capacity to fulfill this potential. Alan Hyde, *Who Speaks for the Working Poor?: A Preliminary Look at the Emerging Tetralogy of Representation of Low-Wage Service Workers,* 13 Cornell J.L. & Pub. Pol'y 599 (2004).

31. *Contractor for Major Clothing Lines Cited for More Than $5 Million in Unpaid Wages,*

Press release, July 23, 2008, *available at* http://www.labor.state.ny.us/pressreleases/2008/July23_2008.htm.

32. *See* http://www.gapinc.com/public/SocialResponsibility/sr_factories.shtml.

33. Steven Greenhouse, *Among Janitors, Labor Violations Go with the Job,* N.Y. TIMES, July 13, 2005, at A1; Steven Greenhouse, *Illegally in the U.S., and Never a Day Off at Wal-Mart,* N.Y. TIMES, Nov. 5, 2003, at A1 [hereinafter Greenhouse, *Illegally*].

34. Unions and other employee advocates have argued strongly for building owners' status as joint employers under various labor laws. *See* Goldstein et al., *supra* note 8, at 1142–43.

35. Steven Greenhouse, *3 Chains Agree in Suit over Janitors' Wages and Hours,* N.Y. TIMES, Dec. 7, 2004.

36. *See, e.g.,* Greenhouse, *Illegally, supra* note 33.

37. *Id.*

38. Interview with Janet Herold, Service Employees International Union, May 9, 2007.

39. Interview with Lilia Garcia, Executive Director, MCTF Sept. 14, 2004 [hereinafter Garcia Interview].

40. *Id.*

41. *Id.*

42. *See* Steven Greenhouse, *Labor Department Wins $1.9 Million in Back Pay for Janitors,* N.Y. TIMES, Aug. 26, 2004, at A16.

43. Garcia Interview, *supra* note 39.

44. Greenhouse, *Labor Department Wins, supra* note 42.

45. Garcia Interview, *supra* note 39.

46. Memorandum from Barry J. Kearney, Assoc. Gen. Counsel, NLRB, to Celeste Mattina, Reg'l Dir., Region 2, NLRB, regarding Rest. Opportunities Ctr. of N.Y., Cases 2-CP-1067, 2-CP-20643, 2-CP-1071, 2-CB-20705, 2-CP-1073, and 2-CB-20787 (Nov. 30, 2006), *available at* http://www.nlrb.gov/shared_files/Advice%20Memos/2006/2-CP-1067.pdf

47. This unpublished administrative decision was referred to and relied upon by the NLRB General Counsel; *see id.,* n. 8.

48. *CIW Anti-Slavery Campaign,* http://www.ciw-online.org/slavery.html.

49. About CIW, http://www.ciw-online.org/about.html.

50. The boycott and agreement are described on the CIW's Web site, http://www.ciw-online.org/agreementanalysis.html. Quotes in the following paragraph are from this site.

51. *Id.*

52. *Id.*

53. Press release, http://www.ciw-online.org/CIW_McDonald's_Release.html.

54. *Id.*

55. *Burger King Corp. and Coalition of Immokalee Workers to Work Together,* Press Release, May 23, 2008, *available at* http://www.ciw-online.org/BK_CIW_joint_release.html.

56. For the SEC's decisions, along with the underlying shareholder proposals and the companies' responses, see McDonald's Corp. (S.E.C. No-Action Letter), March 22, 2007, *available at* 2007 WL 895066; Burger King Holdings, Inc. (S.E.C. No-Action Letter), Sept. 26, 2007, *available at* 2007 WL 2838961.

CHAPTER 6. PRINCIPLES OF SELF-REGULATION FOR THE U.S. WORKPLACE

1. *See* JOHN BRAITHWAITE & PETER DRAHOS, GLOBAL BUSINESS REGULATION 28 (2000).

2. For an overview of some, *see* Kimberly D. Krawiec, *Organizational Misconduct: Beyond the Principal-Agent Model,* 32 FLA. ST. U. L. REV. 571, 585–91 (2005) [hereinafter *Organizational Misconduct*]; Jody Freeman, *Private Parties, Public Functions and the New Administrative Law,* 52 ADMIN. L. REV. 813, 831–35 (2000).

3. *See* CHRISTOPHER STONE, WHERE THE LAW ENDS (1975).

4. *See, e.g.,* Daniel R. Fischel & Alan O. Sykes, *Corporate Crime,* 25 J. LEGAL STUD. 319, 322 (1996); Lewis Kornhauser, *An Economic Analysis of the Choice between Enterprise and Personal Liability for Accidents,* 70 CAL. L. REV. 1345 (1982); Reinier Kraakman, *Corporate Liability Strategies and the Costs of Legal Controls,* 93 YALE L.J. 857 (1984).

5. *See* Samuel Issacharoff, *Regulating after the Fact,* 56 DEPAUL L. REV. 375 (2007).

6. For a careful and complex argument for combining strict corporate liability for harms with explicit duties to engage in certain precautions or policing, *see* Jennifer Arlen & Reinier Kraakman, *Controlling Corporate Misconduct: An Analysis of Corporate Liability Regimes,* 72 N.Y.U. L. REV. 687 (1997).

7. *See* Krawiec, *Organizational Misconduct, supra* note 2, at 580–81.

8. *See* Jennifer Arlen, *The Potentially Perverse Effects of Corporate Criminal Liability,* 23 J. LEG. STUD. 833 (1994); Arlen & Kraakman, *supra* note 6; V. S. Khanna, *Corporate Liability Standards: When Should Corporations Be Held Criminally Liable?,* 37 AM. CRIM. L. REV. 1239 (2000).

9. Krawiec, *Organizational Misconduct, supra* note 2; Kimberly D. Krawiec, *Cosmetic Compliance and the Failure of Negotiated Governance,* 81 WASH. U. L.Q. 487 (2003) [hereinafter *Cosmetic Compliance*].

10. John Conlisk, *Why Bounded Rationality?,* 34 J. ECON. LITERATURE 669 (1996); Herbert A. Simon, *Rational Decision Making in Business Organizations,* 69 AM. ECON. REV. 493 (1979); Owen D. Jones, *Time-Shifted Rationality and the Law of Law's Leverage: Behavioral Economics Meets Behavioral Biology,* 95 NW. U. L. REV. 1141, 1142 (2001).

11. For a summary of the evidence that extrinsic motivations, positive and negative, often crowd out pro-social impulses toward cooperation and civic virtue, see Margit Osterloh & Bruno S. Frey, *Corporate Governance for Crooks? The Case for Corporate Virtue,* in CORPORATE GOVERNANCE AND FIRM ORGANIZATION 191–211 (Ganna Grandori ed., 2004). See also Margaret M. Blair & Lynn A. Stout, *Trust, Trustworthiness, and the Behavioral Foundations of Corporate Law,* 149 U. PA. L. REV. 1735 (2001); Robert A. Kagan, Neil Gunningham, & Dorothy Thornton. *Explaining Corporate Environmental Performance: How Does Regulation Matter?,* 37 LAW & SOC. REV. 61–63 (2003); Dan M. Kahan, *The Logic of Reciprocity: Trust, Collective Action, and Law,* 102 MICH. L. REV. 71, 78–80 (2003). These findings are related to the insight that people are more disposed to abide by rules if they feel fairly and respectfully treated by the rule enforcers. See Tom R. Tyler, *Trust and Law Abidingness:A Proactive Model of Social Regulation,* 81 B.U. L. REV. 361, 368–69 (2001).

12. *See, e.g.,* Tom R. Tyler et al., *Armed, and Dangerous (?): Motivating Rule Adherence among Agents of Social Control,* 41 LAW & SOC'Y REV. 457, 462–63 (2007); Valerie Braithwaite

& John Braithwaite, *Democratic Sentiment and Cyclical Markets in Vice,* 46 BRIT. J. CRIM-
INOLOGY 1110, 1111 (2006); Darren Sinclair, *Self-Regulation versus Command and Control? Beyond False Dichotomies,* 19 LAW & POL'Y 529 (1997).

13. For an overview of the literature on "New Governance," *see* Orly Lobel, *The Renew Deal:
The Fall of Regulation and the Rise of Governance in Contemporary Legal Thought,* 89
MINN. L. REV. 342 (2004).

14. "Reflexive law," a term coined in Gunther Teubner, *Substantive and Reflexive Elements
in Modern Law,* 17 LAW & SOC'Y REV. 239 (1983), is one term for an influential conception of modern law that, in the words of one American legal scholar, "emphasizes the limits of law in the face of complexity [and] proposes an alternative approach to law reform. It focuses on enhancing self-referential capacities of social systems and institutions
outside the legal system, rather than direct intervention of the legal system itself through
agencies, highly detailed statutes, or delegation of great power to courts." Eric W. Orts,
Reflexive Environmental Law, 89 Nw. U. L. REV. 1227, 1232 (1995).

15. Among exceptions, *see* Lobel, *The Renew Deal, supra* note 13; Susan Sturm, *Second Generation Employment Discrimination: A Structural Approach,* 101 COLUM. L. REV. 458 (2001).

16. *See, e.g.,* IAN AYRES & JOHN BRAITHWAITE, RESPONSIVE REGULATION: TRANSCENDING
THE DEREGULATION DEBATE (1992); RALF ROGOWSKI & TON WILTHAGEN, eds., RE-
FLEXIVE LABOUR LAW: STUDIES IN INDUSTRIAL RELATIONS AND EMPLOYMENT REGULA-
TION (1994); ARCHON FUNG, DARA O'ROURKE, & CHARLES SABEL, CAN WE PUT AN
END TO SWEATSHOPS? (2001); Dara O'Rourke, *Outsourcing Regulation: Analyzing Non-
Governmental Systems of Labor Standards and Monitoring,* 31 POL'Y STUD. J. 1 (2003);
Orly Lobel, *Beyond Experimentation: Governing Occupational Safety in the United States
(or Core and Periphery in Regulation Governance), in* NEW GOVERNANCE AND CONSTI-
TUTIONALISM IN EUROPE AND THE UNITED STATES (Grainne De Burca & Joanne Scott
eds., 2006).

17. Michael C. Dorf, *The Domain of Reflexive Law,* 103 COLUM. L. REV. 384, 391 (2003).

18. For skeptical views of reflexive law and self-regulation in the context of workplace regulation, *see* Harry W. Arthurs, *Private Ordering and Workers' Rights in the Global Economy: Corporate Codes of Conduct as a Regime of Labour Market Regulation, in* LABOUR
LAW IN AN ERA OF GLOBALIZATION 471, 485–87 (Joanne Conaghan et al. eds., 2002);
Adelle Blackett, *Global Governance, Legal Pluralism and the Decentered State: A Labor
Law Critique of Codes of Corporate Conduct,* 8 IND. J. GLOBAL LEGAL STUD. 401, 406–
18 (2001); Krawiec, *Organizational Misconduct, supra* note 2. Blackett criticizes the code
of conduct approach for often lacking both an external regulatory dimension and an independent monitoring system, two features that I also insist are crucial. *Id.* at 411–12.
Krawiec similarly criticizes reliance on internal compliance systems as likely to promote
"cosmetic compliance"; but the systems she criticizes lack built-in safeguards of efficacy
proposed here.

19. *See, e.g.,* Donald C. Langevoort, *Monitoring: The Behavioral Economics of Corporate Compliance with Law,* 2002 COLUM. BUS. L. REV. 71 (2002); Cristie L. Ford, *Toward a New
Model for Securities Law Enforcement,* 57 ADMIN. L. REV. 757 (2005).

20. *See, e.g.,* Langevoort, *Monitoring, supra* note 19.

21. *See* AYRES & BRAITHWAITE, *supra* note 16; JOHN BRAITHWAITE, REGULATORY CAPITAL-
ISM: HOW IT WORKS, IDEAS FOR MAKING IT WORK BETTER (2008); JOHN BRAITHWAITE,
RESTORATIVE JUSTICE AND RESPONSIVE REGULATION (2002); John Braithwaite, *Enforced
Self-Regulation: A New Strategy for Corporate Crime Control*, 80 MICH. L. REV. 1466
(1982); JOHN BRAITHWAITE, TO PUNISH OR PERSUADE: ENFORCEMENT OF COAL MINE
SAFETY (1985).

22. AYERS & BRAITHWAITE, *supra* note 16, at 22–27.

23. *Id.* at 33–35.

24. *Id.* at 51–53.

25. *Id.* at 35–40.

26. *Id.* at 60–68.

27. *Id.* at 21.

28. *Id.* at 54–57.

29. *Id.* at 57–60.

30. *Id.* at 59. For a simplified two-track version of this approach to occupational safety and
health, *see* Neil A. Gunningham, *Towards Effective and Efficient Enforcement of Occupational Health and Safety Regulation: Two Paths to Enlightenment*, 19 COMP. LAB. L. &
POL'Y J. 547, 549–56 (1998).

31. AYRES & BRAITHWAITE, *supra* note 16, at 59, 106, 126.

32. *Id.* at 59.

33. BRAITHWAITE, REGULATORY CAPITALISM, *supra* note 21.

34. *Id.* at 94–95. The problem that those small, marginal firms pose for the Responsive Regulation model was highlighted by FIONA HAINES, CORPORATE REGULATION: BEYOND
"PUNISH OR PERSUADE" (1997).

35. BRAITHWAITE, REGULATORY CAPITALISM, *supra* note 21, at 65.

36. CHRISTINE PARKER, THE OPEN CORPORATION: EFFECTIVE SELF-REGULATION AND
DEMOCRACY 63–77 (2002) [hereinafter OPEN CORPORATION]; Christine Parker, *Meta-
Regulation: Legal Accountability for Corporate Social Responsibility?*, in THE NEW COR-
PORATE ACCOUNTABILITY: CORPORATE SOCIAL RESPONSIBILITY AND THE LAW (Doreen
McBarnet, Aurora Voiculescu, & Tom Campbell eds., 2007) [hereinafter *Meta-Regula-
tion*].

37. PARKER, OPEN CORPORATION, *supra* note 36, at ix. *See also* Wayne Gray & John T.
Scholz, *Does Regulatory Enforcement Work? A Panel Analysis of OSHA Enforcement*, 27
LAW & SOC. REV. 177–213 (1993); Neil Gunningham, Dorothy Thornton, & Robert A.
Kagan, *Motivating Management: Corporate Compliance in Environmental Protection*, 27
LAW & POLICY 289–316 (2005); Robert A. Kagan, Neil Gunningham, & Dorothy
Thornton. *Explaining Corporate Environmental Performance: How Does Regulation Mat-
ter?*, 37 LAW & SOC. REV. 51–90 (2003); Jodi L. Short & Michael W. Toffel, *Coerced
Confessions: Self-Policing in the Shadow of the Regulator*, 24 J. LAW, ECON., & ORG. 45
(2008).

38. PARKER, OPEN CORPORATION, *supra* note 36, at ix. See also sources cited at note 11.

39. PARKER, OPEN CORPORATION, *supra* note 36, at ix.

40. *Id.* at x–xi.

41. *See* Thomas J. Donohue, President, U.S. Chamber of Commerce, *How Government Can Really Help Workers* (Aug. 2000), *available at* http://www.uschamber.com/press /opeds/0008donohuelaborday.htm.

42. For a thoughtful exploration of the importance and legal treatment of employee informants, or "whistleblowers," within a New Governance paradigm, *see* Orly Lobel, *Citizenship, Organizational Citizenship, and the Laws of Overlapping Obligations,* Cal. L. Rev. (forthcoming 2009).

43. *See* Clyde Summers, *Effective Remedies for Employment Rights: Preliminary Guidelines and Proposals,* 141 U. Pa. L. Rev. 457, 496–97 (1992).

44. Elletta S. Callahan & Terry M. Dworkin, *The State of State Whistleblower Protection,* 38 Am. Bus. L.J. 99 (2000); Elizabeth C. Tippett, *The Promise of Compelled Whistleblowing: What the Corporate Governance Provisions of Sarbanes-Oxley Mean for Employment Law,* 11 Emp. Rts. & Emp. Pol'y 1 (2007).

45. On the public goods problem in labor standards enforcement, *see generally* Louise Sadowsky Brock, *Overcoming Collective Action Problems: Enforcement of Worker Rights,* 30 U. Mich. J.L. Reform 781, 791–94 (1997).

46. *See* Ayres & Braithwaite, *supra* note 16, at 106, 126.

47. Richard B. Freeman & James L. Medoff, What Do Unions Do? (1984).

48. *See* Roger I. Abrams & Dennis R. Nolan, *Toward a Theory of "Just Cause" in Employee Discipline Cases,* 1985 Duke L.J. 594, 594 n.1. (1985).

49. On the chronic shortage of inspectors and resources, *see* Thomas O. McGarity & Sidney A. Shapiro, Workers at Risk: The Failed Promise of the Occupational Safety and Health Administration 41–42 (1993); Thomas O. McGarity, *Reforming OSHA: Some Thoughts for the Current Legislative Agenda,* 31 Hous. L. Rev. 99, 101–02 (1994); Orly Lobel, *Interlocking Regulatory and Industrial Relations: The Governance of Workplace Safety,* 57 Admin. L. Rev. 1071, 1080–81 (2005).

50. *See* Braithwaite, To Punish or Persuade, *supra* note 21, at 15–40 (1985).

51. MSHA is required by law to inspect all mines twice yearly and underground mines four times yearly; a 2003 evaluation found that MSHA on average completed between 80 percent (all mines) and 98 percent (coal mines) of the required inspections. *See* U.S. Dep't of Labor, MSHA, *Mine Inspection Program Evaluation,* Sept. 30, 2003, *available at* http://www.msha.gov/readroom/foia/specialreports/icfinspectionreport/mshamine inspectionprogramevaluationreport.pdf. By contrast, as of 2007, OSHA had about 1,100 inspectors to cover some 8.9 million work sites. *See* OSHA Fact Sheet, http://www.osha .gov/as/opa/oshafacts.html. Over 59 percent of OSHA's inspections were of construction worksites. *Id.*

52. Braithwaite, Regulatory Capitalism, *supra* note 21, at 92.

53. Steven Greenhouse, The Big Squeeze: Tough Times for the American Worker 226–27, 235–37 (2008).

54. Braithwaite, Regulatory Capitalism, *supra* note 21, at 94–97.

55. *See, e.g.,* Samuel Issacharoff & Geoffrey P. Miller, *Will Aggregate Litigation Come to Europe?,* 62 Vand. L. Rev. 179 (2009); Richard A. Nagareda, *Aggregate Litigation across the Atlantic and the Future of American Exceptionalism,* 62 Vand. L. Rev. 1 (2009).

56. In principle, that is what OSHA promises. In practice, inspections and enforcement

actions have sometimes been focused on larger and more visible establishments, which tend to have better compliance than smaller and more marginal establishments. *See* David Weil, *Enforcing OSHA: The Role of Labor Unions,* 30 Indus. Rel. 20, 23 (1991). As of 2007, OSHA reported that 56 percent of its inspections were of the "high hazard/targeted" type and 59 percent of its inspections were in construction; http://www .osha.gov/as/opa/oshafacts.html. In the case of FLSA enforcement, the agency's traditional tendency to rely on complaints rather than on agency-initiated targeted enforcement tends to skew enforcement away from low-wage sectors and toward overtime violations affecting higher-wage workers. *See* Weil, *supra* at 7–8. In the late 1990s, the agency did shift more of its attention to low-wage industries. *Id.* at 12.

57. *See, e.g.,* Weil, *supra* note 56, at 30; Gregory R. Watchman, *Safe and Sound: The Case for Safety and Health Committees under OSHA and the NLRA,* 4 Cornell J.L. & Pub. Pol'y 65 (1994).

58. William L. Keller et al., International Labor and Employment Laws (2d ed. 2003 & supp.); Clyde W. Summers, *Worker Dislocation: Who Bears the Burden? A Comparative Study of Social Values in Five Countries,* 70 Notre Dame L. Rev. 1033, 1067–68 (1995).

59. Braithwaite, Regulatory Capitalism, *supra* note 21, at 94–97.

60. Fung et al., *supra* note 16, at 1–3. "Ratcheting Labor Standards" is a specific application of the theory underlying "Rolling Rule Regimes"; *see* William H. Simon, *Solving Problems vs. Claiming Rights: The Pragmatist Challenge to Legal Liberalism,* 46 Wm. & Mary L. Rev. 127, 187–92 (2004); it, in turn, is a crucial element of what Dorf and Sabel call, in the public law context, "Democratic Experimentalism." *See* Michael C. Dorf & Charles F. Sabel, *A Constitution of Democratic Experimentalism,* 98 Colum. L. Rev. 267 (1998).

61. Indeed, Fung, O'Rourke, and Sabel point to the problems of underenforced labor standards in the United States as part of their case for a fundamentally different approach to regulation. Fung et al., *supra* note 16, at 13–14.

62. *Id.* at 16–17.

63. *Id.* at 17.

64. *Id.* at 9–11.

65. *Id.* at 17.

66. *Id.* at 7. For a review of the evidence of consumer "demand for labor standards," *see* Kimberly Ann Elliott & Richard B. Freeman, Can Labor Standards Improve under Globalization? 28–45 (2003). They conclude that consumers are willing, to varying but significant degrees, to penalize brands associated with poor labor practices, though they are less inclined to reward those associated with good practices. *Id.* at 31–32. They also find some evidence that firms suffer—in their share prices, for example—when they are identified with exploitative labor conditions. *Id.* at 40–42.

67. Fung et al., *supra* note 16, at 16–18.

68. *Id.* at 32.

69. Braithwaite, too, has recognized the importance of harnessing those corporate regulatory energies. *See* Braithwaite, Regulatory Capitalism, *supra* note 21, at 94–97.

70. Maria Gillen, *Note, The Apparel Industry Partnership's Free Labor Association: A Solution to the Overseas Sweatshop Problem or the Emperor's New Clothes?,* 32 N.Y.U. Int'l L. & Pol. 1059, 1103 (2000).

71. Fung and his co-authors leave room for, but do not require, governmental mandates both from within the developed countries and from the developing countries. *See* FUNG ET AL., *supra* note 16, at 34. The private, non-state-centered approach to international rights enforcement is both a strength and a weakness. *See* Paul Redmond, *Transnational Enterprise and Human Rights: Options for Standard Setting and Compliance,* 37 INT'L L. 69, 90–95 (2003).

72. Critics of the privatized code of conduct approach to sweatshops argue that these systems risk undermining the growth of local state regulatory agencies by sidestepping them. *See* Mark Barenberg, *Toward a Democratic Model of Transnational Labour Monitoring?, in* REGULATING LABOUR IN THE WAKE OF GLOBALISATION: NEW CHALLENGES, NEW INSTITUTIONS 37 (Brian Bercusson & Cynthia Estlund eds., 2007); Arthurs, *supra* note 18; BRAITHWAITE, REGULATORY CAPITALISM, *supra* note 21, at 95–97; Blackett, *supra* note 18, at 419–20, 427–29.

73. *See* FUNG ET AL., *supra* note 16, at 35.

74. *See, e.g.,* Barenberg, *supra* note 72, at 7–8; Blackett, *supra* note 18, at 436; ELLIOTT & FREEMAN, *supra* note 66, at 69–72; Linda Shaw & Angela Hale, *The Emperor's New Clothes: What Codes Mean for Workers in the Garment Industry, in,* CORPORATE RESPONSIBILITY AND LABOUR RIGHTS: CODES OF CONDUCT IN THE GLOBAL ECONOMY 101, 104–05 (Rhys Jenkins, Ruth Pearson, & Gill Seyfang eds., 2002).

75. Shaw & Hale, *supra* note 74, at 101, 104–05.

76. *Sewing a Seam of Worker Democracy in China,* FIN. TIMES, Dec. 12, 2002, at 14 (quoting Doug Cahn, director of human rights programs for Reebok). *See also* Shaw & Hale, *supra* note 74, at 104.

77. *See* ELLIOTT & FREEMAN, *supra* note 66, at 71–72.

78. For criticisms of the reliance on self-regulation, *see* William W. Bratton, *Enron and the Dark Side of Shareholder Value,* 76 TUL. L. REV. 1275, 1282–88 (2002); William W. Bratton & Joseph A. McCahery, *Regulatory Competition, Regulatory Capture, and Corporate Self-Regulation,* 73 N.C. L. REV. 1861, 1892–98 (1995). For a more favorable view, *see* Harvey L. Pitt & Karl A. Groskaufmanis, *Minimizing Corporate Civil and Criminal Liability: A Second Look at Corporate Codes of Conduct,* 78 GEO. L.J. 1559, 1647 (1990).

79. On the centrality of these outside monitors or "gatekeepers" in guarding against corporate misconduct, *see* John C. Coffee, Jr., *Gatekeeper Failure and Reform: The Challenge of Fashioning Relevant Reforms,* 84 B.U. L. REV. 301, 308 (2004).

80. Zohar Goshen & Gideon Parchomovsky, *The Essential Role of Securities Regulation,* 55 DUKE L.J. 711, 723–24, 726, 737 (2006).

81. *See* Coffee, *Gatekeeper Failure, supra* note 79, at 318–23.

82. Sarbanes-Oxley Act 201–301, 303, Pub. L. No. 107–204, 116 Stat. 745, 771–777, 778 (codified in scattered sections of 15 U.S.C.); Lyman P. Q. Johnson & Mark A. Sides, *The Sarbanes-Oxley Act and Fiduciary Duties,* 30 WM. MITCHELL L. REV. 1149, 1155–57 (2004).

83. Sarbanes-Oxley (1) prohibited auditors from engaging in certain other lucrative forms of business with corporate clients; (2) created a new Public Company Accounting Oversight Board to oversee public accountants; and (3) imposed new liabilities on auditors. For a summary of major provisions, *see* John C. Coffee, Jr., *A Brief Tour of the Major Reforms in the Sarbanes-Oxley Act,* ALI-ABA CONTINUING LEGAL EDUCATION, Dec. 5, 2002.

84. Sarbanes-Oxley Act 404, 15 U.S.C.A. §7262; Donald C. Langevoort, *Internal Controls after Sarbanes-Oxley: Revisiting Corporate Law's "Duty of Care as Responsibility for Systems,"* 31 J. Corp. L. 949, 954–55 (2006).

85. The criminal prohibition is codified at 18 U.S.C. §1514(A) (2000); civil enforcement provisions appear in §806(b) of the Act.

86. On the role prescribed for the SEC by Sarbanes-Oxley, *see* Coffee, *Brief Tour, supra* note 83, at 153–55.

87. *See* Coffee, *Gatekeeper Failure, supra* note 79, at 318–23.

88. *See* Christian Leuz et al., *Why Do Firms Go Dark? Causes and Economic Consequences of Voluntary SEC Deregistrations* (ECGI–Fin. Working Paper No. 155/2007, 2006), *available at* http://www.ssrn.com/abstract=592421; Ehud Kamar et al., *Going-Private Decisions and the Sarbanes-Oxley Act of 2002: A Cross-Country Analysis* (U.S.C. Ctr. in Law, Econ. & Org., Research Paper No. C06–5, 2006), *available at* http://www.ssrn.com/abstract=901769.

89. On moves to mitigate Sarbanes-Oxley's costs for smaller companies, *see* Joseph A. Grundfest & Steven E. Bochner, *Fixing 404,* 105 Mich. L. Rev. 1643, 1649–57 (2007).

90. *See* Richard E. Moberly, *Sarbanes-Oxley's Structural Model to Encourage Corporate Whistleblowers,* 2006 B.Y.U. L. Rev. 1107, 1127 (2006); Richard E. Moberly, *Unfulfilled Expectations: An Empirical Analysis of Why Sarbanes-Oxley Whistleblowers Rarely Win,* 49 Wm. & Mary. L. Rev. 65 (2007). Of course, it is impossible to know either how much justified whistleblowing or how much actionable retaliation against whistleblowers is actually going on. A completely effective whistleblower protection law would deter reprisals and would generate no meritorious claims at all. It would be foolish to assume that is what explains the very low incidence and success rate of claims, but it would be equally foolish to conclude from those facts that the law has entirely failed in its mission.

91. Moberly, *Unfulfilled Expectations, supra* note 90.

92. *See* Jeffrey N. Gordon, *The Rise of Independent Directors in the United States, 1950–2005: Of Shareholder Value and Stock Prices,* 59 Stan. L. Rev. 1465 (2007); Donald C. Langevoort, *The Social Construction of Sarbanes-Oxley,* 105 Mich. L. Rev. 1817, 1835–37 (2007).

93. *See, e.g.,* Laura Albareda, *Corporate Responsibility, Governance and Accountability: From Self-Regulation to Co-Regulation,* 8 Corp. Governance 430 (2008). The term has also been used within the realm of public governance, especially within the European Union, to describe "a process through which 'concerned parties' agree upon the best solution for regulation in their respective fields." *See* Philipp Steinberg, *Agencies, Co-Regulation and Comitology—And What about Politics? A Critical Appraisal of the Commission's White Paper on Governance* (NYU School of Law, Jean Monnet Center, Working Paper No. 6/01), *available at* http://www.jeanmonnetprogram.org/papers/01/012901.html.

CHAPTER 7. EMPLOYEE REPRESENTATION

1. *See* Richard Freeman & James Medoff, What Do Unions Do? (1984).

2. *See, e.g.,* David Weil, *Enforcing OSHA: The Role of Labor Unions,* 30 Indus. Rel. 20, 28 (1991).

3. American Rights at Work, *Workers' Rights Statistics, available at* http://americanrights atwork.org/publications/statistics (last visited May 7, 2009); Peter D. Hart Research Associates for AFL-CIO, *Labor Day 2005: The State of Working America,* at 6 (2005), available at http://www.aflcio.org/aboutus/laborday/upload/ld2005_report.pdf (last visited May 7, 2009).

4. U.S. Department of Labor, Bureau of Labor Statistics, *Labor Force Statistics from the Current Population Survey, Union Affiliation Data* (chart 42, p. 252), *available at* http://www.bls.gov/cps/cpsaat42.pdf (2008) (last visited May 7, 2009).

5. For a rich collection of recent essays on these questions from an economic perspective, *see* WHAT DO UNIONS DO? A TWENTY-YEAR PERSPECTIVE (James T. Bennett & Bruce E. Kaufman eds., 2007).

6. Freeman and Medoff attributed a significant share of the decline in union representation to increased employer resistance. *See* FREEMAN & MEDOFF, *supra* note 1.

7. Bruce E. Kaufman, *What Do Unions Do? Evaluation and Commentary,* in BENNETT & KAUFMAN, *supra* note 5, at 548.

8. *Id.*

9. *Id.*

10. Richard B. Freeman & Joel Rogers, WHAT WORKERS WANT (2d ed. 2006).

11. *See, e.g.,* Robert J. Flanagan, *Has Management Strangled U.S. Unions?,* in BENNETT & KAUFMAN, *supra* note 5, at 459–91.

12. Kaufman, *supra* note 7, at 548–49.

13. I testified in favor of the Employee Free Choice Act during the 2007 Senate hearings. *See Testimony of Cynthia L. Estlund before the Senate Committee on Health, Education, Labor, and Pensions,* March 27, 2007, *available at* http://help.senate.gov/Hearings/2007 _03_27_a/Estlund.pdf.

14. For an analysis of the mandatory arbitration provision, *see* David Broderdorf, *Overcoming the First Contract Hurdle: Finding a Role for Mandatory Interest Arbitration in the Private Sector,* 23 LAB. LAW. 323 (2008).

15. *See* Bryan O'Keefe, *A Union Revival? Unions Look to Democrats to Enact Sweeping Legislative Agenda,* Labor Watch (Capital Research Center, Feb., 2008), *available at* http://www.capitalresearch.org/pubs/pdf/v1201821607.pdf; Brian Wingfield, *Fears of a Union Renaissance,* Forbes.com, 6/5/2008, *available at* http://www.forbes.com/business /2008/06/05/labor-congress-teamsters-biz-beltway-cx_bw_0605labor.html.

16. Steven Greenhouse, *After Push for Obama, Unions Seek New Rules,* N. Y. TIMES, Nov. 8, 2008.

17. Michael L. Wachter, *Labor Unions: A Corporatist Institution in a Competitive World,* 155 U. PA. L. REV. 581, 583 (2007); CHARLES B. CRAVER, CAN UNIONS SURVIVE: THE REJUVENATION OF THE AMERICAN LABOR MOVEMENT 42–47 (1993); Samuel Estreicher, *Labor Law Reform in a World of Competitive Product Markets,* 69 CHI.-KENT L. REV. 3, 4–5 (1993); Leo Troy, *Is the U.S. Unique in the Decline of Private Sector Unionism?,* 11 J. LAB. RES. 111, 113–20 (1990).

18. Unions' modest adverse impact on profits, recognized two decades ago by FREEMAN & MEDOFF, WHAT DO UNIONS DO?, *supra* note 1, was verified in a recent review of the

economic literature. *See* Barry T. Hirsch, *What Do Unions Do for Economic Performance?*, in BENNETT & KAUFMAN, *supra* note 5, at 211–14.

19. The union premium varies by sector, state, occupation, and demographic group and has declined in recent decades, but it persists. David G. Blanchflower & Alex Bryson, *What Effect Do Unions Have on Wages Now and Would Freeman and Medoff Be Surprised?*, in BENNETT & KAUFMAN, *supra* note 5, at 103–06. Higher wages and better benefits are at the heart of proponents' policy arguments for unionization. *See* AFL-CIO, *Union Pay Is Higher in Nearly All Occupational Groups, available at* http://www.aflcio.org/joinaunion/why/uniondifference/uniondiff5.cfm (last visited May 7, 2009); AFL-CIO, *Unions Raise Wages—Especially for Minorities and Women, available at* http://www.aflcio.org/joinaunion/why/uniondifference/uniondiff4.cfm (last visited May 7, 2009); AFL-CIO, *Union Workers Have Better Health Care and Pensions, available at* http://www.aflcio.org/joinaunion/why/uniondifference/uniondiff6.cfm (last visited May 7, 2009); Lawrence Mishel & Matthew Walters, *How Unions Help All Workers* (Econ. Pol'y Inst. Briefing Paper No. 143, 2003), *available at* http://www.epi.org/publications/entry/briefingpapers_bp143 (last visited May 7, 2009).

20. *See* Blanchflower & Bryson, *supra* note 19, at 108; Hirsch, *supra* note 18, at 214; Kaufman, *supra* note 7, at 550. For an accessible summary of the argument and the data, *see* Jeffrey M. Hirsch & Barry T. Hirsch, *The Rise and Fall of Private Sector Unionism: What Next for the NLRA?*, 34 FLORIDA ST. U. L. REV. 1133, 1140–45 (2007).

21. Wachter, *supra* note 17, at 627.

22. *Id.* at 626, 634.

23. *See* Cynthia L. Estlund, Response, *Are Unions Doomed to Being a "Niche Movement" in a Competitive Economy?*, 155 U. PA. L. REV. PENNUMBRA 101 (2007), *available at* http://www.pennumbra.com.

24. *See* FREEMAN & ROGERS, WHAT WORKERS WANT, *supra* note 10.

25. Others have explored the possibilities for nonexclusive union representation and its role in the enforcement of employment laws. *See* CHARLES C. HECKSCHER, THE NEW UNIONISM: EMPLOYEE INVOLVEMENT IN THE CHANGING CORPORATION 8, 177, 189–90 (1988); Marion Crain, *Images of Power in Labor Law: A Feminist Deconstruction,* 33 B.C. L. REV. 481, 530–32 (1992); Charles B. Craver, *The Vitality of the American Labor Movement in the Twenty-first Century,* 1983 U. ILL. L. REV. 633, 655; Alan Hyde et al., *After Smyrna: Rights and Powers of Unions That Represent Less Than a Majority,* 45 RUTGERS L. REV. 637, 648–51 (1993); James Gray Pope, *Labor-Community Coalitions and Boycotts: The Old Labor Law, the New Unionism, and the Living Constitution,* 69 TEX. L. REV. 889, 916–17 (1991); Clyde Summers, *Unions without Majority—A Black Hole?,* 66 CHI.-KENT L. REV. 531, 532 (1992).

26. Charles J. Morris, *Members-Only Collective Bargaining: Rejecting Conventional Wisdom,* LERA: PERSPECTIVES ONLINE COMPANION, *available at* http://www.lera.uiuc.edu/Pubs/Perspectives/onlinecompanion/Fall05-morris.htm (last visited May 7, 2009); Jim McKay, *Union Tries a Very Old (New) Tactic to Organize Dick's Workers,* PITT. POST-GAZETTE, Sept. 4, 2005.

27. CHARLES J. MORRIS, THE BLUE EAGLE AT WORK: RECLAIMING DEMOCRATIC RIGHTS IN THE AMERICAN WORKPLACE 9–10 (2004).

28. Lisa Schur, *The Blue Eagle at Work: Reclaiming Democratic Rights in the American Workplace,* 31 LAB. STUD. J. 107, 108 (2006) (book review); John M. True, *The Blue Eagle at Work: Reclaiming Democratic Rights in the American Workplace,* 26 BERKELEY J. EMP. & LAB. L. 181 (2005) (book review); Carol Brooke, *Nonmajority Unions, Employee Participation Programs, and Worker Organizing: Irreconcilable Differences?,* 76 CHI.-KENT L. REV. 1237, 1239–40 (2000); Julius Getman, *The National Labor Relations Act: What Went Wrong?; Can We Fix It?,* 45 B.C. L. REV. 125, 136 (2003); David Rosenfeld, *Worker Centers: Emerging Labor Organizations—Until They Confront the National Labor Relations Act,* 27 BERKELEY J. EMP. & LAB. L. 469, 504–10 (2006).

29. Memorandum from Barry J. Kearney, Assoc. Gen. Counsel, NLRB, to Gerald Kobell, Reg'l Dir., Region 6, NLRB, regarding Dick's Sporting Goods, Case 6-CA-34821 (June 22, 2006), *available at* http://www.nlrb.gov/shared_files/Advice%20Memos/2006/6-CA-34821(06-22-06).pdf.

30. *See* Richard B. Freeman & Joel Rogers, *Open-Source Unionism: Beyond Exclusive Collective Bargaining,* WORKINGUSA, Spring 2002, at 8. *See also* RICHARD B. FREEMAN, AMERICA WORKS: CRITICAL THOUGHTS ON THE EXCEPTIONAL U.S. LABOR MARKET 90–92 (2008).

31. *See* Chapter 5.

32. *See* Matthew W. Finkin, *Employee Representation outside the Labor Act: Thoughts on Arbitral Representation, Group Arbitration, and Workplace Committees,* 5 U. PA. J. LAB. & EMP. L. 75, 99 (2002).

33. *See* IAN AYRES & JOHN BRAITHWAITE, RESPONSIVE REGULATION: TRANSCENDING THE DEREGULATION DEBATE 59 (1992); DAVID I. LEVINE, WORKING IN THE TWENTY-FIRST CENTURY, POLICIES FOR ECONOMIC GROWTH THROUGH TRAINING, OPPORTUNITY, AND EDUCATION 150–52 (1998).

34. *See, e.g.,* PAUL C. WEILER, GOVERNING THE WORKPLACE: THE FUTURE OF LABOR AND EMPLOYMENT LAW 300–06 (1990); Hirsch & Hirsch, *supra* note 20, at 1166–68; Stephen F. Befort, *A New Voice for the Workplace: A Proposal for an American Works Councils Act,* 69 MO. L. REV. 607, 651 (2004); Thomas A. Kochan, *Updating American Labor Law: Taking Advantage of a Window of Opportunity,* 28 COMP. LAB. L. & POL'Y J. 101, 113 (2006). For accounts of works councils in Europe, *see* Joel Rogers & Wolfgang Streeck, *Worker Representation Overseas: The Works Council Story, in* WORKING UNDER DIFFERENT RULES (Richard B. Freeman, ed., 1994).

35. *See* Befort, *supra* note 34, at 635–41.

36. Wolfgang Streeck, *Works Councils in Western Europe: From Consultation to Participation, in* ROGERS & STREECK, *supra* note 34.

37. *See* WEILER, *supra* note 34, at 283–95.

38. Befort, *supra* note 34, at 642.

39. So, for example, Weiler would allow a union, where there is one in place, to serve as the consultative body; where there is no union in place, he would give works councils a right to strike. WEILER, *supra* note 34, at 290–94. Befort would do neither, in hopes of maintaining the cooperative orientation of the works council. Befort, *supra* note 34, at 642–43.

40. *See* Befort, *supra* note 34, at 643–46.
41. *See* Cynthia Estlund, *Something Old, Something New: Governing the Workplace by Contract Again,* 28 COMP. LAB. L. & POL'Y J., 351, 353 (2007).
42. *See* Hirsch & Hirsch, *supra* note 20.
43. *See* LEVINE, *supra* note 33, at 154–55; Orly Lobel, *Interlocking Regulatory and Industrial Relations: The Governance of Workplace Safety,* 57 ADMIN. L. REV. 1071 (2005).
44. *See supra* Chapter 4.
45. *See* Finkin, *supra* note 32, at 99. Those laws escape federal preemption only if they can be construed as providing for committees that are sufficiently independent of the employer to comport with Section 8(a)(2). Jerry M. Hunter, Gen. Counsel, NLRB, Guideline Memorandum Concerning Electromation, Inc., 309 NLRB No. 163, (1993), *available at* http://www.nlrb.gov/shared_files/GC%20Memo/1993/gc%2093–94.pdf.
46. FREEMAN & ROGERS, WHAT WORKERS WANT, *supra* note 10, at 152.
47. *Id.* at 60–63. *See also* Larry Cohen & Richard W. Hurd, *Fear, Conflict, and Union Organizing, in* ORGANIZING TO WIN: NEW RESEARCH ON UNION STRATEGIES 181 (Kate Bronfenbrenner et al. eds., 1998); Michael H. Gottesman, *In Despair, Starting Over: Imagining a Labor Law for Unorganized Workers,* 69 CHI.-KENT L. REV. 59, 62–68 (1993).
48. Ayres and Braithwaite stipulate that employee committees must have real power to play their appointed role, but they do not explain how that might be possible. *See* AYRES & BRAITHWAITE, *supra* note 33, at 126–27.
49. On how this provision inhibits experimentation in labor relations more generally, *see* Cynthia Estlund, *The Ossification of American Labor Law,* 102 COLUM. L. REV. 1527, 1544–51 (2002).
50. For an analysis of the effect of Section 8(a)(2) on employee health and safety committees, *see* Orly Lobel, *Agency and Coercion in Labor and Employment Relations: Four Dimensions of Power in Shifting Patterns of Work,* 4 U. PA. J. LAB. & EMP. L. 121 (2001); Lobel, *Interlocking Regulatory and Industrial Relations, supra* note 43.
51. Rafael Gely, *Where Are We Now?: Life after Electromation,* 15 HOFSTRA LAB. & EMP. L. J. 45, 50–51 (1997).
52. U.S. Dep't of Labor, Occupational Safety and Health Administration, *Voluntary Protection Programs (VPP): Policies and Procedures Manual,* Directive No. CSP 03–01–003 (2008); Hunter, Guideline Memorandum Concerning Electromation, Inc., *supra* note 45.
53. Michael H. LeRoy, *Can TEAM Work? Implications of an Electromation and DuPont Compliance Analysis for the TEAM Act,* 71 NOTRE DAME L. REV. 215, 244–51 (1996).
54. Hirsch & Hirsch, *supra* note 20, at 1163.
55. For a thorough analysis of the history and purposes of Section 8(a)(2), *see* Mark Barenberg, *Democracy and Domination in the Law of Workplace Cooperation: From Bureaucratic to Flexible Production,* 94 COLUM. L. REV. 753 (1994).
56. *See* Estlund, *Ossification, supra* note 49, at 1540–44.
57. *See* Lori A. Nessel, *Undocumented Immigrants in the Workplace: The Fallacy of Labor Protection and the Need for Reform,* 36 HARV. C.R.-C.L. L. REV. 345, 348 (2001); Marianne Staniunas, Comment, *All Employees Are Equal, But Some Employees Are More Equal Than Others,* 6 U. PA. J. LAB. & EMP. L. 393, 399–400 (2004).

58. LEVINE, *supra* note 33, at 151.
59. David Weil, *Are Mandated Health and Safety Committees Substitutes for or Supplements to Labor Unions?* INDUS. & LAB. REL. REV. 339, 340 (1999); David Weil, *Mandating Safety and Health Committees: Lessons from the States, in* INDUSTRIAL RELATIONS RESEARCH ASSOCIATION 47th ANNUAL PROCEEDINGS, 273–81 (1995); Gregory R. Watchman, *Safe and Sound: The Case for Safety and Health Committees under OSHA and the NLRA,* 4 CORNELL J.L. & PUB. POL'Y 65, 82–89 (1994); Lobel, *Interlocking Regulatory and Industrial Relations, supra* note 43, at 1128; Randy S. Rabinowitz & Mark M. Hager, *Designing Health and Safety: Workplace Hazard Regulation in the United States and Canada,* 33 CORNELL INT'L L.J. 373 (2000).
60. *See* Finkin, *supra* note 32, at 99.
61. Calls for loosening the proscriptions of Section 8(a)(2) are plentiful. *See* Chapter 2, note 28.
62. *See* LEVINE, *supra* note 33.
63. That is the proposal of Hirsch & Hirsch, *supra* note 20, at 1158–62. They would condition their proposal on concurrent reforms that strengthen employees' right and ability to choose independent union representation. *Id.* at 1162–65.
64. *See generally* JANICE FINE, WORKER CENTERS: ORGANIZING COMMUNITIES AT THE EDGE OF THE DREAM (2006). For an illuminating account of one such worker center, its role in enforcing workers' statutory rights, and its relation to trade unions, *see* Jennifer Gordon, *We Make the Road by Walking: Immigrant Workers, the Workplace Project, and the Struggle for Social Change,* 30 HARV. C.R.-C.L. L. REV. 407 (1995).
65. *See* FINE, *supra* note 64.
66. *See supra* Chapter 5.
67. The Section 2(5) problem has been explored by others. *See* Alan Hyde, *New Institutions for Worker Representation in the United States: Theoretical Issues,* N.Y.L. SCH. L. REV. 385, 406–07 (2005–06); Eli Naduris-Weissman, *The Worker Center Movement and Traditional Labor Laws: A Contextual Analysis,* U.C. Berkeley Lab. & Emp. Research Fund, 2–3 (2008), *available at* http://repositories.cdlib.org/lerf/WorkCentersThesis/; Rosenfeld, *supra* note 28.
68. 29 U.S.C. § 152(5) (2007).
69. *See supra* Chapter 2.
70. Memorandum from Barry J. Kearney, Assoc. Gen. Counsel, NLRB, to Celeste Mattina, Reg'l Dir., Region 2, NLRB, regarding Rest. Opportunities Ctr. of N.Y., Cases 2-CP-1067, 2-CP-20643, 2-CP-1071, 2-CB-20705, 2-CP-1073, and, 2-CB-20787 (Nov. 30, 2006), *available at* http://www.nlrb.gov/shared_files/Advice%20Memos/2006/2-CP-1067.pdf [hereinafter GC Memo].
71. "Labor organizations" must adopt a constitution and bylaws with detailed provisions affecting membership, assessments, fines, discipline, use of funds, audits, meetings, selection of officers, and authorization of bargaining demands and strikes; and they must file annual financial reports detailing assets, liabilities, receipts, salaries, loans, and disbursements. 29 U.S.C. § 431(a) (2007).
72. *See* Naduris-Weisman, *supra* note 67. Section 3(i) of the LMRDA includes the broad language of Section 2(5) of the NLRA and adds "and any conference, general committee,

joint or system board, or joint council . . . which is subordinate to a national or international labor organization or local central body." 29 U.S.C. §402(3)(i) (2007). Under Section 3(j), that includes unions that are certified collective bargaining representatives, as well as entities made up of unions, such as national and international labor federations, labor councils, and the like. Regulations interpret the term "labor organization" to include only organizations within one of the five Section 3(j) categories. 29 C.F.R. § 454.4(a).

73. GC Memo, *supra* note 70.

74. Steele v. Louisville & Nashville R.R. Co., 323 U.S. 192 (1944); Edward J. DeBartolo Corp. v. Fla. Gulf Coast Bldg. & Constr. Trades Council, 485 U.S. 568 (1988); NLRB v. Fruit & Vegetable Packers Warehousemen, Local 760, 377 U.S. 58 (1964).

75. FINE, *supra* note 64, at 9–11, 33.

76. *Id.*

77. *See* PAUL FRYMER, BLACK AND BLUE: AFRICAN AMERICANS, THE LABOR MOVEMENT, AND THE DECLINE OF THE DEMOCRATIC PARTY (2008).

78. *See* Steele v. Louisville & Nashville R.R. Co., 323 U.S. 192 (1944).

79. The plaintiff must show that his or her union's conduct was arbitrary, capricious, or discriminatory; negligence alone does not breach the duty of fair representation. The law thus creates a "formidable hurdle[]" for plaintiffs. *See* David L. Gregory, *Union Liability for Damages after Bowen v. Postal Service: The Incongruity between Labor Law and Title VII Jurisprudence,* 35 BAYLOR L. REV. 237, 249 n.72 (1983).

80. That is shown by the historical success of labor unions in bargaining for and overseeing fair grievance arbitration processes. Unions' performance in processing the grievances of women and minorities was more spotty and was the subject of many legal challenges under both Title VII and the duty of fair representation. But the basis for those laws and those challenges lies in the unions' exclusive control of employee grievances. That is not a factor outside the union setting.

81. *See* Steven A. Ramirez, *Diversity and the Boardroom,* 6 STAN. J.L. BUS. & FIN. 85, 93–96 (2000).

82. On the history, *see* LIZABETH COHEN, MAKING A NEW DEAL: INDUSTRIAL WORKERS IN CHICAGO 1919–1939 (1990).

83. Ruben J. Garcia, *New Voices at Work: Race and Gender Identity Caucuses in the U.S. Labor Movement,* 54 HASTINGS L.J. 79, 113–14 (2002).

CHAPTER 8. ARCHITECTURE AND ELEMENTS OF CO-REGULATION

1. *See* Chapter 4, *supra.*

2. False or misleading statements about compliance with standards of social responsibility may give rise in some states to liability for "false advertising" or misleading business practices. *See, e.g.,* Kasky v. Nike, Inc., 45 P.3d 243 (Cal. 2002), cert. dismissed as improvidently granted, 539 U.S. 654 (2003).

3. ARCHON FUNG, DARA O'ROURKE, & CHARLES SABEL, CAN WE PUT AN END TO SWEATSHOPS? (2001).

4. If employers make promises to their workers—for example, in an employee handbook

—those promises might be enforceable by workers themselves under the state law of the employment contract. However, employers generally can and do avoid the prospect of legal enforcement by avoiding explicitly promissory language and by including a clear disclaimer of contractual intent (while perhaps providing for internal enforcement or grievance procedures). *See supra* Chapter 3.

5. *See generally* Law and New Governance in the EU and the US (Gráinne de Búrca & Joanne Scott eds., 2006); David M. Trubek, *New Governance and Legal Regulation: Complementarity, Rivalry, and Transformation,* 13 Colum. J. Eur. L. 539 (2007); Jason M. Solomon, *Law and Governance in the 21st Century Regulatory State,* 86 Tex. L. Rev. 819 (2008) (reviewing Law and New Governance, *supra,* and Lisa Heinzerling & Mark V. Tushnet, The Regulatory and Administrative State: Materials, Cases, Comments [2006]).

6. For a description of these systems within garment manufacturing, *see* David Weil, *Regulating Noncompliance to Labor Standards: New Tools for an Old Problem,* 45 Challenge 47, 34–36 (2002).

7. Michele Micheletti & Dietlind Stolle, *Mobilizing Consumers to Take Responsibility for Global Social Justice,* 611 Annals Am. Acad. Pol. & Soc. Sci. 157, 172 (2007).

8. R. H. Coase, *The Nature of the Firm,* 4 Economica 386, 388, 393–94 (1937).

9. For example, Katherine V. W. Stone, From Widgets to Digits: Employment Regulation for the Changing Workplace 67 (2004).

10. *See* Annette Bernhardt, Siobhán McGrath, & James DeFilippis, *Unregulated Work in the Global City: Employment and Labor Law Violations in New York City* 29, 49 (2007) (a report by Brennan Ctr. for Justice at N.Y. U. Sch. of Law).

11. *Id.* at 34.

12. For example, Sharon Rabin-Margolioth, *Cross-Employee Redistribution Effects of Mandated Employee Benefits,* 20 Hofstra Lab. & Empl. L.J. 311, 313 (2003).

13. Richard B. Freeman & James L. Medoff, What Do Unions Do? 78–93 (1984); Bernhardt et al., *supra* note 10, at 57. A recent study confirmed that unions tend to reduce wage inequality and that declining union membership had contributed to greater inequality. *See* David Card, Thomas Lemieux, & W. Craig Riddell, *Unions and Wage Inequality, in* What Do Unions Do? A Twenty-Year Perspective 114, 152–53 (James T. Bennett & Bruce E. Kaufman eds., 2007).

14. Retirement plan tax benefits under the Internal Revenue Code require that "contributions or benefits . . . do not discriminate in favor of highly compensated employees." I.R.C. §401(a)(4) (2000).

15. *See* Clyde W. Summers, *Contingent Employment in the United States,* 18 Comp. Lab. L.J. 503, 515–16 (1997).

16. Bernhardt et al., *supra* note 10, at 28–29.

17. *Id.* at 34.

18. *Id.* at iii.

19. *Id* at 34.

20. The aim of the FLSA and its definition of "employ" and expansion of joint employer liability is exhaustively explored in Bruce Goldstein, Marc Linder, Laurence E. Norton,

II, & Catherine K. Ruckelshaus, *Enforcing Fair Labor Standards in the Modern American Sweatshop: Rediscovering the Statutory Definition of Employment,* 46 UCLA L. Rev. 983, 1106 (1999).

21. *Id.* at 1089–1100.
22. *Id.* at 1055–61.
23. *Id.* at 1161.
24. *Id.* at 987.
25. Nationwide Mut. Ins. Co. v. Darden, 503 U.S. 318, 326 (1992).
26. For example, Goldberg v. Whitaker House Coop., Inc., 366 U.S. 28, 33 (1961).
27. Goldstein et. al., *supra* note 20, at 1010–15.
28. *See* Cal. Lab. Code § 2810 (West 2004).
29. The permeability I have in mind here is more modest than what Christine Parker envisions. *See* Christine Parker, The Open Corporation: Effective Self-Regulation and Democracy (2002). I have in mind only the observability of firms' practices, not (yet) firms' receptivity to public values.
30. In addition to the sources and examples cited in Chapters 4 and 5, *see* Sonia Gioseffi, *Corporate Accountability: Achieving Internal Self-Governance through Sustainability Reports,* 13 Cornell J. L. & Pub. Pol'y 503, 528–29 (2004)
31. *See* Chapter 6.
32. *See* Jill Esbenshade, Monitoring Sweatshops: Workers, Consumers, and the Global Apparel Industry (2004); Dara O'Rourke, *Monitoring the Monitors: A Critique of Corporate Third-Party Labour Monitoring, in* Corporate Responsibility and Labour Rights: Codes of Conduct in the Global Economy (Rhys Jenkins, Ruth Pearson, & Gill Seyfang eds., 2002).
33. Just one aspect of the challenge is seen in employers' ability to ban union organizers from their property and from access to workers. *See* Cynthia Estlund, *Labor, Property, and Sovereignty after Lechmere,* 46 Stan. L. Rev. 305, 306–08 (1994).
34. *See, e.g.,* Clean Air Act, 42 U.S.C. § 7622(d); Energy Reorganization Act, 42 U.S.C. § 5851(d); False Claims Act, 31 U.S.C. § 3730(h); Safe Drinking Water Act, 42 U.S.C. § 300j–9(i)(4); Toxic Substances Control Act, 15 U.S.C. § 2622(d).
35. *See, e.g.,* Occupational Safety & Health Act, 29 U.S.C. § 660(c); Federal Mine Safety & Health Act, 30 U.S.C. § 815(c); Civil Rights Act of 1964, 42 U.S.C. § 2000e-3; Age Discrimination in Employment Act, 29 U.S.C. § 623; Family and Medical Leave Act, 29 U.S.C. § 2615(a); Fair Labor Standards Act, 29 U.S.C. § 2615(a).
36. The Supreme Court has established a virtual presumption, for example, that a federal law prohibiting discrimination (on the basis of race, sex, or other protected trait) implicitly prohibits retaliation against employees who complain of discrimination. *See, e.g.,* CBOCS West v. Humphries, 128 S.Ct. 1951 (2008); *Gomez-Perez v. Potter,* 128 S.Ct. 1931 (2008); Jackson v. Birmingham Bd. of Ed., 544 U.S. 167 (2005); Sullivan v. Little Hunting Park, Inc., 396 U.S. 229 (1969). The tort of wrongful discharge in violation of public policy may also supply a remedy for employees who suffer reprisals for reporting violations of the law or for asserting their rights under the law. *See supra* Chapter 3, pp. 70–71.

37. *See* Orly Lobel, *Citizenship, Organizational Citizenship, and the Laws of Overlapping Obligations,* 97 Cal. L. Rev. 433, 489 (2009). In the case of Europe, weaker legal protections for whistleblowers may reflect not only the presence of unjust dismissal laws that provide greater background job security for dissenters, as discussed below, but also a unique postwar experience with secret police: governments' "excessive reliance on informants created a culture of suspicion and duplicity." *Id.* at n. 350 (citing Alexandra Natapoff, *Snitching,* 73 U. Cin. L. Rev. 645 [2004]).
38. *See* Theodore J. St. Antoine, *The Changing Role of Labor Arbitration,* 76 Ind. L. J. 83, 97–98 (2001).
39. *See* Cynthia Estlund, *Wrongful Discharge Protections in an At-Will World,* 74 Tex. L. Rev. 1655, 1070–78 (1996).
40. *See* Lobel, *supra* note 37.
41. *See supra* Chapter 6.
42. *See* Richard E. Moberly, *Unfulfilled Expectations: An Empirical Analysis of Why Sarbanes-Oxley Whistleblowers Rarely Win,* 49 Wm. & Mary L. Rev. 65 (2007); Richard E. Moberly, *Sarbanes-Oxley's Structural Model to Encourage Corporate Whistleblowers,* 2006 B.Y.U. L. Rev. 1107.
43. Moberly, *Unfulfilled Expectations, supra* note 42, at 65.
44. *See generally* Lobel, *supra* note 37.
45. *See id.*
46. *Id.* at pp. 444–46.
47. Garcetti v. Ceballos, 126 S. Ct. 1951 (2006). For my own ruminations on *Garcetti, see* Cynthia Estlund, *Harmonizing Work and Citizenship: A Due Process Solution to a First Amendment Problem,* 2006 Sup. Ct. Rev. 115; Cynthia Estlund, *Free Speech Rights That Work at Work: From the First Amendment to Due Process,* 54 UCLA L. Rev. 1463 (2007).
48. *See* Terry M. Dworkin & Elletta S. Callahan, *Internal Whistleblowing: Protecting the Interests of the Employee, the Organization, and Society,* 29 Am. Bus. L.J. 267, 281 (1991). *See also* Lobel, *supra* note 37.
49. Lobel, *supra* note 37, at 464.
50. *Id.* at 461–67.

CHAPTER 9. GETTING THERE FROM HERE

1. U.S. Sentencing Commission, Guidelines Manual (Nov. 2004) USSG 8B2.1.
2. Jennifer Arlen & Reinier Kraakman, *Corporate Misconduct: An Analysis of Corporate Liability Regimes,* 72 N.Y.U. L. Rev. 687 (1997).
3. *Id.* at 726–30.
4. Arlen and Kraakman distinguish between two kinds of self-regulatory behavior: precautions, which aim to prevent misconduct, and self-policing, which aims to discover, disclose, and correct misconduct. *Id.* at 699. Both are part of the broader notion of self-regulation as it is used here (and are also part of the Federal Sentencing Guidelines' definition of "effective compliance").
5. Cynthia Estlund, Working Together: How Workplace Bonds Strengthen a Diverse Democracy 166 (2003).

6. *See* Michael Dorf & Charles Sabel, *A Constitution of Democratic Experimentalism*, 98 COLUM. L. REV. 267, 314 (1998); JOHN BRAITHWAITE, REGULATORY CAPITALISM: HOW IT WORKS, IDEAS FOR MAKING IT BETTER 150–52 (2008); CHRISTINE PARKER, THE OPEN CORPORATION: EFFECTIVE SELF-REGULATION AND DEMOCRACY (2002).

7. *See* Alison D. Morantz, *Has Devolution Injured American Workers? State and Federal Enforcement of Construction Safety*, 25 J. L. Econ. & Org. 183 (2009).

8. *See* Charles Sabel & William Simon, *Destabilization Rights: How Public Law Litigation Succeeds*, 117 HARV. L. REV. 1015 (2004). The term "destabilization rights" comes from ROBERTO MANGABEIRA UNGER, FALSE NECESSITY: ANTI-NECESSITARIAN SOCIAL THEORY IN THE SERVICE OF RADICAL DEMOCRACY 530–35 (1987). Sabel and Simon define destabilization rights as "claims to unsettle and open up public institutions that have chronically failed to meet their obligations and that are substantially insulated from the normal processes of political accountability." Sabel & Simon, *supra*, at 1020. They address mainly public service providers—schools, prisons, public housing agencies, and the like. But the concept applies equally well to regulatory agencies.

9. Richard Freeman also sees lessons in the success of antidiscrimination law for the reform of other workplace policies. *See* RICHARD B. FREEMAN, AMERICA WORKS: CRITICAL THOUGHTS ON THE EXCEPTIONAL U.S. LABOR MARKET 94–96 (2007).

10. Courts have upheld the arbitrability of such claims. *See, e.g.*, Carter v. Countrywide Credit Indus., Inc., 362 F.3d 294, 296–97 (5th Cir. 2004); Poteat v. Rich Prods. Corp., 91 Fed. Appx. 832, 834 (4th Cir. 2004); Adkins v. Labor Ready, Inc., 303 F.3d 496, 505–06 (4th Cir. 2002); Kuehner v. Dickinson & Co., 84 F.3d 316, 319–20 (9th Cir. 1996).

11. Courts have varied in their treatment of class-action waivers within arbitration agreements. Most courts reject a categorical treatment and ask how the waiver affects the viability of the particular claims in question. *See* Discover Bank v. Superior Court, 113 P.3d 1100 (Cal. 2005); Genry v. Superior Court, 37 CAL. RPTR. 3d 790 (Cal. Ct. App. 2006); Shroyer v. New Cingular Wireless Services, Inc., 498 F.3d 976, 981–83 (Cal. 2007); Kinkel v. Cingular Wireless LLC, 857 N.E.2d 250 (Ill. 2006). This approach allows employers to deter meritorious claims by setting up a procedural hurdle to their adjudication. But it is not as bad as upholding such waivers in spite of their tendency to preclude the effective vindication of some nonwaivable employment rights. *See* Cynthia Estlund, *Between Rights and Contract: Arbitration Agreements and Non-Compete Covenants as a Hybrid Form of Employment Law*, 155 U. PA. L. REV. 379 (2006).

12. Cal. Lab. Code §2698–99 (West 2004).

13. On PAGA and its history, *see* Erich Shiners, *Chapter 221: A Necessary but Incomplete Revision of the Labor Code Private Attorneys General Act*, 36 McGEORGE L. REV. 877 (2005); Leonora M. Schloss & Cari A. Cohorn, *Assessing the Amended Labor Code Private Attorneys General Act*, 28 L.A. LAWYER 13 (Feb. 2006).

14. Professor Susan Sturm has explored the institution of internal organizational reforms, which may include ongoing consultation with independent experts, as part of the remedy for large-scale employment discrimination litigation. Susan P. Sturm, *Second Generation Employment Discrimination: A Structural Approach*, 101 COLUM. L. REV. 458, 462–63 (2001). She has argued that these "structural" remedies—some of which resemble privately monitored self-regulation—effectively extend the reach of law and antidis-

crimination norms to uncover and alter subtly discriminatory practices that traditional remedies do not. I agree but stress the importance of particular institutional checks against cosmetic compliance.

15. Thomas v. Total Health Home Care Corp., No. 2493 (Philadelphia Co. Ct. of Common Pleas 2008).

16. The FLSA itself allows for collective actions, a form of opt-in group action. *See* 29 U.S.C. 216(b) (2000). Parallel state statutes may permit opt-out "class actions" for the same claims. *See, e.g.,* Ansoumana v. Gristede's Operating Corp., 201 F.R.D. 81, 88–89 (S.D.N.Y. 2001).

17. *See* Gretchen Agena, Comment, *What's So "Fair" about It?: The Need to Amend the Fair Labor Standards Act,* 39 Hous. L. Rev. 1119, 1128 (2002); Mark J. Neuberger, *Punching the Clock Is Not So Simple,* Nat'l L.J., Jan. 13, 2003, at B8; Brooke A. Masters & Amy Joyce, *Suits on Overtime Hitting Big Firms: Employers Paying to Settle Many Cases,* Wash. Post, Feb. 21, 2006, at D01; Gerald L. Maatman, Jr., *Annual Workplace Class Action Litigation Report: Significant Federal Employment Discrimination Litigation and EEOC Pattern or Practice Rulings,* 58 Lab. L.J. 53 (2007).

18. News release, *Wal-Mart Details Progress toward Becoming a Leader in Employment Practices* (June 4, 2004), *available at* http://walmartstores.com/FactsNews/NewsRoom /4645.aspx, last visited Jan. 3, 2009.

19. An in-house audit from several years ago shows Wal-Mart's ability to monitor itself. For coverage of the in-house audit and Wal-Mart officials' reactions to it, *see* Steven Greenhouse, *In-House Audit Says Wal-Mart Violated Labor Laws,* N.Y. Times, Jan. 13, 2004.

20. *See* Chapter 1.

21. Thus far, the only reported decision to consider the issue rejected this argument. *See* Martin v. Ind. Mich. Power Co., 292 F. Supp. 2d 947, 947–57 (W.D. Mich. 2002). On the other hand, these policies played a key role in Wal-Mart's successful defeat of class certification in litigation over its wage and hour practices. *See* Order, In re Wal-Mart Wage and Hour Employment Practices Litigation, 2:06-CV-00225-PMP-PAL (D. Nev. 6/20/08).

22. *See* Thomas O. McGarity, *Reforming OSHA: Some Thoughts for the Current Legislative Agenda,* 31 Hous. L. Rev. 99, 115–17 & n. 109 (1994); William Dorsey, *An Overview of Whistleblower Protection Claims at the United States Department of Labor,* 26 J. Nat'l Ass'n Admin L. Judges 42, 98–112 (2006).

23. *See* Guido Calabresi, The Costs of Accidents: A Legal and Economic Analysis 135–44 (1970).

24. On the undercompensatory and underdeterrent features of workers' compensation, *see, e.g.,* William J. Maakestad & Charles Helm, *Promoting Workplace Safety and Health in the Post-Regulatory Era: A Primer on Non-OSHA Legal Incentives That Influence Employer Decisions to Control Occupational Hazards,* 17 N. Ky. L. Rev. 9, 10–16 (1989).

25. Emily A. Spieler, *Perpetuating Risk? Workers' Compensation and the Persistence of Occupational Injuries,* 31 Hous. L. Rev. 119, 196 (1994).

26. The intentional torts exception to the exclusivity of workers' compensation usually requires an actual purpose to harm, though some jurisdictions allow tort liability in cases of gross negligence. *See* 6 Arthur Larson & Lex K. Larson, Larson's Workers

COMPENSATION LAW 103.03, 103.04 (2005); Restatement (Third) of Torts: Liab. for Physical Harm 1 reporter's note, at 13–14 (Proposed Final Draft No. 1, 2005).

27. For cases recognizing this tort action, *see* Kinzel v. Discovery Drilling, Inc., 93 P.3d 427, 437–38 (Alaska 2004); Reed v. Municipality of Anchorage, 782 P.2d 1155, 1158–59 (Alaska 1989); Motarie v. N. Mont. Joint Refuse Disposal Dist., 907 P.2d 154, 157 (Mont. 1995); D'Angelo v. Gardner, 819 P.2d 206, 216–17 (Nev. 1991); Cloutier v. Great Atl. & Pac. Tea Co., 436 A.2d 1140, 1144–45 (N.H. 1981); Cerracchio v. Alden Leeds, Inc., 538 A.2d 1292, 1296 (N.J. App. Div. 1988); Kulch v. Structural Fibers, Inc., 677 N.E.2d 308, 329 (Ohio 1997). Most courts have held that OSHA does not preempt state wrongful discharge actions. *See* Schweiss v. Chrysler Motors Corp., 922 F.2d 473, 475 (8th Cir. 1990); McElroy v. SOS Int'l, Inc., 730 F. Supp. 803, 806–07 (N.D. Ill. 1989); Hentzel v. Singer Co., 188 CAL. RPTR. 159, 165–67 (Cal. Ct. App. 1982). *But see* Hines v. Elf Atochem N. Am., Inc., 813 F. Supp. 550, 552 (W.D. Ky. 1993); Braun v. Kelsey-Hayes Co., 635 F. Supp. 75, 80 (E.D. Pa. 1986). Some courts have held that apart from preemption, state common law precludes a tort action where a federal or state statute provides an "adequate" remedy for the discharged employee and that OSHA provides such a remedy. *See* Miles v. Martin Marietta Corp., 861 F. Supp. 73, 74 (D. Colo. 1994); King v. Fox Grocery Co., 642 F. Supp. 288, 290 (W.D. Pa. 1986); Grant v. Butler, 590 So. 2d 254, 257 (Ala. 1991); Burnham v. Karl & Gelb, P.C., No. CV 940537069S, 1997 WL 133399, at *6 (Conn. Super. Ct. Mar. 7, 1997); Walsh v. Consol. Freightways, Inc., 563 P.2d 1205, 1208–09 (Or. 1977). Other courts have held that OSHA does not provide an adequate remedy. Flenker v. Willamette Indus., Inc., 967 P.2d 295, 300 (Kan. 1998); Antlitz v. CMJ Mgmt. Co., No. CIV.A. 96–2618C, 1997 WL 42396, at *1 (Mass. Super. Ct. Jan. 30, 1997); Shawcross v. Pyro Prods., Inc., 916 S.W.2d 342, 344–45 (Mo. Ct. App. 1995).

28. David Vogel, THE MARKET FOR VIRTUE: THE POTENTIAL AND LIMITS OF CORPORATE SOCIAL RESPONSIBILITY 77–82 (2005).

Index

ADEA. *See* Age Discrimination in Employment Act (ADEA)

affinity groups. *See* employee representation, minority groups and

AFL-CIO, 113, 114; Working America project, 169

Age Discrimination in Employment Act (ADEA), 89

agency by agency approach, 224–25

aggregate litigation. *See* litigation

Alliance for Fair Food, 125

"American Works Councils Act," 171

antidiscrimination law: Civil Rights Act, Title VII and, 11, 68–70, 85; employee rights and, 68–74. *See also Burlington Industries v. Ellerth;* Civil Rights Act of *1964; Faragher v. City of Boca Raton;* internal antidiscrimination policies; *Kolstad v. American Dental Association*

antiharassment policies. *See* internal antidiscrimination policies

antiretaliation laws. *See* whistleblower protections

Anti-Slavery Campaign (CIW), 123

anti-sweatshop movement, 16, 95, 97–103, 159, 198; monitoring agreements and, 107–8, 155; Ratcheting Labor Standards and, 151–53

arbitration, 89–92; class-action waivers and, 293n11; consumer claims and, 269n80; "Due Process Protocol" and, 92; minority concerns and, 188; "repeat player effect" and, 269n85; wage and hour practices and, 227

Arlen, Jennifer, 218–19

Ayres, Ian, 140, 141, 144, 148, 170, 172. *See also* Responsive Regulation

Banana Republic, 116

Befort, Stephen, 171

BKC. *See* Burger King Corp. (BKC)

Blackett, Adelle, 278n18

O'Rourke, Dara, 150, 152. *See also* Ratcheting Labor Standards (RLS)

Ortiz, Julia, 61, 68

OSG (Organizational Sentencing Guidelines). *See* Federal Sentencing Guidelines for Organizations

OSHA. *See* Occupational Safety and Health Act of *1970* (OSHA); Occupational Safety and Health Administration (OSHA)

OSHRC. *See* Occupational Safety and Health Review Commission (OSHRC)

outsourcing, 199–203. *See also* "employer," definition of; "super-employers"

OWBPA. *See* Older Workers' Benefits Protection Act (OWBPA)

PAGA. *See* Labor Code Private Attorneys General Act (PAGA; California)

Parker, Christine, 141–42, 223, 291n29

pension plans, 58, 95

Polaroid Corp., 37

Pooters, Drew, 61–62

poultry-processing industry, 66–67

preemption doctrine, 41–44, 59, 287n45

private initiatives. *See* contractual strategies; neutrality agreements; worker centers

private rights of action, 109; doctrinal strategy and, 231–33, 235; promotion of co-regulation through, 225–36; remedial strategy and, 228–31; whistleblowers and, 159–60, 233. *See also* contractual strategies; litigation

Private Securities Litigation Reform Act of *1995* (PSLRA), 158, 160

PSLRA. *See* Private Securities Litigation Reform Act of *1995* (PSLRA)

qui tam litigation, 147

Ratcheting Labor Standards (RLS), 25, 150–55, 203

rational actors, and deterrence model, 133–38, 218–21

"reflexive" law, 17, 136–37, 278n14

regulated self-regulation: corporate social responsibility and, 93–103; deregulation and, 13–14, 17, 77–78; employee rights and, 20, 68–74, 82–92; enforcement and, 20, 82–92; labor standards and, 19–20, 78–82, 190–96; litigation threat and, 226–27; movement toward, 11–19; New Governance framework and, 132–38; nonexclusive union representation and, 168–69; opportunities for employees in, 17–18, 22–24; reliance on internal regimes and, 137–38; requirements for effectiveness and, 20–24; Responsive Regulation framework and, 139–50; risks for employees in, 17–19. *See also* co-regulation; self-regulation

remedies: FLSA and, 55–57; job security and, 72–73; NLRA and, 32, 33–34, 37, 39–40, 42, 46, 47; remedial strategies under co-regulation and, 228–31; underenforcement of OSHA and, 64–67; unregulated work and, 67–68; wage and hour law and, 60–64, 108–10, 112–16, 145–47, 205, 227–28, 230–31; whistleblower protections and, 70. *See also* enforcement

Rentway, 61, 62

"repeat player effect," 269n85. *See also* arbitration

representation gap, 162–63; effectiveness of unions and, 163–64; works councils and, 170–71. *See also* employee representation; low-wage workers

"representation remedy," 221

reprisals, fear of: co-regulation and, 207–12; internal disclosures and, 176–77, 179, 210–12; union representation and, 165. *See also* whistleblower protections

Responsive Regulation, 21, 25, 203, 217–18; employee representation and, 142–